MACINTOSH METHODOLOGIES IN THEORY AND PRACTICE

A technical guide for experienced users

formerly *Macs For Dummies*

BY D. WELCH POGUE

Includes advanced treatment of these topics:
- ◆ Invoking the commencement of A/C 120V electric power to the CPU unit
- ◆ Propelling the cursor-control module on a horizontal plane
- ◆ Insertion and removal of magnetic-oxide data storage media

Look, we use the word *Dummies* on the cover with affection and a twinkle in the eye. Still, we understand if you're not thrilled about leaving a book on your desk called *Macs For Dummies*.

We hear you. And we've got the perfect solution: just rip off the real cover of the book! This phony cover will be all that's left. Leave it on your desk in plain sight, so everybody will know what a computer whiz you are.

References for the Rest of Us

COMPUTER BOOK SERIES FROM IDG

Are you intimidated and confused by computers? Do you find that traditional manuals are overloaded with technical details you'll never use? Do your friends and family always call you to fix simple problems on their PCs? Then the ... *For Dummies*™ computer book series from IDG is for you.

... *For Dummies* books are written for those frustrated computer users who know they aren't really dumb but find that PC hardware, software, and indeed the unique vocabulary of computing make them feel helpless. ... *For Dummies* books use a lighthearted approach, a down-to-earth style, and even cartoons and humorous icons to diffuse computer novices' fears and build their confidence. Lighthearted but not lightweight, these books are a perfect survival guide for anyone forced to use a computer.

Already, hundreds of thousands of satisfied readers agree. They have made ... *For Dummies* books the #1 introductory level computer book series and have written asking for more. So, if you're looking for the most fun and easy way to learn about computers, look to ... *For Dummies* books to give you a helping hand.

IDG BOOKS

MACS
FOR
DUMMIES ®
3RD EDITION

by David Pogue

Foreword by John Kander

IDG
BOOKS

IDG Books Worldwide, Inc.
An International Data Group Company

Foster City, CA ◆ Chicago, IL ◆ Indianapolis, IN ◆ Braintree, MA ◆ Dallas, TX

Macs For Dummies,® 3rd Edition

Published by
IDG Books Worldwide, Inc.
An International Data Group Company
919 E. Hillsdale Blvd.
Suite 400
Foster City, CA 94404

Library of Congress Catalog Card No.: 94-73282

ISBN: 1-56884-239-2

Printed in the United States of America

10 9 8 7 6 5 4 3 2

3A/RQ/QS/ZV

Distributed in the United States by IDG Books Worldwide, Inc.

Distributed by Macmillan Canada for Canada; by Computer and Technical Books for the Caribbean Basin; by Contemporanea de Ediciones for Venezuela; by Distribuidora Cuspide for Argentina; by CITEC for Brazil; by Ediciones ZETA S.C.R. Ltda. for Peru; by Editorial Limusa SA for Mexico; by Transworld Publishers Limited in the United Kingdom and Europe; by Al-Maiman Publishers & Distributors for Saudi Arabia; by Simron Pty. Ltd. for South Africa; by IDG Communications (HK) Ltd. for Hong Kong; by Toppan Company Ltd. for Japan; by Addison Wesley Publishing Company for Korea; by Longman Singapore Publishers Ltd. for Singapore, Malaysia, Thailand and Indonesia; by Unalis Corporation for Taiwan; by WS Computer Publishing Company, Inc. for the Philippines; by WoodsLane Pty. Ltd. for Australia; by WoodsLane Enterprises Ltd. for New Zealand.

For general information on IDG Books in the U.S., including information on discounts and premiums, contact IDG Books at 800-434-3422 or 415-655-3000.

For information on where to purchase IDG Books outside the U.S., contact IDG Books International at 415-655-3021 or fax 415-655-3295.

For information on translations, contact Marc Jeffrey Mikulich, Director, Foreign & Subsidiary Rights, at IDG Books Worldwide, 415-655-3018 or fax 415-655-3295.

For sales inquiries and special prices for bulk quantities, write to the address above or call IDG Books Worldwide at 415-655-3000.

For information on using IDG Books in the classroom, or ordering examination copies, contact Jim Kelly at 800-434-2086.

is a registered trademark of
International Data Group

About the Author

Ohio-bred David Pogue never touched a computer — nor wanted to — until Apple Computer suckered him into it by selling Macs half-price at Yale, from which he graduated *summa cum laude* in 1985. Since then, Pogue has merged his two loves — the musical theatre and Macs — in every way he could dream up: by writing manuals for music programs like Finale; by being the computer-consultant guy for Broadway musicals; by teaching Mac music seminars around the country; and by becoming the Mac guru to every Broadway and Hollywood creative-type he could get his hands on — Mia Farrow, Carly Simon, Mike Nichols, Stephen Sondheim, and others.

In his other life, Pogue is a straight-ahead theatre musician, having conducted 1½ Broadway shows (the second one flopped out of town), played piano for some Off-Broadway productions, and composed a number of small-time musicals. In his other life, he's a magician, and teaches courses in magic in New York City.

And in his *other* other life, Pogue is a Contributing Editor for *Macworld* magazine. His column, *The Desktop Critic,* appears in the magazine each month.

He's also responsible for *MORE Macs For Dummies*, the sequel to this book; and, with his former Yale roommate and current *Macworld* writer, Joseph Schorr, Pogue wrote the 1100-page, 3-disk, fact-filled best-seller, *Macworld Mac & Power Mac SECRETS,* 2nd Edition.

In between crises, Pogue wrote a novel called *Hard Drive* — a Macintosh techno-thriller, published by the Berkley Publishing Group. It's available in four languages, was optioned for film, and was named "notable book of the year" by the *New York Times*.

Pogue's résumé also boasts some *real* accomplishments, like winning the Ohio spelling bee in seventh grade, being the only nonlawyer in three generations, and getting a Viewer Mail letter read on David Letterman.

Pogue responds to every piece of correspondence he receives. Turnaround time for E-mail is one day (on America Online, his name is *Pogue*). Turnaround time for U.S. Mail roughly matches the gestation period of a Holstein cow.

Welcome to the world of IDG Books Worldwide.

IDG Books Worldwide, Inc. is a subsidiary of International Data Group, the world's largest publisher of computer-related information and the leading global provider of information services on information technology. IDG was founded more than 25 years ago and now employs more than 7,000 people worldwide. IDG publishes more than 220 computer publications in 65 countries (see listing below). More than fifty million people read one or more IDG publications each month.

Launched in 1990, IDG Books Worldwide is today the #1 publisher of best-selling computer books in the United States. We are proud to have received 3 awards from the Computer Press Association in recognition of editorial excellence, and our best-selling *...For Dummies*™ series has more than 12 million copies in print with translations in 25 languages. IDG Books, through a recent joint venture with IDG's Hi-Tech Beijing, became the first U.S. publisher to publish a computer book in the People's Republic of China. In record time, IDG Books has become the first choice for millions of readers around the world who want to learn how to better manage their businesses.

Our mission is simple: Every IDG book is designed to bring extra value and skill-building instructions to the reader. Our books are written by experts who understand and care about our readers. The knowledge base of our editorial staff comes from years of experience in publishing, education, and journalism — experience which we use to produce books for the '90s. In short, we care about books, so we attract the best people. We devote special attention to details such as audience, interior design, use of icons, and illustrations. And because we use an efficient process of authoring, editing, and desktop publishing our books electronically, we can spend more time ensuring superior content and spend less time on the technicalities of making books.

You can count on our commitment to deliver high-quality books at competitive prices on topics consumers want to read about. At IDG, we value quality, and we have been delivering quality for more than 25 years. You'll find no better book on a subject than an IDG book.

John J. Kilcullen

John Kilcullen
President and CEO
IDG Books Worldwide, Inc.

Acknowledgments

I can't tell you how much I've appreciated the patience of everyone whose projects got back-burnered for the sake of this book: Carol Person and Adrian Mello of *Macworld;* Freddie Gershon and the gang at Music Theatre International; Joe, Allison, and Max; my fiancée, the lovely Dr. O'Sullivan; and Poppa, for whose creative chromosomes I'll thank him personally at his 105th birthday.

Thanks to the unbelievably supportive, enthusiastic people at IDG Books: publisher John Kilcullen; editors Corbin Collins and Jim Grey; and everyone in the sprawling universe of IDG Books voicemail. Thanks, too, to Londa Holsinger for her borrowed wit.

Above all, thanks to my students: the ranks of born-again Mac nuts whose first steps, questions, and impressive strides constitute my research.

(The Publisher would like to give special thanks to Patrick J. McGovern, without whom this book would not have been possible.)

Credits

Executive Vice President, Strategic Product Planning and Research
David Solomon

Editorial Director
Diane Graves Steele

Acquisitions Editor
Megg Bonar

Brand Manager
Judith A. Taylor

Editorial Managers
Tracy L. Barr
Sandra Blackthorn
Kristin Cocks

Editorial Assistants
Tamara S. Castleman
Stacey Holden Prince
Kevin Spencer

Acquisitions Assistant
Suki Gear

Production Director
Beth Jenkins

Project Coordinator
Cindy L. Phipps

Pre-Press Coordinators
Tony Augsburger
Steve Peake

Project Editors
Jim Grey
Corbin Collins

Editors
Andy Cummings
Kathy Simpson

Technical Reviewer
Dennis Cohen

Production Staff
Paul Belcastro
Linda M. Boyer
Mary Breidenbach
Chris Collins
Tyler Connor
Carla Radzikinas
Dwight Ramsey
Patricia R. Reynolds
Gina Scott

Proofreader
Charles A. Hutchinson

Indexer
David Heiret

Book Design
University Graphics

Cover Design
Kavish + Kavish

Contents at a Glance

Table of Contents

Foreword

*It is certainly no surprise to me that I was asked to write the Foreword for this book. After all, I was David Pogue's first dummy. When we met seven years ago, I was an aging composer, wearily putting quill pen to parchment, surrounded by mountains of erasers. The world of computers was as foreign to me as the craters of the moon.

Then along came Mr. Pogue, fresh from Yale, who guided me patiently and painlessly into the joyful world of Macintosh. He made it all seem so simple. And the Mac, my new friend, was helpful as well, with little admonitions like, "Are you sure you want to do this?" or apologies like, "I'm sorry I can't find this. If you find it for me, I promise I'll remember where it is next time." I was soon convinced that this machine really cared about me. In a short time, I became a mouse maniac.

Since then, I have written the scores for three musicals, two films, and countless letters of complaint to my Congressmen on this wonderful contraption, thanks to my two wise, kind friends, David and the Mac.

In this book, you'll find many reminders, explanations, and shortcuts. *Macs for Dummies*, 3rd Edition, will stay by me at my desk. After all, once a dummy . . .

John Kander

John Kander, with lyricist Fred Ebb, has written the scores for Cabaret; Chicago; Zorba; New York, New York; *and the Tony award-winning musical* Kiss of the Spider Woman.

Introduction

• •

A Formal Welcome to the 20th Century

Something has driven you to learning the computer — your friends, your job, or fate. In any case, you couldn't have chosen a better time; technology and price wars have made computers comprehensible, affordable, and almost fun. The Macintosh is the primary example.

In 1984, the ad people called the Macintosh "the computer for the rest of us." The implication was that *other* computers were hard to learn. Previous computers required you to learn jargon, have technical skill, and memorize dumb keyboard codes. The Macintosh was as simple as a toaster — nothing to assemble, nothing to install, no manual to puzzle through.

And sure enough, the first Mac pretty much fit that description. Its factory-sealed case meant that you didn't have to install any parts (like you do on IBM-style computers). Unless you were a real soldering gunslinger, the first Macintosh wasn't expandable. It was a complete, self-contained unit. You unpacked it and plugged it in. Like a toaster.

But Apple Computer learned about a funny catch-22 in the computer business. The people who influenced computer sales (like computer magazines and consultants) *liked* the jargon, the keyboard codes, the messy circuit board stuff! These were people who prided themselves on having *mastered* the convoluted, dim-witted design of pre-Mac computers . . . people who not only didn't appreciate the simplicity of the Macintosh but actually *resented* it. In reviews, editorials, and interviews, the Powers That Were kept saying that the Macintosh would never survive unless Apple opened it up. Let people expand it, customize it, juice it up, just like IBM owners had been required to do for years.

Alas, that movement pushed the Mac out of its "computer for the rest of us" mold. Suddenly, there were more models. They became available in separate modular pieces, so you had more to shop for. The computer weenies who ruled the press started imposing all their terminology and tech-talk on this poor little machine. Macintosh user groups sprang up — they're everywhere now — where you'd hear talk like, "How can I accelerate my 25 MHz SE/30 to get a decent frame rate out of QuickTime two-point-oh?" or "How much RAM do I need for virtual memory on my 80-meg Quantum?"

The Mac wasn't a toaster anymore.

Why a Book for Dummies?

Today, the Mac sometimes seems almost as intimidating as the computers it was supposed to replace. The way the magazines and techno-nerds throw jargon around, you'd think the Mac was the private property of the dweeby intelligentsia all over again.

It's not. You hold in your hands a primal scream: "It's *not* as complicated as they try to make it sound!" Really, *truly,* almost everything said by the computer whizzes of the world is more complicated than it has to be. (Ever study psychology? A person who uses jargon where simple English would do is trying to underscore the listener's ignorance.)

This book is designed to help you

- ✔ Translate the tech-talk into useful information
- ✔ Weed out the stuff you'll never need to know
- ✔ Navigate the hype when it comes to buying things
- ✔ Learn the Macintosh and get useful things done

By the way, of *course* you're not a dummy. Two pieces of evidence tell me so: for one thing, you're learning the Mac, and for another, you're reading this book! But I've taught hundreds of people how to use their Macs, and an awful lot of them start out saying they *feel* like dummies when it comes to computers. Society surrounds us with fast-talking teenagers who grew up learning English from their Nintendo sets; no wonder the rest of us sometimes feel left out.

But you're no more a dummy for not knowing the Mac than you were before you knew how to drive. Learning the Mac is like learning to drive: after a lesson or two, you can go anywhere your heart desires.

So when we say *Dummies,* we're saying it with an affectionate wink. Still, if the cover bothers you even a little — I'll admit it, you wouldn't be the first — please rip it right off. The inner cover, we hope, will make you proud to have the book lying out on your desk.

How to Use This Book
(Other Than as a Mousepad)

If you're starting from the very, *very* beginning, read this book from the end — with **Appendix A,** where you can find out how to buy a Mac (and which one to get) without getting scammed. It also contains an idiot-proof guide to setting up your computer.

Chapter 1 assumes that you do, in fact, have a Mac, and that it's been plugged in. You'll find out how to turn it on and off, for starters. In 10 minutes (or 20 if you're trying to watch TV simultaneously), you'll have mastered the raw basics of driving your Mac.

Then there's something, if you'll forgive me, called **Chapter 1$^1/_2$.** It's my attempt to play down the technical nature of the topic — the difference between memory and disks — by not devoting a full scary chapter to it.

Chapter 2's a Mac lesson for the absolute beginner: how to use the mouse (and what a mouse *is*), how to use menus — that kind of thing. In **Chapter 3,** you'll do some actual work; it includes a word processing lesson that won't destroy your self-esteem.

Once you've got your ideas typed into the computer, you'll want to print your work; that's one of the Mac's strong suits. **Chapter 4** lays bare the mysteries of printing and using typefaces.

Chapter 5 has the all-important "Faking Your Way Through the Top Ten Programs," an indispensable guide for anybody who wants to look cool without actually expending any effort. And speaking of software, **Chapter 6** explains those icons inside the all-important System Folder and attempts to answer man's primal question: "What *is* all that junk?"

In **Chapter 7,** you get to read about all the expensive equipment you can plug *into* the Mac: modems, scanners, and all that good stuff. By the time you get to **Chapter 8,** you'll be ready to start sailing with a priceless potpourri of sizzling shortcuts. You'll find out about the creative vandalism the Mac lets you do: colorizing the screen, recording your own sounds, and using utility programs that help you get extra mileage out of your computer. **Chapter 9,** "Screamingly Important Things That Nobody Tells You," is new in this edition. It reveals everything you need to survive a day-to-day Mac existence — but that people expect you to learn the hard way.

If you were clever enough to buy a Performa — a special breed of Macintosh that comes with preinstalled software and has some special features for beginners — then **Chapter 10** has your name on it. Likewise, for the peripatetic among us, PowerBook owners will thrill to the insights of **Chapter 11.** It shows you, among other things, how to coax every last milliwatt of juice from your laptop's batteries.

When anything goes wrong, turn to **Chapter 12,** "When Bad Things Happen to Good Machines," the mother of all troubleshooting sections. It identifies the snafus you're most likely to encounter, how to prevent them, and what to do about them. Read **Chapter 14** when the stuff in this book is starting to seem old hat, and you're ready to push off into the wider world of computing, and when you're willing to sink still more money into your Mac — to upgrade it. (There *is* no Chapter 13, just as there's no Floor 13 in American office buildings.)

The book winds down with **Appendix B**, the Resource Resource (which has contact info for a number of important Mac companies and organizations), and **Appendix C**, the Techno-Babble Translation Guide. (You'd probably call it a glossary.)

Macintosh conventions

Macintosh conventions? Sure. They're called Macworld Expos, and there's one in Boston and one in San Francisco each year.

Conventions in this book

Oh, *that* kind of convention. First, I'm going to satisfy those beginners who have a recessive geek gene in their DNA, those who actually *want* to learn more about what's going on under the hood, with occasional sidebars on technoid topics. They'll be clearly marked with titles like "Stuff you'll never need to know." Unless you're actually interested, rest assured that you can live a rich and rewarding life without ever reading a word.

Second, so that we'll be eligible for some of the more prestigious book-design awards, I've marked some topics in the main text with these icons:

Nerdy stuff that's OK to skip but will fascinate the kind of people who read Tom Clancy novels.

You can never, *ever* damage your Mac by "doing something wrong" (other than by pouring Diet Coke into the air vents or something). Occasionally, though, I'll alert you that there's a potential risk to your work.

The former Speaker of the House. Also a shortcut so you can show off.

Denotes an actual You-Try-It Experience. Hold the book open with a nearby cinder block, put your hands on the computer, and do as I say.

Indicates a deep glimpse into the psychology of Mac users: why people who already *know* how to use the damn things, for example, love to intimidate people who *don't*.

Why a Mac?

If there's one single *atom* of computer phobia in your bloodstream, but you need a computer, get a Macintosh. Trust me. And trust the 12 million former computer phobes who are now happily computing away.

A confirmation of your taste and intelligence

You've heard it a thousand times: the Macintosh is the most user-friendly computer. What does that *mean?* In concrete terms?

For one thing, there's a lot less to install and set up. When you buy an IBM-type computer, for example, you spend your first weekend hunched over an open computer case filled with wiring. You squint at the manual that's filled with techno-babble and get depressed that you, a well-educated, perfectly good English speaker, can't understand the first thing it's saying. With a Macintosh, of course, you basically just plug it in and press the On switch.

And another thing: there's a lot less to memorize when you use a Macintosh. Because the commands are all listed on the screen, you don't have to remember that Control-Alt-Escape-semicolon is the Print command. In the IBM world, of course, every single program has different commands in different places with different keys you press to activate them. Out of 10,000 Macintosh programs, there are probably five that don't have exactly the same major commands in exactly the same places with exactly the same keyboard shortcuts.

There are a bunch of other reasons you've done the right thing to go for the Mac — the screen looks better, it's easy to expand, it's the easiest to learn, and it has all kinds of high-tech goodies like a microphone for recording your own sounds. Of course, the last reason that a Mac is superior *is* that it's superior; it entitles you to gloat about owning the world's most hip, technologically evolved, shrewd computer.

Apple and obsolescence

Apple is the gigantic Silicon Valley computer company that started out as a couple of grungy teenagers in a garage. It's the target of incredible love and hate from the Macintosh community. Each time Apple introduces a new Macintosh model, it's faster, more powerful, and less expensive than the model *you* already bought. Thus, the mixed passions — people love Apple for coming up with such great products but feel cheated at having paid so much for a suddenly outdated machine.

Feel whatever you want, of course. But if you're going to buy a computer, accept the fact that your investment is going to devalue faster than real estate in Three Mile Island.

Here's a promise: No matter how carefully you shop or how good a deal you get on a Macintosh today, your model will be *discontinued by Apple in two years.* (It'll still *work* just fine, and be more or less up-to-date, for about five years.) Yeah, I know — it's a cruel, irritating fact, but it's a fact nonetheless.

With that quick and inevitable computer death looming, how can people psych themselves into laying out $2,000 for a computer? Simple: They believe that in those few short years, the computer will speed them up enough, and enhance their productivity enough, to cover the costs easily.

That's the theory, anyway.

Part I
For the Absolute
Mac Virgin

The 5th Wave   By Rich Tennant

THE COMMITTEE FOR THE PROLIFERATION OF MACINTOSH
COMPUTERS FINALLY PAYS A VISIT TO LARRY.

In this part...

There are three general ways to learn how to work your Mac. You can prevail upon the good graces of your local computer dealer, who, having pocketed your money already, would just as soon have you blow away. You can read the manuals, which have about as much personality as a walnut. Or you can read a book like this one. (Then again, no book is quite like this one.)

Tough choice, huh?

In this part, you'll learn, as kindly and gently as possible, what you need to know to get up and running on your Mac system — and nothing else. So take off your thinking cap and enjoy your journey through this utopia we call the Mac world.

Chapter 1

How to Turn On Your Mac
(and What to Do Next)

• •

In This Chapter

▶ How to turn your Mac on (and off)

▶ Confronting weird new words like *mouse* and *menu*

▶ Doing windows

▶ Mindlessly opening and closing folders

• •

*1*f you haven't bought a Mac yet, go *immediately* to Appendix A. Don't speak to any salesperson until you've read it.

If you have bought a Mac, but it's sitting in cardboard boxes on your living-room floor, read the second half of Appendix A, where you'll be gently guided through the not-harrowing-at-all experience of plugging everything in.

At this moment, then, there should be a ready-to-roll Mac on your desk and a look of fevered anticipation on your face.

Box Open. Now What?

Switching the Mac on

In this very first lesson, you'll be asked to locate the On button. To keep life interesting, Apple has decreed that This Switch Shall Be In a Different Place on Every Different Mac Model. Fortunately, after you know where yours is, it'll pretty much stay in that spot for as long as you own your Mac.

There are five possible places you'll find the power switch. Here goes:

A keyboard button	*Every* Mac keyboard has this key in the upper-right corner. It has a left-pointing triangle on it: On many of the world's Macs, this key turns the machine on. If yours doesn't, you must have one of the other on-switch locations.
Back-panel switch	Feel around on the ends of your Mac's back panel. On many Macs, especially smallish or inexpensive ones, there's a plastic rocker switch back there. If you look at it, the On position is marked by a straight line, and the Off position is marked by a circle. Nobody can ever remember which is which. You may want to think of it this way: the *O* stands for *Off.* (Of course, it also stands for *On* . . . and they wonder why people are intimidated by computers?)
Round front-panel button	A couple of models (610, 6100) have a round nub of an On/Off button on the front panel, on the right side.
Back-panel pushbutton	PowerBook laptops only. If your model number begins with a 1, you have to flip open the back panel, which is a pain. You'll then see the round, concave power button. (If your PowerBook model number begins with a 5, you turn it on with the triangle-labeled key on your keyboard.)
Keyboard pushbutton	PowerBook Duos only. There's a rubber capsule-shaped button on the keyboard; it's your On switch. (There's an identical button on the back.)

Was your hunt for the elusive On Switch successful? Then turn the Mac on! You should hear a ding or a chord, and after a few seconds, an image appears on the screen.

When one On switch just isn't enough

A private sidebar only for owners of the Color Classic, LC 500-anything, or Performa 500-anything.

Your model actually has *two* power switches. First, there's a rocker switch on the back; it allows the current to reach the Mac. Turn it on today and forget it forever.

But turning on that back-panel switch doesn't actually start up your Mac. To do that, you *then*

have to press that power key on the keyboard . . . you know, the one with the triangle on it.

Oh, and by the way, your Mac's monitor goes off by itself if you don't use the computer for awhile. To wake it up when you come back from lunch, click the mouse button. (Read on for details on mice and buttons.)

What you'll probably see

After a moment, you should see the smiling Macintosh on the screen. It looks like this:

A few seconds after that, the words "Welcome to Macintosh" appear. Then the gray or tinted full-screen pattern, called the *desktop,* appears. Congratulations! You've arrived.

Skip ahead to "Your First Moments Alone Together."

Techie terms not worth learning

You may occasionally hear cocky teenagers tell you to "boot up." No, they're not taking you fly-fishing. That's computerese for turning on the Mac. You also hear people say *power up, start up,* and just *boot.*

Furthermore, after the computer is on, you're sometimes asked to turn it off and on again. This is called *rebooting,* or *restarting,* or sometimes *turning it off and on again.*

What you might see

The very first time you turn on your Mac, there's a chance that you'll see a disk with a blinking question mark like this:

The Mac, in its charming, universal, picture-based language of love, is trying to tell you that it can't find a disk to start up from. More specifically, it can't find an electronic *System Folder,* which is where the Mac's instructions to itself live. (You'll find more about this all-important folder in Chapter 6.)

If you see the blinking question mark icon, you've just met your first computer problem. Proceed directly to Chapter 12, "When Bad Things Happen to Good Machines." This problem, and many others, is explained — and solved — for you there.

What you might not see

Finally, there's a very remote possibility you might see *this* when you turn on the Mac:

In this case, your monitor is upside-down.

Your First Moments Alone Together

As any gadget lover can tell you, the most exciting period of appliance ownership comes at the very beginning. You're gonna love this stuff.

The 5th Wave — By Rich Tennant

"THERE! THERE! I TELL YOU IT JUST MOVED AGAIN!"

The big turn-off

Before we get into 3-D color graphs, space-vehicle trajectories, and DNA analysis, maybe you'd better learn how to turn the Mac off.

If you turned on your Mac with a back-panel rocker switch, then you already know how to turn it off; use the same switch.

If, on the other hand, you turn on your Mac by pressing a triangle key on your keyboard, pressing that key again won't turn the Mac off. You have to find the tiny, round, pea-sized On/Off button at the rear of the machine — it's on the left as you look at the back of the machine.

But turning off the Mac by chopping off its power is a no-no, according to Apple (although I've never heard of it hurting anything). The preferred method is to use the Shut Down command; we'll get to that in a moment.

Moving the mouse

The mouse is the gray, soap-sized plastic box on the desk beside your keyboard. Having trouble visualizing it as a rodent? Think of the cord as its tail, and (if it helps you) draw little eyeballs on the sloping side facing you.

Now then, roll the mouse across the desk (or mouse pad), keeping the cord pointed away from you. See how the arrow pointer moves across the screen? For the rest of your life, you'll hear that pointer called the *cursor.* And for the rest of your life, you'll hear moving the mouse called *moving the mouse.*

Try lifting the mouse off the desk and waving it around in midair like a remote control. Nothing happens, right? The mouse only controls the cursor when it's on a flat surface. (A ball on the bottom of it detects movement and moves the cursor accordingly.) That's a useful feature — it lets you pick up the mouse when you run out of desk space, but the cursor will stay in place on the screen. Only when you set the mouse down and begin to roll it again will the cursor continue moving.

If you have a PowerBook, by the way, you don't have a mouse. Studies have shown that rolling a gray, soap-sized plastic box across the thigh of the guy next to you on the airplane can have, ergonomically and socially speaking, unpleasant results. Therefore, you've been given, instead, either a *trackball* (essentially an upside-down mouse) or a *trackpad.* The principle is the same: roll your fingers away from you, and the cursor moves up the screen. Instead of a square mouse button, you have one or two jumbo buttons nestled against the ball or pad. (If you've got two buttons, they're identical in function.)

I won't mention this distinction again, because if you're smart enough to have bought a PowerBook, you're smart enough to translate future references to the mouse into trackball or touchpad terms.

What's on the menu?

Let's try some real computing here. Move the cursor up to the white strip at the top of the screen. It's called the *menu bar,* named after a delightful little pub near Cupertino. Touch the arrow on the word Special.

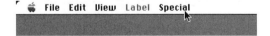

Pointing to something on the screen in this way has a technical term: *pointing*. (Think you're going to be able to handle this?)

Now put your index finger on the button on the mouse, and press the button down. Hold it down. Don't let go.

If all went well, you should see a list of commands drop down from the word Special, as shown in the following figure. Keep holding down the button.

```
 Special
  Clean Up Window
  Empty Trash

  Eject Disk        ⌘E
  Erase Disk...

  Restart
  Shut Down
```

Congratulations — you've learned how to *click the mouse* (by pressing the button), and you've also learned to *pull down a menu* (the list of commands). Try letting go of the mouse button; the menu disappears.

Shutting down

Click the word Special (in the menu bar) again. This time, when the list of commands appears, *keep the button pressed* and roll the mouse downward so that each successive command turns black. In Mac jargon, you're *dragging* the mouse (moving with the button pressed). And when each menu command turns black, it's said to be *highlighted*.

The only commands that don't get highlighted are the ones that are dimmed, or "grayed out." They're dimmed because they don't make any sense at the moment. For example, if there's no disk in the floppy-disk drive, choosing Eject Disk wouldn't make any sense (and it wouldn't work, either). So the Mac makes it gray, which means it's unavailable to you.

Roll the mouse all the way down to the words Shut Down so that they're highlighted.

If you've had enough for one session, release the mouse button — the Mac turns itself off.

Hey, you've only read a few pages, and already you can turn your Mac on and off! *Told* you it was no harder than a toaster.

If your thirst for knowledge is unquenched, and you want to slog ahead with this lesson, then don't let go of the button yet. Instead, slide the cursor *off* the menu in any direction, and *then* let go of the mouse button. The menu snaps back up like a window shade and nothing else happens. (A menu command only gets activated when you release the mouse while the cursor is *on* a command.)

When you're ready to forge forth, read on.

Moving things around on the desktop

Take a look around the Mac screen. You've already encountered menus (those words File, Edit, View, and so on at the top of the screen). Near the upper-right corner of the screen, you should see an *icon* (a small symbolic picture). If your Mac is brand new, that icon is called Macintosh HD.

For budget-Mac owners only

If your Mac model gets turned on by a switch on the back panel, this blurb's for you.

When you use the Shut Down command, your computer doesn't go all the way off. Instead, it just tells you (with a message on the screen) that it's *ready* to be turned off. Now you have to reach around to the back and physically push the switch off, to the – position. (Or was it the ○ position?)

Icons represent everything in the Mac world. They all look different: one represents a letter you wrote, another represents the Trash can, another represents a floppy disk you've inserted. Here are some examples of icons you'll probably be seeing before long:

You can move an icon by dragging it. Try this:

1. Point to the Trash icon.
2. Drag it to a new position (move the mouse while the button's down).

Hey, this thing isn't so technical after all, right?

Other than the fact that there's a Trash can, nobody's really sure why they call this "home-base" screen the desktop. It has another name, too: the *Finder*. It's where you file all your work into little electronic on-screen file folders, so you'll be able to *find* them again later.

Used in a sentence, you might hear it like this: "Well, no wonder you don't see the Trash can. You're not in the Finder!"

Icons, windows, and Macintosh syntax

Point to the hard-disk icon (a rectangular box, probably called Macintosh HD — for Hard Disk) in the upper-right corner of the screen. A hard disk is like a massive floppy disk. It's the filing cabinet that contains all your work, all your files, and all your software.

So how do you see what's in it? Where do you get to see its table of contents?

It turns out that any disk icon can be *opened* into a window, where you'll see every item inside listed individually. The window has the same name as the icon you opened.

Before we proceed, though, it's time for a lesson in Macintosh syntax. Fear not; it's nothing like English syntax. In fact, everything you do on the Macintosh has this format: noun-verb. Shakespeare it ain't, but it's sure easy to remember.

Let's try a noun-verb command, shall we?

1. Click the hard-disk icon in the upper-right corner of the screen.

It should turn black, indicating that it's *selected.* Good job — you've just identified the *noun.*

2. Move to the File menu and choose Open.

You guessed it — Open is the *verb.* And, sure enough, your hard disk *opens* into a window, where you can see its contents.

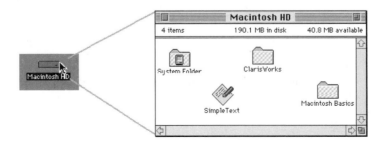

Did any of that make sense? In the world of Macintosh, you always specify *what* you want to change (using the mouse), and then you use a menu command to specify *how* you want it changed. You'll see this pattern over and over again: *select* something on the screen and then *apply* a menu command to it.

Look over the contents of your hard-drive window. See the following figure. (Everybody's got different stuff, so what you see on your screen won't exactly match these illustrations.) There are all kinds of neat things you can do to a window. They're worth learning — you're going to run into windows *everywhere* after you start working.

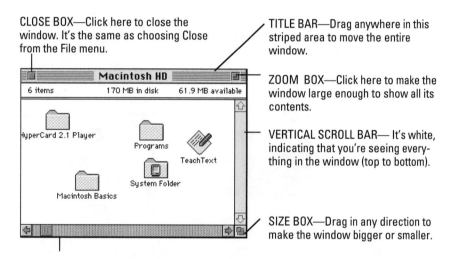

CLOSE BOX—Click here to close the window. It's the same as choosing Close from the File menu.

TITLE BAR—Drag anywhere in this striped area to move the entire window.

ZOOM BOX—Click here to make the window large enough to show all its contents.

VERTICAL SCROLL BAR— It's white, indicating that you're seeing everything in the window (top to bottom).

SIZE BOX—Drag in any direction to make the window bigger or smaller.

HORIZONTAL SCROLL BAR—It's gray, indicating that you're not seeing everything in the window (there's something off to the side). You can drag the little square from side to side to adjust your view of the window.

Go ahead and try out some of the little boxes and scroll bars. Click them. Tug on them. Open the window and close it again. No matter what you do, *you can never hurt the machine by doing "the wrong thing."* That's the wonderful thing about the Macintosh: it's the Nerf appliance.

Now try this. Make sure your hard drive window is open. See the System Folder? Even if you don't, here's a quick way to find it: quickly type *SY* on your keyboard.

Presto, the Mac finds the System Folder (which happens to be the first thing that begins with those letters) and highlights it, in effect dropping it in front of you, wagging its tail.

All systems are go

If nothing happened when you typed SY, your Mac may not be using the trendy behind-the-scenes software known as *System 7.* Absorb the wisdom of Chapter 6 if you care what this means.

However, it *is* worthwhile to know what version of this so-called "system software" your Mac uses. Fortunately, it's easy to find out.

Get a pencil.

See the Apple logo in the upper-left corner of the screen? That's no ordinary logo. It's actually a menu, just like the ones you've already experienced. Point your arrow cursor tip on the apple, hold the button down continuously, and watch what happens.

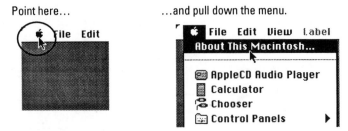

As with any menu, a list drops down. This one, however, has an extremely useful command. It's so important that it's separated by a dotted line from the mere mortal list items after it. It's *About This Macintosh.*

Slide the pointer down until About This Macintosh turns black, and then release the mouse button. A window appears:

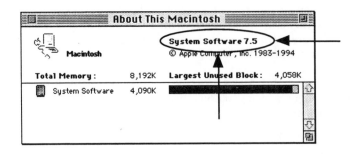

As the preceding figure indicates so subtly, this window reveals what version of the System software you have. It's either 6-point something or 7-point something. (It may even be 7-point-something-*point*-something, indicating that Apple uses a math even newer than New Math.)

In any case, this is a number you'll need to know later in this book and later in your life. Therefore, take this opportunity to write it onto your Cheat Sheet (the yellow cardboard sheet inside the front cover). There's a little blank for this information in the upper-left corner of your card, where it says your System version.

The main question is: do you have System 7 (-point anything) or System 6 (-point anything)? The answer will make a big difference, both to your understanding of this book and to your ability to get dates at computer-club meetings.

Because all Macs made since 1991 come with System 7, for the rest of this book I'm going to assume that you're using System 7 (or 7.1 or 7-point-anything). If your Mac is really old, and you've got System 6, watch the margins for special notes that refer to the differences between the two systems.

Double-clicking in theory and practice

Anyway, moving on: try pressing the arrow keys on your keyboard — right, left, up, down. The Mac highlights neighboring icons as you do so.

Suppose that you want to see what's in the System Folder. Of course, using your newfound noun-verb method, you could (1) click the System Folder to select it, and then (2) choose Open from the File menu.

But that's the sissy way. Try this power shortcut: point to the System Folder icon so that the tip of the arrow cursor is squarely inside the picture of the folder. Keeping the mouse still, click twice in rapid succession. With stunning originality, the Committee for the Invention of Computer Terminology calls this advanced computing technique *double-clicking.*

If all went well, your double-click opened a new window, showing you the contents of the System Folder. (If it didn't work, you probably need to keep the mouse still or double-click faster.)

Remember this juicy golden rule: *Double-click means "open."*

In your Mac life, you'll be asked (or tempted) to click many an item on-screen: buttons that say "OK"; tools that look like paintbrushes; all manner of multiple-choice buttons. In every one of these cases, you're supposed to click *once*.

Only when you want to *open* something do you double-click. Got it?

Multiple windows

Now you should have two windows open on the screen: the hard-disk window and the System Folder window. (The System Folder window may be covering the first one; they're like overlapping pieces of paper on a desk.)

Try this: Click the title bar of the System Folder window (just one click; remember that double-clicking is used exclusively for opening something). Drag the title bar downward until you can see the hard drive window behind it. See the following figure.

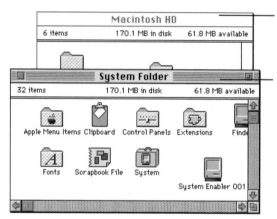

You can tell that this window is in back because its title bar is white. Just click anywhere in the window to bring it to the front.

You know that this window is the top window because its title bar is striped.

Take a stress-free moment to experiment with these two windows: click the back one to bring it forward; then click the one that was in front to bring it to the front again.

If you need any more help fooling around with these windows, the Macintosh manual has a complete tutorial.

Using a list view

There's one more aspect of windows that will probably make Type A personalities squirm with delight. Up 'til now, you've been viewing the contents of your disk as a bunch of icons. Nice, but wouldn't it be neat to see things alphabetically?

1. Make sure the System Folder is the active window (the one in front).

    We're going to use the System Folder because it's got a lot of stuff in it.

    Next, you're going to use a menu. Remember how to choose a menu command? Point to the menu's name and hold down the mouse button.

2. Locate the View menu at the top of the screen. From it, choose By Name.

Suddenly, the big icons are replaced by a neat alphabetical list of the window's contents.

The easiest homework you've ever had

To reinforce your budding mouse skills, here's a pathetically easy assignment. Find the icon in your hard drive window called either Macintosh Basics or Mouse Practice. (Macintosh Basics/Mouse Practice comes with every Mac sold in the last few years. If you can't find it anywhere, call up whatever store sold you the Mac and ask about it. And if you still can't get ahold of it, don't sweat. I'll try to hit most of the same points as we go along.)

It's a clever, animated introduction to the Mac, and it shows you America's favorite computer skills (the ones you just learned): pointing, clicking, and dragging.

For would-be weenies only (nonessential info)

When you view a window's contents in a list, each folder *within* the window is marked by a tiny triangle. The triangle points to the right.

You can open one of these folders-within-the-folder in the usual way, if you wish — by double-clicking. But it's much more satisfying for neat freaks to click the *triangle* instead. In the following figure, the before-and-after view of the Control Panels folder (inside the System Folder) shows how much more organized you can be.

When you click the triangle, in other words, your window becomes like an outline. The contents of that subfolder are indented. To "collapse," or close, the folder, click the downward-pointing triangle.

One more trick: See the words Size, Kind, and so on (at the top of the window)? Click any of these words. Instantly the Mac re-sorts everything in the window, based on the word you clicked. Example: Click Size, and you'll see the largest files listed first.

System Folder		
17 items	22.5 MB in disk	54.3 MB available
Name	Size	Kind
▷ ☐ Apple Menu Items	105K	folder
☐ Clipboard	56K	file
▷ ☐ Control Panels	291K	folder
▷ ☐ Extensions	1,235K	folder
☐ Finder	356K	file
☐ Note Pad File	3K	file
▷ ☐ Preferences	20K	folder
▷ ☐ PrintMonitor Documents	zero K	folder

System Folder		
22 items	22.5 MB in disk	54.3 MB available
Name	Size	Kind
▷ ☐ Apple Menu Items	105K	folder
☐ Clipboard	56K	file
▽ ☐ Control Panels	78K	folder
☐ Color	12K	contr
☐ General Controls	17K	contr
☐ Monitors	41K	contr
☐ Mouse	9K	contr
▷ ☐ Extensions	1,235K	folder

Here's how you use the Macintosh Basics program:

1. Open the Macintosh Basics (or Mouse Practice) folder, if necessary, by pointing to it and double-clicking.

2. Point to the little Macintosh Basics man (or Mouse Practice Woman) and double-click *that*.

From there, just follow the instructions on the screen. Turn down the corner of this page, and pick up here when you're ready to go on. By the time you finish, you'll have earned your MMA — Master of Mouse Activity.

Pit stop

Shut the Mac down now, if you want (by choosing the Shut Down command from the Special menu — but you knew that). Chapter $1^1/_2$ is something of a chalk-talk to help you explain what's really happening inside the computer's puny brain.

Top Ten Similarities Between You and Your Mac

Before you move boldly forward to the next chapter, ponder the significance of the following frightening similarities between you and your computer.

1. Both weigh between 5 and 15 pounds when first displayed in public.

2. Both have feet on the bottom.

3. Both have slots to provide adequate ventilation of the innards.

4. Both react to the movement of a nearby mouse.

5. Both sometimes crash when asked to do too much at once.

6. Both have a central button.

7. Both light up when turned on.

8. With considerable effort, both may be made to work with IBM computers.

9. Both may be connected to a phone line for days at a time.

10. Both have a built-in 1.4MB SuperDrive. (Well, OK, *you* probably don't, but you don't want to be *exactly* like your computer, do you?)

Chapter 1½
High-Tech Made Easy

How a Mac Works

I'm a little worried about sticking this chapter so close to the front of the book. Plenty of people firmly believe that the Mac has a personality — that when something goes wrong, the Mac is being cranky; and when a funny message appears on the screen, the Mac is being friendly. Don't let the following discussion of cold, metal, impersonal circuitry ruin that image for you; the Mac *does* have a personality, no matter what the wireheads say.

For the first time, you're going to have to roll up your brain's sleeves and chew on some real, live computer jargon. Don't worry — you'll feel coolly professional and in control by the time it's over. And it's a short chapter. Only *half* a chapter, really. That should make it easier to contemplate reading pages of chalk talk.

Storing things with floppy disks

Human beings, for the most part, store information in one of two places. Either we retain something in our memory — or, if it's too much to remember, we write it down on the back of an envelope.

Computers work pretty much the same way (except they're not quite as handy with envelopes). They can either store what they know in their relatively pea-brained *memory,* which I'll cover in a moment, or they can write it down. A computer writes stuff down on computer disks.

The most common kind of disk is the floppy disk. Unfortunately for your efforts to understand the Mac, its floppy disks aren't floppy, and they're not disks. They're actually hard plastic squares, $3\frac{1}{2}$ inches on a side.

Inside the protective hard shell, though, there's a circle of the same shiny brown stuff that cassette tapes are made of. (I suppose that means there really is a floppy disk in there.) Anyway, instead of recording a James Taylor song or a Bruce Willis movie, as audio or videotapes would do, the computer records your documents: a letter to Aunt Millie, your latest financial figures, or notes for your novel.

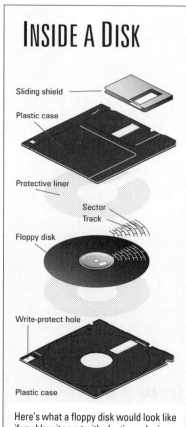

Inside a Disk

Sliding shield

Plastic case

Protective liner

Sector

Track

Floppy disk

Write-protect hole

Plastic case

Here's what a floppy disk would look like if you blew it apart with plastic explosives. In the middle, sandwiched between the two protective Stridex pads, there lies a shiny plastic disk to which you entrust your sacred data.

Floppy disks come in several capacities, but even the largest one only holds about 1,000 pages' worth of data. That may seem like a lot, but that's just text. Pictures, for instance, take up much more space; that same floppy disk can probably only hold one or two color pictures. You can see, then, that floppies aren't very handy for storing lots of information.

Conceptualizing the hard disk

Every Mac made since 1987 has an even better storage device built inside it — a *hard disk.* The concept of a hard disk confuses people because it's hidden inside the Mac's case. Since you can't see it or touch it, it's sort of conceptual — like beta-carotene or God, I guess. But it's there, spinning quietly away, and a hefty chunk of your Mac's purchase price pays for it.

Hard disks differ from floppy disks in a few critical ways. A hard disk delivers information to the computer's brain about ten times faster, holds about 100 times more, and costs about 500 times as much. (Floppies are dirt cheap.)

Why all this talk of disks? Because this is where your life's work is going to live when the computer is shut off. Don't be confused if you hear the terms *hard disk* and *hard drive* used interchangeably — they're the same thing.

Understanding memory

OK. Now we get to the good stuff: how a computer really works. I know you'd just as soon not know what's going on in there, but this is mental broccoli: it's good for you, and later in life, you'll be glad you were forced to digest it. If, at this point, your brain is beginning to hemorrhage, skip this section and find serenity in Chapter 2.

There's actually a significant difference between a *Mac's* memory and *your* memory (besides the fact that yours is probably much more interesting). When the Mac is turned off at night, it forgets *everything*. It becomes a dumb, metal-and-plastic doorstop. That's because a computer's memory, just like yours, is kept alive by electrical impulses. When you turn off a Mac, the electricity stops.

Therefore, each time you turn on a Mac, it has to re-learn everything it ever knew, including the fact that it's a computer, what kind of computer it is, how to display text, how many days until your warranty expires, and so on. Now we arrive at the purpose of those disks we've been droning on about; that's where the computer's knowledge lives when the juice is off. Without a disk, the Mac is like someone with a completely hollow skull (and we've all met *that* type). If you're ever unlucky enough to experience a broken hard drive, you'll see how exciting a Mac can be without any disks: it shows a completely gray screen with a small blinking question mark in the middle. (I've met a few people like *that*, too.)

When you turn on the Mac, there's whirring and blinking. The hard disk inside begins to spin. When it hits about 3,600 rpm, the Mac starts reading the hard disk — it "plays" the disk like a record player. It finds out: "Hey, I'm a Mac! And this is how I display text!" and so on. The Mac is reading the disk and copying everything it reads into *memory*.

Memory is really neat. After something's in memory, it's instantaneously available to the computer. The Mac no longer has to read the disk to learn something. Memory is also expensive; it's really a bunch of complicated circuits etched onto a piece of silicon the size of a stick of gum.

Because it's expensive, most people's Macs have far less memory than disk space. For example, even if your hard disk holds every issue of *National Geographic* ever published, you're probably only going to *read* one article at a time. So the Mac reads "African Tribal Women: Pierced Noses in the Desert" from

The 5th Wave   **By Rich Tennant**

"IT'S NOT THAT IT DOESN'T WORK AS A COMPUTER,
IT JUST WORKS BETTER AS A PAPERWEIGHT."

your hard disk, loads it into memory, and displays it on the screen. So it doesn't matter that your Mac's memory doesn't hold as much as your entire hard disk; the hard disk is used for *long-term, permanent* storage of *lots* of things, and memory is used for *temporary* storage while you work on *one thing at a time.*

Who's Meg?

You often hear computer jocks talk about megs. Only rarely are they referring to Meg Ryan and Meg Tilly. Meg is short for *megabyte.* So is the abbreviation MB. (*Mega*=1,000,000 and *byte*=an iota of information so small it takes about eight of them to specify the letter A.)

What's highly confusing to most beginners is that memory (fast, expensive, temporary) and hard-disk space (permanent, slower) are measured in the *same units:* megabytes. A typical Mac has four or eight megs of memory (silicon chips), but 120 or 250 megs of hard-disk space (spinning platters).

With this vital fact in mind, see if you can answer the following paradoxical dinner party question:

"*How many megs* does your Macintosh have?"

The novice's answer: "Um . . . say, have you tried those little cocktail weenies?"

The partly-initiated's reply: "I . . . I think 80?"

The truly enlightened response: "What do you mean, how many megs? Are you referring to *memory* or to *hard-disk storage space?* Here, have a cocktail weenie."

Understanding RAM

Let's add another term to your quickly growing nerd vocabulary list. It pains me to teach you this word because it's one of those really meaningless terms that was invented purely to intimidate people. Trouble is, you're going to hear it a lot. You may as well be prepared.

It's *RAM.* You pronounce it like the goat. RAM is memory. A typical Mac has four or eight megs of RAM (in other words, of memory).

Incidentally, this might be a good time to find out how much RAM *you* have. Here's how to find out.

Turn on your Mac.

Remember the Apple menu? The fruit in the upper-left corner of the screen? Pull down that menu as you did in Chapter 1. Once again, slide the pointer down until About This Macintosh turns black, and then release the mouse button.

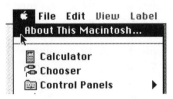

A window appears.

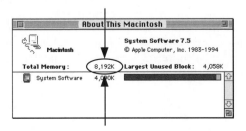

Why they call it RAM

You know what an *acronym* is, right? It's a bunch of initials, like M.A.D.D. or SALT Treaty . . . or RAM.

When the Committee for Arbitrary Acronyms ratified the abbreviation RAM, it probably stood for

Random Abbreviation for Memory. Today, it supposedly stands for Random Access Memory.

Whatever *that* means.

The number shown in the preceding figure is how much RAM your Mac has. If you lop off everything after the comma (only mentally, please), you're left with the number of *megs* of RAM. It's probably 4, 5, 8, or 16 megs. Older Macs may have less; high-powered expensive ones may have more.

In any case, this is a statistic you'll enjoy reviewing again and again. Therefore, take this opportunity to write this number, too, onto your Cheat Sheet at the front of the book. There's a little blank for this information, nearby where you wrote your System-software version.

Putting it all together

OK. Now that you know where a computer's information lives, let me take you on a tour of the computer's guts. Let's get into our little imaginary Disney World tram. Keep hands and feet inside the car at all times.

When you turn on the Mac, as noted earlier, the hard disk spins, and the Mac copies certain critical information into its memory. So far, the Mac only knows that it's a computer. It doesn't know anything else that's stored on your hard disk. It doesn't know about African Tribal Women, or your new screenplay, or how much you owe on your credit card — yet.

To get any practical work done, you now have to transfer the article (or screenplay, or spreadsheet) into memory; in Macintosh terminology, you have to *open a file*. In Chapter 2, you find out how easy and idiot-proof this is. Anyway, after you open a file, it appears on the screen. (It's in memory now.)

While your document is on the screen, you can make changes to it. This, of course, is why you bought a computer in the first place. You can delete a sentence from your novel or move a steamy scene to a different chapter (the term for this process is *word processing*). If you're working on your finances, you can add a couple of zeros to your checking-account balance (the term for this process is *wishful thinking*). All without any eraser crumbs or whiteout.

Perceptive readers (who haven't already gotten bored and gone off to watch TV) will recognize that you're making all these changes to what's in *memory*. The more you change the screenplay that's up on the screen, the more it's different from that *permanent* copy that's still on your disk, safe and sound.

At this point, you're actually in a pretty precarious position. Remember that memory is sustained by electricity. In other words, if your four-year-old mistakes the Mac's power cord for a handy suckable plaything and jerks it out of the wall, then the electricity stops, the screen goes blank, and all the changes you've made disappear forever. You're left with the original copy on the disk, of course, but any work you've done on it vanishes, along with anything else in the Mac's memory.

However, every Mac program has a simple command, called Save, that saves your work back onto the hard disk. That is, the computer updates the original copy that's still on the hard disk, and you're safe. Even if a sun storm wipes out all power plants in the Northern Hemisphere and your Mac goes dark, your novel or letter or spreadsheet is safe on the disk. Most people use the Save command every five or ten minutes so that their work is always up to date and preserved on the disk. (You learn how to use the Save command in Chapter 3.)

"I lost all my work!"

So that you'll quit worrying about it, the precariousness of memory accounts for the horror stories you sometimes hear from people who claim that they lost their work to a computer. "I was on volume Y of the encyclopedia I've been writing," they'll say, "and I lost all of it because of a computer glitch!"

Now you can cry crocodile tears and then skip back to your office with a smirk. *You* know what happened. They probably worked for hours with some document on the screen but forgot to use the Save command. Then, when the unthinkable happened — someone tripped on the power cord — sure enough, all the changes they'd made got wiped out. A simple Save command would have stored everything neatly on the hard disk.

Top Ten Differences Between Memory and a Hard Disk

May you never confuse memory with a hard disk again.

1. You usually buy memory two or four megs at a time. Hard disks come in 40-, 80-, and 160-meg sizes (and on up).

2. Memory comes as chips on a little minicircuit board. A hard disk is a big box made of metal (and sometimes encased in plastic).

3. You can only install memory inside the computer (something you usually hire a local guru to do). A hard disk may be inside the Mac (an *internal* drive) or a separate box you just plug into the back (an *external* drive).

4. Memory delivers information to the Mac's brain almost instantly. The hard disk sometimes seems to take forever.

5. Memory is sometimes called RAM. A hard disk has no abbreviation.

6. Not every Mac has a hard disk (about 11 people still use very old models with nothing but floppy disks). But every Mac has memory.

7. When the Mac is reading some information off a hard disk, a little light on the computer's case may flicker on and off (on the front of most Macs, or on the case of an external hard disk). You can't tell when the Mac is getting information from RAM.

8. As a very general rule, RAM costs about $40 per meg, and hard drive space averages about $2 per meg.

9. Memory's contents disappear when you turn off the computer. A disk's contents stay there until you deliberately throw them away.

10. You can trick the Mac into thinking that some of your *hard-disk* space is RAM (called *virtual memory*). You can also trick the Mac into thinking that some of your RAM is a disk (called a *RAM disk*). (Actually, I guess this is really a similarity, not a difference. Oh well. Both of these advanced techniques are described in your Mac manuals, more or less. Neither is important except to power-users; most people don't use either one. I'm already sorry I brought it up.)

Chapter 2
Doing Windows, Getting Floppy

● ●

In This Chapter

▶ All about windows, folders, and icons

▶ Learning keyboard shortcuts

▶ Working with floppy disks

▶ Tips on using windows and floppy disks to raise your social status

● ●

Becoming Manipulative

All of the clicking and dragging and window-shoving you learned in Chapter 1 is, in fact, leading up to something useful.

Foldermania

I've said that your hard disk is like the world's biggest filing cabinet. It's where you store all your stuff. But a filing cabinet without filing *folders* would be about as convenient to handle as an egg without a shell.

The folders on the Mac screen don't occupy any space on your hard drive. They're electronic fictions whose sole purpose is to help you organize your stuff.

Mr. Folder

The Mac provides an infinite supply of them. Want a folder? Do this:

From the File menu, choose New Folder.

Ooh, tricky, this machine! A new folder appears. Note that the Mac gracefully proposes "untitled folder" as its name. (Gotta call it *something*, I suppose.)

Notice something else, though: the name is *highlighted* (black). Remember our earlier lesson? Highlighted = selected = ready for you to *do* something. When *text* is highlighted, the Mac is ready for you to *replace* it with anything you type. In other words, you don't even have to backspace over it. Just type away.

1. Type *USA Folder*. Press the Return key.

   The Return key tells the Mac that your naming spurt is over.

   Now, to see how folders work, create another one.

2. Choose New Folder from the File menu again.

   Another new folder appears, once more waiting for a title.

3. Type *Ohio*. Press Return.

USA Folder

Ohio

You're going to create one more empty folder. But by this time, your wrist is probably weary from the forlorn trek back and forth to the File menu. Don't you wish there were a faster way to make a folder?

There is.

Keyboard shortcuts

Pull down the File menu, but don't select any of the commands in it yet. See that weird notation to the right of some of the commands?

```
┌─────────────────────────┐
│ File                    │
│ New Folder        ⌘N    │
│ Open              ⌘O    │
│ Print             ⌘P    │
│ Close Window      ⌘W    │
│                         │
│ Get Info          ⌘I    │
│ Sharing...              │
│ Duplicate         ⌘D    │
│ Make Alias        ⌘M    │
│ Put Away          ⌘Y    │
│                         │
│ Find...           ⌘F    │
│ Find Again        ⌘G    │
│                         │
│ Page Setup...           │
│ Print Window...         │
└─────────────────────────┘
```

Get used to 'em. They're *keyboard shortcuts,* and they appear in almost every menu you'll ever see. You're by no means obligated to use them, but you should understand that they let you select certain menu items without using the mouse.

When you type, you press the Shift key to make a capital letter, right? They call the Shift key a *modifier key* because it turns ordinary, well-behaved citizen keys like 3 and 4 into madcap symbols like # and $. Welcome to the world of computers, where everything is four times more complicated. Instead of having only *one* modifier key, the Mac has *four* of them! Look down next to your spacebar. There they are: in addition to the Shift key, one says Option, one says Control, and another either says Command or has a little ⌘ symbol on it.

It's that little cloverleaf symbol that appears in the File menu. Next to the New Folder command, it's ⌘-N. That means:

1. While pressing the ⌘ key down, press the N key. Then release everything.

   Bam! You've got yourself another folder.

2. Type *Michigan* and press Return.

   You've just named your third folder. So why have you been wasting a perfectly good afternoon (or whatever it is in your time zone) making empty folders? So you can pretend you're getting organized.

3. Drag the Ohio folder on top of the USA Folder.

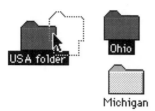

Make sure that the tip of the arrow actually hits the center of the USA Folder so that the folder becomes highlighted. When it turns black, let go of the Ohio folder — and watch it disappear into the USA Folder. (If your aim wasn't good, you'll now see the Ohio folder sitting *next* to the USA Folder; try the last step again.)

4. Put the Michigan folder into the USA Folder in the same way — by dragging it on top of the USA Folder.

As far as you know, though, those state folders have *disappeared*. How can you trust me that they're now neatly filed away?

5. Double-click the USA Folder.

Yep. Opens right up into a window, and there are your two darling states, nestled sweetly where they belong.

Unimportant sidebar about other menu symbols

Besides the little keyboard-shortcut symbols at the right side of a menu, you'll occasionally run into a little downward-pointing arrow, like this:

Font
Avant Garde
Bookman
Chicago
Courier
Futura
Garamond
Geneva
Hartel
Helvetica
Monaco
Palatino
Symbol
▼

That arrow tells you that the menu is so long, it doesn't even fit on the screen. The arrow is implying that there are still more commands in the menu that you're not seeing. To get to them, carefully roll the pointer down the menu all the way to that down-pointing triangle. Don't let it scare you: The menu commands will jump upward, bringing the hidden ones into view.

If you were to double-click one of the *state* folders, you'd open *another* window. (Having a million windows open at once is nothing to be afraid of. If you're a neatness freak, it might make you feel threatened, but it's easy enough to close them — remember the close box in the upper-left corner of each one.)

OK, so how do you get these inner folders *out* again? Do you have to drag them individually? That would certainly be a bummer if you had all 50 folders in the USA Folder.

Turns out there are several ways to select more than one icon at a time.

6. Click above and to the left of the Ohio folder (Example 1, below). Without releasing the mouse, drag down and to the right so that you enclose both folders with a dotted rectangle (Examples 2 and 3).

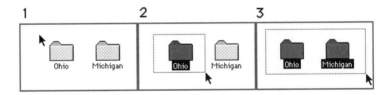

Release the mouse button when you've got both icons enclosed.

Now that you have several folders selected, you can move them en masse to another location.

7. Drag the Ohio folder outside of the USA Folder window. The Michigan folder goes along for the ride.

This was a somewhat unproductive exercise, of course, because we were only working with empty folders. It gets much more exciting when you start working with your own documents. All of these techniques work equally well with folders and with documents.

God never closes a window

When you opened the USA folder, did you notice how its icon changed texture? After you double-clicked it, the icon turned dark and sort of grainy.

It's supposed to do that. When you double-click *any* icon to make its window appear, the icon itself turns into a grainy silhouette. That's your visual clue that it's been opened.

The icon won't collapse back into its normal, more attractive state until you close the corresponding window. (Can't find it? Then double-click the already-opened icon *again.* Its window will pop to the fore.)

Yet to be opened   Already opened

USA Folder   USA Folder

Cartridge   Cartridge

Macintosh HD   Macintosh HD

How to trash something

Here's one more icon-manipulation trick you'll probably find valuable.

1. Close the USA Folder by clicking its close box.

2. Then drag the folder on top of the Trash can in the lower-right corner of the screen.

Don't let go until the Trash can actually turns black (when the tip of the arrow cursor is upon it). When you do let go, notice how the Trash can bulges, a subtle reinforcement of how important it thinks your stuff is. Anyway, that's how you throw things out on the Mac: just drag them on top of the Trash can.

Technically, you've really only put that stuff in Oblivion Waiting Room; it doesn't disappear when it goes into the Trash. It'll sit there forever, in a bulging trash can.

Eminently skippable trivia

The method of selecting several icons by dragging a rectangle around them is fine if all the icons are next to each other. But how would you select only the icons that begin with the letter A in this picture?

You can't very well enclose the A's by dragging the mouse — you'd also get all the *other* icons within the same rectangle.

The power-user's secret: Click each one *while pressing the Shift key.* As long as you're pressing Shift, you continually add additional, non-adjacent icons to the selection. (And if you Shift-click one by accident, you can *de*select it by Shift-clicking *again.* Try it!)

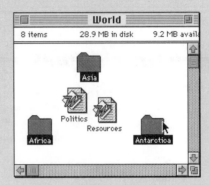

If you need to rescue something, just double-click the Trash to open its window; drag whatever-it-was right back onto the screen.

So if putting something into the Trash doesn't really delete it, how *do* you really delete it? Choose Empty Trash from the Special menu.

Trash and System 6

If you're using System 6 (did you take the test in Chapter 1 to find out?), then the Trash can *doesn't* sit there, bulging, until you Empty Trash. It gets emptied automatically when you turn off the Mac, and sometimes sooner.

A truly trivial trash tidbit for techies

Don't tell anybody, but *even after* you've Emptied the Trash, your file *still* isn't really gone forever. There are programs (like Norton Utilities and Central Point MacTools) that can unerase a file that's been trashed, as long as you haven't used your Mac much since then. That's useful to remember in case (1) you ever trash something by mistake, or (2) you're a spy.

Fun with Floppies

For our next trick, you're going to need a floppy disk. If you didn't buy a box of blank disks with your Mac, you're going to need some eventually. Call up Mac Connection and order some. They're cheap and you'll have them by tomorrow morning. (Phone number is in the Resource Resource at the back of the book.)

Take your first disk. Hold it flat. You're going to slip it into the Mac *metal side* first, *label side* up.

1. Put the floppy disk into the *disk drive slot,* which is the thin horizontal slit on the front of your Mac (or the side of your PowerBook). Keep pushing it in until the Mac gulps it in with a satisfying *kachunk.*

   If it's a brand new disk, or not a Mac disk, you'll probably see this message:

   Go ahead. Click Initialize. (If you're asked whether you want to make it *single-sided* [the kind of disk that's way obsolete] or *double-sided,* select double-sided — unless you're going to be sending this disk to someone who bought a Mac in 1984 and immediately moved to Borneo.)

   You're then asked to name the disk; type a name, click OK, and then wait about 45 seconds while the Mac prepares the disk for its new life as your data receptacle.

A floppy factoid barely worth reading

You know how an audio cassette has that small plastic tab, which you can pry out to prevent your little sister from accidentally recording over the tape?

Well, a floppy has the same thing (a tab, not a sister). In the corner of the disk, on the back, there's a little square sliding tab. On a disk, you don't actually have to pry out the tab (this is

progress); you can just slide it back and forth. When you slide the tab so that you can see through the hole, you've *locked* the disk, and you can't erase it or trash any of its contents.

When you slide the tab so that it *covers* the hole, the disk is unlocked, and you can erase it, trash it, or copy new stuff onto it.

If it's *not* a new disk — for example, if you're using one of the disks that came with your Mac — the floppy-disk icon shows up on the right side, just beneath your hard-disk icon:

To see what's on the disk, double-click the icon. As you've no doubt tired of hearing repeated, a *double-click* on a disk icon *opens* its contents window.

You're about to learn how to copy stuff from your hard drive onto a floppy disk (and vice versa). This is important stuff: In your lifetime, you'll do a lot of copying from floppy disks *to* your hard drive (such as when you buy a new program and want to put it on your hard drive). And if you're smart, you'll also do a lot of copying onto floppies *from* your hard drive (such as when you make a backup copy of all your work, in preparation for the inevitable day when your hard disk calls in sick).

2. Double-click your hard-disk icon.

   If its window was closed, it now opens. If the window was open but hidden behind the floppy-disk window, the hard-disk window now pops to the front.

3. Drag the Ohio folder on top of the floppy-disk icon.

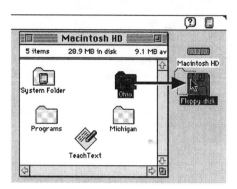

If you already trashed your Ohio folder, no big deal. Choose New Folder from the File menu (or press ⌘-N) to create a new folder. Drag that instead.

The point is that, on a Macintosh, making a copy of something is as easy as dragging it to the disk you want it copied onto. You can also drag something into the disk's *window* (instead of onto its *icon*).

Copying something *from* a floppy *to* your hard disk is equally easy. Open the floppy-disk window (by double-clicking the floppy-disk icon). Then drag whatever icons you want from the window onto the hard-disk icon (or into the hard-disk window).

For example, in the illustration below, two files are being copied from a floppy disk — not just into the hard-disk window, but into a *specific folder* on the hard disk:

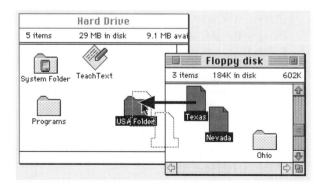

You can make as many copies of a file as you want without ever experiencing a loss of quality. You're digital now, kids. It's not like copying tapes, where each copy of a copy is a little bit worse than the previous generation. The ten-thousandth copy of your novel will be just as spicy as the first. (That makes software companies nervous; some unscrupulous people make a regular habit of making themselves free copies of their friends' expensive software.)

OK, so you've made a backup copy of your fourth-quarter report, or you've just copied a new program onto your hard disk. Now what? How do you get the disk out?

Well, you wouldn't be alone in guessing that you use the Eject Disk command in the Special menu. But you'd be wrong, more or less. The Eject Disk command does spit out the disk — but it leaves the disk's *icon* on the screen so that the Mac thinks it's still available. The minute you try to go on with your work, the Mac will start displaying messages demanding that you give the disk back to it.

A much better way to get rid of the disk is to select it (noun) and choose *Put Away* (verb) from the File menu. That makes the disk pop out, *and* its image disappears from the screen. (If you care, there's a keyboard shortcut for Put Away: ⌘-Y.)

More disk stuff you don't really need to know

The big floppy-disk makers, like Sony and Fuji, churn out disks by the trainload. They have a big market; both Macs and IBM-type computers use these 3½-inch disks.

The thing is, not all computers *format* the floppies in the same ways. Imagine that a little floppy-disk gnome runs around while the disk is being "initialized," making chalk-mark boundaries for the storage of your files. Well, Mac gnomes and IBM gnomes space their disk-surface boundary lines differently — an IBM disk will appear unreadable to a Mac, and vice versa. So Sony and Fuji and the other disk companies don't bother preformatting these disks for you since they don't know what kind of computer you have, and besides it's too much trouble.

As noted in Chapter 1½, disks come in three capacities, although all the disks look almost alike: the old 400K, or *single-sided* disks; 800K, or *double-sided* disks; and 1.4MB, or *high-density* disks. That is a *lot* of storage for such a little disk; 1.4 megabytes is around 1400K, or 3.5 times as much as the original single-sided disks. High-density disks are marked with the letters CH, for some reason:

Well, OK, it's really supposed to be an upside-down *HD,* for high-density, but the logo designer had a bad night. Anyway, all *recent* Macs can read high-density disks, but there are millions of Mac Pluses and older SE models that can't. So when you exchange disks with somebody with an older Mac, give them 800K (double-sided) disks unless you've made sure they can handle the HD ones.

Dweebs' Corner: Alternative disk tips

Another way to remove a floppy disk is to drag its icon to the Trash can! Yes, yes, I *know* it looks like you're erasing the entire disk. It looks that way to *every* first-time Mac user. But you're not— this action just pops out the disk.

Every now and then, you'll have a situation where a disk won't come out of the drive. If the Mac is still running, hold down the ⌘ and Shift keys together, and press 1. (This works even if you're not at the

desktop/Finder.) Even less frequently than that, you'll have a disk in the drive and the Mac will be *off.* In that case, turn on the Mac while pressing the mouse button down continuously until the Trash can appears.

And if *that* doesn't pop the disk out, straighten a paper clip. Push it slowly but firmly into the tiny pinhole to the right of the disk drive slot. That'll shove the disk out.

Top Ten Window, Disk, and Trash Tips

Staggering through the basics of using your Mac unattended is one thing. Shoving around those on-screen windows and icons with Gretzky-esque grace is quite another. Master the following and then invite your friends to come over some evening to watch.

1. To rename an icon or disk, click carefully on its name. Wait for a second or so, until a rectangle appears around the name. That's your cue to type away, giving it a new name. Press Return when you're done.

1. **2.** **3.**

It works a little differently in System 6. Just click an icon and start typing. No rectangle, no waiting.

2. If you're looking at a windowful of file icons, you can select one by typing the first couple of letters of its name.

3. Don't forget that you can look at a window's contents in a neat list (choose "by Name" from the View menu). Once in a list view, when a folder is highlighted, you can press ⌘→ to expand it (as though you'd clicked the triangle to view its contents) and ⌘← to collapse it again.

4. In System 7, every time you choose Empty Trash from the Special menu, the Mac asks you if you're absolutely sure. If you'd prefer to simply vaporize the Trash contents without asking, select the Trash icon. Choose Get Info from the File menu and click the "Warn before emptying" checkbox so that the X disappears.

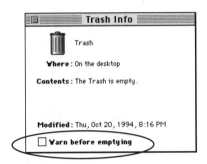

5. If you're trying to make a copy of a floppy disk, and you only have one floppy-disk drive, you'll find that the Mac can only copy a little bit at a time. It winds up asking you to insert one disk, then the other; one disk, then the other . . . until your wrists are swollen and bleeding.

   A better, faster idea: Copy the entire disk to your *hard disk,* eject the floppy, insert the blank floppy, and then copy the stuff from the hard disk to the new floppy. Using the hard disk as an intermediate holding tank in this way eliminates the disk swapping. (Just trash the superfluous copy from your hard disk when it's all over.)

6. If you have a very important document, you can prevent it from getting thrown away by accident. Click its icon. Choose Get Info from the File menu. Select the Locked checkbox. Now, even if you put it in the Trash and try to empty the Trash, the Mac will simply tell you that there's a locked item in the Trash, which it won't get rid of.

7. You already know how to copy a file from one disk to another. You can copy it on the *same* disk, too. Click the icon and choose Duplicate from the File menu.

   Or, while pressing the Option key, drag the icon onto a new window or folder.

8. Isn't it frustrating to open a window that's too small to show you all of its contents?

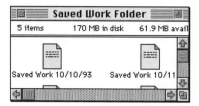

Of course, you could spend a weekend fussing with the scroll bars, trying to crank the other icons into view. Or, using error-and-trial, you could drag the lower-right handle (the resize box) to make the window bigger.

There's a much quicker solution. Click the *zoom box* in the upper-right corner of the window. The Mac automatically makes the window *exactly* large enough to show all of the icons.

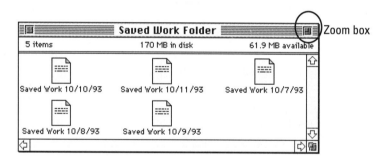

9. You don't have to be content to leave the Trash stranded way down there at the bottom of your screen. You can move it anywhere you want, just by dragging it. That's especially handy if you're lucky enough to have one of those screens the size of a Cineplex Odeon and don't feel like packing a week's worth of supplies every time you want to make a Journey to the Trash Corner.

10. You don't have to eject disks and clean up your windows before you shut down the computer. The disks pop out automatically, and the windows will be right where you left them the next time you turn on the Mac.

Chapter 3

Actually Getting Some Work Done

● ●

In This Chapter

▶ What software is, for those who care

▶ Copying and pasting

▶ Your very first word processing lesson

▶ Saving your work for posterity

▶ Desk accessories and the fruit-shaped menu they're listed in

● ●

*T*he Mac is like a VCR. The disks you slide into the Mac are like the tapes you slip into your VCR. Without tapes (disks), the VCR (Mac) is worthless. But with tapes (disks), your VCR (Mac) can take on any personality.

A VCR might let you watch a Western one night, home movies another, and a *60 Minutes* exposé about a corrupt Good Humor man another night. In the same way, your Mac can be a typing instructor, a checkbook balancer, or a movie-editing machine, depending on the software you buy. Each piece of software — usually called a program, but sometimes known as an *application* — is like a different GameBoy cartridge: It makes the Mac look, feel, and behave differently. The average Mac user winds up using about six or seven different programs regularly.

Obsolescence Therapy II

Your relationship with a software company doesn't end when you buy the program. First, the company provides a technical help staff for you to call when things get rocky. Some firms are great about this — it's a toll-free number that's answered immediately by a smart, helpful, customer-oriented technician. More often, though, sending out an SOS is a long-distance call . . . and a long-distance five- or ten-minute wait before somebody can help you. How can you find out how good a company's help line is? By asking around and reading the reviews in *Macworld* and *MacUser* magazines.

Like the computers themselves, software applications are continually being improved and enhanced by their manufacturers. Just as in owning a computer, owning a software program isn't a one-time cash outlay; each time the software company comes out with a new version of the program, you'll be offered the chance to get it for a small "upgrade fee" of $25 or $99, for example.

You'd think people would get fed up with this endless treadmill of expenses and just stick with the version they've got, refusing to upgrade to successive versions. Some manage it. Most people, however, succumb to the fear that somehow they'll be left behind by the march of technology, and wind up forking over the upgrade fees once a year or so.

Credit Card Workout #2: Buying Software

(Credit Card Workout #1, by the way, was buying the computer.)

Unless you actually bought (or received) some software when you got your Mac, you won't be able to do much more than admire the Mac's contribution to the décor. So unless you bought a Performa model, which comes with a handsome bonus gift of software preinstalled on your hard disk, get ready for another buying spree.

Names and numbers

After you spend a while with Macs, you start to notice some peculiar naming conventions in software. First of all, all programmers must have broken spacebars, because you never see spaces between words in the names of programs: PageMaker, MacPaint, WriteNow, and even MyAdvancedLabelMaker (I'm not making these up). Today, having a space in your title is like clipping your nails on the bus: it's simply not done by our kind of people.

You learn to tell how recent a program is by the version number after its name. What begins as

WordMeister Version 1 becomes WordMeister 1.5 when its maker adds a spelling checker to the program, for example. Then they add built-in help messages and call it WordMeister 1.5.2. I don't know where the idea of *multiple* decimal points came from, but it's pretty dumb. It's only a matter of time before we'll start seeing ads for things like MacFish 2.4.9.6 and PageMan 3.6.5.4.2.1.

Oh, and when a program gets upgraded too many times, the company adds the word Pro to its name.

Of course, every Mac comes with *some* software. For example, each Mac comes with the System software (on white floppy disks or on a compact disc) that it needs for its own internal use. It comes with some miniprograms, like the Calculator and the Note Pad, called *desk accessories.* None of this free software will make you very productive on the day you set up your computer.

Software, for the most part, is expensive. The most popular Mac word processing program, for example, is Microsoft Word, and the lowest price I've seen for it is $300. If you plan to do number crunching, over 80 percent of Mac users use the spreadsheet Microsoft Excel (another $300). Want a database for handling order forms, tracking phone calls, and creating merged form letters? Check out the fantastic FileMaker Pro (around $200).

There are lower-priced alternatives, of course. If you really want to do your homework, read a few recent issues of *Macworld* and *MacUser* for some guidance. WriteNow, for example, is a super, fast, easy-to-use word processing program, and it's only $150. It can even exchange files with Microsoft Word. Unfortunately, you may feel a little bit left out with one of the underdog programs since almost all the talk, help, and articles will be about the big three (Word, Excel, and FileMaker).

If you're on a budget and don't much care about being in the vanguard, you can get a lot of power in the form of an *integrated* program like ClarisWorks — which is the kind of program you get when you buy a Mac Performa. For the cost of a single program, you get several programs mashed into one: word processor, database, spreadsheet, drawing program, and so on. Of course, a Works-type program doesn't do any one thing as well as a separate program does, but it does everything pretty well. (Especially ClarisWorks.)

El Cheapo software

Once you've read Chapter 7, and you've decided it might be fun to plug your Mac into the telephone line to dial up faraway computers, you may stumble onto another kind of software: *shareware.* These are programs written by individuals, not software companies, who make them freely available on "electronic bulletin boards." You can grab them, via telephone, and bring them to your own Mac. And get this: only the *honor system,* for heaven's sake, compels you to pay the authors the $15 or $20 they're asking for.

Sure, you usually get what you pay for; shareware often has a homemade, not-quite-ready-for-prime-time feel to it. On the other hand, some of it's really terrific: ZTerm, for use with a modem, has won awards; CompactPro and StuffIt, used to make files take up less space on the disk, are classics; and there are acres and acres of sounds, pictures, clip art, and games available on dial-up services like America Online and CompuServe.

In any case, you definitely need a word processor. Most people could use an address book program like Super QuickDex and a calendar/reminder program like Now Up-to-Date. And then there are graphics: if you want to draw or paint, read Chapter 5 for some explanations and suggestions.

Where to get it

There are two places to buy software: via mail order and at a store. At a store, you can heft the actual box, tap a live human being on the shoulder to ask questions, and ask other customers what they've had luck with. In some stores you can even try out the software on a real live Mac, so you won't wind up buying something you don't need.

On the other hand, mail-order companies give much bigger discounts; most take returns after you've opened the box; they don't charge sales tax; and, of course, you don't have to fire up the old Volvo. You get your stuff delivered to your door by the next day (the overnight shipping charge is usually $3 per order).

At the risk of sounding like a broken CD, I'm going to direct you to the Mac magazines like *Macworld* and *MacUser* for more info on mail-order companies. They're called things like Mac Connection, Mac Zone, and Mac Warehouse. They all have toll-free phone numbers, and their catalogs and ads all appear in every single issue of those magazines. (Their numbers also appear in Appendix B, the Resource Resource.) Overnight mail-order companies like these are truly one of the bright spots in the Mac world. You can call Mac Connection, for example, until *3:30 a.m.* and get your new programs by mid-morning (seven hours later). After being around them awhile, you'll start to wish there were overnight mail-order grocery stores, gas stations, and dentists.

In this chapter, you're going to do some word processing. That's what 90 percent of Mac users do the most of (when they're not hang gliding, housing the homeless, and saving the environment, I mean). I have no way of knowing what software, if any, you bought with your computer. Maybe you already have a word processing program, maybe not. (Look over your pile of boxes. If there's one that says Microsoft Word, WriteNow, WordPerfect, Nisus, or anything that ends with *-Works,* then you have a word processor.) If you don't have a word processor yet, call up a mail-order company and order one right now so you'll be able to work with it tomorrow.

Until Federal Express delivers your new software, however, let me show you some of the basic principles of the computer. To make sure you've got the same thing on your screen that I do, we'll start off by using the built-in programs that came with your Mac.

Your very first software

There are several menus across the top of the screen (remember these?). As you get to know the Mac, you'll discover that their wording changes from program to program. Right now, they say File, Edit, View, Label, and Special; in a word processor they might say File, Edit, Font, Size, and Format, and so on. The menu names (and the commands listed in those menus) are tailored to the function of the software.

There's one menu that's *always* on your screen, though: our friend the Apple menu (the at the left edge of the menu bar). Among other things, this menu provides immediate access to some useful miniprograms known as *desk accessories.* Desk accessories are sure fire, nonthreatening, and fun — perfect for your first baby steps into the world of software.

Desk Accessories

Let's start simple. Move your cursor up to the menu and choose Calculator. The Calculator pops up in a tiny window of its own.

The Calculator

Using the mouse, you can click the little calculator buttons. The Mac gives you the correct mathematical answer, making you the owner of the world's heaviest and most expensive pocket calculator.

What's neat is that you can also type the keys on your *numeric keypad,* the block of number keys off to the right side of your keyboard. As you press these real keys, you can watch the on-screen keys in the Calculator window get punched accordingly. Try it out!

(Of course, a PowerBook doesn't *have* a numeric keypad. Still, the numbers on the top row of regular alphabet keys works just as well.)

Desk accessory details you can get by without

The Calculator, along with other miniprograms like the Note Pad, Key Caps, and so on (all in the menu), is called a desk accessory. It's always available to you, no matter what Mac activity you're in.

In the olden days of System 6, the Apple menu *only* contained desk accessories. They were small, inexpensive, and cute. One of the special features in System 7, however, is that you can stick anything you want into that menu: full-fledged software applications, a disk icon, a folder, a document you work on a lot, a sound, and so on. (Some people wind up with *very* long Apple menus.)

Want to know the secret of making your own menu in System 7? Check it out: Point to your hard drive icon in the upper-right corner of the screen, and double-click. Now double-click your System

Folder icon. Inside *that*, you'll find a folder called Apple Menu Items. (Pretty cryptic, I know.)

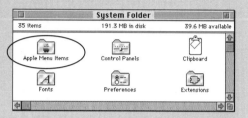

Go ahead and drag any icon into this folder: another folder, a letter, your word processing program, whatever; instantly it appears in the Apple menu for easy access.

(It's better still to put an *alias* of your icon in there, but Chapter 8, where aliases are explained, is still miles away.)

Take a moment to reinforce your love of windows: by dragging the *title bar* (where it says "Calculator"), move the Calculator window into a new position. If you were good and tired of looking at it, you could also make the Calculator go away by clicking its close box (in the upper-left corner, like on all windows).

But don't close the Calculator just yet. Leave it open on the screen.

The Note Pad

Now go to the menu again, and this time choose Note Pad. Instantly, the world's most frill-free word processor appears on the screen.

You'll learn more about word processing in the next section. For now, we're just going to do some informative goofing around. With the Note Pad open on your screen, type a math problem, like this:

37+8+19*3-100

(In the computer world, the asterisk * means "times," or multiply.) If you make a mistake, press the big Delete key at the upper-right corner of your keyboard. This means "Backspace."

Now, by dragging the Note Pad's title bar, move it so that you can see the Calculator window, too.

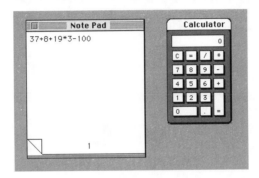

You're going to use two programs at once, making them cooperate with each other — one of the most remarkable features of the Mac.

Selecting text

This is about to get interesting.

Using the mouse, position the pointer at the left side of your equation (below, top). Press the button and drag, perfectly horizontally, to the right (middle). Release the mouse when you've highlighted the entire equation (bottom).

$$][37+8+19*3-100$$

$$\boxed{37+8+1\&*3-100}$$

$$\boxed{37+8+19*3-100}\ ][$$

You've just *selected* some text. Remember in Chapter 1 when you *selected* an icon — and then used a menu command? Struggling, as always, to come up with a decent analogy, I likened this *select-then-operate* sequence to building a noun-verb sentence.

Well, it works just as well with text as it does with icons. You've now high-lighted, or selected, some text. The Mac now knows what the noun is — what it's supposed to pay attention to. All you have to do is select a verb from one of the menus. And the verb du jour is *Copy*.

The cornerstone of human endeavor: Copy and Paste

Choose Copy from the Edit menu.

Thunder rolls, lightning flashes, the audience holds its breath . . . and abso-lutely nothing happens.

Behind the scenes, though, something awesomely useful occurred. The Mac looked at the selected equation and memorized it, socking it away into an invisible storage window called the *Clipboard*. The Clipboard is how you transfer stuff from one window into another and from one program into an-other. (Some programs even have a Show Clipboard command, in which case I take back the statement about the Clipboard being invisible.)

Now then. You can't *see* the Clipboard at this point, but in a powerful act of faith, you put your trust in me and you believe that it contains the highlighted material (the equation).

The Application menu

Do you see the tiny Note Pad icon at the right end of your menu bar? It's next to that question mark thing.

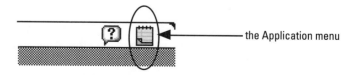

the Application menu

Don't go bug-eyed searching for it. If it's not there, then you don't have System 7. (Check your Cheat Sheet, where, in theory, you wrote down this information while reading Chapter 1.) The Application menu, as well as the question mark icon, are both elements of System 7.

This icon actually represents a menu — the Application menu, of course. It lists all the programs you have running at once.

At this moment, you have *three* programs running at once: the Note Pad, the Calculator, and the famous Finder (or desktop).

You multitasking maniac, you.

Choose Calculator from the Application menu.

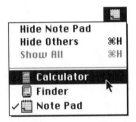

The Calculator window comes to the front, and the icon in the upper right changes to look like a Calculator.

Those of you still awake will, of course, object to using the Application menu to bring the Calculator forward. You remember all too plainly from Chapter 1 that simply *clicking* in a window brings it to the front, which would have required less muscular effort.

Absolutely right! You may now advance to the semifinals. However, learning to use the Application menu was a good exercise. There are going to be many times in your life where the program that's in front covers up the *entire* screen. So *then* how will you bring another program forward, big shot? That's right. You won't be able to *see* any other windows, so you won't be able to click one to make it active. You'll have to use the Application menu.

In any case, the Calculator is now the active application. (*Active* just means it's in front.) Now then: Remember that intricate equation that's still on the Mac Clipboard? Instead of having to type an equation into the Calculator by punching keys, let's just paste it in.

1. Press the Clear key on your Mac keyboard or click the C button on the Calculator.

   You just cleared the display. We wouldn't want your previous diddlings to interfere with this tightly controlled experiment.

2. From the Edit menu, choose Paste. Watch the Calculator!

If you looked in time, you saw the number keys flashing like Las Vegas at midnight. And with a triumphant modesty, the Mac displays the answer to your math problem. (It should be 92.)

Did you get what just happened? You typed out a math problem in a word processor (the Note Pad), copied it to the Clipboard, and pasted it into a number-cruncher (the Calculator). Much of the miracle of the Mac stems from its capability to mix and match information among multiple programs in this way.

It's a two-way street, too. You can paste this number back into the word processor.

1. From the Edit menu, choose Copy.

   But wait! There was already something on the Clipboard. Where is the Mac supposed to put this *new* copied info?

   On the Clipboard, of course. And whatever was there before (your equation) gets nuked. The Clipboard contains exactly one thing at a time — whatever you copied *most recently*.

2. From the Application menu, choose Note Pad (or just click the Note Pad window).

   The Note Pad is now the active application.

3. Type this:

   Dear son: You owe me $

   Stop after the $ sign. Move the mouse up to the Edit menu.

4. From the Edit menu, choose Paste.

Bingo! The Mac pastes in the result from the Calculator (which it had ready on the Clipboard).

Incidentally, whatever's on the Clipboard stays there until you copy something new or until you turn off the machine. In other words, you can paste it over and over again.

5. For a second time, choose Paste from the Edit menu.

Another 92 pops into the window.

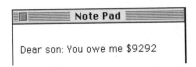

By now, you're probably cradling your wrist, which no doubt aches from all those trips to the menu. Although what you're about to learn is, technically speaking, a *power-user technique,* it will save you all kinds of time and chiropractor bills.

You don't have to use the menu to issue a command like Copy or Paste. If you wish, you can use a keyboard shortcut to do the same thing. You may remember having used the ⌘ key in Chapter 2 to issue commands without using the mouse.

And how are you supposed to remember which letter key corresponds to which command? Well, usually it's mnemonic: ⌘+P for Print, ⌘+O for Open, and so on. But you can cheat; try it right now. Pull down the Edit menu, but don't let go of the mouse button.

There's your crib sheet, carefully listed down the right side of the menu. Note that the keyboard shortcuts for all four of these important commands (Undo, Cut, Copy, Paste) are adjacent on the keyboard: Z, X, C, V.

C is Copy. And V, right next to it, is Paste. Let go of the mouse button and let's try it.

1. While holding down the ⌘ key, type a V.

   Bingo! Another copy of the Clipboard stuff (92) appears in your Note Pad. (In the future, I'll just refer to a keyboard shortcut like this as "⌘-V.")

2. Press ⌘-V again.

   Yep, that kid's debt is really piling up. He now owes you $92,929,292.

   But after all, he's your son. Why not just let him pay 10 percent down on the amount he owes you? In other words, why not *undo* that last 92 pasting?

3. From the Edit menu, choose Undo.

   The most recent thing you did — in this case, pasting the fourth 92 — gets undone.

Rewriting history is addicting, ain't it?

Remember, though, that Undo only reverses your *most recent* action. Suppose you (1) copy something, (2) paste it somewhere else, and then (3) type some more. If you choose Undo, only the typing will be undone (step 3), *not* the pasting (step 2).

There are some other DAs, too. (Like everything in the Mac world, it's cooler to call something by its initials. DA = desk accessory.) Play around with (and look up in your Macintosh owner's guide) the Puzzle, the Alarm Clock, Key Caps, and all that stuff.

Control Panels

There's one item in your Apple menu that *isn't* a DA. It says Control Panels, and all it does is open up your Control Panels folder. And what exactly is your Control Panels folder? Well, it's a folder that lives inside your System Folder. It contains a bunch of icons, each of which controls some aspect of your Mac. Choose Control Panels from the ⌘ menu to make this window appear:

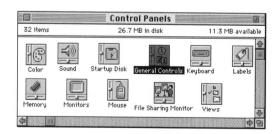

Everybody's got a slightly different set of control panels, so your screen may look different. In any case, I'll show you around one control panel; then you can take it from there.

1. Quickly type *GE* on your keyboard.

   Remember this handy trick? You can select one icon in a folder just by typing the first couple of letters of its name. In this case, you get the General Controls window.

   (If your Mac has System 6, you have to scroll through the icons until you see the one you want; the letter-typing business is a perk of System 7.)

2. Double-click General Controls.

   The General Controls window opens. It looks like . . . well, rather like a control panel. These controls govern the way your Mac works; you can customize your working environment, to a certain extent, or change the time, or whatever. (This window may look slightly different if you have a Performa or System 7.5.)

The Desktop Pattern is the shading that fills the background, behind the windows and stuff. You can change the design; see Chapter 8 for details.

When you type (as in the Note Pad), the Mac marks your place with a blinking *insertion point.* These buttons control how fast it blinks, in the event that the blinking rate has been triggering those inconvenient seizures.

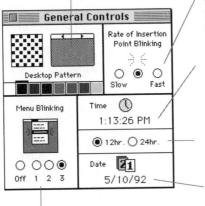

Click a number to change the time. Usually, when you buy a Mac, it's set to California time, so double-check this.

Click "24 hr." if you are a military-type person who wakes up at 0600 hours each morning.

Click a number to change the date.

When you choose a command from a menu (and release the mouse), the command blinks. This setting controls how many times. How did we *live* before we had this?

All right — close the General Controls window by clicking the close box in the upper-left corner; enough fooling around. Time to get some work done. (Fortunately, *working* on the Mac is almost as much fun as goofing off.)

Word Processing 101

If you have a word processing program, install it onto your hard disk now, if you haven't already done so. You'll find the instructions at the beginning of its manual.

Find the program's icon on your hard disk. It may be inside a folder, which you can open by double-clicking. In any case, after you find the word processing program icon, double-click it; you'll be presented, after a moment, with a blank white screen.

If you don't have a word processor yet, you can use your discount word processor, the Note Pad; choose its name from the menu.

Top three rules of word processing

The first rules of typing on a computer are going to be tough to learn, especially if you've been typing for years. But they're crucial. Here they be:

- ✔ **Don't press the Return key at the end of each line.** I'm dead serious here. When you type your way to the end of a line, the next word will *automatically* jump down to the next line. If you press Return in the middle of a sentence, you'll mess everything up.

- ✔ **Only put ONE space after a period.**

- ✔ **Don't use the L key to make the number 1.** All right, this one's not so crucial to your future happiness. Still, your Mac, unlike the typewriter you grew up with, actually has a *key* dedicated to making the number 1. If you use a lowercase L instead, the 1 will look funny, and your spelling checker will choke on it every time.

See here?

There are two spaces after this sentence. It looks sort of wide.
There's only one space after this one. Looks pretty good.

If those statements give you uncontrollable muscular facial spasms, I don't blame you. After all, I'm telling you to do something that you were explicitly taught *not* to do by your sharp-tongued high school typing teacher.

Nonetheless, don't put two spaces after a period. Typewriters print letters onto paper by slapping tiny metal blocks against a ribbon, and every block (every letter) is the same width — including the space. But on a Mac, every letter has a different width; look how much wider this W is than this I, for example. On the Mac, a space is *already* extra-wide, thus saving you that precious calorie you would have exerted to press the spacebar a second time.

There are a few other rules, too, but breaking them isn't serious enough to get you fired. So let's dig in. Make sure you have a blank piece of electronic typing paper open in front of you — either a new, untitled word processing screen or the Note Pad.

You should see a short, blinking, vertical line at the beginning of the typing area. They call this the *insertion point*. It shows you where the letters will appear when you start to type.

The point of no returns

Why aren't you supposed to hit Return at the end of each line?

First time in print! An actual example of the kind of mess you can get into by pressing Return after each line of text.

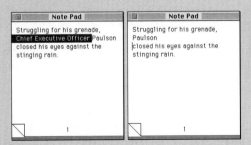

At left: the original passage. Suppose you decide to remove Paulson's title, "Chief Executive Officer," since everybody already knows what kind of guy he is (left). But suppose you'd been foolish enough to press Return after each line of text; if you remove those three highlighted words, the word *Paulson* flops back to the left side of the line, but the rest of the sentence stays where it is, looking dumb (right).

On the other hand, if you *hadn't* put Returns into your text, you'd get the figure below, where everything looks peachy.

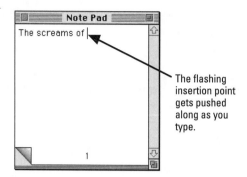

The flashing insertion point gets pushed along as you type.

Type the passage below. If you make a typo, press Delete, just like Backspace on a typewriter. *Don't* press Return when you get to the edge of the window. Just keep typing, and the Mac will create a second line for you. Believe. *Believe.*

> *The screams of the lions burst Rod's eardrums as the motorboat, out of control, exploded through the froth.*

See how the words automatically wrapped around to the second line? They call this feature, with no small originality, *word wrap.*

But suppose, as your novel is going to press, you decide that this sleepy passage really needs some spicing up. You decide to insert the word *speeding* before the word *motorboat.*

Remember the blinking cursor — the insertion point? It's on the screen even now, blinking calmly away at the end of the sentence. If you want to insert text, you have to move the insertion point.

There are two ways to move the insertion point. First, try pressing the arrow keys on your keyboard. You can see that the up- and down-arrow keys move the insertion point from line to line, and the right- and left-arrow keys move the insertion point across the line. Practice moving the insertion point by pressing the arrow keys.

If the passage you want to edit is far away, though (on another page, for example), using the arrow keys to move the cursor is inefficient. Your fingers would be bloody stumps by the time you finished. Instead, use the mouse:

1. Using the mouse, move the cursor (which, when it's near text, looks like this ⌶) just before the word *motorboat.* Click the mouse.

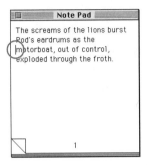

This is as confusing as word processing ever gets — there are *two* little cursors, right? There's the blinking insertion point, and there's this one ⏋, which is called an *I-beam* cursor.

In fact, they're quite different. The blinking insertion point is only a *marker,* not a pointer. It always shows you where the next typing will appear. The I-beam, on the other hand, is how you *move* the insertion point; when you click with the I-beam, you set down the insertion point.

In other words, editing stuff you've already typed, on the Macintosh, is a matter of *click, then type.*

2. Type the word *speeding.*

The insertion point does its deed, and the Mac makes room on the line for the new word. A word or two probably got pushed onto the next line. Isn't word wrap wondrous?

So much for *inserting* text: you click the mouse (to show the Mac *where*) and then type away. But what if you need to delete a bunch of text? What if you decide to *cut out* the first half of our sample text?

Well, unless you typed the challenging excerpt with no errors, you already know one way to erase text — by pressing the Delete key (which is called Backspace on some keyboards). Delete takes out one letter at a time, just to the left of the insertion point.

That's not much help in this situation, though. Suppose that you decide to take out the first part of the sentence. It wouldn't be horribly efficient to backspace over the entire passage just so you could work on the beginning.

No, instead you need a way to edit any part of your work, at any time, without disturbing the stuff you want to leave. Once again, the Macintosh method, noun-then-verb, saves the day. Try this:

1. Using the mouse, position the I-beam cursor at the beginning of the sentence.

   This takes a steady hand; stay calm.

2. Click *just* to the left of the first word and keep the mouse button pressed down. Drag the I-beam cursor — *perfectly horizontally,* if possible — to the end of the word *as.*

   As you drag, the text gets highlighted, or *selected.* You've done this once before, in your copy-and-paste lesson.

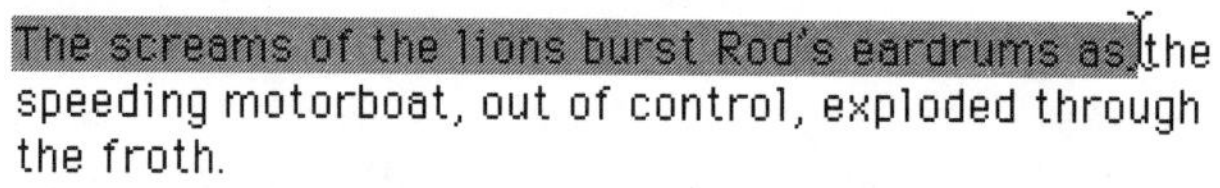

   ```
   The screams of the lions burst Rod's eardrums as the
   speeding motorboat, out of control, exploded through
   the froth.
   ```

   If you accidentally drag up or down into the next line of text, the highlighting jumps to include a big chunk of that additional line. Don't panic; without releasing the mouse button, simply move the cursor back onto the original line you were selecting. This time try to drag more horizontally.

If you're especially clever and forward-thinking, you'll have selected the blank space *after* the word *as,* as well. Take a look at the illustration above.

All right, in typical Mac syntax, you've just specified *what* you want to edit by selecting it (and making it turn black to show it's selected). Now for the verb:

1. Press the Delete key.

   Bam! The selected text is gone. The sentence looks pretty odd, though, since it doesn't begin with a capital letter.

2. Using the mouse, position the cursor just before (or after) the letter *t* that begins the sentence. Drag it sideways across the letter so that it's highlighted.

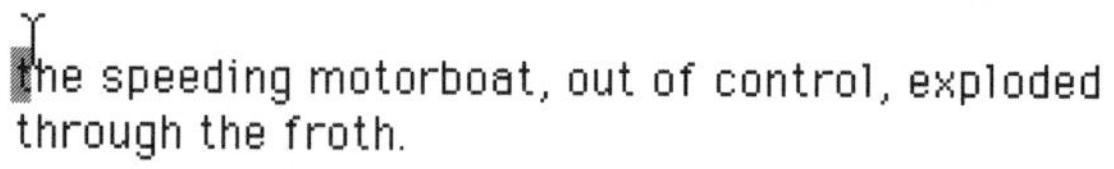

   ```
   the speeding motorboat, out of control, exploded
   through the froth.
   ```

   Here comes another ground rule of word processing. See how you've just selected, or highlighted, the letter *t?* The idea here is to capitalize it. Of course, using the methods for wiping out (and inserting) text that you learned earlier, you could simply remove the *t* and type a *T.* But since you've selected the *t* by dragging through it, replacing it is much easier:

3. Type a capital *T.*

The selected text gets replaced by the new stuff you type. That, in fact, is the fourth ground rule: *Selected text gets replaced by the new stuff you type.* As your Macintosh life proceeds, keep that handy fact in mind; it can save you a lot of backspacing. In fact, you can select 40 pages of text so that it's all highlighted and then type *one single letter* to replace all of it. Or you could *select* only one letter but replace it with 40 pages of typing.

Take a moment now for some unsupervised free play. Try clicking anywhere in the text (to plant the insertion point). Try dragging through some text: if you drag perfectly horizontally, you select text just on one line (below left). If you drag diagonally, you get everything between your cursor and the original click (below right).

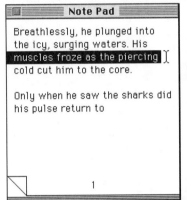
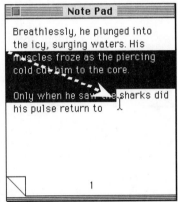

You deselect (or, equally poetically, unhighlight) text by clicking the mouse. Anywhere at all (within the typing area).

Here's about the most fabulous word processing shortcut ever devised: Try pointing to a word and then double-clicking the mouse! You've easily selected *exactly* that word without having to do any dragging.

As you experiment, do anything you want with any combination of drags, clicks, double-clicks, and menu selections. It's nice to know — and you might want to prepare a fine mahogany wall plaque to this effect — that *nothing you do with the mouse or keyboard can physically harm the computer.* Oh, sure, it's possible to erase a disk or wreck one of your documents or something, but none of that requires a visit to a repair shop. You can't *break* the computer by playing around.

A word processing rule-ette

You know, by now, that your mouse pointer looks like this — Ɪ — whenever it's near text. And you know, by now, that you use this cursor to *click* wherever you want to type next.

But suppose you want to add some words way down the page, like this:

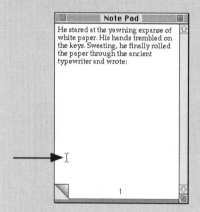

You'll discover pretty quickly that the Mac won't let you type there. The rule is: you can click your cursor anywhere on the page *that already has typing on it*. But if you try to click down *below*, in the white space, you're out of luck; the blinking

insertion-point cursor simply jumps back up to the end of what you've already typed. In its ornery way, the Mac enforces its own rule of writing: No jumping ahead, bub.

Of course, you *can* skip down the page if you want some words to appear there. But you have to *type your way* down the page first. That's why God invented the Return key. Press it over and over again until your little insertion-point cursor is blinking merrily away at the bottom of the page — or wherever you tell it to go — and *now* start typing.

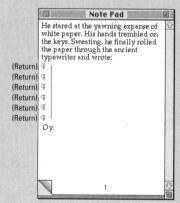

Form and format

For the rest of this lesson, you're going to need a real word processor. Sorry, kids, the Note Pad will only get you so far in life.

One of the most important differences between a typewriter and its replacement — the personal computer — is the sequence of events. When you use a typewriter, you set up all the formatting characteristics *before* you type: the margins, the tab stops, and (for typewriters with interchangeable type heads) the type style.

But the whole point of a word processor is that you can change anything at *any* time. Many people type the text of an entire letter or proposal or memo into the Mac and *then* format it. When you use a typewriter, you might discover, after typing the entire first page, that it's *slightly* too long to fit, and your signature will have to sit awkwardly on a page by itself. With a Mac, you'd see the problem and nudge the text a little bit higher on the page to compensate.

Word processing has other great advantages: no crossouts; easy corrections that involve no white-out and no retyping; a permanent record of your correspondence that's electronic, not paper, and so it's always easy to find; a selection of striking typefaces — at any size; paste-in graphics, and so on. I think it's safe to say that once you try it, you'll never look back.

The return of Return

With all the subtlety of a Mack truck, I've taught you that you're forbidden to use the Return key *at the end of a line.* Still, that rectangular Return key on your keyboard *is* important. You press Return at the end of a *paragraph,* and only there.

To the computer, the Return key works just like a letter key — it inserts a *Return character* into the text. It's just like rolling the paper in a typewriter forward by one notch. Hit Return twice, and you leave a blank line.

The point of Return, then, is to move text higher or lower on the page. Check this example, for instance.

Return characters move text down on the page. So, if you want to move text up on the page, drag through the blank space so that it's highlighted (above left); of course, what you've really done is select the usually invisible Return characters. If you delete them, the text slides up the page (right).

Seeing the unseen

I said that Returns are *usually* invisible. However, every time you press the Return key, the Mac actually does plop down a symbol onto your screen. Same thing with the spacebar. Same with the Tab key.

You'll have to check your own word processor's manual to find out the exact command, but virtually every word processor lets you see these markings. The command may be called Show Invisibles; in Word, the command is called Show ¶. In any case, the result looks something like this:

♦   "Alison—my·god,·not·that!·Anything·but·that!"¶

♦   But·it·was·too·late.·She·had·already·disappeared.¶

Combine this knowledge with your advanced degree in Inserting Text (remember? you click to place the blinking insertion point and then type), and you can see how you'd make more space between paragraphs or push all the text of a letter down on the page.

Appealing characters

Another big-time difference between word processing and typing is all the great *character formatting* you can do. You can make any piece of text **bold,** *italic,* underlined, all of the above, and more. You also get a selection of great-looking typefaces — only a few of which look like a typewriter. By combining all these styles and fonts randomly, you can make any document look absolutely hideous.

Here's the scheme for changing some text to one of those character formats: noun-verb. Sound familiar? Go for it:

1. Select some text by dragging through it.

   Remember, you can select a single word by double-clicking it; to select a bunch of text, drag the cursor through it so that it turns black. You've just identified *what* you want to change.

   Each word processor keeps its Bold, Italic, and Underline commands in its own specially named menu; it may be called Font, or Style, or Format. Drag your cursor through each menu name, reading the commands on each menu as it drops down, until you see the character formats like bold and italic.

The efficiency zealot's guide to power typing

Because you *can* format text after you've typed it doesn't mean you *have* to. Most power-users get used to the keyboard shortcuts for the common style changes, like bold and italic. They're pretty easy to remember: In nearly every word processing program, you get bold by pressing ⌘-B, and italic with ⌘-I.

What's handy is that you can hit this key combo just *before* you type the word. For example, without ever taking your hands off the keyboard, you could type the following:

He stared at the **Delinquent Birds** folder. No: it *was not* happening!
↑ ↑ ↑ ↑
⌘-B ⌘-B ⌘-I ⌘-I

In other words, you hit ⌘-B once to turn bold *on* for the next burst of typing, and ⌘-B again to turn it off — all without ever having to use a menu.

2. From the Font menu (or Format menu, or whatever it's called in your program), choose Bold.

   Or Shadow or Outline or whatever. You've just specified *how* you want to affect the selected text.

You can apply several of these formats to the same text, too, although you won't win any awards for typographical excellence. Try changing the typeface, also; the various fonts are called things like Chicago, Geneva, Times, and so on. Changing fonts works the same way: Select text and then choose the font.

And sizes — same deal: Select some text and then choose a type size from your word processor's menu. (Again, the name of the menu may vary. But for specifics on Microsoft Word and ClarisWorks, see Chapter 5.) The font sizes are measured in points, of which there are 72 per inch. Works out nicely, too — a Mac monitor has 72 *screen* dots per inch, meaning that 12-point type on the screen really is 12-point,

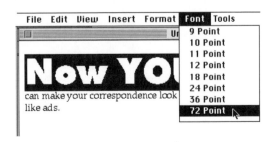

Before you know it, you'll have whipped your document into mighty handsome shape.

Getting rid of the black

Text changes color as you drag across it, right? This is called highlighting.

A panicked phone call from a novice Mac owner recently alerted me to a strange fact: nobody ever tells you *how to make the text white again!* It's not in the manuals, it's not in the books, it's not in the menus.

To make text white again (unselected), *click the mouse* anywhere in the window.

Dr. O'Sullivan grinned as she unwrapped the bandages from his face. Flakes of dried blood crumbled from his twisted, hideous	Dr. O'Sullivan grinned as she unwrapped the bandages from his face. Flakes of dried blood crumbled from his twisted, hideous
Just click anywhere...	...to get rid of the highlighting.

There. I think I just made the world a better place.

Formatting paragraphs

Where type styles and sizes can be applied to any amount of text, even a single letter, *paragraph formatting* affects a whole paragraph at once. Usually these styles are easy to apply. To select a paragraph, you don't have to highlight all the text in it. Instead, you can just click *once,* anywhere, within a paragraph to plant the insertion point. Then, as before, choose the menu command that you want to apply to that entire paragraph.

This figure shows some of the different options every word processor provides for paragraph formatting — left-justified, right-justified, fully justified and centered.

Her heart pounding, she looked toward the door. It swung open with a creak. The stench hit her first—an acrid, rotting swamp smell. She covered her mouth with the blood-soaked handkerchief and stepped backward, her naked back pressed hard against the fourposter.

Her heart pounding, she looked toward the door. It swung open with a creak. The stench hit her first—an acrid, rotting swamp smell. She covered her mouth with the blood-soaked handkerchief and stepped backward, her naked back pressed hard against the fourposter.

Her heart pounding, she looked toward the door. It swung open with a creak. The stench hit her first—an acrid, rotting swamp smell. She covered her mouth with the blood-soaked handkerchief and stepped backward, her naked back pressed hard against the fourposter.

Her heart pounding, she looked toward the door. It swung open with a creak. The stench hit her first—an acrid, rotting swamp smell. She covered her mouth with the blood-soaked handkerchief and stepped backward, her naked back pressed hard against the fourposter.

There are other ways you can control paragraphs, too. Remember in high school when you were supposed to turn in a 20-page paper, and you'd try to pad your much-too-short assignment by making it two-and-a-half spaced? Well, if you'd had a Mac, you could have been much more sneaky about it. You can make your word processed document single-spaced, double-spaced, quadruple-spaced, or any itty-bitty fraction thereof. You can even control how tightly together the letters are placed, making it easy to stretch or compress your writing into more or fewer pages.

Take this opportunity to toy with your word processor. Go ahead, really muck things up. Make it look like a ransom note with a million different type styles and sizes. Then, when you've got a real masterpiece on the screen, read on.

Someone Save Me!
(Working with Documents)

It might terrify you — and it should — to find out that you've been working on an imaginary document. It's only being preserved by a thin thread of streaming electrical current. It doesn't exist yet, to be perfectly accurate, except in your Mac's *memory*.

You may recall from the notes you took on Chapter $1^{1}/_{2}$ that *memory is fleeting*. (Specifically, I mean computer memory, but if you find a more universal truth in my words, interpret away.) In fact, the memory is wiped away when you turn the Mac off — or when your coworker's trip over the power cord turns it off for you. At that moment, anything that exists on the screen is gone forever.

Therefore, almost every program has a Save command. It's always in the File menu, and its keyboard shortcut is always ⌘-S.

When you save your work, the Mac transfers it from transient, fleeting, electronic memory onto the good, solid, permanent disk. There your work will remain, safely saved. It will still be there tomorrow. It will still be there next week. It will still be there ten years from now, when your computer is so obsolete it's valuable again.

Therefore, let's try an experiment with your ransom note document on the screen. From the File menu, choose Save.

Uh-oh. Something weird just happened: The Mac presented you with a box full of options. It's called a *dialog box* because the computer needs to have a little chat with you before proceeding. (If you have a Performa, it says "Documents" at the top of this window.)

What the Mac mainly wants to know is: "Under what name would you like me to file this precious document, Masssssster?"

And how do you know this? Because in the blank where it says "Save as," there's a proposed title that's *highlighted* (selected already). And what do you know about highlighted text? *Anything you start typing will instantly replace it.*

The Mac, in its cute, limited way, is trying to tell you that it needs you to type a title. Go ahead, do it: Type *Ransom Note.*

At this point, you could just click the Save button. The Mac would take everything in perilous, fleeting memory and transfer it to the staid, safe hard disk, where it would remain until you're ready to work on it some more.

However, there's a bunch of other stuff in this dialog box. Especially since this is the Numero Uno source of confusion to beginners, I think a tour of the Save File box is in order.

OK, OK, not all programs

The occasional program—Word, for example—doesn't propose a title (like "Untitled 1") in the text box of the Save as dialog box. Instead, you just see the little blinking insertion point in the empty blank. The message is the same, though: "Type your title *here."*

Navigating the Save File (and Open File) box

You've already learned about the way your computer organizes files: with folders and with folders *in* folders. Remember this little exercise, where you put state-named folders inside the USA folder?

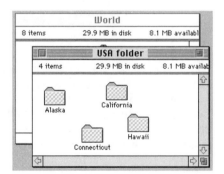

Well, the point of all the complicated-looking stuff in the Save File box is a miniature version of that same folder-filing system. Suppose you see this when you're trying to save your file:

Look at the open-folder "menu" (in a rectangle above the list). It tells you that you're viewing the contents of the USA folder. (If you have a Performa, you always see the Documents folder at this point.) In other words, if you click the Save button, you'll file your new Ransom Note document in the USA folder, mixed in among the state folders.

But suppose you want to file the Ransom Note document in one of the state folders. You already know how you open a folder — by double-clicking it — so you'd point to Alaska, for example, and double-click.

Now the open folder "menu" above the list says Alaska, and you can see the stuff inside the Alaska folder. Most of their names are dimmed because they're all *documents;* the only things whose names are black in this dialog box are folders. (The Mac wants to know where you want to put your new document. Since you can't very well store one document inside *another* document, the document names are grayed out and unavailable, and only the folder names are black and available.)

OK. So now you're viewing the contents of the Alaska folder. What if you change your mind? What if you decide that the ransom note should really go in the World folder — the one that *contains* the USA folder?

You must retrace your steps. That's what the little open folder menu is all about (the open folder icon is in front of the word *Alaska*). They call this doohickey a *pop-up menu:* it's a menu, but it's not at the top of the screen. The small black triangle beside the name Alaska tells you: "Click me!"

Sure enough, when you click the word Alaska (above left), you see the list of all the nested folders you had to travel through to get here (above right). This is where things get a little weird: The list is *upside-down* from the path you took!

In other words, if you were in the Finder instead of in this Save File dialog box, you started at the Desktop level (gray background). You'd have double-clicked the hard-disk icon to open its window. Then you'd have double-clicked the World folder to open that, and the USA folder inside of that, and finally the Alaska folder. If you look at the menu picture above, you'll see that, sure enough, your entire folder path is listed. You can view the entire hierarchy of folders — as long as you get used to the fact that the list is upside-down, and the outer levels (the hard disk and the Desktop) are listed at the bottom.

Therefore, if you wanted to file the ransom note in the World folder (below, right), you'd simply slide down the pop-up menu list and choose World (below, left).

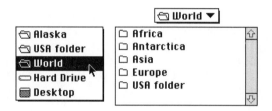

Then, at long last, when you're viewing the contents of the folder you want to save the file in, you can click the Save button.

For the purposes of following along with this exercise, double-click a folder — any folder — to store your file in. And then click Save.

Your file gets snugly tucked away into the folder whose contents you're viewing. Want proof, O Cynic? All you have to do is choose Finder from the Application menu. Remember, the Application menu is the icon at the upper-right side of the screen. It lists all the programs that are running at once.

When you choose Finder, our friends the folders, windows, and Trash can pop up. If you wanted to make sure your file really exists, and it really got put where you wanted it, you could now double-click your way through folders until you found it. In our example, your ransom note would be in the World folder:

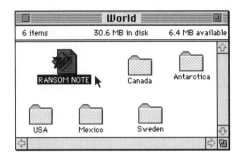

Why are we kicking this absolutely deceased horse? Because the same folder-navigation scheme (where you see an upside-down list of nested folders) is used for *retrieving* files you've already created. You need to know how to climb up and down your folder tree, as you'll see in a moment, if you ever want to find your files again.

Closing a file, with a sigh

You've created a ransom note. It's got all kinds of text and formatting. You've saved it onto the disk so that it'll be there tomorrow. In a moment, you'll get a chance to prove it to yourself.

Click the close box in the upper-left corner of the window. Once.

In the Mac's universal language of love, clicking the small square up there means close the window, as you'll recall. If all went well, the window disappears.

How to find out what the heck you're doing

This gets sort of metaphysical. Hold on to your brain.

Just because you closed your *document* doesn't mean you've left the *program*. In fact, if you pull down the Application menu at the right side of the screen, you'll see that the word processing program is, in fact, still running. (It's the one with a check mark beside it; your word processing program may be different.)

Worrywarts' corner

From the way I've described the terrifyingly delicate condition of a document that's on the screen (that you haven't saved to disk yet) — that is, precariously close to oblivion, kept alive only by electric current — you might think that closing a window is a dangerous act. After all, what if you forgot to save some work? Wouldn't closing the window mean losing that critical memo?

Not really — if you try to close a document, the Mac won't *let* you proceed until it asks you if you're *sure* you want to lose all the work you've done. It will say something like:

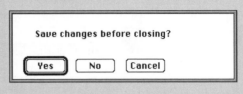

Click Yes if you do want to save your work. Click No if you were only goofing around or showing off your Mac to somebody and don't want to preserve your labors.

Click Cancel if you change your mind completely about closing the document and want to keep working on it.

You could bring the Finder to the front by choosing its name from the Application menu — without exiting the word processor. They both can be running at the same time, but only one can be in front.

In fact, that's the amazing thing about the Mac (using System 7). You can have a bunch of programs all running at once. The more memory your Mac has, the more programs you can run simultaneously.

What gets confusing is that one program (say, your word processor) may be active, but you'll *think* you're in the Finder. After all, you'll see your familiar icons, Trash, folders, and so on. You have to understand that all of this is simply *shining through* the emptiness left by your word processor, which has no windows open at the moment. If a window *were* open, it would cover up the desktop behind it.

Right now, for instance, I realize that it's hard for you to believe that you're using a word processor, when there are no words on the screen. But you have three clues as to what program you're using:

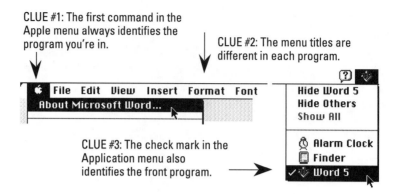

For the moment, I want you to stay in your word processing program.

Those crazy relationships: Parents and kids

OK. You've typed a ransom note. Using the Save command, you turned that typing on your screen into an icon on your hard disk. Now it's time for a concept break.

There are two kinds of files on your hard disk right now: *programs* (sometimes called *applications*) and *documents.* A program never changes; it's like a Cuisinart on your kitchen counter, sitting there day after day. Documents are what you *create* with a program — they're the coleslaw, crushed nuts, and guacamole dip that come out of the Cuisinart. You pay money to buy a program. Once you own it, you can create as many documents as you want, for free.

For example, you could use the Word Proc-S-R program (above top) to create all the different word processing documents below it and thousands more like them. If you love analogies as much as I do, you can think of the application as the mommy and the documents as the kiddies.

Here's what their family relationships are like:

1. Double-click the *program* icon when you want to open a brand new, untitled, clean-slate document.

2. Double-click a *document* icon to open that document. Unbeknownst to you, double-clicking a document simultaneously opens the program you used to create the document.

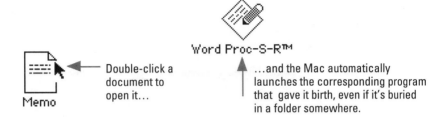

Word Proc-S-R™

Double-click a | ...and the Mac automatically
document to | launches the corresponding program
open it... | that gave it birth, even if it's buried
| in a folder somewhere.

Memo

This may seem unimpressive to you. But in the dark days of DOS and other scary pre-Macintosh computers, there was no such automatic program-launching. You'd have to know what program you used to create the document, launch it first, and *then* retrieve a document. And even then, you'd have to remember what you named it, exactly, and type that name precisely on the screen.

Fetch: How to retrieve a document

Let's return to our increasingly fruitful exercise with the ransom note, shall we?

Let's pretend it's tomorrow. Yawn, stretch, fluff your hair (if any). You find out that the person you've kidnapped actually comes from a wealthy Rhode Island family, and so you can demand much more ransom money. Fortunately, you created your ransom note on the Mac, so you don't have to retype anything; you can just change the amount you're demanding and print it out again.

But if you've been following the steps in this chapter, then there's *no* document on the screen. You're still *in* your word processing program, though (or should be; look for the check mark in the Application menu). So how do you get your ransom note file back?

Like this:

1. Choose Open from the File menu.

A dialog box appears. You probably remember dialog boxes — in fact, you probably remember this one. It looks just like the Save dialog box, where you were asked to give your document a title. This one, navigationally speaking, works exactly the same way.

Double-click a folder to see what's in it.

Use this pop-up menu to see what folder *this* folder is inside of.

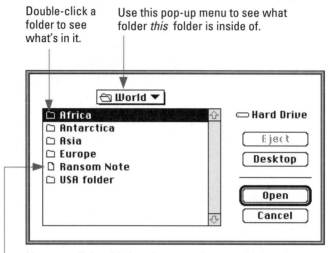

You can tell that this is a document because its icon isn't a folder. You can open it by double-clicking its name.

Unfortunately for my efforts to make this as instructional as possible, if you've been following these steps, your ransom note is staring you in the face right now. It's in whichever folder you saved it into. The Mac is nice that way — it remembers the most recent folder you stashed something in and shows you that location the next time you try to save or open something. (Unless you have a Performa, which shows you the Documents folder, no matter what.)

If you want to emerge from this experience a better person, pretend you can't find your ransom note. Pull down the pop-up menu and jump to your hard-disk level:

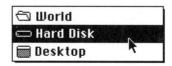

An easy way to avoid learning this stuff

This business about the "Save Where?" dialog box is, as anybody will tell you, the most confusing thing about the Mac. After years of experience, a few professional beginners have adopted the following cheat — and they never lose another file.

Whenever you save a file, and you're faced with the Save dialog box, *click the Desktop button first.* Only then should you click the Save button.

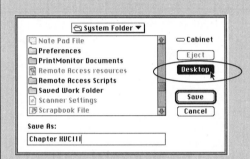

Go ahead, ask it. "What's the point?"

Easy: When you're done working for the day, and you return to the desktop, you won't have to wonder what folder your document's icon fell into. Your new file will be sitting right there, *on the desktop,* in plain sight.

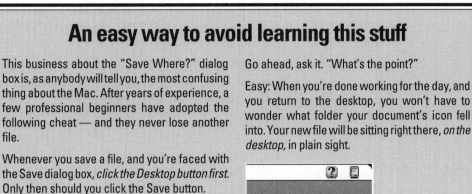

At this point, it's child's play to drag the icon into the folder you *want* it in.

Now the display changes to show you the contents of your hard disk:

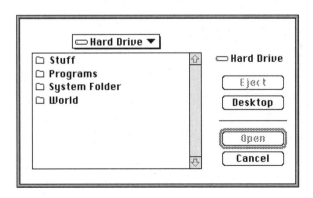

And from here, you know how to get back into the World folder, don't you? Correct — double-click the World folder, and you're right back where you started.

2. Double-click the ransom note.

This is what you've been working up to all this time. The ransom note appears on your screen in its entirety. Now, at last, you can edit it to your heart's content.

Save Me Again!

To continue this experiment, make some changes to your document. Once again, you have to worry about the fact that your precious work only exists in a fragile world of bouncing electrons. Once again, turning the Mac off right now means you'll lose the *new* work you've done. (The original ransom note, without changes, is still safe on your disk.)

Therefore, you have to use that trusty Save command each time you make changes that are worth keeping. (For you desk potatoes out there, remember that ⌘-S is the keyboard shortcut, which saves you an exhausting trip to the menu.) The Save dialog box will *not* appear on the screen each time you use the Save command (like it did the first time). Only the very first time you save a document does the Mac ask for a title (and a folder location).

As mentioned in Chapter 1½, you've probably heard horror stories about people who've lost hours of work when some glitch made their computers crash. Well, usually it's their own darned fault for ignoring the two most important rules of computing:

Rule 1. Save your work often.

Rule 2. See Rule 1.

"Often" may mean every five minutes. It may mean after every paragraph. The point is to do it a lot. Get to know that ⌘-S shortcut, and type it reflexively after every tiny burst of inspiration.

Ever notice how you can control the weather? If you haul around an umbrella all day, it won't rain. If you forget the umbrella, it's Noah's flood.

It's precisely the same with computers. If you save your work often, you'll wonder why you bother; nothing will ever go wrong. The day — no, the *minute* you forget to save something you've typed, you'll get something called a system crash and lose your entire document into the electronic ether.

Learning to be a quitter

Now you know how to start a new document, edit it, save it onto the disk, reopen it later, and save your additional changes. You know how to launch (open, or run) a program — by double-clicking its icon or by choosing its name from the ¢ menu. You've discovered the fact that you can have more than one program open at once, which can be handy when you need to copy numbers from the Note Pad and paste them into the Calculator (for example).

But now you have to learn to get out of a program when you're finished for the day. It's not terribly difficult: Choose Quit from the File menu.

If the word processor was the only program you were running, then you return to the Finder. If you were running some other programs, then you just drop down into the next program. It's as though the programs are stacked on top of each other; take away the top one, and you drop into the next one down.

The other most important rule of computing

Duty compels me to keep this chapter going just long enough to preach one other famous word of advice to you: Back up.

To *back up,* or to *make a backup,* means to make a safety copy of your work.

When you're in the Finder, the documents you've worked on appear as icons on the hard disk. Your hard disk is like a giant-sized floppy disk. Like any of us, these disks occasionally have bad hair days, go through moody spells, or die. On days like those, you'll wish you had made a *copy* of the stuff on the hard disk, so your life won't grind to a halt while the hard disk is being repaired.

Remember the cruel gods that make the computer crash when you don't save your work frequently? Those same deities have equal powers over your hard disk, and an equal taste for irony. That is, if you don't back up, your hard disk will *certainly* croak. On the other hand, if you back up your work at the end of every day or every week, nothing will ever go wrong with your hard disk, and you'll mumble to yourself that you're wasting your time.

Life's just like that.

The idiot-proof guide to backing up

Put a blank floppy disk in the disk drive. (If it's a brand new disk, you'll be asked to *initialize* it [prepare it for use by a Mac]; do it.)

Now select the icons of the documents you want to back up. Drag them, together or one by one, onto the floppy disk icon. If the floppy fills up, insert another one and continue. Label the floppy disks *Backup* (and note the date). Keep them away from magnets and telephones.

If this starts to get tedious, buy a backup *program,* which essentially backs up automatically. DiskFit, Redux, and Retrospect are some popular backup programs. If you have a Performa, you already own a backup program, you lucky dog, called Apple Backup.

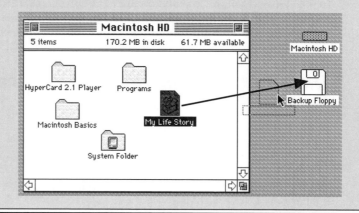

Top Ten Word Processing Tips

1. Select a word by double-clicking — and then, if you keep the mouse down on the second click and drag sideways, you select additional text in complete one-word increments.

2. Never, never, never line up text using the spacebar. It may have worked in the typewriter days, but not anymore. For example, you may get things lined up like this on the screen:

   1963   **1992**   **2001**
   Born   Elected President   Graduated college

Yet, sure as death or taxes, you'll get this when you print:

1963 1992   2001
Born   Elected President   Graduated college

So instead of using spaces to line up columns, use *tab stops* instead. Learn how your word processor does tabs and use 'em!

3. You can select all the text in your document at once by using the Select All command (to change the font for the whole thing, for example). Its keyboard equivalent is almost always ⌘-A.

4. Aesthetics Rule of Thumb: Don't use more than two fonts within a document. (Bold, italic, and normal versions of a font only count as one.) Talk about ransom notes!

5. Don't use underlining for emphasis. You're a typesetter now, babe. You've got *italics!* Underlining is a cop-out for typewriter people.

6. The box in the scroll bar at the right side of the window tells you, at a glance, where you are in your document:

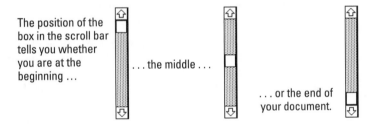

The position of the box in the scroll bar tells you whether you are at the beginning ...

... the middle ...

... or the end of your document.

By dragging that box, you can jump anywhere in the document.

There are two other ways to move around:

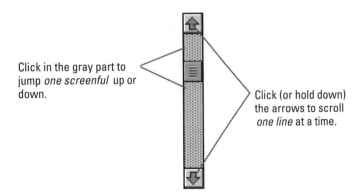

Click in the gray part to jump *one screenful* up or down.

Click (or hold down) the arrows to scroll *one line* at a time.

7. You've already learned how to *copy* some text to the Clipboard, ready to paste into another place. Another useful technique is to *cut* text to the Clipboard. Cut works just like Copy, except it snips the selected text out of the original document. (Cut-and-paste is how you *move* text from one place to another.)

8. It's considered uncouth to use "straight quotes" and 'straight apostrophes.' They hearken back to the days of yore (the days of your typewriter, that is). Instead, use "curly double quotes" and 'curly single quotes' like these. (See the difference?)

   You can produce curly double quotes by pressing Option-[(left bracket) and Shift-Option-[(right bracket) for the left and right ones, respectively. The single quotes (or apostrophes) are Option-] and Shift-Option-], for the left and right single quotes, respectively.

   But good heavens — who can remember all that? That's why every word processor I've ever heard of (like ClarisWorks or Word) has an *automatic* curly quote feature, which is a much better solution.

9. If there's an element you want to appear at the top of every page, like the page number, or the date, or *The Mister Rogers Story, Part VII: The Early Years,* don't try to type it onto each page. Not only is that a waste of effort, but the minute you add or delete text from somewhere else, this top-of-the-page information will become middle-of-the-page information.

   Instead, use your word processor's *running header* feature — it's a little window into which you can type whatever you want. The program automatically displays this info at the top of each page, no matter how much text you add or take away. (There's also such a thing as a *running footer,* which appears at the *bottom* of the page, as well as a *running politician,* which you want to avoid at all costs.)

10. You know how to select one word (double-click it). You know how to select a line (drag horizontally). You know how to select a block of text (drag diagonally through it). By now, you're probably about to reach Selection-Method Overload.

    But none of those techniques will help when you want to select a *lot* of text. What if you want to change the font size for *ten pages'* worth? Don't tell me you're going to sit there dragging the cursor through 117 screens of text.

    Instead, try this two-part tip. First, click at the *beginning* of the stuff you want to highlight so that the insertion point is blinking there.

    Now scroll to the *end* of what you want to highlight. Hold down the *Shift key* with one hand, and click the mouse with the other. Magically, everything between your original click and your Shift-click gets highlighted!

1. Click...

2. Shift-click...

3. ...and everything in between gets selected.

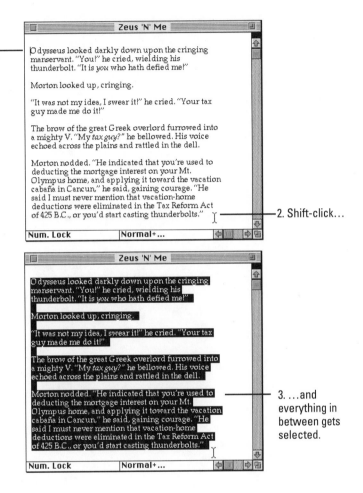

Chapter 4

A Quiet Talk About
Printers, Printing, and Fonts

I hope you're seated for this chapter. In fact, I hope you're leaning way back with your feet up and a daiquiri in your hand.

Because there's no greater source of confusion and irritation for the beginning Mac user than understanding printers and fonts, and how to get the best of the latter from the former. After dropping $1,000 on a laser printer, some people still get jaggedy, irregular type in their printouts. Others aren't able to print at all — they get error messages. And still others have been printing their correspondence for years, in happy ignorance, using the Chicago font — the heavy black type style that's used in the Mac menus.

It's time to make some sense of it all. If possible.

Credit Card Workout #3: A Printer Primer

Printers come in all kinds of configurations and prices. You can spend next to nothing and get a "dot-matrix" printer whose printouts are so jagged that they look like Dante's *Inferno* written in Braille. Or you can spend a thousand clams or so and get a laser printer whose printouts look like they were typeset.

The ImageWriter-saurus

Talk about a dinosaur. This honorable senior citizen is called a *dot-matrix* printer because it prints by firing little pins against a ribbon that strikes the paper. The resulting collection of dots form the letters.

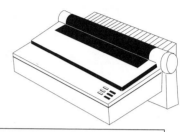

The ImageWriter is slowish and so noisy that people used to buy *mufflers* for them. The print quality isn't anything to write home about (and it's only barely good enough for letters home. See the print samples below). About the only thing ImageWriters are any good for is printing onto multiple-page forms (like Fed Ex labels).

ImageWriter
StyleWriter
LaserWriter

The StyleWriter

Yes, Virginia, there *is* a high-quality printer that won't bleed you dry: the Apple StyleWriter II. Its quality almost matches a laser printer's. It's very small, very lightweight, and almost silent. You can feed all kinds of nonliving things through it: tagboard, envelopes, sheet metal, whatever. And it costs less than $350.

So what's the catch? Well, for people who are used to laser printers, the StyleWriter II's speed — two pages per minute — seems pretty slow. (They shouldn't complain; the original StyleWriter only printed half a page per minute!) Still, the StyleWriter II is so compact, quiet, and inexpensive that it's hard to resist. It prints grays (such as photographs) beautifully, too.

Both the StyleWriter II and its popular $300 rival, the Hewlett-Packard DeskWriter, are *inkjet* printers. They create a printed image by spraying a mist of ink. Therefore, the printing isn't laser-crisp if your stationery is even slightly absorbent. Note, too, that inkjet-printed pages smear if they ever get the least bit damp, making them poor candidates for use during yacht races.

Laser printers

If you can afford to pay something like $900 for a printer, some real magic awaits you: *PostScript laser printers.* Don't worry about the word PostScript for now. Just look for the word PostScript in the printer's description, as though it's some kind of seal of approval.

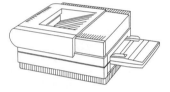

A PostScript printer, like most of Apple's LaserWriter models, can print any text, in any style, at any size, and at any angle, and everything looks terrific. PostScript laser printers can also print phenomenal-looking graphics, like all the diagrams in Macintosh magazines. They're quick, quiet, and hassle-free; most can print envelopes, mailing labels, and paper up to legal-size (but not tagboard).

Remember the old saying, "The power of the press is limited to those who have one"? Well, the combination of a Mac and a laser printer is what put the Mac on the map because it turns anybody into a self-publisher. If you can afford a PostScript printer, get it. If you're a small-time operation — a home business, for example — get the cheapest PostScript laser printer you can find. Almost all laser printers between $800 and $1,400 have exactly the same quality printouts.

If you're going to print mainly normal-looking text without fancy graphics, you can save some bucks by getting one of the LaserWriter printers that *isn't* PostScript, such as the LaserWriter Select 300.

How to Print

I'm going to assume that you've happily purchased a printer. If it's already hooked up, and you've made some successful printouts already, fast-forward to the end of this section.

Plugging in a 'Writer

If you bought an ImageWriter, StyleWriter, or other 'Writer, a cable (printer-to-Mac) probably came with the printer. It's a no-brainer to connect them; there's only one possible place to plug the cable into the printer. The other end goes into the back of the Mac; there's a little round jack with a printer icon. (Be careful not to plug it into the nearly identical jack next to it, which is marked with a telephone icon.)

Plug your printer here

Of course, you also need to plug your new appliance into the wall.

Plugging in a laser printer

If you bought a laser printer, believe it or not, you probably did *not* get a cable with it. Like anything precious in the computer jungle, it'll take some bush-whacking through the technical underbrush to get at the explanation.

When Apple invented the LaserWriter — the very first PostScript laser printer — they charitably recognized that not every company could afford a $7,000 printer to sit beside each desk. They had a great idea, though: Invent a system where several Macs could all plug into the *same* printer.

Ladies and gentlemen, I hereby introduce you to the word *network*.

The connectors that attach these Macs to a single shared printer are called, for example, PhoneNet or ModuNet. (There are many brands, but people generally call them PhoneNet connectors. Sometimes, not quite accurately, people call them LocalTalk connectors. No matter what you call 'em, they're the same connections you use to hook Macs up to each *other* — but that's a topic for the sequel.)

What's great about PhoneNet-type connectors is that you string ordinary *telephone wire* between them. If you decide to move your printer into the next room, no big deal — just buy a longer piece of phone wire from Radio Shack.

A PhoneNet connector   A piece of phone wire

This is all relevant only if you believe that you *must* have a network in order to plug a Mac into a laser printer. And, in fact, that's exactly what the salespeople would like you to believe.

But here's another money-saving *Macs For Dummies* secret: You only need all that fancy wiring *if* you plan to share your laser printer with other Macs.

If it's just you, your Mac, and a cup of coffee, get a plain old ImageWriter II or StyleWriter cable for $15. After all, one Mac and one printer hardly qualify as a *network*. Put the other $35 into a skiing weekend or something.

Anyway, if you do get the more expensive connectors, plug one into the back of the printer and the other into the printer jack in the back of the Mac. Then connect the connectors using the phone wire. And if you're just going to use a StyleWriter cable, see "Plugging in a 'Writer."

The Chooser: Where Mac meets printer

The hardest part of printing on a Mac comes at the very beginning — an unfortunate fact for the novice who simply wants to get going. You have to take this step no matter what brand or kind of printer you've just connected, or you won't be able to print a thing.

When you first plug a printer into the Mac, it's not smart enough to notice that it's got a new friend. Therefore, after the Mac is connected to the printer, turn on both machines. Now choose Chooser from the menu. You should see something like this:

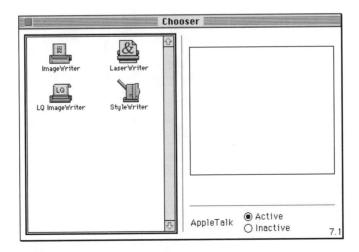

Your screen may look different, of course. The icons that appear in the left half of the window depend upon which *printer drivers* have been placed in your System Folder. A printer driver is a little piece of software that teaches the Mac how to communicate with a specific printer. Its name and its icon match the printer itself, as you can tell, sort of, from the figure above.

If you see a printer driver icon in the Chooser window that matches your printer, you're in luck! Click it.

If you have a laser printer, you should see its actual name show up in the *right* side of the Chooser window (if it's turned on), as shown here:

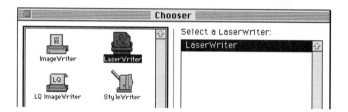

If, on the other hand, you have a StyleWriter, you'll see a choice of jacks, as shown below. If you plugged your StyleWriter into the printer jack as instructed above, click (obviously) the printer icon.

If you plugged the StyleWriter into the printer jack of your Macintosh...

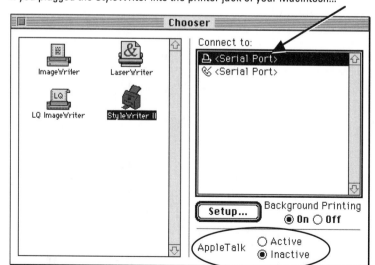

...be sure "AppleTalk" is set to Inactive.

Good going! Everything's coming up roses. If the names of *several* printers show up on the right, then you're either part of an office network with several printers, or you're an unexpectedly wealthy individual. Congratulations. Click the one you want to print on.

If you don't see your printer's icon (or *any* icons) in the left half of the Chooser window, somebody's taken them off your Mac. No matter — re-install all these icons by running the Installer on your original white System-software disks (or the startup compact disc). Now you can repeat this Chooser business, and everything should go fine.

If things *still* aren't going well — for example, if you click the driver icon, but your printer's name doesn't show up in the right side of the window — then see Chapter 12.

Anyway, once you click a printer driver icon, a couple of things happen. If you're selecting a laser printer, you may be told to turn on *AppleTalk.* AppleTalk is related to LocalTalk, the networking system mentioned earlier; remember that if you have a laser printer, you're supposedly part of a network even if just one Mac is attached to it. So make sure the little AppleTalk setting (in the lower-right corner of the dialog box) is Active if you have a laser printer. Conversely, make sure AppleTalk is *inactive* if you have a StyleWriter.

When you close the Chooser, you get a soon-to-be-annoying alert message:

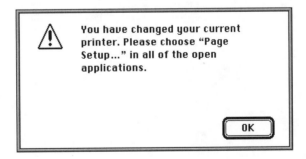

You have changed your current printer. Please choose "Page Setup..." in all of the open applications.

OK

It tells you (as if you didn't know) that you've just changed to a new printer. Its advice, though, is sound. After you select a printer driver, choose Page Setup from your File menu. A dialog box appears. Don't *do* anything in this box; just click OK.

You've just introduced the Mac to its new printer. All of this is a one-time operation, by the way. Unless you have to switch printers or something, you'll never have to touch the Chooser again.

Special FX with QuickDraw GX

Do you have System 7.5? Check your Cheat Sheet, where (if you read Chapter 1) you wrote down this information.

Anyway, one of System 7.5's fancy new features is called *QuickDraw GX*. The initials stand, as you can probably imagine, for nothing at all.

Good old QD GX is actually a pretty ingenious piece of software, even though (a) it takes up a huge chunk of your Mac's memory, (b) it doesn't get installed automatically when you install System 7.5 (you have to run a special GX installer), and (c) most of its features don't work yet.

Someday, GX will revolutionize Macintosh printing, typefaces, color, screen display, and more. Today, the only way it might make a dent in your destiny is with *desktop printer icons.* For people with more than one printer available, this is a great feature. Instead of slogging off to the Chooser to specify a printer, you just drag the *icon* of whatever you've typed on top of an icon that represents a *printer,* as shown here.

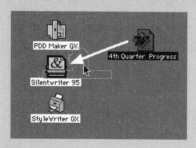

If you double-click one of these printer icons, you see a list of the files waiting to be printed on that printer.

There are a million other new features of GX, too. For example, a lot of high-falutin' typography is built into GX — glitzy new type-twisting features that happen automatically as you type. Here are some examples:

Automatic correct-looking fractions!   Automatic swashes!

"Put ½ of that fish back in the vats,"

Automatic fancy initials!   Automatic letter-pair tightening (kerning)!

These and other magical GX technologies require special, smartened-up GX *fonts.* That's OK; you can buy them today. (You'll be reading about fonts shortly.) But the GX magic *also* requires special, smartened-up GX *programs,* such as word processors. And those are *not* available today. Unfortunately, it may be a long time before software companies update their stuff to make it GX-compatible.

Until they do, and typographic utopia arrives, the only advantage you gain by installing QuickDraw GX is that desktop-printer business. Be sure you're willing to dedicate 1.5 of your Mac's precious few megs of memory to this handy feature; that's what GX takes for itself.

Background printing

In the Dark Ages of the 1980s, when you printed something, the printer's soul took over your Mac's body. You couldn't type, you couldn't work, you couldn't do anything but stare at the sign on the screen that said "Now printing." It was a dark and stormy era, a time of wild and rampant coffee breaks. Only when the paper came out of the printer were you allowed to use your computer again.

Since then, some clever engineer at Apple figured out how to allow *background printing*. When you use this handy feature, the Mac sends all the printing information, at a million miles per hour, into a *file* on your hard disk. It then immediately returns its attention to you and your personal needs.

Then, quietly, behind the scenes, the Mac shoots a little bit of that file to your printer at a time. It all happens during the microseconds between your keystrokes and mouse clicks, making it seem as though the Mac is printing in the background. In time, the printer receives all the information it needs to print, the paper comes gliding out, and you've been able to keep working the whole time.

The 5th Wave   By Rich Tennant

"WELL, MR. BOND, I GUESS THIS IS FAREWELL. LOWER...THE...LASER...PRINTER!"

In practice, there are a few chilly background printing realities to consider. First, a document takes much *longer* to print in the background than it would if the Mac devoted all of its brain power to printing. Similarly, making your Mac concentrate on two things at once also bogs down what *you're* doing; while something's being printed in the background, you can outtype your word processor, windows seem to take longer to open, and so on.

Turning the Background Printing feature on and off is easy. Select Chooser from the menu. In the lower-right side of the box, you'll see the On/Off buttons. Go for it.

I mention this tidbit so that you'll remember it when you're in a serious hurry for a printout. When it's 1:55 p.m. and the meeting is at 2:00. Or you're leaving the house anyway and want to make sure your printout is ready when you get back. In all of these cases, it would be wise to turn *off* background printing to ensure that you get your printout as fast as possible.

After all that: How you actually print

OK. Suppose that your printer is finally plugged in and, via the Chooser, has been introduced to the Mac. The moment has arrived: you'd actually like to *print* the thing.

Choose Print from the File menu. This dialog box appears; it looks different depending on your printer, but the one pictured below is typical of what you see if you have a laser printer:

LaserWriter "Silentwriter 95"		7.1.1	Print
Copies: 1 Pages: ⊙ All ○ From: [ ] To: [ ]			Cancel
Cover Page: ⊙ No ○ First Page ○ Last Page			
Paper Source: ⊙ Paper Cassette ○ Manual Feed			
Print: ⊙ Black & White ○ Color/Grayscale			
Destination: ⊙ Printer ○ PostScript® File			

The main thing you do in this dialog box is tell the Mac which pages of your document you want it to print. If you just want page 1, type a *1* into *both* the From and To boxes. If you want page 2 to the end, type *2* into the From box and leave the To box empty.

Specify how many copies you want by clicking and typing a number in the Copies box.

Using the Tab key in dialog boxes

Now would be a good time, I suppose, to mention what the Tab key does in dialog boxes. Suppose that you want to print *two* copies of page 3. Instead of using the mouse to click in each number box on the screen, you can just press Tab to jump from box to box.

Therefore, you'd just type *2* (in the Copies box); press Tab, type *3* (in the From box); press Tab, type *3* again (in the To box). And the mouse just sits there gathering dust.

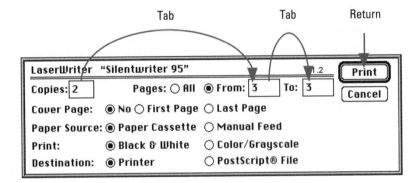

Anyway, after you're done filling out the options in this box, you can either click the Print button *or* press the Return key. (Pressing Return is always the same as clicking the outlined button.) The Mac should whir for a moment, and pretty soon the printout will come slithering out of your printer.

If you can't get anything to work right, check Chapter 12 for trouble-sleuthing tips.

Canceling printing

If you want to interrupt the printing process, ⌘-period does the trick — that is, while pressing the ⌘ key, type a period. Several times, actually. Even then, your printer will take a moment (or page) or two to respond to you.

A Guide to Jagged Printouts

This is really going to be "A Guide to *Avoiding* Jagged Printouts." Just wanted to grab your attention.

But listen: if your printouts look great, you're done. Outta here. Finito. Go on to the next chapter. This section gets a little dense, and it's only here if you need it or, God forbid, if you *want* to know what's going on behind the scenes.

You see, to understand why lettering sometimes prints out jaggedly, you must suffer through a description of the three different font formats that may lurk inside your Mac.

Font format 1: Bitmapped fonts

When the Mac first appeared, every typeface (which Apple calls a *font*) was formed of dots in a particular arrangement. It was a "map" of dots, if you will (and even if you won't). It was therefore called a *bitmapped* font. (So why don't they call it a *dotmap?* You kidding? That'd be too easy to understand.)

These fonts were named after cities: New York, Geneva, Athens, and so on.

The Mac screen, then and now, has 72 tiny square dots per inch. (To make sure as many people as possible are left in the dark, everybody abbreviates "dots per inch" as *dpi.*) This screen resolution worked out incredibly well: the only Mac printer — the ImageWriter — *also* printed 72 dots per inch. In other words, each dot you saw on the screen produced a corresponding dot on the page. For the first time in the history of computers, you got a printout that looked *exactly* like what you saw on the screen.

The ten great city fonts

All of the original Mac bitmapped fonts are still around. If you're a System 7 user, you probably only see a few of them in your font menus — the Installer doesn't automatically give you all of them. (The remaining fonts are tucked away on your Fonts disk; drag them onto your System Folder to install them.)

Here, for the sake of history, are the city-named, non-PostScript fonts. Note the little jaggies at the edges, even though they've been printed by the most expensive printer in the world. (The picture font is Cairo.)

New York   San Francisco   Athens
London   Venice   ✂🖉🖐🎗
Monaco   Chicago
Geneva   Los Angeles

In an inspired burst of cutesiness, the term *WYSIWYG* was born, which supposedly is pronounced wizzy-wig and stands for "what you see is what you get."

There are two drawbacks to bitmapped fonts. First, 72 dots per inch may sound, at first, like a plethora of dots . . . dots aplenty . . . a veritable dotfest. But believe it or not, 72 dpi is still too coarse to produce smooth printouts. You can still see the chunky square dots that compose each letter.

Second, if you think about it, you'll realize that a bitmapped font can only be printed clearly at a single size — the size at which its designer arranged the dots to look good. True, each bitmapped font usually comes in a *selection* of different sizes, each painstakingly mapped to screen dots — usually 10-point, 12-point, 14-point, 18-point, and 24-point sizes. But if you try to select an in-between type size, you get pretty gross-looking results.

For example, 12- and 24-point below looks fine, but no 17-point New York font bitmap comes with your Mac, as evidenced by the chunky example in the middle:

New York at 12-point size

New York at 17-point size

New York at 24-point size

Which sizes are in stock?

After reading the discussion of bitmapped fonts, you may wonder how you can tell for sure which bitmapped font sizes have been included in a set. Just consult the Font Size menu in one of your programs, as shown at right.

If a point size number is hollow, you've got it. If it's black, you don't, and the type will look squashed and blocky on the screen.

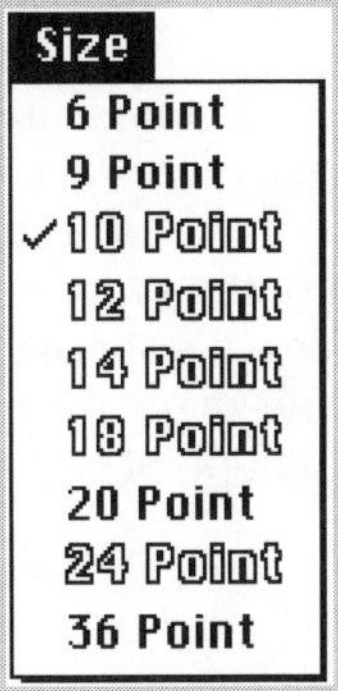

Size
6 Point
9 Point
✓10 Point
12 Point
14 Point
18 Point
20 Point
24 Point
36 Point

Therefore, if you're getting crummy-looking text in your printouts, the first possibility is that you've used a bitmapped font — one with a city name — in your document. (And if it looks *really* wretched, you're probably using it at a non-predesigned point size.) For example, London, Venice, and Los Angeles are the names of fonts that come on the Fonts disk with every Mac. But they're destined to be forever jagged. Change the font to a non-city–named font, and read on.

Font format #2: PostScript fonts

The world changed when Apple created the LaserWriter printer. Its resolution was *300* dots per inch — over four times sharper than the ImageWriter.

The main thing about the LaserWriter, though, was the new technology called PostScript that was built into it. They call PostScript a "page description language." It was invented by a little California company called Adobe. Once Apple saw how cool PostScript was, they struck a deal with Adobe to build PostScript technology into each laser printer. (By the way, there is such a thing as a *non-PostScript* laser printer. There are even a couple *nonlaser* PostScript printers. But in *general,* and in this chapter, "PostScript printer" = "laser printer.")

You can read all kinds of things about how PostScript works. But all *you* need to know is that:

> ✔ A PostScript laser printer means the end of jaggies. It can create extremely sharp, clear printouts that look published.
>
> ✔ To print sharp text on a PostScript laser printer, you have to use special fonts. (They're called, of course, *PostScript* fonts.)
>
> ✔ PostScript fonts can be printed at any size or angle — no matter how big, small, or absurdly stretched — with equal clarity.

PostScript fonts, unlike bitmapped ones, don't print text by specifying the placement of each dot on the page (below, left). Instead, the Mac thinks of each letter in a PostScript font as a hollow outline (below, right). The printer fills in that outline with solid black. Since a PostScript printer thinks of fonts by their shapes, it's simple to tell the printer "Make this bigger"; it just multiplies the outline-shape by a point size number you specify. Printouts of 12-point, 35.8-point, and 128-point type all look equally sharp on a PostScript printer.

Unfortunately, there are *two parts* to each PostScript font. There's a regular bitmapped font, with all the usual problems of ugliness-at-strange-sizes, for use on the screen. (It's sometimes, therefore, called a *screen font.*) And there's a separate file, called a *printer font,* that you put in your System Folder.

The printer fonts have the same names as the screen fonts, with the last letters lopped off. In your word processor's Font menu you might see Palatino Roman — but in your System Folder, there'll be a printer-font file called PalatRom. (If there's a Fonts folder *inside* your System Folder, then *that's* where you'll find these printer files.) For *each* type family, like Futura, you need a whole rat's nest of printer-font files in your System Folder: one each for **bold,** *italic,* ***bold italic,*** and so on. In the following figure, you can see a suitcase icon (which contains the screen fonts) and its associated printer fonts.

N Helvetica Narrow

HelveNar   HelveNarBol   HelveNarBolObl   HelveNarObl

Anyway, this is all leading up to explaining a second (and more common) cause of jagged type. If you've used PostScript (non-city-named) fonts in the document you're printing, and they're not looking terrific in the printout, then the appropriate printer-font file is missing or in the wrong place (i.e., not in the System Folder).

"And where," I can almost hear you asking, "am I supposed to *get* this piece of font that you claim I'm missing?"

"Well," you can almost hear me replying, "no PostScript fonts *come with* your Mac! So if you have a PostScript font, either you or somebody else *bought* it (or, um, copied it from somebody) and installed it on your Mac." Therefore, seek the missing printer-font file on the original font disk.

Font format #2½: Adobe Type Manager

As I mentioned, PostScript fonts look stunning in your laser printouts. But text on your *screen* still looks horrible if you use oddball sizes, like 17-point type, because you're still looking at a plain, old bitmapped font. Then, too, you only get this gorgeous print if you use a *PostScript laser printer.* If you tried to save some diñero by buying, say, a StyleWriter printer, then PostScript fonts gain you absolutely nothing. It's Jagged-Edgeville all over again.

So Adobe, the company that dreamed up PostScript, introduced a clever little gizmo called Adobe Type Manager, or ATM. (At last you know that Mac people don't actually go to cash machines a lot. Half the time they say "ATM" they're *not* talking about automated teller machines.)

ATM makes type on the *screen* look sharp at any size, just the way a PostScript printer does. The secret: It consults the printer font in your System Folder, decides what each letter should look like based on its *outline*, and draws it on the screen. Better yet, ATM works the same magic for nonlaser printers like the StyleWriter. ATM makes PostScript fonts print sharp, clear, and terrific at any size on those printers, too. Here's a 111-point capital R, Before ATM (left) and After:

The price: ATM takes up a good chunk of memory, and it slows down the screen display a bit. Still, at $99 per copy, Adobe sold a gazillion copies of ATM, and then promptly bought the state of Nevada for its employee parking lot.

Fortunately, Apple eventually persuaded Adobe to *give away* ATM. Unfortunately for everybody who'd paid $99 for it, you can now get ATM for a mere $7.50 shipping charge. (Call 800-776-2333.) You also get ATM free with System 7.5.

I mention ATM so that you'll know what it is, of course. But I also want you to know what to do if a PostScript font, *even* with ATM, *still* looks lousy on the screen. If that happens, it's the same problem as jagged PostScript printouts: you're missing the printer-font file for the typeface in question.

Here's where things get hairy. It turns out that there usually *are no* printer-font files for the standard ten PostScript fonts (Times, Helvetica, Helvetica Narrow, Palatino, Avant Garde, Bookman, New Century Schoolbook, Courier, Symbol, or

Zapf Chancery). Because these are so standard, their printer-font information comes *built into* virtually every laser printer made. Of course, that doesn't do ATM much good. It needs *printer fonts,* man, *printer fonts.* And it needs them in the System Folder. And guess what else? The version of ATM that Adobe so sanguinely sells you for $7.50 *doesn't include* printer-font files for that basic set!

Therefore, if you want smooth text on the screen (or on your nonlaser printer), you have three choices:

1) Get the $7.50 version of ATM and buy some fonts to go with it (or get some fonts from a user group, as described later).

2) Get the package called Adobe Type Basics, which contains ATM, the printer files for those 35 built-in fonts, and a handful of bonus fonts, for about $130.

3) Bail out of PostScript fonts altogether, and consider TrueType fonts instead (read on).

Font format 3: TrueType fonts

I'll mention this third font format only to avoid negligence suits. I mean, it *is* a font format — in fact, it's the one you most likely have — but you cannot *possibly* get jagged type from it, either on paper or on the screen.

It's TrueType. It's a special kind of font that Apple invented relatively recently. It has all the advantages of PostScript fonts (smooth type at any size). Yet it eliminates the problems associated with the PostScript scheme. Instead of having two separate files — one for the printer and one for the screen — TrueType fonts are self-contained. Likewise, instead of cluttering up your life with a separate font for each style variation (bold, italic, and so on), all the styles in a TrueType font are built into that one font suitcase file. And finally, instead of needing ATM for crisp, on-screen type at any size — a potentially costly add-on — TrueType fonts always look good on the screen automatically.

A TrueType font, therefore, *never* looks or prints jagged.

Incidentally, when TrueType appeared, everybody said "Ooh, font fight!" Everybody geared up for a big tragic rivalry between TrueType and PostScript. People also expected all kinds of system crashes and goofy-looking printouts if both font types were installed at once. None of it happened. The two technologies coexist just fine. Yet despite its convenience, TrueType didn't blow PostScript off the map for two reasons.

✔ *There weren't many fonts in this new format.* Apple provides a half dozen with every System 7 Mac, and you can buy hundreds of others from font companies. But by the time TrueType was invented, people had invested thousands of dollars in PostScript typefaces. Most people muttered that they couldn't afford to build a type library from scratch again.

✔ *TrueType is only a font technology.* PostScript, on the other hand, is a *graphics* technology. It can do much more than manipulate text. It can also create lines, circles, patterns, wild shadings, and three-dimensional re-creations of Marilyn Monroe standing over an air shaft. Indeed, two of the most famous professional graphics programs of all time, Illustrator and FreeHand, are PostScript drawing programs. TrueType, which deals only with type, can't possibly replace all the flexibility of PostScript.

G Whiz: GX formats

Technically, your foray into font formats isn't finished yet. If you're using System 7.5 (see Chapter 6), and you've installed QuickDraw GX (as described in a previous sidebar), you've got two formats to go. Yes, that's right: just when your tension headache was going away after reading about so many font formats, GX introduces TrueType GX and PostScript GX.

When you first install GX, all your *existing* fonts get converted to GX fonts automatically. Actually, TrueType GX and PostScript GX fonts work just like regular TrueType and PostScript fonts. Those old-fonts-converted won't offer anything new with QuickDraw GX (except to work with it).

If you *buy* fonts that began life as GX fonts, however, they may well come with hundreds of extra letters and symbols—additional alphabets complete with enough swashes and fancy capitals to make your grocery list look like the Declaration of Independence.

Oh, yeah: there's one other way that GX fonts impact your life. Whereas a PostScript font normally comes in several parts (a screen-font suitcase file accompanied by several printer-font files), a PostScript *GX* font just looks like a suitcase by itself. The handful of funnily-named printer-font files (HelvNar, PalatRom, etc.) are absorbed into the suitcase file itself. In other words, the days of misplacing or losing your printer-font files are over forever.

On the other hand, now a TrueType GX font suitcase looks exactly like a PostScript GX font suitcase. There's no way to tell them apart just by looking. Of course, since it's impossible to lose your printer-font files, and since ATM gets installed automatically with QuickDraw GX, it no longer makes any *difference* whether a font is TrueType or PostScript; it will look smooth on screen, and print out smoothly on paper, in either case.

ID'ing a font

So: in practical terms, there are *three* kinds of fonts: bitmapped, PostScript, and TrueType. In your quest to understand what you've got on your computer, and to straighten out whatever jagged-printout problems you might be having, here's your own personal Guide to Font Identification.

If you have System 7

If your Mac uses System 7 (that is, 7-point-anything), and you haven't added any new fonts yourself, then everything's TrueType. On a System 7 Mac, even the city-named fonts (like Chicago, Geneva, and New York), which are usually presumed to be bitmapped fonts, are actually TrueType ones. No matter *what* kind of printer you own, TrueType fonts look great when printed, and you don't have to worry about point sizes or printer-font files or any of that jazz.

You can prove this to yourself by opening your System Folder and double-clicking the System file itself (or your Fonts folder if you have one). Then double-click a suitcase icon. If you now choose By Icon from the View menu, you'll see TrueType fonts displayed with this special icon (see all those little A's?):

New York

Now, it's remotely possible that you or somebody you love has enhanced your Mac with additional fonts. Here are the basic System 7 fonts: Times, Helvetica, Monaco, Chicago, Geneva, Palatino, Courier, Symbol. Buy a printer and you usually get Helvetica Narrow Zapf Chancery, Zapf Dingbats, Avant Garde, New Century Schoolbook, and Bookman.

If you have any fonts not in this list, then it's a sure thing you've got extra fonts. If they have a city name (like Los Angeles), they're bitmapped fonts, and they'll look cruddy no matter what kind of printer you use.

If you have extra fonts that *don't* have city names, they're either PostScript or TrueType fonts. Open your System file (or Fonts folder), as I mentioned a moment ago, and decide for yourself by looking at each font's icon.

Just remember that if the font is a PostScript font, it'll only look terrific when you print *if* you also have the corresponding printer-font files in your System or

Fonts folder.

There are 35 exceptions to that generalization — the 35 type styles *built into* your laser printer. These fonts *don't* need printer files in your System Folder. (Although *Oblique* and *Demi* may sound like part of a sleazy trapeze act, they

Times Roman	New Century Schoolbook	Helvetica Roman
Times Bold	Roman	**Helvetica Bold**
Times Italic	**New Century Schoolbook**	*Helvetica Oblique*
Times Bold Italic	**Bold**	***Helvetica Bold Oblique***
	New Century Schoolbook	
Avant Garde Roman	*Italic*	Helvetica Narrow Roman
Avant Garde Demi	***New Century Schoolbook***	**Helvetica Narrow Bold**
Avant Garde Italic	***Bold Italic***	*Helvetica Narrow Oblique*
Avant Garde Demi Italic		***Helvetica Narrow Bold Oblique***
	Palatino Roman	
Bookman Roman	**Palatino Bold**	*Zapf Chancery*
Bookman Demi	*Palatino Italic*	
Bookman Italic	***Palatino Bold Italic***	αβχδεφγηιφκ (Symbol)
Bookman Demi Italic		
	Courier Roman	❀❂✳❉✳✳❊ (Zapf Dingbats)
	Courier Bold	
	Courier Italic	
	Courier Bold Italic	

are in fact the trendy words for *Italic* and *Bold,* respectively.) Here's the list:

If there's a font in your font menu that doesn't appear in this list (other than city-named fonts), then it didn't come with the Mac. You're going to need the printer-font file equivalent of it in your System Folder.

One more word of advice, ye lucky laser printer user: Nobody's ever gone to hell for this, but it's a good idea not to let the TrueType and PostScript versions of the *same* font coexist on your system. Make a decision to go with the TrueType versions or the PostScript versions, and stand by it — and remove the duplicates.

If you have System 6

First of all, it's extremely unlikely that you have any TrueType fonts. You *can't* use TrueType fonts, in fact, unless you've put a special file, called the *TrueType init,* into your System Folder, which you'd probably remember doing.

Therefore, it's very simple. If your font has a city name, it's going to look lame

And if the font *doesn't* have a city name, it's a PostScript font. It'll look great when printed on a laser printer *if* (1) it's one of the Built-In 35 or (2) you have the corresponding printer-font files installed.

The output upshot

If you just bought a new Mac, you have nothing to worry about. Whether you know it or not, *all* of your fonts are TrueType fonts, which do their elfin-magic behind the scenes. And no matter what printer you own, you can rest easy knowing that TrueType will give you the highest quality printouts it's capable of. End of story.

Things only get more complicated if you (1) crave more variety, (2) find fonts in your font menu that *you* didn't put there, or (3) have a Mac running System 6.

If any of those conditions are true for you, use this table to help you figure life out.

Your Mac	Your printer	Use TrueType fonts?	Use PostScript fonts?	Use city-named fonts?
System 7	PostScript laser	Sure	Yes, with ATM and the printer-font files in your System Folder	Yup ('cause they're really TrueType)
System 7	StyleWriter, DeskWriter, non-PostScript laser	You betcha	Yes, with ATM and the printer-font files in your System Folder	Go for it ('cause they're really TrueType)
System 6	PostScript laser	No*	Yes, with ATM and the printer-font files in your System Folder	No way
System 6	StyleWriter, DeskWriter, non-PostScript laser	No*	Yes, with ATM and the printer-font files in your System Folder	Only if you have the appropriate point size installed (see the sidebar on page 101)

*Unless you have System 6.0.7 *and* the TrueType INIT, as described earlier.

A Veritable Font-u-copia

So where do you get additional fonts? The universal response to that kind of question is, of course: Buy them. Those on a budget, however, can still get tons of great fonts. If a white Fonts disk came with your Mac, for example, there are about a dozen interesting extra ones. (Alas, they're all the bitmapped kind.)

Or you can call up your local user group and pay about $5 for a disk full of new fonts. Or if you have a modem (as described in Chapter 7), you can dial up America Online or another online service and help yourself to as many fonts as your typographical taste buds can tolerate.

How to install a font in System 7

Quit all your programs (if you're running any) before trying this.

Drag the font file icon on top of the System Folder icon. That goes for both printer-font files and screen font files, if it's a PostScript font you're installing. (Do *not* drag them into the open System Folder *window.* Do not drag them to the Trash can. Do not collect $200.)

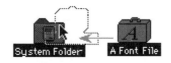

The only sidebar about user groups

Just in case the term "user group" caught you by surprise, here's the lowdown.

There are hundreds of these things—Macintosh User Groups, or MUGs. They're called things like LAMUG, NYMUG, and THUG (for the LA, NY, and The Hudson organizations, respectively). Each is a teeming hotbed of Mac enthusiasts of all different levels. They usually meet monthly, crank out a newsletter a month, and charge low annual dues. Each is also a dandy place to get your questions answered, your purchases previewed, and your social cravings slaked.

To find out which group is closest to you and your Mac, call Apple's user-group hotline, 800-538-9696.

How to install a font in System 6

If you're using System 6, installing fonts is much uglier and more difficult. I'll make the effort, but you should feel free to consult your original, crumbling Mac manuals for more patient instructions.

Find the program called Font/DA Mover. It's either on your hard disk someplace or still on the white Apple disks that came with your Mac. Double-click the icon. You'll see two lists. One side lists all the fonts you *already* have in your System. The other side is probably empty.

Click the Open button on the empty side, and navigate your way to the font you want to install. Double-click its name; you return to the main Font/DA Mover window. Drag through the names of the fonts you want to install and then click the Copy button. (To remove fonts from your system, drag through their names on the System side of the list and click Remove.) And then think about getting System 7, where installing fonts isn't such a pain.

You'll see a message alerting you that the Mac is going to install the font for you. Just smile, wave, and click OK.

How to remove a font

First of all, remind yourself what system-software version you've got. (Did you write it on this book's Cheat Sheet, as instructed in Chapter 1?)

If you've got System 7.0 or System 7.0.1 (or the "p" Performa versions of those), open the System Folder and then double-click the System *file* icon itself.

If you have System 7.1 or later (or a "p" version thereof), open your System Folder and then open the Fonts folder therein.

In any case, you'll now see a list of your fonts in a window:

System		
61 items	34 MB in disk	4 MB available
Name	Size	Kind
Geneva 18	5K	font
Geneva 20	7K	font
Geneva 24	9K	font
Helvetica	60K	font
Helvetica 9	11K	font
Helvetica (bold)	58K	font
Helvetica 10	10K	font
Helvetica 12	11K	font
Helvetica 14	11K	font

To see what a font looks like, double-click it; a little window opens, displaying a line from classical literature, displayed in the font you're investigating.

To remove a font, just drag it out of the window. Put it onto the desktop. Or put it into some other folder — or right into the Trash can.

Top Ten Free Fun Font Factoids

1. Every Mac comes installed with **Times, Helvetica, Courier** (which looks like an electric typewriter), **Symbol** (a bunch of Greek symbols), **New York, Chicago** (the font used for menu names), **Geneva** (the font used for icon names in the Finder), and **Monaco** (a *monospaced* font, where every letter is exactly the same width; Monaco looks ugly on-screen but looks OK when printed). The Mac won't let you remove the last three; it uses them for various things on the screen.

2. Some of the bitmapped fonts that come with the Mac correspond to PostScript fonts. New York is pretty much like Times; Geneva is sort of like Helvetica; and Monaco is a lot like Courier (they're both monospaced).

   If you have a non-System 7 Mac, and you try to print a document prepared in New York, Geneva, or Monaco, the Mac will, at your request, *substitute* the PostScript equivalents (Times, Helvetica, Courier) automatically. ("At your request" means that, when you choose Page Setup from the File menu and encounter a dialog box, you make sure that Font Substitution is selected.)

   However, you're much better off not using this feature. When the Mac does this font substitution for city-named fonts, it doesn't account for the fact that New York and Times (for example) have different *letter widths*. So you get really weird word spacing in the printout because the Mac tries to *position* every word in the same place (below, right) as it's shown on the screen (below, left).

   "Agatha!" I screamed, my lungs   "Agatha!"   I screamed,   my lungs
   bleeding and raw from the   bleeding   and raw   from   the
   violent pounding of the vicious   violent   pounding   of the vicious
   surf spray.   surf   spray.

   Much better idea: Format your documents with laser fonts to begin with! Unless you like the look of free-floating words in space, keep Font Substitution clicked off.

3. Ten font families are built into most PostScript laser printers. They are, as you'll recall, Times, Helvetica, Helvetica Narrow, Avant Garde, Palatino, Bookman, New Century Schoolbook, Symbol, Zapf Chancery, and Zapf Dingbats.

Any PostScript font that doesn't appear on this list has to be *downloaded* (transferred) to the printer each time you turn on the printer and try to print. As such, they're called *downloadable* fonts. That's why their printer-font files have to sit in your System Folder, where the Mac will know where to find them.

Downloadable fonts impact your life in several ways. First, you have to buy them. Second, documents that use downloadable fonts take more time to print; the Mac has to teach the printer what each character looks like.

Third, if you use several downloadable fonts in a document, it may not print at all. The printer's memory will get filled up with font information even before the Mac starts to send the document. The result: The printer keeps saying "Wait, wait, I'm not ready yet . . ." to the Mac, and the Mac keeps saying "Ready? Ready? Here it comes . . .", until you get disgusted and flip one of them off. (Marriage counseling for computer equipment is not yet available outside California.)

The solution, of course, is to reformat your document using the built-in fonts (Times, Helvetica, and so on) instead of downloadable ones — or to install more memory into your printer. (You'll find more nitty-gritty on this topic in Chapter 12.)

4. Choose Page Setup from the File menu. The Page Setup dialog box has a handful of very useful options — what paper size you plan to use, for example, or how much you want your document enlarged or reduced.

In the upper-right corner, though, there's a nifty Options button (if you have a laser printer). Click it. Up comes a dialog box:

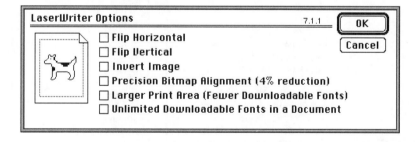

To get a little preview of each option, click the appropriate checkbox and watch the helpful Dogcow illustrate the effect on your printout.

Most noteworthy, though, is the item called Larger Print Area. The average laser printer can only print to within $1/2$ inch of the page edge. Select Larger Print Area, though, and you gain $1/4$ inch all the way around — a very useful gain for graphics, music, page layout, and other kinds of printing.

5. Suppose that you select some text and make it bold. Then you try to print, but the text keeps coming out as *non*bold on the printed page.

The problem is that some PostScript typefaces, notably Zapf Chancery, *don't have* a bold version. (Zapf Chancery doesn't even have an italic style since it's already sort of italic.)

6. Adobe's PostScript typefaces each include a complete bitmapped screen font for each type style — bold, italic, and so on. Unfortunately, each style name appears in your Font menu prefaced by an initial: "I Times Italic, B Times Bold, BI Times Bold Italic," and so on.

Who came up with this dumb idea, I can't tell you. But I do know that your font menu lists fonts alphabetically. The result is that each typeface's style variations aren't listed together — they're scattered all over the darned menu, as shown on the left below. Your only chance of getting things into shape is to buy a utility program that combines them into family groups on your menu, with the style variations listed in a submenu (right):

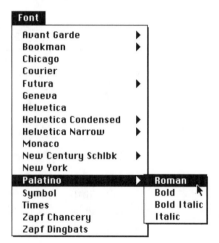

The Dogcow

No Mac book would be complete without at least a passing acknowledgment of the Dogcow.

His name, need I point out, stems from the fact that nobody can precisely figure out what kind of animal he is. In the inner sanctum of Apple Computer Corporation, it is said that, late at night, you can hear the sound made by the Dogcow: Moof!

One such utility is sold by (guess who?) Adobe. Because they probably concocted the inconvenient font-naming scheme just so they could sell their utility program to correct it, I'm not going to play along by telling you what the thing is called. Instead, I'm going to recommend WYSIWYG Menus, an even better utility. It's part of the Now Utilities package (see Appendix B, the Resource Resource).

7. In MacWrite II and some other word processing programs, you can actually see the names of the fonts in your font menu *in* those typefaces, like this:

```
Font
Avant Garde
Avant Garde Demi
Bookman
Chicago
Courier
Futura
Garamond Book
Geneva
H Futura Heavy
```

There are a few other ways to get this feature, all of which involve spending some money. Suitcase II, Now Utilities, and MenuFonts are a few programs that add this feature to any program you own.

8. When you first buy your laser printer, you may have noticed (and sworn at) the fact that it spits out a "startup page" every time you turn it on. This startup page contains a host of extremely unimportant information, like the number of pages you've printed in the printer's lifetime (including the useless startup page in your hand). Meanwhile, the Brazilian rain forests keep getting smaller.

You can tell the printer not to waste that paper and ink, if you want. Use the little program called LaserWriter Utility or LaserWriter *Font* Utility; it's on the disks that came with your Mac. (If you have some version of System 7 before System 7.5, it's on a disk called Tidbits.)

Double-click LaserWriter Utility, and choose Start Page Options from the Utilities menu. Click Off, and savor the fact that you made the world a better place for your grandchildren.

9. If you have something important to print, keep in mind that you don't actually have to *own* a laser printer to get that professional look. Even if you use an ImageWriter or other 'Writer at home, you can always take your disk in to an "output bureau" (a high-tech copy shop) and pay a certain amount per page for laser-printed (or even higher quality) printouts. But if you do so, just remember the golden rules of which fonts to use, as described earlier in this section.

10. Want to look good the next time you're hanging out with a bunch of type geeks? Then learn to bandy about the terms *serif* (pronounced SAIR-iff) and *sans serif* (SANNZ sair-iff).

A serif is the little protruding line built onto the edges of the letters in certain typefaces. In the *serif font* pictured in the top example here, I've drawn little circles around some of the serifs:

Terrif serifs
Sans-serif

A *sans serif* font, on the other hand, has no little protuberances, as you can see by their absence in the little square (in the lower example above). Times, Palatino, and the font you're reading are all serif fonts. Helvetica, Geneva, and the headlines in most newspapers are sans serif fonts. And that information, plus 32¢, will buy you a first-class postage stamp in the United States.

Part II
Increasing Your Coolness Quotient

The 5th Wave   By Rich Tennant

"WELL, RIGHT OFF, THE RESPONSE TIME SEEMS A BIT SLOW."

In this part...

*E*ither you've faithfully plowed through the personality-
enriching material so far, nursing your inner child (the
one that always wanted to use a computer), and are now
ready for more . . .

. . . or you've just skipped over a lot of stuff to get here.
Either way, you won't be disappointed: the mind-blowing
Faking Your Way Through the Top Ten Programs will be your
survival guide for maintaining status in the office, and *More
Stuff to Buy and Plug In* will help you unleash your Mac's
potential (and unload your wallet).

Chapter 5

Faking Your Way Through the Top Ten Programs

In This Chapter

▶ Faking your way through ClarisWorks

▶ Faking your way through graphics programs like MacPaint, MacDraw, and Canvas

▶ Faking your way through word/page processing programs like Word, PageMaker, and QuarkXPress

▶ Faking your way through famous number/data crunchers like Excel and FileMaker

*T*his chapter is a survival guide for stranded-on-a-desert-island, filling-in-for-Mr.-Big, my-son's-at-school-but-I-need-to-print-out-something, the-computer-just-arrived-but-the-board-meeting-is-in-two-hours, in-a-computer-store-to-try-something-but-don't-know-how-it-works situations.

I'm going to assume that you know the basics by now. If you ever were a dummy to begin with, at this point you're only a *demi*-dummy: you already know how to save files and retrieve them (from Chapter 3) and how to use fonts and print (from Chapter 4). And if you want to do something fancier than what I'll be showing you, I'm assuming that you do have access to either (a) the manuals or (b) whoever got you into this mess to begin with.

Macintosh users are notorious for not reading their software manuals. They're actually belligerently *proud* of the fact that they never read manuals. Of course, two years down the line, one user will look at another user's techniques and intone, astounded, "I never knew it could do *that!*"

You're welcome to join this cult of instant gratification, with this chapter as your guide — but at least read the manual for your word processor (or whatever program you spend the most time in).

The one thing this section *isn't* for is to help you use an illegal copy of one of these programs. Humor me on this; living in New York City is dangerous enough without worrying that some scary-looking goons in trench coats and dark glasses are gonna show up at my apartment accusing me of encouraging software piracy.

HyperCard ... Not!

In earlier printings of *Macs For Dummies,* this chapter started with HyperCard because HyperCard used to come free with every Mac. HyperCard is often described as a "software Erector set" because you could create lots of neat things with it: an address book, a planning calendar, a recipe book, and so on.

At the time, you could also buy HyperCard from Claris Corporation — for $200. I guess not too many people were buying, though. Why would they, when they already had a free copy of the program?

So a funny thing happened near the end of 1992: without saying a word to anyone, Apple stopped giving away HyperCard with each Mac. Instead, they substituted a stripped-down doodad they call HyperCard Player. You can't use the Player to design your own cool miniprograms. All the Player can do is open *other* people's HyperCard files. In fact, beginning with System 7.5, you don't even get HyperCard Player.

Since HyperCard was yanked out of the Software Top Ten, I'm going to spend the following pages teaching you about a much more popular program: ClarisWorks. If you bought a Performa Mac or PowerBook 150, ClarisWorks probably came already installed on your hard disk. Rub it in, you lucky so-and-so. ClarisWorks is definitely one of the top ten programs, and it's a durned fine program.

One final caution forever

You're about to start using actual programs to do actual work. You have now entered the Computer Age. No refunds. No U-turns. No exit.

I've witnessed hundreds of beginners embark on this brave adventure. And I've watched some of them get very disgruntled, develop nervous tics, and eventually give the computer to a neighborhood preteen.

The reason is simple: they fall into the bad habit of *double-clicking menus.*

Utterly understandable, I concur. And yet utterly wrong. Double-clicking menu commands will get you utterly into trouble.

Quick recap: what you're supposed to do is point to a menu title (such as File, View, or Edit) and *press the mouse button.* Leave it down. Leave it down.

Slide down the list of menu commands until the one you want turns black.

Now: *just let go.* Do not click. Just let go.

Remember that *double-clicking* is only used to *open something;* never to choose from a menu.

ClarisWorks

ClarisWorks is Swiss Army Knife software. Just look at all you get, even if you don't know what they are yet: a word processor, a database, and a spreadsheet. *Now* how much would you pay? But wait: you also get a graphics program that can even serve as a basic page-layout system. And if you order now, you even get a little communications program (to use if you own a *modem* — a phone hookup for your Mac).

All of these modules are neatly bundled into a single integrated program. You can write a letter and put a graphic in it; or design a flyer that has a little spreadsheet in it; and so on. This section will be worth reading even if you don't own this particular software because ClarisWorks works exactly like most other Mac programs.

Most of the following stuff applies to all versions ClarisWorks; the stuff near the end, however, is only in version 2.0 and later.

Launching ClarisWorks

Double-click the ClarisWorks icon.

After the Claris logo disappears, you're asked to decide what you want to accomplish. Because you'll face this decision every time you use this program, a rundown may be in order here.

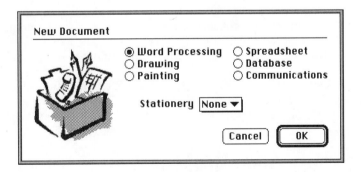

Word Processing: You know what a word processing document is: something you type. A memo, a novel, a ransom note.

Drawing: This is ClarisWorks' version of MacDraw (more later in this chapter). In this kind of document, you toy around with lines, shapes, and colors to produce logos, maps, Hangman diagrams, and other important visuals.

Painting: This is ClarisWorks' version of MacPaint or Photoshop (more on these later in this chapter, too). Painting is another way of making graphics. Unlike the Drawing mode, where you can only create distinct circles, lines, and squares, the Painting tools let you create shading, freeform spatters, and much more textured artwork.

Database: An electronic index-card file, very much like FileMaker (see later in this chapter). You type in your lists — household expenditures; record collections; subscriber list to *Regis & Kathie Lee!* magazine — and the program sorts them, prints them, finds certain pieces of info instantly, and so on.

Spreadsheet: A computerized ledger sheet, almost exactly like Excel (also coming up later). Crunches numbers: calculates your car's mileage per gallon, your bank account, how much of the phone bill your teenage daughter owes, that kind of thing.

Communications: You need this kind of program if you want to use your modem for dialing up (1) local "electronic bulletin boards," (2) a pay-by-the-hour information service like CompuServe, or (3) your local school's computer system. (You *can't* use a program like this to dial up America Online or eWorld. Instead, you have to use a special program provided by those companies. Details to come.)

To make ClarisWorks strut its stuff, I'll show you how to create a thank-you letter. But not just any thank-you letter — this is going to be the world's most beautiful and personalized *form letter.* You're going to merge a list of addresses into a piece of mail, creating what appear to be individually composed letters; thus, the technoid term for what you're about to do is *mail merge.*

Yeah, yeah, I hear ya: form letters aren't exactly what you bought a computer to do. Follow along anyway; this exercise will take you through most of ClarisWorks, and you'll brush up against some features that *will* be useful to you.

Your first database

Suppose you just got married. You were showered with lovely gifts. And now it's your task to write a charming thank-you note to each of your gift givers. You'll begin by typing a list of the gift givers. The ideal software for organizing this kind of information is a *database.*

Therefore, double-click the Database button.

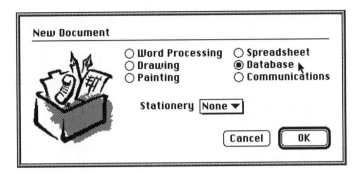

Don't be alarmed. The screen that now appears may look complicated, but it's actually not so bad — it simply wants to know what blanks you'll be wanting to fill in for each person in your list (name, address, gift type, and so on).

You're about to type names for these blanks (which the program calls *fields*). As always, if you make a typo, just press the Delete key to backspace over it. Here we go:

1. Type *First Name*. Press the Return key. (Pressing Return is the same as clicking the Create button.)

2. Type *Last Name*. Press Return.

3. Type *Address*. Press Return. (See how you're building a list?)

4. Type *Gift*. Press Return.

5. Type *Adjective*. Press Return. (In this blank, you'll eventually type a word that describes the glorious present this person gave you.)

6. Finally, type *Part of House*. (You'll see why in a moment). Press Return.

Your masterpiece should look something like this:

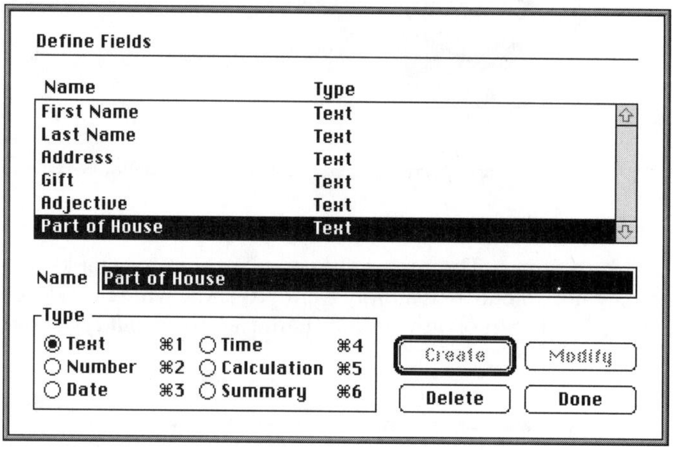

Define Fields

Name	Type
First Name	Text
Last Name	Text
Address	Text
Gift	Text
Adjective	Text
Part of House	**Text**

Name [Part of House]

┌Type────────────────────────────┐
◉ Text ⌘1 ○ Time ⌘4	[Create] [Modify]
○ Number ⌘2 ○ Calculation ⌘5	
○ Date ⌘3 ○ Summary ⌘6	[Delete] [Done]

7. Click the Done button in the lower-right corner. The dialog box goes away.

When you see what you've created, things should make a little bit more sense. You've just created the blanks (oh, all right, *fields*) to be filled in for each person in your list.

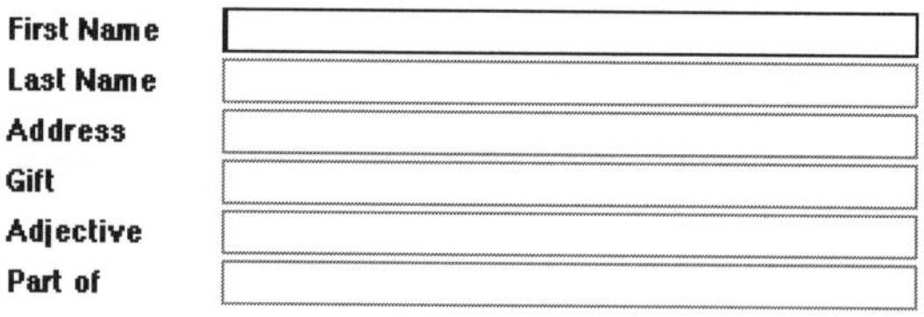

First Name	
Last Name	
Address	
Gift	
Adjective	
Part of	

Data entry time

This is important: To fill in the fields of a database (like this one), just type normally. To advance from one field to the next — from "First Name" to "Last Name," for example — *press the Tab key*. Do not press the Return key, as every instinct in your body will be screaming to do. You'll discover why in a moment. (You can also move to a new field by clicking in it, but the Tab key is quicker.)

So here goes:

1. Make sure you can see a dotted-line rectangle for each field, like the ones in the preceding figure. If not, press the Tab key. The little blinking cursor should be in the "First Name" blank. (If it's not, click there.)

2. Type *Josephine*. Press the Tab key to jump to the "Last Name" field.

First Name	Josephine
Last Name	
Address	
Gift	

3. Type *Flombébé*. (See "Accent heaven" on the next page.) Again, press Tab. Now you're in the Address blank.

4. Type *200 West 15th Street*. Ready to find out what the Return key does?

   Go ahead: *Now* press Return. Note that you don't advance to the next blank; instead, the program thoughtfully makes *this* box bigger, so there's room for another line of address.

First Name	Josephine
Last Name	Flombébé
Address	200 West 15th Street
Gift	New York, NY 10010
Adjective	
Part of	

If you ever hit Return by *mistake,* intending to jump to the next blank (but just making this blank bigger), press the Delete key.

5. Go ahead and type *New York, NY 10010.* Then press Tab. (And don't worry that the second line of the address immediately gets hidden. The information you typed is still there.)

6. Type *acrylic sofa cover* (and press Tab); *practical* (and press Tab); *living room* (and stop).

You've just filled in the information for your first gift sender. So that this won't take all day, let's pretend that it was a *very* small wedding, and you only received gifts from three people.

But let's see, we need a new set of fields, don't we? Come to think of it, wouldn't life be sweeter if there were a computer *term* for "set of fields"? By gumbo, there is! A set of fields is called a *record.*

Accent heaven

Ah, mais oui, mon ami. C'est vrai, c'est la vie, c'est le résumé.

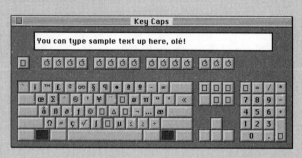

I know what you're thinking: *What a smooth, sophisticated guy to be able to speak French like that!* Thank you.

But you're also thinking: How did he get those cool accent marks? Very easily — and you, having been smart enough to choose a Mac over all its inferior competitors, can do it too.

The Mac has a ton of these special characters. Look at your keyboard — I bet you don't see ©, or ™, or •, or ¢, or any other useful symbols Mac people use all the time. That's because they're hidden. The secret that unlocks them is . . . the Option key.

It works like the Shift key: while pressing Option, you type a key. Here are some popular ones:

To get this . . .	Press Option and type this . . .
©	g
™	2
ç	c
¢	4
¡	1
£	3
•	8
®	r
†	t

Anyway, there are dozens of these things. What's nice to know is that you have a complete built-in cheat sheet that shows their locations on the keyboard. It's the Key Caps desk accessory, which is in your menu.

Open it up and take a look. Now try pressing the Option key.

So *that's* where all those little critters live!

Anyway, there's one more wrinkle to all this. A few symbols, called *diacritical marks* (that's not a computer term, it's a proofreading one, I think) can be placed over *any* letter. They include the markings over this ü, this é, this è, and so förth. Since the Mac doesn't know ahead of time which vowel you're going to type, creating these is a two-step process:

1. While pressing Option, type the key as shown here:

To get this . . .	Press Option and type this . . .
é	e
ü	u
è	`
ñ	n
î	i

When you do this, *nothing will happen*. In other words, no marking appears on the screen — until you do step 2.

2. Type the letter you want to appear under the diacritical marking.

Only now does the entire thing — letter and marking — appear on the screen. So if you think about it, typing the six-letter word *résumé* requires eight keystrokes. *C'est formidable, ça!*

I wouldn't bother with that term if it didn't crop up in the next set of instructions.

1. From the Edit menu, choose New Record.

2. A new record ("set of fields") appears, and you're ready to type the second person's information. Type anything you want, or copy the example below, but remember to press Tab at the end of each piece of information. (Oh, and if you want a second line for the address, press Return. Make up a town and state; you're a creative soul.)

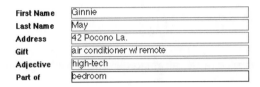

First Name	Ginnie
Last Name	May
Address	42 Pocono La.
Gift	air conditioner w/ remote
Adjective	high-tech
Part of	bedroom

3. Once again, choose New Record from the Edit menu. Type a third set of information, perhaps along these lines:

First Name	Suzie
Last Name	Khiou
Address	1 Doormouse Ave.
Gift	Harley
Adjective	expensive
Part of	garage

4. Fabulous! You're really cooking now. As a final wise step, choose Save from the File menu. Type *Gift List* as the name of your database.

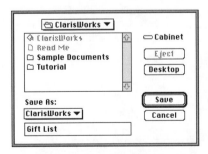

5. Click Save to preserve your database on the hard disk.

You've just created your first database. Having gone through the tedium of typing in each little scrap of information the way the Mac wants it, you can now perform some stunts with it that'd make your grandparents' jaws drop. You can ask it to show you only the names of your friends whose last names begin with Z. Or only those who live in Texas. Or only those whose gifts you've categorized as *fabulous*.

For instructions on finding, showing these lists, and sorting your database, read the section on FileMaker later in this chapter.

Forming the form letter

Next, you're going to write the thank-you note. At each place where you want to use somebody's name (or other gift-related information), you'll ask ClarisWorks to slap in the appropriate info.

1. Choose New from the File menu. (Once again, you're asked to choose the kind of document you want.)

Avoiding the ClarisWorks Excedrin headache

If God uses software, it's probably ClarisWorks. That's how wonderful it is.

However, using ClarisWorks does have its frustrations. Here are a couple of them, and how to avoid them.

The black record syndrome: If you accidentally click one of your records in the area shown below, it turns black. You've actually now *selected* a record.

At this moment, you can do anything you'd do to a highlighted Macintosh object. You can also use the Edit menu to cut, copy, duplicate, or delete this record.

If you've selected this thing by accident, however, your main instinct will probably be to get *rid* of the black highlighting. There's only one way to do that: click in a *field* (the blank where you'd type in information).

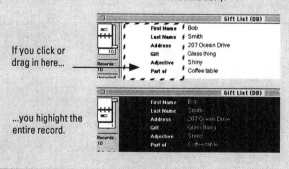

If you click or drag in here...

...you highlight the entire record.

2. Double-click Word Processing.

Now you get a sparkling new sheet of electronic typing paper.

This area
represents
the margins of
the page. You
can't type
here.

Do your typing
here. Press
the Delete
key to fix a
typo.

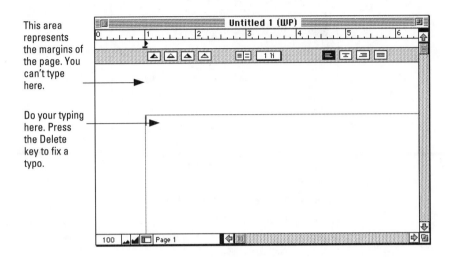

Incidentally, if you have a small-screen Mac like a Classic or a PowerBook, you
probably don't want all that margin area eating up your screen. You can hide it
easily enough: choose Document from the Edit menu. A dialog box appears;
click the Show Margins checkbox to deselect it. And then click OK. Now your
whole screen is filled with typeable area.

Now then — on with the form letter. You'll start the letter with the address, of
course. Yet the address will be *different* on each letter! This is where mail-
merging is handy:

3. From the File menu, choose Mail Merge. When the little window appears,
   you'll see your database name, "Gift List," prominently displayed.

4. Click OK (to tell ClarisWorks that Gift List is the database you want to
   work with).

Now a strange-looking window appears:

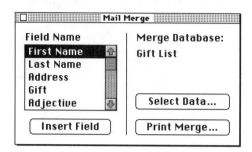

In the scrolling list you see the *field names* from your database. Here's how it works:

5. Point to *First Name* and double-click.

   See what happened? The program popped a placeholder for the First Name right into your letter. When you print, instead of *<<First Name>>*, it will say *Josephine.*

6. Type a space. In the Mail Merge window, point to *Last Name* and double-click. Press Return; then point to the Mail Merge window again and double-click *Address*.

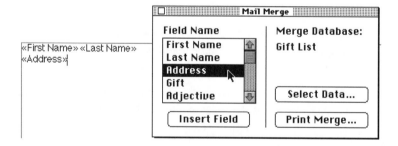

Before you continue typing, you may want to drag the little Mail Merge window off to the right of your screen as best you can. (To move the window, drag its title bar.) You're going to want to see both it and your typing simultaneously.

7. Press Return a couple of times. Type *Dear,* followed by a space.

8. Point to the words *First Name* in the Mail Merge window, as you did a moment ago. Double-click. Type a comma. Your letter should look something like this:

```
«First Name» «Last Name»
«Address»

Dear «First Name»,
```

9. This is where it gets good. Press Return a couple of returns. Type *I nearly cried when I unwrapped the incredible,* followed by a space.

10. Double-click the word *Gift* in the Mail Merge window.

11. Continue typing: *you gave me for my wedding. It is far and away the most* (and now double-click *Adjective* in the Mail Merge window) *gift I will ever receive.*

```
«First Name» «Last Name»
«Address»


Dear «First Name»,

I nearly cried when I unwrapped the incredible «Gift» you gave me for my wedding. It
is far and away the most «Adjective» gift I will ever receive.
```

Are you getting the hang of this? At each place where you want ClarisWorks to substitute a piece of information from your Gift List database, you insert a little <<placeholder>>.

To see the last field name, *Part of House,* you have to use the Mail Merge window's scroll bar. Then finish the letter as follows:

12. Type *It will look sensational in the* (double-click *Part of House* in the Mail Merge window) *of our new home.*

13. Press the Return key twice and finish up like this: *I had to write this personal note to you and you alone, so you'd know how much I treasure your gift above all the others. Love, Marge.*

```
«First Name» «Last Name»
«Address»


Dear «First Name»,

I nearly cried when I unwrapped the incredible «Gift» you gave me for my wedding. It
is far and away the most «Adjective» gift I will ever receive.

It will look sensational in the «Part of House» of our new home.

I had to write this personal note to you and you alone, so you'd know how much I
treasure your gift above all the others.

Love, Marge.
```

Naturally, Emily Post would go instantly bald in horror if she thought you were about to send out a letter that says *Dear First Name.* But through the miracle of computers, when these letters are printed, it'll be impossible to tell that each one wasn't typed separately.

Save from the File menu. Type *Thank-you letter,* and click Save.

The graphics zone: Designing a letterhead

You'll read a lot more about graphics programs in the next couple of sections. But just to show you how you can tie everything together, let's whip up a quick letterhead in the Graphics module.

Choose New from the File menu. Our friend, the New Document dialog box, appears. This time you should double-click the Drawing button.

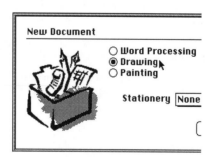

ClarisWorks shows you its drawing window. The grid of dotted lines is there to give things a nice architectural look; it won't appear in the finished printout.

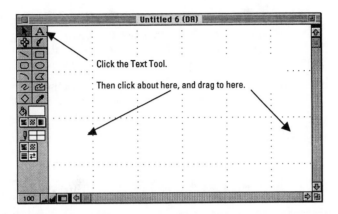

See the tool icons on the left side of your screen? They're pretty much covered in the section on MacDraw, later in this chapter. Now then:

1. Click the text tool — it looks like a letter A — and release the mouse button. Move your cursor onto the drawing area, and drag across the screen, as shown in the figure above.

2. Use the Font menu; choose Times. Use the Size menu; choose 24 Point.

3. Type three spaces and then a long dash. (To make a long dash, hold down the Shift and Option keys, and type a hyphen.) Type *A Very Personal Note*. Type another long dash and then three more spaces.

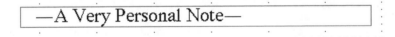

4. Press the Enter key so that handles appear around your text. Using the Alignment submenu of the Format menu, choose Center.

5. Finally, you'll add that elegant white-lettering-against-black look that shows up on so many corporate annual reports. At the left side of your screen, there's a set of odd-looking icons. Find the one immediately below the tiny pouring paint can icon, as shown by the arrow in this illustration:

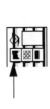
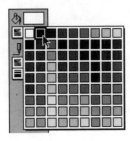

This icon is actually a pop-out palette. Click the icon, but keep the mouse button pressed so that the palette appears. Drag carefully to the right until the pointer is on the solid black square, as shown at right (above). (If you have a black-and-white Mac, choose the *word* "Black.") Release the mouse.

You've just used the Fill palette to color in the entire text block with black. Which is just great, except that now the text is a solid black rectangle! To fix the problem, you need to make the *text white*.

6. From the Text Color submenu of the Format menu, choose White. Ta-da!

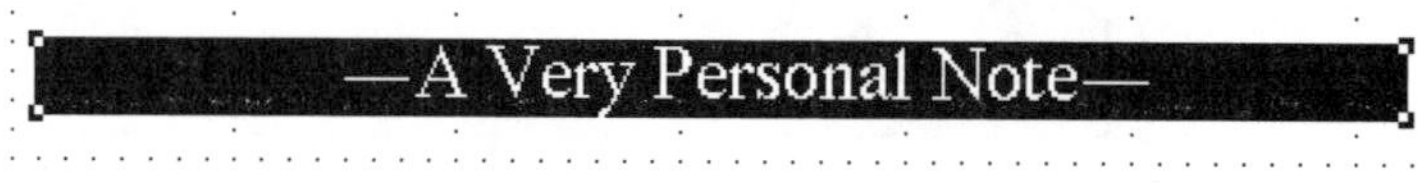

—A Very Personal Note—

You used a ClarisWorks Graphics window to make it easier to manipulate your text. Of course, while you're in the graphics mode, you could actually do some *graphics* . . . you could use any of the other drawing tools to dress up your logo. You could draw a box around this letterhead. You could rotate the whole thing 90 degrees. You could make all kinds of insane diagonal stripes across it.

Keep those creative possibilities in mind when it comes time to design your *real* letterhead.

For control freaks only: The View buttons

Before you leave the drawing window, cast your eyes upon the lower-left corner of the screen. There you'll find this odd-looking array of controls:

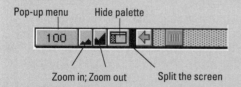

Pop-up menu   Hide palette

Zoom in; Zoom out   Split the screen

As you can tell, ClarisWorks makes it extremely easy to blow up your work. (Obviously I mean *magnify* it; *destroying* it is up to you.) A quick click on either of those little mountain buttons makes the artwork smaller or larger. Or jump directly to

a more convenient degree of magnification by using the percentage pop-up menu (where it says 100 in the figure to the left). You're not changing the actual printed size — only how it's displayed on the screen.

If you're on a small-screen Mac, you can hide that inch-wide strip of tools at the left side of the window by clicking the palette-hiding button, as shown in the figure. Finally, you can see two widely separated parts of the drawing simultaneously by dragging the fat, little black strip, indicated by the words "Split the screen" in the figure, to the right. Now you've got two distinct panes of your masterpiece, which you can scroll independently.

The return of Copy and Paste

All that remains is for you to slap this letterhead into your mail-merge letter.

1. From the Edit menu, choose Copy.

2. Now you have to return to your word processing document. Here's a quick way to pull it to the front: From the Window menu, choose Thank-You Letter (WP).

   (WP stands for Word Processing document, DB stands for Database, DR stands for Drawing, and PT stands for Painting. GR, if you have ClarisWorks 1.0, stands for graphics, which is the same as Drawing.)

   Your letter springs to the fore.

3. From the Format menu, choose Insert Header. (A *header* is an area at the top of every page, above whatever text you've typed. In this case, it looks like an empty text area.)

4. From the Edit menu, choose Paste.

   Et voilà . . . your graphic pops neatly into the header.

You've actually done it: combined a database, a word processor, and a drawing program in a single project! For a real kick, click the Print Merge button. It's on the little floating mail merge window-ette that should still be on the screen. Watch how the program automatically replaces actual names for the <<placeholders>> on the screen.

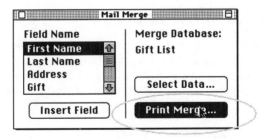

A little paint

There are two excellent features of ClarisWorks I feel it's my duty to mention.

Meet the Painting window (which isn't in ClarisWorks version 1.0). By this time, I trust you know how to get there: choose New from the File menu and then double-click the Painting button.

For pixel-painting landscapes

Don't know about you, but when I first installed ClarisWorks and then tried to paint, it opened up a little-bitty square of white (for me to paint on). And it gave me an error message that said:

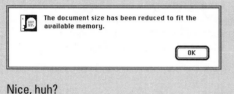

The document size has been reduced to fit the available memory.

OK

Nice, huh?

Anyway, the solution to this problem — and many other Disrespectful-Software Behaviors — is to give the program more memory. This process is explained in excruciating detail in Chapter 12. In the meantime, here's the scoop:

Quit ClarisWorks. Highlight its icon. Choose Get Info from the File menu. In the Size box at the bottom of the Get Info window, you'll see a number (probably something like 900 or 950). Change this number to, say, 1400, and you'll finally be able to paint more than miniatures.

Suddenly, you're in a pixel-blitzing wonderland, where you can create all kinds of "painted" artwork. As you'll discover when you read ahead to the MacPaint section, this kind of artwork has pros and cons. The pro is that you can change the color of *every single dot* on the screen (instead of just drawing circles, lines, and rectangles, which is all you can do in the Drawing window). The con is that you can't move or resize something in a painting after you've laid down the "paint" (which you *can* do in the Drawing window).

A little slide show

One of the strangest and most delicious things people do with a Macintosh is make *slide shows.* These can be self-running (a new "slide" every four seconds, say). They can be controlled by you (a new slide every time you click the mouse button). Most of all, they can be really impressive-looking to your friends.

You're in for another *Macs For Dummies* Bargain-Hunter's Paradise, by the way. Plenty of businesspeople spring $300 to buy a program that does *nothing* but slide shows. (They have a $300 word for it, too: "presentation software.") You, of course, get one in ClarisWorks at no extra charge.

OK, here's how it goes.

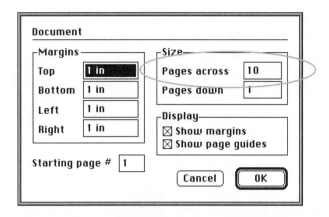

1. Choose Document from the Format menu. In the dialog box that appears, find the Pages Across blank. Type in the number of "slides" you'll want in your show.

2. From the View menu, choose Page View. Now use the scroll bar at the bottom of the screen to shift your view horizontally. You'll see that you've just created a number of side-by-side pages.

Click the "zoom out" button a few times...

...to see miniatures of your pages side by side.

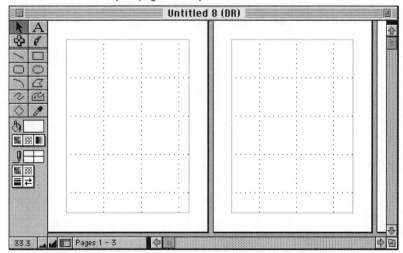

To make your show easier to visualize, click the little "zoom out" button a few times, as shown here.

3. Now (after zooming out, if you wish), fill up each page with artwork or writing. Remember that only the top two-thirds of each letter-sized page will fit on a standard-sized monitor, so don't waste your artistry on the lower part of each page.

(Alternatively, use the Page Setup command to specify a landscape — in other words, sideways — orientation of your "pages.")

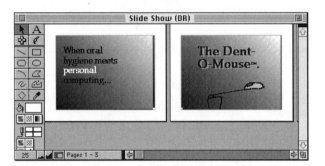

Move from page to page using the horizontal scroll bar. Make sure everything's looking good.

Reduces each slide to fit entirely on your screen.

Click here to make your slide show self-running. (Otherwise, you have to click the mouse to advance the slides.)

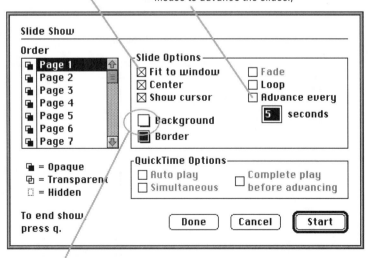

Hold down your pointer on this square to select a background color (to fill in the page margins).

4. Choose Slide Show from the View menu. Set your options up, as shown here:

5. Payoff time. Click the Start button!

   If you set up your slides to advance automatically, just sit back and watch. Otherwise, click the mouse button each time you get sick of the current slide. When you've had enough of the whole affair, press the Q key.

Just think of all you can do with Mac-based slide shows! Tell stories to your kids. Tell stories to your parents. Convince the committee that fourth-quarter earnings are up. Convince the spouse that you need to spend more money on your computer habit … so you can make more slide shows!

That's not all there is

The only parts of ClarisWorks we've left unexplored are the spreadsheet (which I couldn't figure out how to tie in to a thank-you letter) and the Communications module. Spreadsheets are covered under Excel later in this chapter. And if you have a modem and want to learn about the Communications program, then the little extra ClarisWorks manual does a nice job of explaining how to make your phone line a highway to the world of information. Or, if it's worth spending some bucks on, buy *MORE Macs For Dummies*, where the whole world of modem-dialing is covered with astonishing clarity, brilliance, and modesty.

MacDraw, Canvas, ClarisWorks again

MacDraw (now called ClarisDraw), Canvas, SuperPaint, all drafting programs, and the Drawing window in ClarisWorks all work essentially alike. They're called *drawing programs.* As much as that sounds like they'd be the same things as *painting programs,* they're not.

Paint vs. draw

Painting programs create art called *bitmapped* graphics. When you lay down some "paint," it's stored as a bunch of dots. You can erase them, but you can't change the original shape you painted — a circle, say, or a letter of the alphabet — because the Mac no longer thinks of them as a circle or a letter. It just thinks of them as a bunch of painted little dots. The advantage: You have control over each individual dot, and you have dot-manipulation tools like the Spray Can. In the figure below, note (1) the speckled effect, and (2) the fact that you can drag a chunk of circle out of the original collection of dots:

A high-end sidebar barely worth a glance

There's yet a *third* type of graphics program. Ever read *USA Today?* How about *Time* magazine? Well, then, surely you've seen Sunday newspaper Stop-N-Shop ad inserts showing little line drawings of Clorox and Fig Newtons?

The drawings and diagrams in all of these fine publications are typically produced with either FreeHand or Illustrator, called *PostScript* graphics programs. Printouts from these programs are incredibly smooth and high quality. When used with a color printer, these illustration programs can be (and are) used for package designs, brochures, maps, you name it. These two professional programs may be in the top ten, but they sure ain't in the *beginner's* top ten, so I'm not even gonna touch them until this book's sequel — but their operation has much in common with the drawing-type programs described here.

Drawing programs, on the other hand, create *object-oriented* graphics. When you draw a circle, the Mac doesn't store it as a map of black dots. It remembers that you drew a *circle* of a fixed shading and size. That means that you could never speckle it, and you could certainly never erase (or remove) a chunk of it.

But the advantage of drawing programs is that, later, you can return to that circle and move it by dragging it. Or you can overlap another object on top of it — and later change your mind. Or you can change a circle's shading long after you drew it. Or, as shown in the next figure, you can tug a circle's handles to stretch it.

Drawing programs tend to print out with much sharper quality than painting programs.

Drawing concepts

The palette in all of these drawing programs contains the same basic tools. These tools are so common that they even crop up in non-art programs, like databases (FileMaker), word processors (Word), and spreadsheets (Excel). Here's the *Reader's Digest* condensed version:

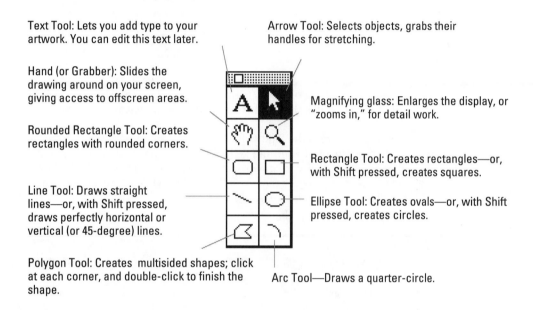

Text Tool: Lets you add type to your artwork. You can edit this text later.

Hand (or Grabber): Slides the drawing around on your screen, giving access to offscreen areas.

Rounded Rectangle Tool: Creates rectangles with rounded corners.

Line Tool: Draws straight lines—or, with Shift pressed, draws perfectly horizontal or vertical (or 45-degree) lines.

Polygon Tool: Creates multisided shapes; click at each corner, and double-click to finish the shape.

Arrow Tool: Selects objects, grabs their handles for stretching.

Magnifying glass: Enlarges the display, or "zooms in," for detail work.

Rectangle Tool: Creates rectangles—or, with Shift pressed, creates squares.

Ellipse Tool: Creates ovals—or, with Shift pressed, creates circles.

Arc Tool—Draws a quarter-circle.

Each program has a few goodies of its own, too, but these basics are always included.

To draw something, click the tool (and release the button), move to a blank part of the screen where you want to place the object, hold down the mouse button, and drag. When you let go, you'll see the new line or shape enclosed by small black *handles*. Using the Arrow Tool, you can drag these handles to stretch or resize the object you just drew. Or click in the middle of it to drag the object to a new location.

Or just click an object to make its handles show. After they appear — letting you know that the object is selected — you can use the menus to change the object's appearance. For example, suppose you draw a thin line (below, left). While it's selected, you can choose a new line thickness (below, middle) from the line thickness palette (every program has one). The result: The same line has a different thickness (below, right).

Using the palette of colors (or of patterns), you can change the color (or pattern) that fills the inside of a shape the same way: select and then apply.

When you press the Shift key while you draw something, the Mac constrains the movement of your mouse to flat or symmetrical movements. For instance, press Shift when you draw a line, and the line will be perfectly horizontal, vertical, or 45-degree diagonal. Press Shift while you draw a rectangle, and it will be a perfect square. And so on.

A mucho major secret for architect-types

The rule for modifying lines, squares, and circles you've made in a drawing program is simple: *select, then apply.* (You've read this before, I believe.) To make a rectangle black, you click it (select it) and then choose a color from a pop-up palette. Select, then apply.

Here's a powerful shortcut. If you use a menu or palette to make a setting *before* you draw something, while no object is selected, you specify the settings for the *next* objects you draw. This illustration should make all clear.

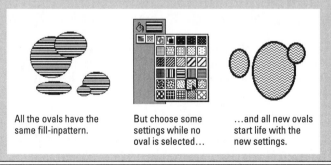

All the ovals have the same fill-inpattern.

But choose some settings while no oval is selected...

...and all new ovals start life with the new settings.

Selecting and grouping multiple objects

In the Finder, after you click one icon, you can select additional icons by Shift-clicking them (that is, clicking them while pressing the Shift key). In a word processor, if you have selected a word, you can extend the selection by Shift-clicking some place later in the paragraph.

Yes, indeed, Mr. Watson, there is a pattern here. This Shift-click-to-extend-a-selection deal is a common Mac technique. Same thing in drawing programs: click to select one object, Shift-click to select others.

After you've got a bunch of objects selected, you can *group* them — combine them into a single new object — using (what else?) the Group command. You can even group groups. You may want to group objects in this way just to make sure their alignment to each other doesn't get disturbed.

Handiest yet, you can *un*group a group, or even ungroup a grouped group of groups. (I'll give you a moment to work on that.) Drawing programs ungroup objects in the same order in which they were grouped. So imagine that you group objects A and B together, and then group object C to the first group. The first time you use the Ungroup command, you'll wind up with the A/B group and the C object loose; apply Ungroup a second time to split up A and B.

Text FX

One of the nicest things about drawing programs is that text is text, and text it remains. Text in a bitmapped program (like MacPaint), on the other hand, turns into a text-shaped collection of painted *dots* instantly. You can't edit the text or change the font or correct a typo, once you're done typing. And the printout looks exactly as jagged as it does on the screen:

A Green Onion

In a drawing program, though, each piece of text remains editable inside its little boundary rectangle. You can change the font or the size of the text or the dimensions of this rectangle at any time. And because the Mac still thinks of it as text (and not dots), it prints out at full text sharpness on a laser printer or StyleWriter:

A Green Onion

After you create a text block, you can paste it into a word processor and drag those little corner boxes. The word processor thinks it's just a plain old graphic and proceeds to squish it any way you like. The result is fantastic text effects you couldn't create in a word processor alone:

A Green Onion

A Green Onion

Beyond these concepts, a drawing program really doesn't require a degree in rocket science. I now release you to your creative juices.

MacPaint, ClarisWorks Yet Again

There are about a dozen of these programs, many of which end with the word *Paint.* Most of them work alike — only the frills differ from program to program. Some programs, such as Super-, Ultra-, and PixelPaint, plus pro-level programs like Photoshop, Painter, Color It, and Studio/32, work in color. They can even be used to retouch photos.

They're called *painting* programs because they produce *bitmapped* artwork. (For a discussion of what that means, see the introduction to the MacDraw section.) Printouts from bitmapped programs tend to be a little bit jagged since the Mac is reproducing the Mac screen when it prints out.

There's not much mystical hidden knowledge to be unearthed in paint programs. Once you've used a tool, you've pretty much mastered it for life. Here, then, is a typical Tool palette. You click a tool (and release), move the cursor to the page, and then drag across your white screen. With this guide — and the all-important Undo command in the Edit menu — you're well on your way to the world's toniest art galleries.

Marquee	[ ]	℘	Lasso
Pencil	✐	A	Text Tool
Spray can	🖌	🖌	Paint brush
Paint bucket	🪣	◭	Eraser
Line Tool	╲	☐	Rectangle
Rounded rectangle	⬭	◯	Ellipse
Polygon Tool	◁	⌐	Arc Tool
Hand grabber	🖐	🔍	Magnifying glass

Marquee and Lasso

These tools don't create any marks on the artwork. Instead, they're *selection* tools. They draw a dotted, shimmering line as you drag the mouse; you're creating an enclosure. Anything within the enclosure — the selected area — will be affected by your next move. For example, you can click within the selection to drag that chunk into a new position. Or press the Delete key to erase it. You can also apply special effects to the selected region, such as Invert (which swaps white areas for black, and vice versa) and Trace Edges (a bizarre one; try it).

There are two important differences between the Marquee and the Lasso. The Marquee always creates rectangular selected areas, *including whatever white space* is inside the rectangle. In the following illustration, you can see that when you drag a rectangular selection on top of a dark object (left), the white part of the selection remains opaque (right):

The Lasso, on the other hand, requires you to draw a circle all the way around the image you're trying to select. When you let go of the mouse, the dotted line snaps like a rubber band inward, enclosing only black regions of your artwork (below left). Therefore, when the selected part is dragged on top of a dark object, the latter shows through the former (below, right):

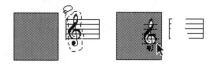

Pencil

The Pencil is pretty tame. Drag across the white area to draw a one-dot-thick line.

There's only one trick to it. If you begin your line by clicking in a *dark* spot, the line you draw will be white, even if you cross over into a white area.

Text Tool

Not much to this one: click in a blank area and start typing. While you're typing, you can press Delete (or Backspace) to fix a typo; in some programs you can even use the mouse to drag through stretches of text for editing. But beware! The instant you click the mouse outside of the text box, your text freezes into a noneditable clump of dots (yes, a *bitmap*).

In most programs, you can double-click the Text Tool icon to set the font and size for your type (before you do the typing). Obviously, after you click the mouse outside the text box (and freeze the text into a bitmap), it's too late to change type characteristics. You have to delete the whole thing if you want to change it.

Of course, bitmaps have some advantages; after selecting one with the Lasso or Marquee, you can apply any *transformation* commands to it (found in a menu): Stretch, Distort, Slant, whatever. See here:

Spray can

Painting at its finest. Drag it across the painting area to create a fine mist of dots, just like an airbrush or spray paint can. Dawdle over an area to make it darker; hurry across the screen for a lighter mist. The color (or pattern) of the spray is whatever color (or pattern) you've selected from the color (or pattern) pop-up menu. In some programs, you can double-click the Spray can icon to produce a dialog box, where you can adjust the rate and size of the spray. For post-pubescent thrills, try drawing a subway car and then spraypaint your name across it.

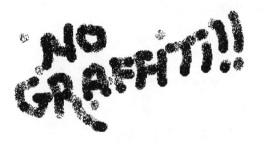

Eraser

Pretty basic. Drag across dark areas to erase them. Don't forget to zoom in (enlarge the screen image, using the Magnifying Glass) for detail work. For more mature thrills, draw your ex-spouse on the screen and then erase his/her head.

Line Tool

Choose a line thickness (there's usually a pop-up menu for this purpose) before you draw. Then drag to create a straight line. If you want a perfectly horizontal, vertical, or 45-degree line, press Shift while you drag. Some programs also let you specify the line's color or pattern.

Rectangle, Ellipse, Polygon, Arc

These shape tools pretty much work alike: drag diagonally to produce the shape. (The Polygon Tool works differently — click once for each corner point of your multisided shape; then double-click to finish the shape.)

In any case, you can usually control both the color (or pattern) of the *interior* of the shape as well as that of the *outline* of the shape by using pop-up color (or pattern) menus. The Line Thickness pop-up menu governs the thickness of the outline. As before, the Shift key is the great constrainer: press it to create a perfect square (with the Rectangle Tool), circle (with the Ellipse Tool), and so on.

Hand grabber

Unless you have a large monitor, you usually can't see a full page of art at once. You can always use the scroll bars to slide your image up or down on your screen. But the Hand grabber is much more direct — just drag in the direction you want to shift the painting.

Each program has its own keyboard shortcut for this handy tool; usually it's the spacebar or the Option key. When this special key is pressed, your cursor turns into the Hand grabber; when you release the key, you return to whatever tool you had previously selected.

Magnifying glass

Click this tool; then click the painting to zoom in and/or enlarge the display for detail work. Of course, you're not actually making anything bigger (in terms of its printout); you're really just magnifying the *screen* image to get more control over those pesky dots. Keep zooming in until you get an idea of how those little dots make up your painting. You can use the Pencil to click the dots either black or white.

To zoom out again or return to normal size, you usually press Option while clicking the painting.

Microsoft Word

Q: Where does an 800-pound gorilla sit?

A: Anywhere it wants.

A Microsoft joke that says a lot

How many Microsoft software programmers does it take to change a lightbulb?

None. They just declare darkness to be the standard.

Refer to this age-old discourse the next time somebody asks you why Microsoft Word, a program with numerous flaws and irritations, is the best-selling Macintosh program of all time. Microsoft is a gargantuan software company in Washington state. They sell so much software that the founder/owner (Bill Gates) is the youngest multibillionaire in history. Probably because of Microsoft's huge presence in the IBM-PC world, it's the 800-pound gorilla in the Mac world, too.

Of course, Microsoft Word isn't *bad.* In fact, it's got some truly wonderful features, one of which is that *everybody* uses Word. (Well, the vast majority does.) That means that when you hand your letter (on a disk) to a friend, you usually don't have to worry whether or not she's got the software needed to read it.

Anyway, you've already absorbed most of the basics of word processing (in Chapter 3). Word has a few fancy features worth learning, though (and does some basic features in interesting ways).

Views

To start a new document, double-click the Word icon. You arrive at a blank screen. Go ahead and start typing your Oscar-winning screenplay. Use the usual word processing techniques (Delete to backspace, drag through text to select it, use the Edit menu to copy and paste, and so on) to whip it into shape.

You'll discover, though, that your piece of paper appears to be endless, as though it's delivered on a never-ending roll of Bounty. That's because you're in Normal view, where you never see a page end. (The end of a page is symbolized by a thin dotted line, but you sort of have to watch for it.) In Normal view, you don't get to see page-related elements like page numbers, either. They're hidden until you go to another view.

If you want to see a more accurate display of what you'll get when you print, choose Page Layout from the View menu. Things start to bog down in Page Layout view — that is, it takes longer to scroll around and visit different corners of your document. But you clearly see where each page ends, and you get to see things like page numbers and multiple columns.

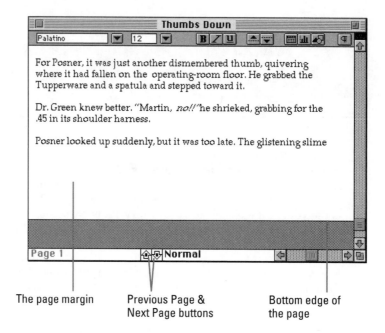

The page margin   Previous Page &   Bottom edge of
                Next Page buttons   the page

There's also an Outline view, which is pretty bizarre. I'll let you cuddle up to the manual for that one.

Finally, there's Print Preview, an absolutely vital and useful view. (Just to make sure the program isn't too easy to use, they've put the Print Preview command in the *File* menu, not the View menu with the others.) In Print Preview you get to see the entire page — in fact, two side-by-side pages — no matter what size monitor you have.

To change the margins

Print Preview also provides the easiest way to adjust the margins. Just drag the small black handles; remember that you're adjusting the margins for *all* the pages when you do this.

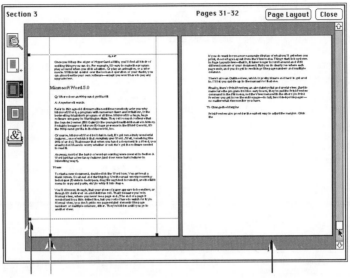

Drag these black handles (and the others like them) to adjust the margins…

…and then click the gray background to see the changes.

Why Word 6 is so awful

I've made an effort to accommodate version 6 of Microsoft Word in this section. However, most of the discussion applies mainly to versions 5.0 and 5.1. If you're wondering why, then you probably haven't tried Word 6.

Word 6 takes half an hour to install onto your Mac. This single program takes up *24 megabytes* of your hard drive ... for those of you scoring at home, that's about 25 percent of the typical hard drive for this one program.

On a Mac of typical speed, Word 6 takes almost *two minutes* just to start up when you double-click it. It takes nearly 10 seconds to bring up the box where you change the typeface. (On a Power Macintosh, Word 6 isn't quite as much of a dead dog, but it's still extremely overblown.) The screen is so filled with toolbars and buttons that your typing area is only about three inches tall.

Most people I know took one look at Word 6 and beat a hasty retreat to the prior version.

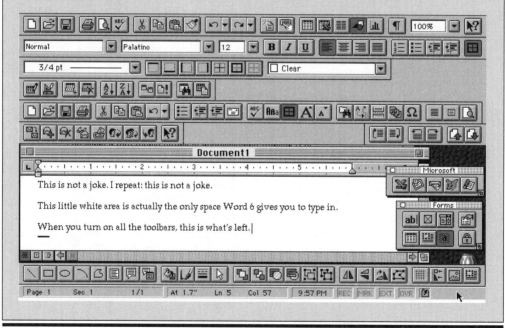

To return to Normal view from Print Preview, click Close.

(Word 6 sufferers: your Print Preview doesn't work like this. To change your margins, use the Document Layout command in the File menu.)

The unbearable lightness of interface

In their efforts to make Word 6 user-friendlier, Word's designers went, methinks, a tad overboard in the visual-interface department. When you launch Word for the first time, you get not one, not two, but *ten* different strips of icons and buttons! I mean, come on.

You could spot this cancer growing even in the earlier versions 5.0 and 5.1. Look at this picture and tell me that you'd know how to work this program on your first time at bat:

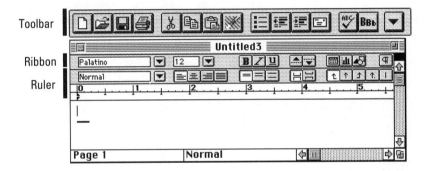

I'll do what I can to clear this up. I'll take each strip of cryptic controls and decipher them for you.

But let me make this clear: here I am, a Board-Certified Power User, and I have most of these things *hidden*. Oh, yes, it's true: you don't have to have these things cluttering up your screen. As we go, I'll mention how you can nuke each of these examples of graphic-interface-run-amok. Thousands of people have *all* of these icon strips turned off. Without these strips, using Word is almost exactly like using a typewriter, and that's 100 percent OK.

The Toolbar

What's the difference between Word 5.1 and previous versions? The primary addition is the Toolbar: a bunch of icon buttons, each of which does exactly the same thing as one of the menu commands. For example, if you click the very first button on the Toolbar, you get a new, blank, empty document. It's exactly the same as choosing New from the File menu.

Here's what the buttons do. (If you have a big screen, you'll see a few additional buttons.)

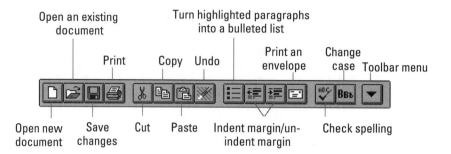

If you're the kind of person who enjoys dismantling the car and then reassembling it from memory, you can, if you wish, rearrange the buttons, or create a different set, using the Customize command on the Toolbar menu (the Toolbar menu is shown in the figure above).

If, however, your main objective is to have as long and happy a life as possible, you may wish to do away with the Toolbar entirely. There are three degrees of non-Toolbar presence. First, you can rotate it 90 degrees, so that instead of taking up a valuable half-inch across the *top* of your screen, it's running down the *side*. To do this, pull down the Toolbar button/menu (as pictured above), and choose Left.

Second, you can get rid of the Toolbar just for today. To do this, choose Toolbar from the View menu.

Finally, you can request that you never again be tormented with the existence of these enigmatic icons. From the Tools menu, choose Preferences. Scroll down until you see Toolbar. Click the icon. At long last, deselect the View Toolbar checkbox. You shan't see the Toolbar again.

(In Word 6, you get rid of those silly toolbars by choosing Toolbars from the View menu. Click the little checkboxes to get rid of the X's.)

The Ribbon: Quick word formatting

When you're in Normal or Page Layout view editing text, there are two information strips across the top of the window. The Ribbon is the top one; the Ruler is below it. (If you don't see these strips, somebody must have hidden them. Choose their names from the View menu.)

For the most part, the Ribbon controls *character formatting*: the size of type, the style (bold or italic), and the font. To make it work, you *first* have to select some text you've already typed — by dragging through it. Of course, you can also make some of these settings just *before* you begin to type.

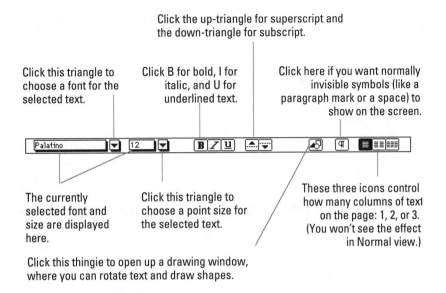

Click the up-triangle for superscript and
the down-triangle for subscript.

Click this triangle to
choose a font for the
selected text.

Click B for bold, I for
italic, and U for
underlined text.

Click here if you want normally
invisible symbols (like a
paragraph mark or a space) to
show on the screen.

The currently
selected font and
size are displayed
here.

Click this triangle to
choose a point size for
the selected text.

These three icons control
how many columns of text
on the page: 1, 2, or 3.
(You won't see the effect
in Normal view.)

Click this thingie to open up a drawing window,
where you can rotate text and draw shapes.

If you ask me, the most useful are the B, I, and U buttons in the middle (for Bold, Italic, and Underline). You can glance at them and know immediately what formatting your next typing will have.

The font and size controls (at the left side) are useful, too, once you figure out that you have to click on the *downward-pointing triangle* to change the setting.

The Ruler: Quick paragraph formatting

Below the Ribbon is the Ruler. These icons make changes to an entire *paragraph* at a time — and remember, a "paragraph" is anything you've typed that ends with a Return. Before you can use the ruler, you must first *select the paragraphs you want to change!*

Nine out of ten novices surveyed find this concept hard to get used to. If you want to indent *one* paragraph, just click anywhere in it so that the insertion point is blinking within it, and then use the Ruler's margin control. If you want to change your *entire document,* like making it double-spaced, start by selecting *everything* (the Select All command in the Edit menu is a quick way to do so), and then use the Ruler.

If you want to affect several paragraphs but not the whole memo, drag through them and then use the Ruler.

The point is to remember the Macintosh mantra: Select, then apply. Select, then apply. . ..

Click one of these 3 icons to make the selected paragraphs single-spaced, one-and-a-half, or double-spaced, respectively.

These are 5 "tab wells." Click for a left, centered, right, decimal, or vertical-rule tab; then click it into place on the ruler to make a tab stop.

Click this triangle to choose a Style for the selected paragraphs.

These 3 icons help you format table margins, if you use Word's Table feature.

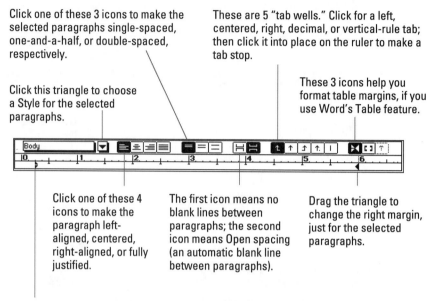

Click one of these 4 icons to make the paragraph left-aligned, centered, right-aligned, or fully justified.

The first icon means no blank lines between paragraphs; the second icon means Open spacing (an automatic blank line between paragraphs).

Drag the triangle to change the right margin, just for the selected paragraphs.

Drag the top *half* of this marker to set the first-line indent for the paragraph; drag the lower half to set the overall left margin.

Be careful on the strip

And here you thought we'd finished talking about all Word's strips. No such luck.

Word's most hazardous feature, as far as you, Most Honorable Newcomer, are concerned, is its *selection bar.* This is a very, very skinny invisible stripe up the left side of the window. You'll know when your cursor has inadvertently wandered in there because your arrow pointer will suddenly start pointing to the *right* instead of left. (This narrow vertical slice is there in *every* version of Word.)

You may find this impossible to believe, but Word's left-margin strip was not, in fact, designed out of pure foaming malice toward new Mac users. It's actually supposed to make editing your work easier by providing some text-selecting shortcuts. Here are a few favorites.

Shortcut 1: Select one line of text by clicking in the selection strip.

Linda choked back the sobs as the explosions shook the scarred earth around her. She fingered the ashy remnants of the glider.
"Happy...happy Groundhog Day, Harry," she murmured noiselessly.

Shortcut 2: To select a paragraph instantly, double-click in the selection strip. (Or triple-click anywhere inside a paragraph.)

Linda choked back the sobs as the explosions shook the scarred earth around her. She fingered the ashy remnants of the glider.
"Happy...happy Groundhog Day, Harry," she murmured noiselessly.

Shortcut 3: To select the entire document, triple-click in the selection strip. (Do this when you want to change the font for the entire memo, for example.)

Linda choked back the sobs as the explosions shook the scarred earth around her. She fingered the ashy remnants of the glider.
"Happy...happy Groundhog Day, Harry," she murmured noiselessly.

As a matter of fact, as long as we're covering different ways to highlight text, here are a couple as free bonuses:

Shortcut 4: Select a certain stretch of text by clicking at the beginning of the part you want and then pressing *Shift* and clicking the end point, even if it is pages and pages away.

Linda choked back the sobs as the explosions shook the scarred earth around her. She fingered the ashy remnants of the glider.
"Happy...happy Groundhog Day, Harry," she murmured noiselessly.

Shortcut 5: Select one sentence by Command-clicking in it (in other words, click while pressing the ⌘ key).

Linda choked back the sobs as the explosions shook the scarred earth around her. She fingered the ashy remnants of the glider.
"Happy...happy Groundhog Day, Harry," she murmured noiselessly.

Moving text by dragging it

One of the coolest features in Word (version 5 and later) is "drag-and-drop" text manipulation. You can highlight some text and simply drag it into a new position without doing the tawdry cut-and-paste routine.

For example, in the sentence below, you select the word *miserable* by double-clicking it. Then point the cursor at the highlighted portion, and drag it carefully into a new position and let go. The result is shown in the lower example.

(If the drag-and-drop deal doesn't work, some vandal probably turned this feature off. Choose Preferences from the Tools menu and turn it back on.)

Page numbers, headers, date-stamping

Suppose there's something you want to appear at the top (or bottom) of every single page (like *TOP SECRET: Destroy this document after Xeroxing*). Go to Normal view. From the View menu, choose Header (or Footer for the bottom of the page). A new window opens. Anything you type in here will conveniently appear at the top of every page.

If you click the little page number icon, Word will put a page number (at the insertion point) on every page. Click the middle icon, which is supposed to look like a calendar, to pop the date into this header. And click the clock to insert the time. Go ahead and use all the normal formatting controls — fonts, sizes, styles — to touch up the header text. If you want to see how it looks, choose Page Layout from the View menu.

Raw power: Style sheets

In this book, you see the same kinds of styles used over and over again. For example, this paragraph has specific margins and type characteristics, but the subhead ("Raw power: Style sheets") looks different. Yet I didn't have to reset all those margins and type styles for every appearance of a subhead. I just used styles.

You can read the manual for the full spiel on styles. But here's the easy way to do it.

Type some text. Format the heck out of it. Fiddle with the indents (see the Ruler diagram a couple pages back). Change the type style. Make it double-spaced or whatever. Adjust the tab stops.

Finally, when it's good and ready, click the Style Name box (at the left side of the Ruler — known as the Formatting Toolbar in Word 6). Give this formatting a style name. Go ahead, just type it. Call it Subhead.

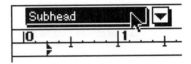

When you press Return, Word will ask you to confirm that you want to create a new Style called Subhead. Click OK.

Now the *next* time you need to format a paragraph this way, don't bother doing all that formatting. Just plop the insertion point anywhere in the paragraph; then, using the small black triangle to the right of the Style name box (on the Ruler), choose Subhead. You've just changed all the formatting characteristics at once. (To switch back to the normal, unformatted style, choose Normal from that same Style menu.)

Now here's the beauty part. Let's say you've got 12,029 subheads in your document. (No *wonder* your editors say you're long-winded.) And now you decide that you want to change the font. For all 12,029 of them.

Fortunately, it's incredibly easy since you assigned them all to one style. Just triple-click *one* subhead to select it. (Triple-clicking highlights the entire paragraph.) Change the font (or make any other changes you want to make).

Global Thermonuclear Politics for Dummies
Think the President makes it look easy? You can, too, once you know the way! The humor makes it all easy to take.

Genetic Engineering for Dummies
Amino acids are your ammo for this engaging, fun-to-read guidebook to the wonders of gene splicing and chromosomal tampering.

Magnetic-Resonance Imaging for Dummies
A lighthearted look at the fast-emerging world of MRI scans and postdigital arthroscopy.

Now, using the Style pop-up menu (that old black triangle again), choose the *same* Style name — Subhead.

Word will ask you what you're doing. Click "Redefine the style based on selection" and then click OK.

In the blink of an eye, all 12,029 occurrences of this style change!

Global Thermonuclear Politics for Dummies
Think the President makes it look easy? You can, too, once you know the way! The humor makes it all easy to take.

Genetic Engineering for Dummies
Amino acids are your ammo for this engaging, fun-to-read guidebook to the wonders of gene splicing and chromosomal tampering.

Magnetic-Resonance Imaging for Dummies
A lighthearted look at the fast-emerging world of MRI scans and postdigital arthroscopy.

Checking your spelling

Click at the beginning of the document. Choose Spelling from the Tools menu. A dialog box appears, in which Word will display each spelling error it finds; click Suggest to see some guesses as to what word you intended. Double-click one to replace the misspelled word in the document.

If none of this happens, and you get some kind of message telling you that the Spelling command isn't installed, then, by gum, the Spelling command isn't installed. (When you first install Word, you're given the choice of which features to include. Thesaurus, Grammar, Hyphenation, and the drawing module are some of the others available. You can install them later, as long as you have the original Word floppy disks.)

How to kill the summary box

One of the most irritating aspects of Word 5 and 5.1 is that stupid Summary Information box that comes up every darned time you save a document. (You don't mind if I vent a little, do you?)

Before you put your fist through the screen, try this. Choose Preferences from the Tools menu. Click the third icon, the one that says Open and Save.

In the main window, click Prompt for Summary Info to deselect it. That's it!

How to kill superfluous commands

While I'm going with my flow of hostility, may I point out how many menu commands Word has that nobody ever uses? *TOC Entry? Link Options? Revert to Style?* Let's be real here.

Fortunately, you don't have to live with them. Unless you're trying to crank out the next Sears catalog on your Mac Plus or something, chances are good you won't be needing indexing and auto-hyphenation features, for example.

Removing a command you never use is incredibly easy. While pressing ⌘ and Option together, press the minus (hyphen) key. Your cursor turns into a big fat minus sign! Handle your mouse with care, now — it's a loaded weapon. Any menu command you touch will *disappear from the menu!*

Before...	After

File		File	
New	⌘N	New	⌘N
Open...	⌘O	Open...	⌘O
Close	⌘W	Close	⌘W
Save	⌘S	Save	⌘S
Save As...		Save As...	
Find File...		Find File...	
Summary Info...			
		Print Preview...	⌘⌥I
Print Preview...	⌘⌥I		

Here's a partial listing of the commands I nuked from my Word 5.1 menus. Depending on how far you intend to let Word take you, you may want to augment this list (or leave some of these alone):

- **File menu:** Summary Info, Print Merge.
- **Edit menu:** Paste Special, Go To, Create Publisher, Subscribe To, Link Options, Edit Object.
- **View menu:** Print Merge Helper, Annotations, Voice Annotations, Play Movie.
- **Insert menu:** Section Break, Voice Annotation, Addresses, Index Entry, Index, TOC Entry, Table of Contents, Frame, Object, Movie.
- **Format menu:** Section, Frame, Revert to Style.

And, by the way, you're not removing these commands from the *program* — you're simply removing them from the *menu listings.* If you ever want to restore Word's menus to their original condition, choose Commands from the Tools menu. Click the Reset button in the lower-right corner of the window that appears.

(OK, OK: in Word 6, choose Customize from the Tools menu. Click Reset All.)

PageMaker

The idea of *page layout* software is amazingly simple. You see a blank page. You dump different kinds of page elements onto it: text, graphics, straight lines, photos, whatever. Then you drag them around like tiles on the page until they're in an attractive arrangement. This, kids, is page layout. Without a single union laborer being paid $180 per hour to paste waxed paper strips onto dummy pages (which is how they used to do page layout), you can publish and distribute your very own *Neighborhood Anarchist Weekly* — you can become a "desktop publisher." And since the Macintosh brought this fun new pastime into people's homes and offices, every magazine, brochure, newsletter, flyer, and newspaper from *USA Today* to *Time* is designed this way.

Starting a new document

Double-click the PageMaker icon. You get a dialog box that asks what size paper you want to use: Letter (8$\frac{1}{2}$-inch × 11-inch), Legal (8$\frac{1}{2}$-inch × 14-inch), or Tabloid (11-inch × 17-inch), which is what the *National Enquirer* uses.

The Master Pages

Some elements of your publication are probably going to appear on every page: the logo, the page number, the issue date. Instead of making you retype *Bathroom Fixture Journal* at the top of every page, you can just type it once, on the Master Pages. To get to the Master Pages, you click the little dog-eared page icons in the far lower left of the window:

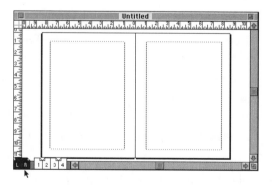

Now you see two blank pages — the Right and Left Master Pages (if your document has facing pages), whose image lurks behind every individual page of your publication. This is where the logo, the page number (which you create using the Text Tool by holding down ⌘-Option and typing a P), the chapter head, or whatever goes.

When you're done working with the Master Pages, click one of the individual page icons (each corresponds to a page of your document) to return to one-page-at-a-time editing.

Adding text

Ideally, you're supposed to write the articles for your newsletter (or whatever) in a word processor like Word. Then go to PageMaker and choose Place from the File menu. A list box appears; find your word-processed article, double-click it, and finally click the mouse (or drag to create a rectangle) on the appropriate starting page. The article spills onto the page, stretching from margin to margin (or filling the rectangle). Now, by grabbing the corner handles, you can resize or reshape the article's layout on the page:

You can also shorten the article's length by dragging the little window shade handle at the bottom, as in the following figure:

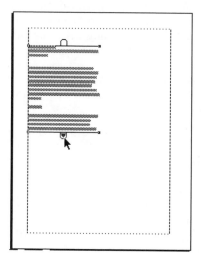

Of course, if you're thinking that an article needs shortening, window-shading it into a shorter *box* is only wishful thinking. All you've done is to place *less* of the article on the page — the rest of it is chopped off but needs to go someplace.

To specify where the rest of the article should go (as in, "continued on page C4"), ⌘-click the "windowshade handle" at the bottom of the text block. The cursor turns into a "loaded text" icon, telling you that the program is ready to pour the remainder of the article wherever your little heart desires. If you *click* someplace, PageMaker will dump the remainder of the article from margin to margin. If you *drag* to create a rectangle, the article will only fill that rectangle, as shown here.

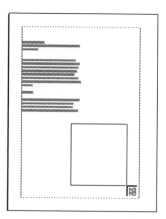

The neatest part of *flowing* text from box to box like this is that if you later have to cut some material from the beginning of the article, the text will flow, snake-like, through every text box it's been poured into. You'll never lose a single precious word.

If you could use some guidance in drawing text boxes, place your pointer in the ruler at the side (or top) of the screen and drag onto the page. A thin "guide" line comes with the pointer, which you can drag into position. (Hint: For consistent pages, place some guides on the *Master Pages,* so they'll be in the same place on every page.) These guides don't print; they're simply straight edges to help you align things, as you can see in the example below.

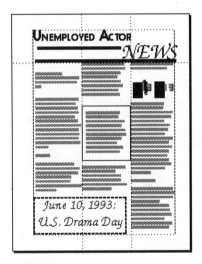

Tweaking to perfection

You can zoom in or out by using the Page menu commands and change the text style by selecting text (with the Text Tool, which looks like an A) and applying fonts, styles, and other attributes using the Type menu. For heavy-duty text editing, you'll want to use the built-in word processor, the Story Editor (choose Edit Story from the Edit menu).

Add straight lines, boxes, and other graphic accents using the appropriate tools on the PageMaker Tool palette; the Element menu controls line thickness and so on. You can either paste in graphics or import them using the Place command in the File menu.

Just remember that the Pointer Tool is what you need to draw, move, resize, delete, shorten, and lengthen text blocks. But you need the Text Tool to do everything that pertains to type, including changing fonts, sizes, styles, line spacing, and so on.

After you become a power-user publishing mogul (God forbid), you may appreciate the Styles palette, which gives you a list of predefined paragraph and text formatting attributes. (See the description of Word to get an idea of why these are useful and how to use them.)

And if you're using PageMaker 5.0 or later, you'll get a kick out of the Control Palette, a veritable carbon copy of the QuarkXPress Measurements Palette (read on!).

QuarkXPress

QuarkXPress is PageMaker's rival. Both have ardent supporters. (In fact, if you're ever on a blind date with a Mac person, it's a sure conversation starter: "So which do you like — Quark or PageMaker?") The differences are getting smaller and smaller, as each company comes out with an update that duplicates the features of the other.

Anyway, this is not the book to solve the great debate. This *is* the book to help you muddle through a few basic tasks when they're thrown at you.

The basics

Quark (for some reason, everybody refers to this program by the name of its company) does pretty much the same thing as PageMaker, but the methods are different. The Tool palette looks like this:

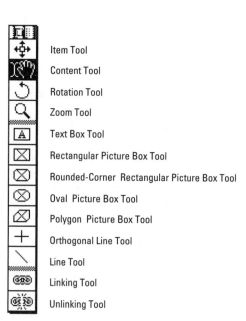

Item Tool

Content Tool

Rotation Tool

Zoom Tool

Text Box Tool

Rectangular Picture Box Tool

Rounded-Corner Rectangular Picture Box Tool

Oval Picture Box Tool

Polygon Picture Box Tool

Orthogonal Line Tool

Line Tool

Linking Tool

Unlinking Tool

The rules of thumb: Use the Item Tool to delete, move, and copy *boxes* (text and picture boxes), but use the Content Tool to resize or edit the *text and pictures themselves*. You can actually leave the Content Tool selected all the time since it's what you use for typing, editing, adjusting text box corner handles, cropping pictures, and so on — and whenever you need to move something, press the ⌘ key and drag. (The ⌘ key switches you temporarily to the Item Tool.)

To create a document, double-click the QuarkXPress icon and then choose New from the File menu. A dialog box appears, where you specify the page size and margins you want; then click OK.

To import some text, click the Text Box Tool and *draw a rectangle*. (You can't paste or import text or graphics in Quark without first drawing a box to contain it.) Quark switches back to the Content Tool automatically; from the File menu, choose Get Text and select the word processing document you want to import. It appears in the selected text box automatically. As in PageMaker, you can now edit the text, drag the text box's corners to adjust its dimensions, and so on.

Linking to page C4

Quark's method of breaking a story up into separate text boxes requires the use of its Linking Tool. First, make sure you've actually drawn both text boxes on the screen, using the Text Block Tool. Now click the Linking Tool. Click the *first* text box and then the *second* text box — that's all there is to it. The text now flows freely from one to the other, even if you edit the text in either box.

What's especially useful about this method of linking is that you can *pre*link text boxes that you've drawn on a Master Page. If you produce a newsletter, for example, that has roughly the same layout month after month, you could design an empty template containing ready-to-go, prelinked, empty text boxes. When those lazy-slob writers are finally ready to turn in their stories, one Get Text command suffices to pour an article into your waiting Quark layout, and all flowing happens instantly.

Master Pages: Rearranging pages

Quark's Document Layout palette shows a thumbnail view of all pages in your document, including any Master Pages. (You can have up to 127 *different* Master Pages, in case each section of your magazine has different common background elements.)

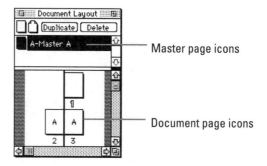

Master page icons

Document page icons

This Document Layout palette serves a number of useful functions:

✔ Double-click a page icon to make the document window jump to that page.

✔ Drag a page icon into a new position to rearrange your pages.

✔ Drag a Master page icon onto a Document page icon to change its background (master) elements.

✔ Double-click a Master page icon to edit that Master page.

✔ Drag a blank page (top left of the palette) or a Master page icon in between two existing Document page icons to insert a new page.

There's a bunch of other stuff the Document Layout window does, but this should get you started, and you can always use the QuarkXPress Help feature to read up on the other features.

Measurement Palette

Choose Measurement Palette from the View menu to see this useful little floating window full of precise numerical controls over the selected object. Click any of these numbers to change them. Try changing the angle for a text box — it's fun!

Excel

Excel is the best-selling Macintosh spreadsheet program. Well, "best-selling" is about the understatement of the decade. (A recent Excel ad headline said, "99 out of 100 spreadsheet users use Excel. What are we doing wrong?")

If you're not familiar with a *spreadsheet,* get psyched — even if you only use 1 percent of its features, Excel can really be a godsend. It's for math, finances, figuring out which of two mortgage plans is more favorable in the long run, charting the growth of your basement gambling operation, and other number-crunchy stuff.

Starting up

Double-click the Excel icon. A blank spreadsheet appears on your screen. It's a bunch of rows and columns, like a ledger book. The columns have letters and the rows are numbered. Each little rectangular cell is called, well, a *cell.* It's referred to by its letter and number: A1, for example.

To type a number into a cell, click the cell with the mouse and begin typing. Note that you don't do your typing (and editing) in the cell itself, unless you have version 5 or later. In all previous versions, all the action is in the editing strip at the top of the window. When you're done typing or editing, press Enter.

Formatting numbers and text

As you enter numbers, don't bother to format them with dollar signs, decimal points, and all that jazz. Formatting can be applied later. For instance, you could enter the following numbers, each of which has a different number of decimal places:

546
213.5
645.88
987.556

Now drag vertically through them with the pointer.

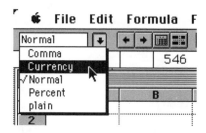

By now you can probably say it in your sleep: In the world of Mac, you select something first and then act on it . . . *Select, then apply.* . . . After the numbers are selected, you can format them all with dollar amounts in one fell swoop. See the little tiny pop-up menu at the upper-left corner of the screen? Choose Currency from this list.

Instantly, Excel formats all the selected numbers as dollar amounts. Note how it adds zeros (or rounds off excess decimal places) as necessary.

Spreading the sheet

Now it gets good. If you've been fooling around so far, erase everything you've done. Drag the cursor diagonally through it and then choose Clear from the Edit menu. We're gonna start you off fresh-like.

Click in cell B3 (that's column B, row 3; a spreadsheet is like a good game of Battleship). Type in *1963*.

To jump into the next cell to the right, press Tab. Or press the right-arrow key. (You move to the *left* by pressing Shift-Tab, or the left-arrow key.) In any case, enter *1973*. Repeat until you've filled in the years as shown below.

You move *down* a row by pressing Return or the down-arrow key. Shift-Return moves you up a row, and so does the up-arrow key. (There's a certain twisted logic to this, isn't there?)

You can also jump to any cell by clicking in it, of course. Now then: Go wild. With these navigational commands under your belt, type in the text and numbers as shown below. (Frankly, it doesn't make any difference *what* numbers you type. I made them all up anyway.)

	A	B	C	D	E	F
1						
2						
3		1963	1973	1983	1993	
4	Quarter 1	1234	2435	3466	8453	
5	Quarter 2	3123	2396	3536	3488	
6	Quarter 3	120	1589	6455	122	
7	Quarter 4	2000	3235	5353	8441	
8						
9	TOTALS:					
10						

Worksheet1

Want to make the top row boldface, as shown in the prceding figure? Drag the cursor through the years. Now click the B button in the ribbon at the top of the screen.

If you haven't guessed, **B** means **Bold**, and *I* means *italic*. (And I mean italic!)

Creating automatically calculating cells

Here comes the juicy part. Click in the Totals row, under the 1963 column of numbers. Click the funny Σ button on the ribbon. It's the Sum button, and it's some button.

In the formula bar at the top of the screen, you'll see that Excel has entered "=SUM(B3:B8)."

In English, the program is trying to say: "The number I'll enter into the cell you clicked (Total) is going to be the sum of . . . well, I suppose you mean the numbers directly *above* the cell you clicked — cells B3 down to B8." Isn't it smart to guess what you mean?

B3	X √	=SUM(B3:B8)

	Fina

	A	B	C
1			
2			
3		1963	1973
4	Quarter 1	$1,234.00	$2,435.00
5	Quarter 2	$3,123.00	$2,396.00
6	Quarter 3	$120.00	$1,589.00
7	Quarter 4	$2,000.00	$3,235.00
8			
9	TOTALS:	=SUM(B3:B8)	
10			

Well, smart, but not quite smart enough. Because you *don't* want the number 1963 included in the total! So you can override Excel's guess by showing it which numbers you *do* want totaled . . . by dragging through them. Try it. While the dotted-line rectangle is still twinkling, drag vertically through the four cells *below* 1963. Then press Enter.

B9		=SUM(B4:B7)

	A	B	C
1			
2			
3		1963	1'
4	Quarter 1	$1,234.00	$2,435
5	Quarter 2	$3,123.00	$2,396
6	Quarter 3	$120.00	$1,589
7	Quarter 4	$2,000.00	$3,235
8			
9	TOTALS:	6477	
10			

Neat, huh? Excel automatically totals the four numbers you selected. But that's only the half of it. Now click one of the cells below the 1963 heading — and *change the number.* That's right, type a totally different number. (And press Enter when you're done typing. You always have to press Enter to tell Excel you're done working in a cell.) Voilà — the total *changed* automatically!

This is the origin of the phrase "What-if scenario." You can sit here all day, fiddling with the numbers in the 1963 column. As soon as you change a number and press Enter, the total will update itself. That's why it's so easy to compute a mortgage at 10 percent for five years and see if it's better than one at 8 percent for seven years (or whatever).

Fill right, feel right

Now then. You have three other columns to contend with. Do you have to redo the Σ business each time? Nope. You've already explained to Excel how the Total row should work: it should add up the four numbers above it, *not* including the year at the top of the column.

So just take that magic total cell (B9 in the preceding picture) and *copy it* into the three cells to its right. Excel is smart enough to add up the right numbers in each column (no, it won't put the *1963* total into each cell).

Of course, you could use the regular Copy and Paste commands — but that's too tedious. Use the Fill Right command instead. Drag through the Totals row, starting with the 1963 total and extending through the three other years' total cells.

Then, from the Edit menu, choose Fill Right (or press ⌘-R). Bingo! Excel intelligently copies the *formula* from the first cell into the other cells, totaling each column automatically. You may as well know that there's also a Fill Down command, used when you want to copy a formula to a series of cells *below* the one that contains it.

From here to infinity

Using the standard math symbols (+, −, / for division, and * for multiplication), you can build much more complicated auto-calculating cells than the simple SUM function described above. For example, you can use nested parentheses and the whole works. To make a cell calculate how many hours there are in ten years, for example, you'd click on it. Then, in the formula bar at the top of the screen, you'd type *=(24*365)*10* and press Enter. The formula always has to begin with the equal sign, but otherwise your equations can be as complicated as you want.

You can have formula cells that work with numbers from *other* formula cells, too — in the example above, you could create a Grand Total cell that would sum up the 1963, 1973, 1983, and 1993 totals automatically. There are even a few dozen more complex formula elements — financial, statistical, math, and time functions — listed in the Paste Function command (Edit menu), if you're into that kinky stuff.

Making a chart

There are a zillion options for charting, too, but here's the quick-and-dirty approach.

Drag through the table you created earlier — just the data part, not the totals in the bottom row. After this section is highlighted, click the Chart Wizard button on the ribbon, as shown here:

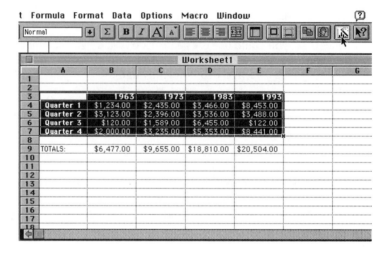

Now the cursor turns into a skinny little crosshair. Excel is waiting for you to show it where, and how big, to make the chart. Drag diagonally across the screen, either below the numbers (if your screen is big enough) or — what the heck — right on top of them. When you let go, a charming little chart pops up. (If a charming little *dialog box* appears instead, click the >> button.) Double-click the chart and then double-click an individual bar to adjust the colors and styles used in the chart.

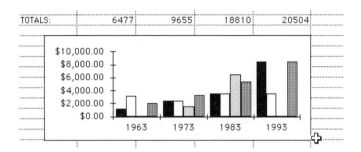

There are also outlining, drawing tools, macros, a database function, and probably a convenient toaster-oven . . . but this was supposed to be a crash course. If you want those frills, you'll have to actually put your nose in the manual.

FileMaker Pro

FileMaker is the king, queen, and princess of *database* programs. A database is just what it sounds like: a base of data — a pile of it, if you will — that you can view in a million different ways. Stop me if you've heard this one. Suppose that you have a mailing list, and you want to know how many people in ZIP code 44122 have last names beginning with M. Or you have a list of 2,000 books and want to sort them by author's name or print a list only showing hardcover volumes, or find out the publisher of a book of which you know only one word of the title. For all these tasks, a database is the way to go.

The really far-out feature of FileMaker is that you can set up several different *views* of the information. Suppose you have a mailing list for a party. You could set up your Data Entry view with great big 18-point bold type, which makes it easier for you to type in those names without your glasses. You'd also want a Mailing Label layout, though, which neatly arranges the addresses side-by-side across the page, in a much smaller type size, so that you can print and mail the invitations. Yet a third layout could be the Name-Tag view; it would place only the person's name (and not the address) in a cute font, preceded by the words "Hello! My name is." Using these different layouts — of the same information — really lets you put the data to work without having to do any retyping.

Step 1: Starting a file

Double-click the FileMaker icon. A dialog box appears, where you're either supposed to open an existing data file or create a new one; click New. In the next dialog box, type a name for your file and click New again.

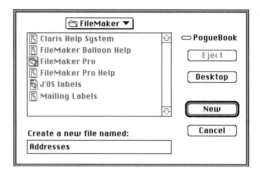

Before you know it, a *really* complex-looking dialog box appears. Brace yourself for a couple more terms. (If you read about ClarisWorks earlier in this chapter, then you'll be on familiar turf here.)

As you design your database, there are two units of information you'll be creating. First of all, there are the individual blanks: the name, the ZIP code, and the state. These are called *fields*. (The International Council of Nerds evidently felt that calling them *blanks* wouldn't have confused people enough.)

A set of fields constitutes one *record*. A record might be a complete name-street-city-state-ZIP set for a mailing list; if there are three people's addresses, there are three records in the database. Still with us?

OK then. In the dialog box now staring you in the face, you're being asked to create the *fields* (the blanks). First type the name of the field; it might be First Name or Last Name or Street or Account Number or Date or Eyebrow Thickness or whatever. Now tell FileMaker what *kind* of data is going to be in this blank, as shown in the following table.

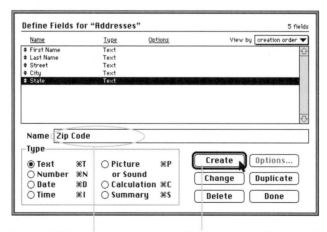

Type a field's name...   ...then click Create to add it to your list.

If you select this data type...	Then this happens...
Text	You can enter any kind of typed data
Number	FileMaker won't let you type letters of the alphabet — only digits.
Date, Time	FileMaker only accepts dates or times in any format.
Picture	You can't type anything into this field, but you can paste a picture.
Calculation	You can't paste or type anything. FileMaker fills in this field automatically by performing math on other fields, like adding the Amount and Tax fields.
Summary	You can't paste or type anything. FileMaker fills in this field automatically by performing math on other fields, like adding them, counting them, or giving you a running total.

For each field you'll want on the screen, then, type a name and select a data type, and click Create. Repeat for the other fields. (If you want FileMaker to auto-matically enter data, like today's date, then click Options just after creating a field.)

Anyway, after you're done defining every blank you'll want to use, click Done. You've just finished step 1.

No Save command!?

Why the heck do you have to name your file *before* you type any information into it? Isn't that exactly opposite from the way most programs work, where you type some stuff and *then* choose Save (and give the file a name)?

Yup.

In FileMaker, though, you'll actually come to like this feature — the program saves your data *automatically,* without your having to remember. The result: Your data is always up to date, even when something goes wrong.

A calculated maneuver

If you created a Calculation field, a dialog box will appear as soon as you click Create. In this box, you can build the equation you want FileMaker to use. It usually involves other fields — which are listed at the upper left — combined with the +, −, / (divided by), and * (times) symbols. For example, if you're crazy enough to live in New York City, you would define the Sales Tax field as *Purchase Amount * 1.0825* (8.25 percent is the sales tax rate).

Step 2: Data entry

At this point, you can start typing away to input data. The rules are simple: It's just like a word processor, so you use the Delete key to backspace over a typo, cut, copy, and paste selected text, and so on. To advance to the next field, press Tab. To jump back to the previous field, press Shift-Tab. To create a new, blank record (for a new person's address, say), choose New Record from the Edit menu. (Again, for a complete illustrated tour of this process, see the ClarisWorks section a few pages back.)

As you create more records, the little open book icon at the upper left will indicate that it has more and more "pages," each of which is a record. This little diagram shows the four ways you can navigate your pile of data.

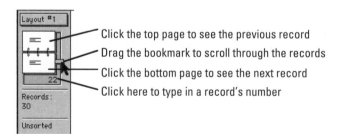

Click the top page to see the previous record
Drag the bookmark to scroll through the records
Click the bottom page to see the next record
Click here to type in a record's number

If your goal, in reading this section, is to perform the joyous task of entering data, this may be all the info you'll need. Put down this book and get busy. If, on the other hand, you want to create a database of your own, or if you're supposed to modify an existing database, you may want to learn step 3.

Step 3: Designing a layout

When you first create a new FileMaker file and define some fields, the program creates a simple default arrangement of the blanks so that you can type in some data. The default arrangement looks like this:

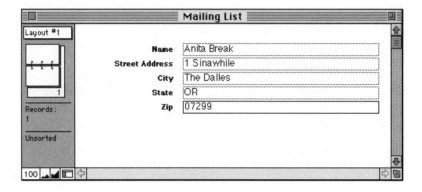

But suppose you want those same fields arranged in a more mailing-labelish layout, like this:

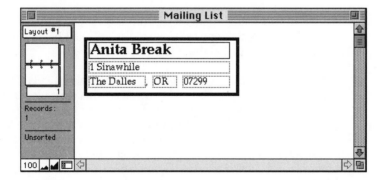

To accomplish this, you must enter the Layout Zone. Choose Layout from the Select menu. You enter a view that looks a lot like MacDraw (or any other drawing program). And, in fact, all the tools (line, rectangle, blah blah blah) work exactly as they do in a graphics program.

So: click the Arrow Tool. Drag the fields around (make sure you can tell the difference between a field and its *label,* which you may or may not want to appear on the screen). Or click a field and then change its type style from the Format menu.

Since you can have as many different arrangements of your information as you want, use this pop-up menu to select the Layout you want to edit.

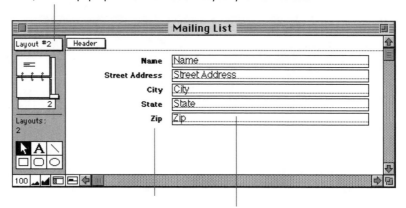

These are field labels. They don't have to appear in a layout if you don't want them to.

These boxes represent the fields themselves. To resize one, click and then drag a corner handle. To move one, drag it by its center.

If you want to see more than one record at a time (when you're in data entry mode), drag the little Body tag upward until it's just below your fields, and choose View as List from the Select menu.

Remember, too, that you can *delete* a field from a particular layout. For example, if you're creating "Hello! My name is" stickers, you certainly don't need each person's phone number to appear on his or her badge (unless it's *that* kind of party). So you can delete the phone number field from the layout; you do *not* lose any data you've typed in. The phone number field still *exists* — just not in this layout. Using the New Layout command in the Edit menu, you can create another layout . . . and another . . . and so on, until you've had your fill of data rearrangement.

When you're finished designing layouts, return to data entry mode by choosing Browse from the Select menu.

Finding

Once you've got some data typed in, you can manipulate it in all kinds of fun and exciting ways. Choose Find from the Select menu to get what appears to be a blank layout. Type what you're looking for into the appropriate blanks. For example, if you're trying to find everybody who lives in ZIP code 90210, you'd fill out the Find dialog box this way:

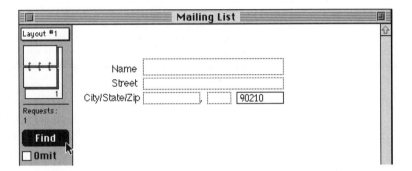

Then click the Find button. After about one second, you'll be returned to Browse (data entry) view, where you'll see the results of your search. This is important — FileMaker is *hiding* the records that *didn't* match your search requirements. You haven't lost them; they're just out of sight until you choose Find All from the Select menu. You can prove this to yourself by consulting the little book at the left side of the screen. It will say "Records: 194, Found: 22." That means FileMaker still knows there are 194 addresses in your mailing list, but only 22 have ZIP code 90210 (and they're all attractive teenage models on a major TV show).

Sorting

To sort your records, choose Sort from the Select menu. FileMaker needs to know how you want to sort your records: by first name, ZIP code, nose length, or what? On the left side, you see a list of all the fields in your database; just double-click the one by which you want to sort.

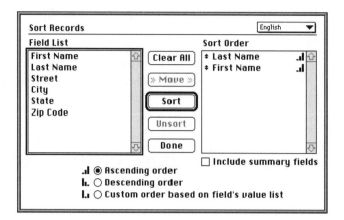

(If you want to sort by last name and then sort by first name *within* each common last name, double-click First Name.) Finally, click Sort.

Sorting is the one major drag with FileMaker, by the way. As you're about to discover, FileMaker doesn't *keep* your stuff in the sorted order! Every time you add a record or search for something, all your records jump back into the order in which you first entered them! You have to use the Sort command over again every time you want things sorted again.

Other steps

There's a million other cool things FileMaker can do. For example, it can look up a piece of info (like a phone number) from *another* FileMaker file and copy it into the appropriate place in *this* file. FileMaker also has a powerful Scripts command, which works a lot like a macro program (see "QuicKeys," following). In other words, you can make the program find all names added since last week, sort them by last name, switch to the Mailing Label layout, and print them — all with a single command from the Scripts menu. These rarefied pleasures are not, however, for the unenlightened. Grab whichever is closest — the manual or your resident computer guru person.

QuicKeys

QuicKeys is a *macro program.* (Bet you'd been hankering for some more lingo, hadn't you?)

A macro is an automated series of mouse or keyboard steps, which you'd otherwise have to perform manually. It's a shortcut, bub. Mouse and keyboard tasks aren't particularly strenuous, of course, except that sometimes you can get tired of performing them, especially if you have to repeat the same steps over and over again.

Typical examples: You have to type a password into some program every day. Or you're asked to open each of 1,000 documents, change the font to Times 96-point bold, print, and save. Or you always sign your letters "With fondest and most lingering feelings of warmth and mutual support, Ingrid." All of these tedious and repetitive tasks can be automated using a macro program like QuicKeys so that only a *single keystroke* (of your choosing) triggers the Mac to do the chore itself.

QuicKeys is the easiest System 7-compatible macro program, and it can perform some amazing stunts. For example, you can make it open up a certain program or document with the touch of a key. It can type out the time or the date when you press another key. And so on. Here be the basics.

Teaching by example

The easiest way to create a macro is the voyeur method: You do whatever-it-is *manually,* while QuicKeys watches.

For example, if you've just installed QuicKeys, you should see "QuicKeys" listed in your ⌘ menu. When your pointer reaches those words, a *submenu* pops out to the right; choose Record Sequence from that submenu.

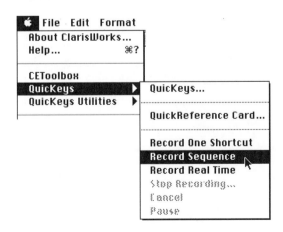

(These figures illustrate version 3.0 of QuicKeys. Other versions look similar enough for you to figure out what's happening, I'm guessing.)

Suddenly, a little blinking microphone appears where the normally is. This is QuicKeys's signal to you that it's paying attention. While you have such an attentive student, perform the task, or series of tasks, you'd like it to learn. Some examples:

  ✔ Type your return address.

  ✔ Empty the Trash can.

  ✔ Print, then Save, and then Quit.

  ✔ Choose Bold, then Italic, and then 12-point from the font menus.

  ✔ Open the Calculator desk accessory, choose a menu command, flap your arms, or whatever.

As you teach QuicKeys what you want it to do, there's just one caveat: If you want it to click something, make sure that whatever-it-is will always be in the *same place* on the screen. Suppose that you drag an icon to the Trash can. When QuicKeys later tries to repeat what you did, it will click futilely in empty space and drag *nothing* to the Trash can — because that icon is no longer there. Good bets for macros that involve clicking, therefore, are menus, desk accessories, and Tool palette icons — all of which are always in the same screen location.

Anyway, when you're done doing the task yourself, go back to the QuicKeys menu item in your menu and choose Stop Recording from the submenu. The following box (or something like it) appears:

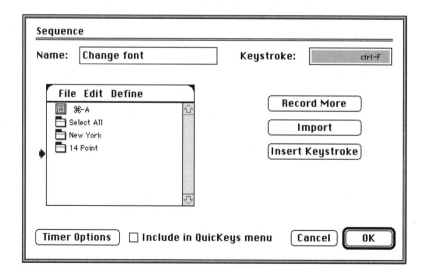

In the Name box, type a short description of what this macro is supposed to do. Press Tab to jump to the Keystroke box.

Then press the key (or keys) on your keyboard that you want to be the *trigger*. A great choice for a trigger key, by the way, is one of those otherwise useless function keys (F1, F2, and so on) that the IBM world is so bonkers about. If your keyboard has them, they're at the top of your keyboard. Another idea: Use the otherwise useless *Control* key (sometimes labeled *Ctrl*), which you've probably never even noticed. For example, you might make Control-Q save your document and then quit. Or Control-R could type your return address.

In the lower-left quadrant of the screen, you can see QuicKeys's list of the individual steps that constituted this macro. Each type of action — a mouse click, text typed on the keyboard, a menu item selected — is represented by a different icon. You can cut, copy, paste, or delete these, but that's really a topic for your pal, the manual, to cover.

When you're done setting up the name and trigger key for this macro, click OK twice, and you're in business. Whenever you press the trigger key you specified, QuicKeys will perform that series of tasks by itself in very frantic succession. It's really something to see, too — you'll think your Mac has been inhabited by a ghost who's had way too much coffee.

Opening QuicKeys

For more specific, or more complex tasks, you may want to program macros manually (and not by example). For this, you can create a macro in the QuicKeys control panel.

There are several ways to bring up this panel. First, choose QuicKeys from your menu and then choose QuicKeys from the submenu. Alternatively, you can choose Control Panels from the menu, double-click the QuicKeys icon, and then click Open. Either way, you wind up facing a screen like this:

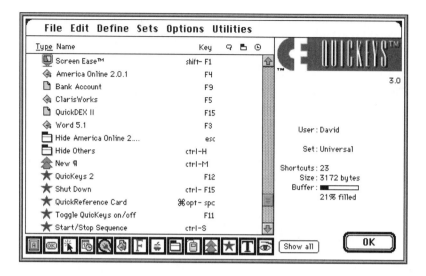

The key to creating a macro manually is the Define menu that appears within this panel. It lists 13 kinds of macros, as follows.

An *Alias Keystroke* is a letter substitution. You type a W, but a P appears on the screen. That's a dumb example, of course, but that's the idea. A more useful use: Get QuicKeys to type a *period* instead of a > symbol every time you press Shift-period so that you don't keep typing "Born in the U>S>A>" by accident. (Don't confuse this kind of alias with what's called an alias by Apple in System 7. You'll find out about *that* kind of alias in Chapter 8. Sorry to interrupt.)

A *Button* is an on-screen button, like OK or Cancel. QuicKeys can click such a button automatically. What's especially nifty is that QuicKeys even knows — in the case of a checkbox-type button — whether the button is on or off. You can tell it to click a checkbox *only* if it's not already selected, for example.

A *Click* is a mouse click or a mouse drag. When you choose this from the Define menu, you'll be asked to *do* the click or drag so that the program gets the idea.

Date/Time types out the current date or time, in your choice of several formats.

Extensions are pretty neat. They're plug-in special-feature macros. One extension flips your color monitor to black and white (or back again), saving you a tedious trip to the Monitors control panel. Another extension changes printers for you, in case you have more than one connected to your Mac. Once again, QuicKeys has chosen a particularly unfortunate term: an *extension* is actually a special self-loading program in System 7 that you'll read about in Chapter 6. If you last that long.

Anyway, look through the various Extensions submenus. You'll find several extremely useful ready-to-go QuicKeys. They include *ScreenEase* (which switches your monitor from black and white to color, or vice versa); *Folders* (which opens a specific folder on your hard drive); *SpeakerChanger* (which adjusts your speaker's volume at the touch of a key); *Message* (which produces a dialog box that says anything you want); and *Choosy* (which switches printers, saving you a trip to your Chooser desk accessory).

A *File Launch* macro automatically opens a file, or a program, of your choice. It's peachy because you don't even have to know where the thing's icon is buried on your hard disk. I use Control-W to launch Word. I used Control-D to open the *Macs For Dummies* manuscript while I was writing it.

Don't worry about *FKEYs*. Nobody uses them.

A *Menu Selection* macro pulls down a menu item for you or opens a desk accessory.

Mousies are various self-explanatory mouse actions, like scrolling down in a document, closing a window, or opening a window to full size.

A *Sequence* is several of the other types of macros, strung together. Using this kind of macro, you can construct long and complex macros.

Specials are miscellaneous handy macros. Shut Down, for example, safely turns off your Mac even if you're not in the Finder. And QuickQuotes automatically pops in a curly quote whenever you type in one of those boring straight ones (see "Top Ten Word Processing Tips" in Chapter 3).

Text is how you get QuicKeys to type out some text that's always the same: your end-of-a-letter closing; your return address; boilerplate text of any kind.

Finally, a *Real-Time* macro is one that doesn't zip maniacally through the steps of the macro as fast as its little brain can manage. A Real-Time macro performs the steps you teach it at exactly the same pace, with all the hesitations and mouse movements at which you recorded it. You'd use a Real-Time macro in a painting program to draw a cartoon smile, for example. If you used the Sequence kind of macro instead, QuicKeys would try to save time by drawing a line straight from the beginning point to the end point, which wouldn't look like a smile at all.

Any macro usually needs a little debugging. But once you've mastered the art of putting your Mac on autopilot, you'll save hours of cumulative time which you can use to leave work early and play outside.

Apple File Exchange (and Friends)

Most people will never use this program, so I guess it really doesn't qualify for the top ten. In fact, it's not even made anymore; it's been superseded by much more convenient programs like PC Exchange.

Yet for many years, Apple File Exchange came free with every Mac (it comes on those white System disks); *millions* of people have it. And the few people who need a program like this *really* need it.

What it does

Apple File Exchange converts IBM-compatible PC files to Mac and vice versa. You may have read in the brochures that your floppy-disk drive is a SuperDrive capable of reading both Mac and PC disks — a technical achievement comparable to making a CD player play tapes.

What the brochure *doesn't* say is that it's not quite that easy. You don't slip a PC disk into the drive and watch its icon pop up on your screen. (Especially not the old 5¼-inch *really* floppy disks, which you have to first get transferred to Mac-style 3½-inch hard-shell disks before you can even think about any of this.)

No, what you do is launch Apple File Exchange first. *Now* you can insert a PC disk, and its contents will show up on the right side of the screen:

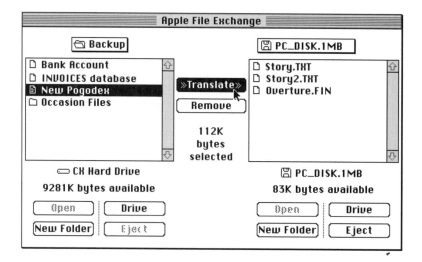

On the left, you see the contents of your hard drive. To convert a file, you just select it by clicking and then click the Translate button, as shown above.

You get exactly one converter included with Apple File Exchange — from MacWrite to DCA format, whatever that is. Actually, you really don't need to worry about converters if you're performing obvious translations: a Mac *text file* to an IBM *text file;* a Microsoft *Word document* to a *Word for Windows document;* a PC *FileMaker file* to a Mac *FileMaker file;* and so on.

Better alternatives

Of course, if you're serious about exchanging files with PCs and PC clones, you're much better off with programs like PC Exchange and MacLink. PC Exchange lets you shove any PC disk into your Mac's disk drive, and the disk's icon shows up on the desktop just as a Mac disk would.

Then, when you double-click a file, MacLink automatically converts it from the hideous, alien PC file format into something your Mac can open — a Word or ClarisWorks document, for example. If you have a *third* program, called Macintosh Easy Open, you're even offered a choice of *several* programs (among those you own) that can open the PC file.

Most of today's Macs, in fact, come with these three programs (PC Exchange, MacLink, Easy Open) included free. System 7.5 comes with them, too. If your Mac (or your System) came with them, then you, you lucky slob, are free from Apple File Exchange tyranny forever.

Too bad you still have to deal with PCs.

Top Ten Programs That Aren't in the Top Ten

For your shopping pleasure and entertainment: a double handful of neat programs that are often discussed at techno-savvy cocktail parties. ("Hi there, baby. Want to come up and see my FreeHand printouts?")

Plug alert: If these additional programs interest you, then so might *MORE Macs For Dummies;* its "Faking Your Way Through Eight More Programs" covers many of them.

1. *FreeHand* or *Illustrator.* Primo, powerful, professional, pricey PostScript graphics programs. Be prepared to read the manual.

2. *Photoshop.* MacPaint on steroids. A stunning, pro-level photo painting program, capable of fantastic transparency effects or undetectably painting your in-laws right out of the family portrait.

3. *Now Up-To-Date.* A sensational calendar program: type your appointments onto the appropriate squares. Up-To-Date can then remind you of them, show your To Do list, and print out gorgeous daily, weekly, or monthly agendas.

4. *Quicken.* The world's greatest and least expensive checkbook/financial program. Perfect for home and very-small-business use. Prints your checks; balances your budget. When stretched, can even do mortgage calculations, profit and loss, and that sort of thing.

5. *Persuasion.* It's called *presentation* software. Lets you quickly and easily assemble slide shows — graphs, bullet charts, colorful diagrams — with a choice of many rich, unified color schemes. Print the slides onto slides or transparencies, or use the Mac itself to give a slide show.

6. *Kid Pix.* Mind-blowing, colorful, audio-equipped version of MacPaint. Designed for kids but equally addictive for adults. The drippy paintbrush runs, the eraser makes scritch-scratch sounds, and when you want to start over, the Dynamite Tool blows up your artwork. About $30.

7. *Myst.* Reason enough to buy a CD-ROM player (which you need for this CD anyway). A spectacular visual treat, and a darned addictive wordless mystery.

8. *Microphone II.* You use this program if you have a modem (a phone hookup for your Mac). Lets you dial friends, bulletin boards, or online services like CompuServe. (More about these things in Chapter 7.)

9. *Super QuickDex.* A sizzlingly fast Rolodex program. Can pull up one person's card out of 2,000 in less than half a second. Can even dial the phone if you have a modem. Easier to use than a hairbrush. If you'll want to do much printing, you may prefer the more feature-laden (but much slower) *Now Contact* or *TouchBase.* They print out your address books in a billion different formats.

10. *Premiere.* For high-horsepower color Macs. This is the program for making your own digital QuickTime movies right on the screen. And what's QuickTime? Like the man said: digital movies right on the screen. See Chapter 7.

Chapter 6

System Folder:
Trash Barge of the Macintosh

- -

In This Chapter

▶ What the System Folder is for

▶ Why System 6 isn't System 7

▶ How to get System 7 if you really want it

▶ Just enough verbiage on System 7.5

▶ What junk you can throw out of your System Folder

- -

*T*here it sits. Only one folder on your hard drive looks like it — or acts like it. It's the System Folder, which holds software that the Mac needs for itself. Every Mac has a System Folder. (Correction: every *functioning* Mac has one.) Yours probably looks like any other folder, except that it's called System Folder and its icon has a tiny Mac Plus drawn in the middle:

System Folder

There are three important reasons for you, the former novice, to know about this vital folder.

First, someday you, like millions of Mac users before you, will attempt to double-click one of the icons inside the System Folder. With gentle, earnest curiosity, you will shyly move your pointer onto something; with a soft, trusting gesture, you'll click your mouse button twice; and with sarcastic venom, the Mac, your former friend, will reward you with nothing but a meaningless error message.

You get this message because much of the stuff in the System Folder *isn't for you!* It's information *for* the Mac, *by* the Mac. Information — notes it takes — to serve you, its master. I'll give you some specific examples later; for now, suffice it to say that most of the stuff in the System Folder is for the *system* (which explains why Apple hides it away in a folder to begin with).

The second reason you'll be glad you learned about the System Folder is this: you got a brand new computer. It's clean, it's fresh, it's empty. You know for a fact that you haven't put much of anything into it. And yet, one day you open up your System Folder to discover that it's absolutely *crawling* with files! Seething, teeming, overrun with zillions of little icons you've never seen before.

You're perfectly entitled to exclaim, "Jeez, what *is* all this stuff?!" And, before having read Chapter 1½, you might also have exclaimed, like many Mac beginners before you: "For the love o' Mike, all those files are gonna *use up all my memory!*"

Naturally, you now realize the foolishness of this comment. Data resting comfortably on your hard drive doesn't use up *any* memory. It *does,* however, take up *disk space.*

Since disk space, for most of us, is *also* limited, I'm going to show you exactly how much of the System Folder clutter you can safely throw away.

Finally, you should know about the System Folder because it's the nerve center of your whole Mac . . . the heart . . . the brain . . . the headquarters. A Mac without a System Folder is like a car without an engine. A house without a roof. *Groundhog Day* without Bill Murray.

Battle of the Systems

Back in Chapter 1, when you were a rank amateur at this computer thing, I hinted that your Mac may or may not be outfitted with a special feature called System 7. And instead of explaining what that meant, I muttered something along the lines of, "Tell you later." Before we get busy with our System Folder Trash-fest, we need to get this over with.

You know how General Motors comes out with a new model of each of its cars every year? Apple does the same thing: It keeps making minor changes to its computers, trying to make them better (and provide more incentive to buy them).

In 1991, Apple came out with a newer version of the System Folder contents, called System 7. (It replaced the older version, which, with stunning originality, was called System 6.)

System 7 has lots of terrific features, especially for the beginning Mac user. Every Mac sold since early 1991 is equipped with System 7. You'd only have System 6 if you bought your Mac used, or you've had it for a long time.

It's easy to tell which System you have. In Chapter 1, you were supposed to have written down this information on this book's Cheat Sheet; but here's a quick cheat. Look in the upper-right corner of the screen. Do you see this icon ⟨?⟩? If so, you have System 7. Otherwise: System 6.

And if the upper-right of your screen contains a more mod-looking question mark — like this |🔧| — then you have the even more trendy System 7.5. More on that later, too.

Names and numbers

When people say "System 7," they're not being terribly specific. Apple keeps making little changes to System 7. Each time, they rename the thing by changing the digits after the decimal point. First it was called System 7.0. Then they made a few touch-ups and called it System 7.0.1. Incredibly, and confusingly, they then made some *more* improvements and dubbed the result System 7.1 … and then added *more* goodies and called it System 7.5. (If you can believe this, there was actually even something called System 7 *Pro.* What'd they do, run out of decimal points?)

When I was your age, we were taught one decimal point per number. Anyway, if you ignore the additional decimals, you can pretty much figure out which System version is more recent. For example, 7.01 is, technically, a smaller number than 7.1, so it's therefore earlier.

Then there's the issue of *P.* Some system versions have the letter P after them: System 7.1P, for example. That means you have a Performa Mac. More about Performas in Chapter 9.

Finally, there's x. You'll sometimes hear computer people say that something won't work if you have System 7.x. That's shorthand. It means "System 7.0, System 7.0.1, System 7.1, or System 7-point-anything." As opposed, naturally, to System 6.x.

As you'll recall from Chapter 1, there's a quick way to find out what you've got. Go to the menu. Choose About This Macintosh. A window appears. The upper-right corner tells what system version you have.

There's no appreciable difference between versions 7.0 and 7.0.1. The one feature System 7.1 added was a folder called Fonts inside the System Folder. You know all about fonts if you read Chapter 4. Anyway, the Fonts folder makes it much easier for font freaks to add and remove new typefaces to the Mac.

If you've got 7.1.1, 7.1.2, and so on, there are no new features worth mentioning; these are all subtle mutations of System 7.1.

There *are* major differences between Systems 6 and 7, and between 7.1 and 7.5. With your indulgence, then, I'll recap them here.

What's the diff: 6 vs. 7

There are about one zillion and fifty-eight differences between Systems 6 and 7. Here are a few worth mentioning.

✔ **System 7 is slower.** It's true. Everything takes longer in System 7: copying files, emptying the Trash, opening windows, and so on. Oh, and if you've already experienced the horror of an "out of memory" message (see Chapter 12), it's worth noting that System 7 hoards a bigger chunk of your Mac's memory unto itself.

✔ **Icons in System 7 are in color and have a neat 3-D look.** All right, it's not a trip to Bermuda, but it's better than nothing.

✔ **System 7 has those little list-view triangles.** You may have messed with these in Chapter 1.

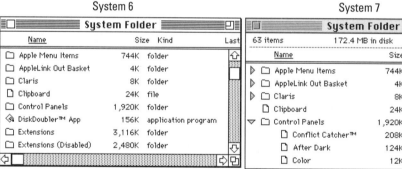

✔ **System 7 has the ⍰ menu.** This little guy is called the *Help menu.* If you're at your Mac, try this now: mouse on up to that ⍰, hold down the button, and choose Show Balloons.

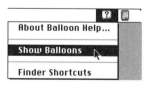

Now roll the cursor around the screen. Don't click — just point to things: icons, windows, disks, the Trash, menus, whatever. As the cursor touches each one, a little cartoon-character balloon pops up. The balloon identifies whatever you're pointing at.

When you're tired of seeing what things are and what they do, go back to the question mark menu. This time, choose Hide Balloons.

This Balloon Help feature always works when you're working at the desktop. It *usually* works when you're using your programs (word processor, and so on).

✔ **System 7's Trash never empties by itself.** You have to choose Empty Trash from the Special menu to make it stop bulging. In System 6, on the other hand, the Trash gets emptied by itself whenever you turn off the Mac.

✔ **In System 7, you can stick anything into the** 🍎 **menu.** In System 6, as you discovered in Chapter 3, the 🍎 menu at the left side of your screen lists miniprograms called desk accessories. But in the newer system, you can make *anything* appear there: a program (such as your word processor itself), a word processing document (like your application to driving school), a folder (your last 14 poetry attempts), and so on.

In fact, *anything that has an icon* can also be listed in your 🍎 menu. Some people's 🍎 menus are longer than their résumés.

Why would you care about listing some folder or file in the 🍎 menu? The primary advantage is efficiency. When you choose an item from the 🍎 menu, it opens immediately, just as though you'd double-clicked its icon. The 🍎 menu is a much more direct way of choosing something than having to burrow into your folders, three deep, trying to locate the icon you want to open.

If you're still wobbly on your Mac feet, and have already supersaturated your brain with computer info, and just want to know how you're supposed to turn the thing off and go to bed, then you might not care in the least about this nicety. If you *are* interested, here's the trick: double-click your System Folder to open it. Inside the System Folder window is another folder called Apple Menu Items.

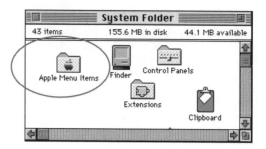

Any icon you drag into this folder appears, *instantly,* in your menu! And, likewise, you can get rid of anything listed in the Apple menu that you don't use much. Just double-click the Apple Menu Items folder and drag the offending item into the Trash (or into another folder).

Anyway, you'll find out more good dirt on System 7 in Chapter 8 and elsewhere. But you probably get the point that System 7 is a newer, more feature-laden edition of the Mac's *operating system.* ("Operating system," by the way, is a terrific-sounding computer term. In fact, I find that simply walking into a public place and very loudly saying "operating system" works wonders when I'm feeling a little depressed.)

What's the diff: 7 vs. 7.5

Apple's 1994 incarnation of the System folder adds 50 new features and takes up a lot more disk space. In addition to all of the features listed above for System 7, you also get:

✔ **Step-by-step instructions (Apple Guide).** Lurking in that ? menu at the top right of your screen is a fascinating source of advice that's geared especially toward You, the Novice. It's called Macintosh Guide.

Choose it from the ? menu to see an index of topics on Mac essentials. These include questions, tasks (like printing and using disks), and definitions.

All you have to do is follow the steps described in the little help window. When you've completed each step, you click the right-arrow button on the screen to see the next step.

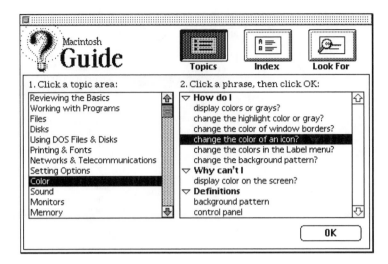

When you're supposed to use the mouse, a big fat red ghostly magic marker draws a circle around whatever you're supposed to manipulate.

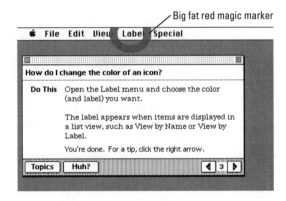

And if you ever get confused by even these patient instructions, you can click the "Huh?" button for an even more basic explanation. It's all pretty wonderful.

More of life's institutions should have "Huh?" buttons.

✔ **Submenus in the Apple menu.** Now you can open a particular control panel without even opening the Control Panels folder. Any folder listed in the Apple menu has submenus that list its contents.

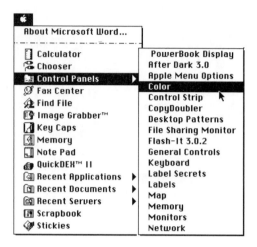

✔ **Roll-up windows.** Just when you'd gotten used to thinking of *menus* as behaving like window shades, now *windows* snap up like window shades. Just double-click a title bar to unclutter your screen. Double-click the floating menu bar — all that remains — to re-expand the window.

Before:

After:

✔ **Stickies and Find File.** The two most useful desk accessories ever born (read "In your Apple Menu Items folder," coming up next).

✔ **QuickDraw GX, PC Exchange, and PowerTalk.** Chapter 4 contains the very few words that need to be said about the powerful, pretty much useless QuickDraw GX. The end of Chapter 5 describes the value of PC Exchange (which is zip, unless you regularly need to use disks from people who are condemned to using IBM-style computers).

PowerTalk is similarly complex, memory-hungry, and useless for the average person who doesn't work at NASA. If you're interested in pursuing these more advanced topics, a whole book awaits you: *System 7.5 For Dummies.* For real.

Handy Clip-N-Save System 7.5 upgrade guide

Across the land, citizens are reaching this page and murmuring quietly to themselves: "Hmm. This System 7.5 thing. Do I want it?"

Probably. Unless you install that QuickDraw GX thing, which you probably won't, System 7.5 *doesn't take up more memory* than regular System 7. No matter how often people repeat that myth to you, it's just not true.

System 7.5 *does* take up more hard-disk space. It can wolf down 10 or even 15 megs of space, depending on how much stuff you leave in your System folder. For example, if you throw away Macintosh Guide, described in this chapter, that's about 2 megs right there.

Now then. In exchange for your $75 (or whatever System 7.5 goes for at Mac Connection these days), you get all the bells and whistles described in this chapter, like Stickies and collapsible windows. (You will *love* Stickies and collapsible windows.) But the faster speed and the stability are much more important.

Once you buy System 7.5, you'll find yourself with an *Upgrade Guide* and a pile of floppy disks (or a CD-ROM, if you have a player). Installing the new System folder is a breeze. For best results, just follow the instructions in the *Upgrade Guide* manual, especially that first step about using your Disk Tools disk. (On the other hand, don't bother with that part about running the Safe Install Utility; it's totally bogus.)

And may all your Stickies be happy ones.

Anyway, the 50 little goodies in System 7.5 make using a Mac 50 tiny shades of easier and more efficient to use.

But as far as most people are concerned, the main selling point of System 7.5 is its increased speed (yes, it's true) and its stability. In other words, fewer system crashes. If you don't have System 7.5 yet, and you care about things like speed, efficiency, and stability, see Chapter 14 for details and warnings about upgrading your Mac.

System-Folder Trash-O-Rama

Who else would be utterly mad enough to utter the following Emperor's-New-Clothes utterance? *Half the stuff in your System Folder is worthless.* It's designed for power users, or people in big corporate networks, or superweenie jet-propulsion scientists and their Mensa-qualifying eight-year-old offspring. Meanwhile, these files are taking up room on *your* hard drive.

Do it right now: double-click your System Folder to open it. (Of course, your System Folder is in your main hard-drive window. Double-click your hard-drive icon first, if need be.) Now click the zoom box, the tiny square in the top-right corner of the System Folder window, so you can see as much of the System Folder contents as possible. As a matter of fact, move your mouse up to the View menu and choose "by Name." That should put everything into a neat list.

System Folder		
32 items	155.6 MB in disk	44.1 MB ava
Name	**Size**	**Kir**
▷ ☐ After Dark Files	1,701K	
▷ ☐ Aldus	1,001K	
▷ ☐ Aldus folder	662K	
▷ ☐ Apple Menu Items	746K	
▷ ☐ AppleLink Out Basket	4K	
▷ ☐ At Ease Items	77K	
☐ ATM Font Database	1,421K	
▷ ☐ Claris	18K	
☐ Clipboard	7K	
▷ ☐ Control Panels	2,188K	
◈ DiskDoubler™ App	158K	
▷ ☐ Extensions	3,406K	
☐ Finder	371K	
▷ ☐ Fonts	2,727K	
▷ ☐ GlobalFax Files	5,506K	
▷ ☐ GlobalFax Personal	32K	
☐ Note Pad File	4K	
▷ ☐ Preferences	1,344K	
▷ ☐ Printer Descriptions	18K	
▷ ☐ PrintMonitor Documents	zero K	

Just *look* at all that junk! *You* sure as heck didn't put it there — what's it *doing* there?

Here's a wonderful, glorious, worth-the-price-of-the-book-right-there list of everything in your typical System 7 System Folder, item by item. I'll tell you which of these things you can safely trash.

Don't have a cow about throwing things away, either. This is *not* like cleaning your attic, where if you toss that box of your drawings from elementary school, you've wounded your inner child forever. No, *this* stuff you can always get *back again* if you need it. It's all on your white System disks that came with your Mac. (If you're a Performa or PowerBook 145 owner, you didn't get System disks; you're supposed to make your own backup of the System Folder. And, as I've mentioned elsewhere, if your Mac has a built-in CD-ROM drive — you'd remember having paid extra for it — you may have received a CD-ROM disc containing the System software instead.)

And if you're not the least bit interested in de-junking your System Folder? That's why we chose to make *Macs For Dummies* a book and not a major motion picture: since it's a book, you don't have to sit through the dull parts.

By the way, you may not find *every* one of these files listed in your System Folder; about half of them are tweaky little bonus features that only come with System 7.5 or later. Likewise, you may find files in your System Folder that *aren't* listed here (especially if your Mac isn't new).

In your Apple Menu Items folder

Let's start off with the stuff in the Apple Menu Items folder, which is, alphabetically speaking, the first thing in your System Folder. You'll recall, of course, that anything in this folder also appears in the ⬛ menu at the left side of your screen.

This is really a two-for-one discussion: each Apple menu item is also a desk accessory like the ones you worked with in Chapter 3. So now you'll get to find out what exactly those things in your ⬛ menu are . . . acquire a deep and sensitive appreciation of their importance and value . . . and *then* throw them away.

Alarm Clock — Try choosing it from your menu right now, if you have it. You'll see that it's a tiny clock. You can leave it open on your screen all day, and always know exactly how much time you're wasting. With some difficulty, you can also use it to set an alarm that goes off at a certain time of day. (Some alarm. All it does is beep once and make your menu icon start flashing at the top left of your screen.)

You can probably trash the Alarm Clock and never miss it. It's not even included anymore in System 7.5. As the song says, does anybody ever really know what time it is?

AppleCD Audio Player, CD Remote — It has Play, Stop, and Rewind controls for playing regular *music* compact discs on your Apple CD-ROM player. If you don't *have* an Apple CD-ROM player, this does you no good whatsoever.

Battery — This DA shows you how much juice is left in your battery. Toss it unless you have a PowerBook.

Calculator, Note Pad — You already know about these desk accessories (see Chapter 3). Leave them for now.

Chooser — You *definitely* need this, as you found out in Chapter 4.

Control Panels — This folder is simply a shortcut (an *alias*) to opening your real Control Panels folder. More on aliases and control panels when the informational flood dries up a little.

Find File — (System 7.5 and later) A turbocharged file-finding feature. Worth its weight in the precious metal of your choice. Just type in what you're looking for, and the Mac finds it . . . *fast.*

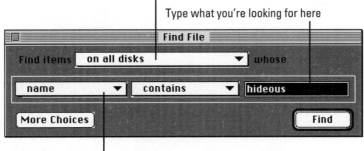

Use this pop-up menu to specify what disks or folders you want to search.

Type what you're looking for here

Use this pop-up menu to specify what kind of info you're looking for (the file's name, date, etc.)

Double-click a found file to open it.

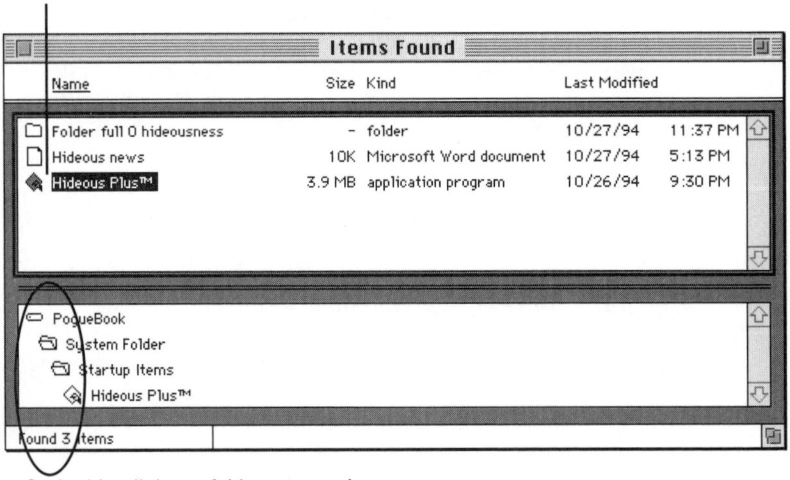

Name	Size	Kind	Last Modified	
Folder full O hideousness	–	folder	10/27/94	11 :37 PM
Hideous news	10K	Microsoft Word document	10/27/94	5:13 PM
Hideous Plus™	3.9 MB	application program	10/26/94	9:30 PM

PogueBook
System Folder
Startup Items
Hideous Plus™

Found 3 Items

Or double-click any folder to open *it.*

Find File shows you a list of files that match what you looked for (see the illustration above). There are three important things you can do now: (1) double-click a file in the list window to open it; (2) drag a file's little icon onto the desktop to move it; or (3) choose Open Enclosing Folder from the File menu to view one of the icons in the folder where it's actually hiding out.

Guard this desk accessory with your life; even when you grow up to be a great big computer whiz, you will *still* forget where you stored a file now and then. (The Find command in the File menu, by the way, brings up the exact same feature.)

Key Caps — Another desk accessory. It helps you find out which combinations of keys you're supposed to press when you want to type wacky symbols like ¢ or ¥ or © (see details in Chapter 5).

Puzzle, Jigsaw Puzzle — Highly silly desk accessories whose Novelty-Wear-Off Quotient is about five minutes. Upon reaching the sixth minute, trash it. (Jigsaw Puzzle comes with System 7.5.)

Scrapbook — This desk accessory is worth keeping. Using Copy and Paste, you can put pictures, sounds, or blocks of text into it for use later. For example, after you spend three weekends designing an absolutely gorgeous logo for yourself, paste it into the Scrapbook. Thereafter, whenever you need that logo again, open the Scrapbook and copy it, so that it'll be ready to paste into your memo or package design.

Stickies — (System 7.5 and later) How did we *live* before Stickies? Sheer, purest genius. Stickies are electronic Post-It notes. That's all. Just choose New Note from the File menu, jot down what you want, and maybe pick a new pastel hue from the Color menu.

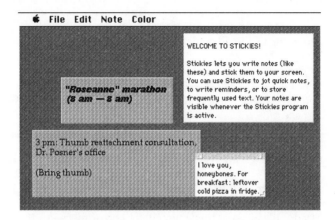

When you try to close Stickies (by choosing Quit from the File menu), you'll be asked nicely if you want the Stickies to reappear each time you turn on the Mac. Say yes, and you'll never forget another dog-grooming appointment.

Shut Down — (System 7.5 and later) The same as the usual Shut Down command. Why a duplicate here in the Apple menu? So that you can get to it without having to quit whatever program you're using at the time. Saves a step when dinner's ready.

In your Control Panels folder

Control Panels is another folder inside your System Folder. As you read in a previous chapter, a control panel is a tiny miniprogram that changes some aspect of the Mac's behavior.

It's very important — and rarely understood — that Apple's control panels *only* do their work when you actually *change* a setting. In other words, it's perfectly OK to make a setting and then throw away the control panel completely. Your setting will remain in effect forever.

If you ever *do* need to change that setting again, you can always use your System disks. The full complement of control panels is on them, and you don't even have to copy them to the Mac to use them.

Apple CD Speed Switch — Slows down your CD-ROM drive to accommodate a very few ancient discs. If you have AppleCD Audio Player under your menu, you don't need this at all.

Apple Menu Options — (System 7.5 or later) This is the little gizmo that provides the submenus in your Apple menu, as described earlier. Also creates, in your Apple menu, folders that track the last bunch of documents and programs you used, which is handy.

At Ease Setup — This control panel lets you choose which icons you want on your big fat At Ease tablecloth. (See Chapter 10 to find out what At Ease is.) If you use At Ease, take note: you need this control panel if you ever want to turn At Ease *off!*

~ATM™ — The first half of Adobe Type Manager (see Chapter 4). It didn't come with the Mac until System 7.5, but an awful lot of people have it anyway.

Auto Power On/Off — Works only with a few Mac models, such as the Power Macintosh 7100 or 8100. Makes them turn off by themselves at a specified time. Try double-clicking this; if you get an error message, throw it out.

AutoRemounter — One of many doodads that's only good for connecting Macs together — in this case, a PowerBook and a regular Mac. (It automatically reconnects the two whenever you wake a sleeping PowerBook.) If you have neither PowerBook nor network, send it Trashward.

Brightness — This control panel doesn't even *do* anything except on a Mac Classic or Classic II. If you have any other model, march this icon directly to the Trash.

Cache Switch — This little software switch has two settings: Compatible and Faster. It's useful exclusively on Macs named Quadra and Centris — and even then, only slightly. (Compatible mode makes your Mac run slower but with fewer problems using really old programs.)

CloseView — Magnifies the screen if you have trouble seeing. Switch it on or off by pressing ⌘-Option-O. The area of enlargement follows around your little pointer, which takes some getting used to. This control panel also lets you make your screen white-writing-on-black, instead of the reverse. If neither of those visual options interests you, out it goes.

Color — If you have a black-and-white Mac, trash this sucker. It's used on color or grayscale Macs to choose what shade you want to use when you highlight some text. (Talk about obscure.) See Chapter 8 for details.

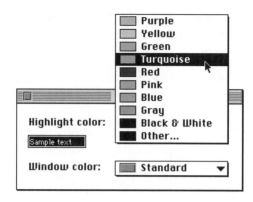

ColorSync System Profile — Trash it.

Control Strip — (System 7.5 or later) For PowerBooks only. Pertains to the nifty floating Control Strip, which gives you one-click access to several battery-saving PowerBook options. It looks like this:

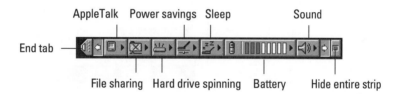

Anyway, this control panel simply makes the Control Strip appear or disappear. You don't really need it, since one click on the Control Strip's tab tucks it away off the edge of your screen anyway.

CPU Energy Saver — Turns off the Mac after you haven't used it for, say, half an hour to save electricity. Only works on Macs that shut off completely when you choose Shut Down from the menu. So if you have an LC, the 6100, or a similar push-button-power-switch model, out this goes.

Date & Time, Numbers — These control panels are for non-Americans. They let you change the way the Mac punctuates numbers and spells dates. For example, when you write down a date in England, you're supposed to put the month *second.* So if Cher's birthday is August 25, you'd say that her 40th birthday was 25/8/83. Along the same lines, the French use *periods* in large numbers instead of commas. You'd say, "Bonjour! You owe moi $1.000.000, Monsieur."

If you're satisfied with the American way of doing things, throw away these control panels. (You only have them if you're using System 7.1 or later anyway. Oh, yeah: before you toss Date & Time in System 7.5 or later, be aware that it's the only remaining method of setting your Mac's clock.)

Desktop Pattern — (System 7.5 or later) Very simple: lets you choose a fancier backdrop pattern for your computer. Lists various textures, fabrics, and, well, kitties.

Easy Access — This control panel is designed for people who have difficulty using a mouse or typing with both hands. If you're coordinated and two-handed, throw this thing away.

Express Modem — The only models that have this control panel are those with a built-in Apple fax modem (or the so-called GeoPort Adapter): a PowerBook, Power Macintosh, or AV model, for example. If you're having trouble sending faxes or using your modem, make sure this switch is set to the *Express Modem* setting, not the External Modem setting.

Extensions Manager — Comes with System 7.5 or later. Here's how it works. As the Mac is starting up, press and hold your spacebar. Suddenly, you'll be shown a list of *everything* listed in this chapter — all the control panels and extensions. By clicking their names, you can decide which of them you'd like to use during the work session that's about to begin.

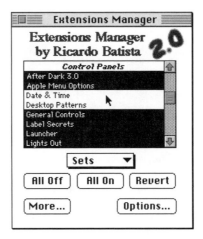

File Sharing Monitor — Another of the slew of control panels that have to do with *networking* (connecting Macs together by wire). If you have no plans to plug your Mac into somebody else's, throw this away. (Instructions for setting up a Mac network are beyond the scope of this book. Networking is not, however, beyond the scope of *MORE Macs For Dummies*.)

General Controls — A useful control panel. (You played with it in Chapter 3.) Set your cursor-blinking speed, and so on. In System 7.5, lets you create a Documents folder to collect every new file you make, just as on a Performa. Details in Chapter 10.

Keyboard — Use this control panel to change how a key behaves when you keep it pressed. Does a held-down key start repeating like thisssssssssss? And how fast?

Many first-time Mac users fare better if they turn the repeating-key feature off. That way, if a book happens to lean on the spacebar while you're on the phone for 20 minutes, you won't hang up to find 536 pages of blank space in the letter you were working on.

If you couldn't care less, throw this one away.

Labels — Look at your menu bar: File, Edit, View, Label, Special. Labels are a way to categorize your files. You just highlight an icon and choose a label from the Label menu (such as In Progress). It's a wonderful, ingenious, fascinating concept. Almost nobody uses it.

Use this control panel, Labels, to change *what* the Labels menu says (instead of Essential, Hot, In Progress, you can change them to say Late, Past Deadline, Hopeless, or whatever). If you don't use labels, which is probably the case, chuck this.

Launcher (or Performa) — You only have this if you have a Performa Mac or System 7.5. You *can* throw it away, but only if you want to de-Performatize your Mac. See Chapter 10 for an explanation.

Map — This control panel is primarily useful for people who do business with different geographical locations. You type a major city's name and click Find, and the Map shows you where that city is. It also tells you how far away it is, and what the time difference is.

If you pretty much stay in your living room, the Map is a good candidate for trashing.

Memory — As the French say, *Ne trashez pas!* You'll need this one. Details on memory, and Memory, in Chapter 12.

Monitors — If you have a black-and-white Mac, throw this out.

If you have a color screen, you use this control panel to switch it between color and black and white.

And why, you may well ask, would you ever want your Mac world in black and white after you've gone to all the trouble and expense of buying a color Mac? Easy — when you set your monitor to black and white, it's *faster.* Much faster. Things like opening windows and scrolling through a document happen about three times quicker in black and white. (They're just not as pretty doing it.)

Mouse — This control panel adjusts how far the cursor moves on the screen relative to how you move the mouse. It may surprise you that moving the mouse one inch does *not* move the cursor one inch on the screen. In fact, the distance the arrow moves depends on the *speed* of your mouse motion.

Try this: move the mouse very slowly across three inches of desk space. The arrow moves three inches. But now *jerk* the mouse across the same three inches. Now the cursor flies across your entire monitor!

Anyway, the Mouse control panel lets you adjust how much of this speed-exaggeration you'll get when you move the mouse. It also lets you decide how fast two clicks must be to be treated as a double-click.

My advice: set the Mouse Tracking to one of the Fast settings, and the double-click speed in the middle. Then throw this control panel away.

Network — Yet another control panel used only for networking. In fact, even if you *have* a network, you can toss this; it's used to switch *between* different kinds of networks, such as Ethernet and LocalTalk (whatever *they* are).

Portable (or PowerBook), PowerBook Display — The first one controls how quickly your laptop Mac goes to "sleep" to conserve battery juice. The second governs what happens when you plug an external monitor into your laptop. Naturally, if you don't have a PowerBook, it's Trash Time for both. (See Chapter 11 for more on PowerBooks.)

PowerBook Setup — For laptops only, needless to say. Has a slider that lets you choose which you'd rather have: a faster computer or a longer-lasting battery charge.

PC Exchange — Lets you shove IBM-computer disks into your Mac. Details at the end of Chapter 5; meantime, if you only work with Macs, send this baby trashward.

Screen — For certain models only (such as LC 500-somethings, Color Classic, Mac TV). Lets you adjust the screen picture since those Macs' screens have no knobs on them. Useless for all other models.

Serial Switch — This thing only works on *one* Mac: the IIfx, which was last on the market in about the Jurassic Period. It's an on/off switch that may make MIDI musical gear work better on that model.

Sharing Setup, Users & Groups — More control panels used only for networking. Throw them away unless you want to connect to other Macs.

Sound — A keeper. It lets you adjust the volume of your speaker. It also lets you choose from among several equally uncouth sound effects for use as your error beep (what the Mac does when you make a mistake). And if your Mac came with a microphone or has one built into the front, then you can record your own embarrassing and gurgly sound effects. Chapter 8 has the scoop.

Speech Setup — Only Macs with AV in their names (such as Quadra 840 AV) come with this control panel. Use this to control how the Mac responds when you talk to it (see Appendix A for details on The Macs Who Listen).

Startup Disk — You'd use this if you had *more than one* hard drive connected to your Mac. You have one hard drive inside the Mac. Some people purchase another one, or a removable-cartridge thing, that plugs into the back. Startup Disk lets you choose which hard drive's System Folder you want to run the show when you next turn on the computer.

If the hard drive in your Mac is your only hard drive, toss Startup Disk.

Text — (System 7.5 or later) Mister Pointless. Would let you choose a language software kit other than English for your computer — if you had any installed. You don't. Throw this away.

Trackpad — Worthless unless you have a PowerBook 500-something. On those laptops, this works just like the Mouse control panel (described earlier) . . . except, of course, it adjusts the *trackpad* sensitivity, not the mouse's.

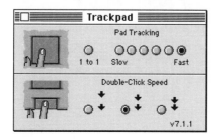

Views — My grandfather's 104 and sharp as a tack. When I showed him my PowerBook last Thanksgiving, he had absolutely no problem using it. But there was one thing that bothered him: the icons' names were too small to read.

Fortunately, I was using System 7. I opened up the Views control panel, typed a new point size as shown below, and handed the Mac back to him. He loved it.

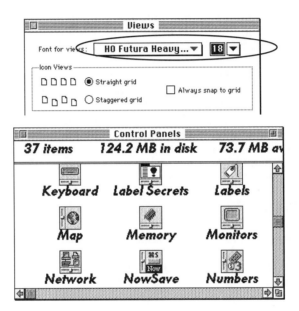

He did remind me, however, that when *he* was growing up, they didn't even have *electricity.*

WindowShade — (System 7.5 or later) This is the gadget that turns on or off that collapsible-window syndrome described earlier, where you double-click a window's title to hide the window (except for the title bar). You don't really need it except to turn the feature on and off.

In your Fonts folder

You only have a Fonts folder if you're using System 7.1 or later. Actually, you probably shouldn't throw away anything in it. See Chapter 4 again for a detailed explanation of what all this junk is.

In your Extensions folder

An *extension* is a little program that runs automatically when you turn on the Mac. It usually adds some little feature to your Mac that you want available at all times: a screen saver, for example, that automatically blanks your screen after a few minutes of inactivity on your part.

Apple CD-ROM, CD Remote Init, Foreign File Access, ISO 990, High Sierra Access, Apple PhotoCD Access, Audio CD Access — Why does Apple's CD-ROM player need so many little extensions? Heaven knows. All I know is that you should toss these if you don't have a CD-ROM.

Apple Guide, Shortcuts — Remember that System 7.5 feature called Apple Guide, in which you're given step-by-step on-screen instructions for doing something? These are the files that contain all the instructions. If you use the Apple Guide feature, leave these here.

AppleShare, File Sharing Extension, Network Extension — Still more doodads for networking Macs together.

AppleScript, Finder Scripting Extension, Scripting Additions — All components of a very technical System 7.5 feature for the kind of person who wouldn't be caught dead reading this book.

A/ROSE — There's a good joke in here somewhere — something about A/ROSE by any other name — but, alas, this extension is useless. Jettison pronto.

AudioVision Extension — Look at your monitor. Does it have speakers built into either side? If not, you don't have the Apple AudioVision monitor, and you can safely send this icon to the great Trash can in the sky.

Basic Color Monitor — This extension lets your Mac work with this one specific low-cost Apple monitor model. If you have any other kind of screen, get rid of this.

Caps Lock — Only for PowerBooks. Because the Caps Lock key on certain models doesn't light up or stay down when you press it, this little extension puts an up-arrow symbol on your menu bar when Caps Lock is engaged. That way, you know when you're about to inadvertently type 46 pages in all caps.

Clipping Extension — (A System 7.5-or-later item.) This is the magic software responsible for a nifty feature called Macintosh Drag & Drop. Here's how it works: Open your Note Pad from the menu. Type something. Drag across what you've typed to highlight it.

Now stick your pointer right into the middle of the highlighted area. Drag it sideways clear out of the window and onto the desktop.

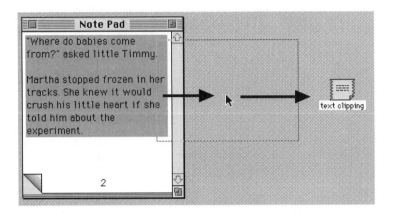

And presto: you've just created a *clipping file* — a little icon on your desktop that contains whatever you dragged there! You could actually drag this little clipping icon *back* into a Note Pad or SimpleText or Scrapbook window to put it there. It's like Copy and Paste: The Next Generation.

ColorSync — If you don't know what this is, you don't need it.

DAL — It's ridiculous that Apple even wastes your time with this. It's for hooking up to gigantic humming mainframes in Houston. Nobody uses it. Toss it.

EM Extension — Another piece of Extensions Manager, described under "Control Panels," earlier in this chapter.

EtherTalk Phase 2 — Sounds suspiciously like something you'd hear uttered on *Deep Space Nine,* doesn't it? Actually, it comes with the fancier models (Quadras, Power Macs, etc.), and it's useless unless you're hooked up to a major office network that uses special Ethernet cables.

Fax Extension, GeoPort Extension, Shared Library Manager, Fax Sender, GeoPort Extension — Believe it or not, you need all this crud just to run your GeoPort Adapter. That's the strange-looking box, which is supposed to act like a fax/modem, that may hang off the back of a Power Macintosh or AV model.

Finder Help — Leave this one alone. It's where the Mac stores the information you get when you use Balloon Help.

Find File Extension — Comes with System 7.5 or later. You want it; trust me. It's responsible for bringing up that wonderful new Find File feature described near the beginning of this endless chapter.

ImageWriter, LaserWriter, StyleWriter II, etc. — Recognize these names? They're various *printers* made by Apple. You only need one of them — the one that matches *your* printer. You should definitely throw away all the others. (More on printers in Chapter 4.)

How come you can't double-click things

Nobody ever explains this. Not one computer book — including, I'm embarrassed to say, the first edition of *this* book — bothers to mention this extremely annoying syndrome.

You see an icon. You double-click it to see what it does. But all you get is this error message:

 The document "Aldus Prep" could not be opened, because the application program that created it could not be found.

OK

This frustrating occurrence, as you've probably discovered, flies violently in the face of the Macintosh Reputation for User-Friendliness.

Actually, if you've read this chapter from the beginning, you already pretty much know the explanation. Half the icons in the System Folder *aren't for you.* They serve as storage cubbies for the computer itself. The "Application not found" message really means "Sorry, bub, authorized personnel only." And it's really nothing to worry about.

If you try to double-click an *extension* icon, the Mac is only slightly more coherent:

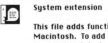 System extension

This file adds functionality to your Macintosh. To add this file's functionality to your Macintosh, place the file in the Extensions folder and then restart the computer.

OK

As noted earlier, *you can't do anything with extensions.* They have no controls for you to change, no pictures to look at, nothing for you at all. They do what they're programmed to do automatically when you turn on the Mac. There's only one thing you can do about it: drag an extension's icon out of the System Folder window (and restart the computer) to get rid of its effects.

So much for clicking things in your System Folder. At other times in your Macintosh computing life, you'll get a similar error message when the thing you're double-clicking is *not* in the System Folder. That's a very different scenario, particularly when you're double-clicking an icon you *know* is a legitimate, user-openable file.

For an explanation of that irritating event, see Chapter 12.

PlainTalk Speech Recognition, TTS Male Voice, TTS Female Voice, SR North American English, SR Monitor, System Speech Rules, PlainTalk Text-To-Speech, etc. — Gad, what a bunch of useless attic clutter. Believe it or not, you need it if you want your Mac to obey spoken orders. This feature, of course, is only available if you have a Power or AV-model Mac. It's described a little more in Chapter 7 and a lot more in *MORE Macs for Dummies.*

PrintMonitor — Definitely leave this. It's actually a program, not an extension, and it's the genie that grants you the miracle of *background printing,* a concept you probably don't understand unless you've read Chapter 4.

QuickDraw GX — The memory-grabbing On switch for QuickDraw GX, a System 7.5-or-later feature described in Chapter 4. I think you're better off without it.

QuickTime — You need this little jobber if you plan to use (or are using) digital movies on the Mac. You know, little flicks that play inside a Triscuit-sized window right on your screen, complete with sound (see Chapter 7). This QuickTime extension is what makes those movies possible. If you have a black-and-white Mac, or you're not a Hollywood wannabe, then save yourself the memory and disk space and send this one to the cutting room floor.

Record Button Extension — This one works with that bizarr-O Apple keyboard, the one that splits in half down the middle for ergonomic comfort. Or whatever. This is the doodad that makes the Record button (on that keyboard) turn on your Mac's sound recording (if the Sound control panel is open). Pretty useless.

Sound Manager — What a misnomer. Doesn't manage sounds at all. Instead, about the only thing you'll notice when this thing is installed is that your error beep — you know, that Simple Beep sound — changes to a glassier, more neutered sound. And some older games stop making sounds. (If that happens, throw this away.) Sound Manager comes with lots of modern software from Apple, like System 7.5.

Tuner — Keep this baby right where it is! This extension repairs some bugs in System 7.0 or 7.0.1, some of which are a wee bit dangerous. If you have any other System version, you can ditch it.

In your Launcher Items folder

You only *have* a Launcher Items folder if your Mac has *Performa* in its name (or if you're running System 7.5). And the purpose of this folder is to let you specify what jumbo icons you want to appear in your Launcher window, the Performa's program-launching bay. See Chapter 10 for the gory details.

In your Preferences folder

The Preferences folder is filled with information, and *none* of it's for you.

Every single file in this folder was put there by *another* piece of software. Let's say you change a setting in your word processor: you always want it to make your typing double-spaced, let's say. Well, where do you suppose the computer stores your new setting? It jots it down in a *preferences file.* And this prefs file lives — wild guess — in the Preferences folder.

Prefs files are famous for frustrating beginners. Because they're for use by your programs, and not by you, virtually every one of them gives you a rude error message if you try to double-click it. *You* simply can't open a Prefs file; only your software can.

Finder Preferences, Photoshop Prefs, ClarisWorks Prefs, etc. — Like I said. Leave these alone, and don't even think about double-clicking them.

DAL Preferences — Out it goes. See DAL, on page 216.

In the Speakable Items folder

There's no possible way you'll find this folder in your System Folder, except under one circumstance: you have a Power Macintosh or a model with *AV* in its name (such as Centris 660AV or Quadra 840AV).

If you're using your Mac's speech-recognition feature — you know, where you talk to your Mac ("Computer: open MacWrite") — you can "teach" your Mac to recognize the names of certain files or folders by putting them, or aliases of them, into this folder. Don't get greedy, though. You're not supposed to put more than about 50 things in here.

Loose in the System Folder

Clipboard — Every time you use the Cut or Copy command in a program, the Mac, according to what you read earlier, socks the selected material away on an invisible Clipboard. Well, guess what: it's not actually invisible. Technically speaking, that info you copied has to be put *somewhere.* This is where: in the Clipboard file.

Little-known fact: you can double-click the Clipboard file to open a window that shows the last thing you cut or copied. (Another little-known fact: the last swallow of a can of soda is 69 percent saliva.)

Finder — This is the most important file on your Mac. Without it, a System Folder is just a folder, and your Mac can't operate. The Finder file is responsible for creating your basic desktop: the Trash, your disk icon, windows, and so on.

System — This is *also* the most important file on your Mac. It contains all kinds of *other* info necessary for the computer to run: your sounds, for example; your fonts (in systems before 7.1); and reams and reams of instructions for the computer's own use. Without a System file, the Mac won't even turn on.

System Enabler — This, too, is the most important file on the Mac. Like the System and the Finder, without this file, your Mac can't even turn on.

However, not every Mac *has* one of these. In fact, only Macs sold in the last couple of years have one: Centris, Quadra, LC III, PowerBook Duos, and a few other recent models. (System 7.5 eliminates the need for most enablers.) If you have one, don't touch it.

PrintMonitor Documents — PrintMonitor, as you read in Chapter 4, has to do with *background printing.* After you use the Print command but before the paper actually starts coming out of the printer, the Mac stores the printout-to-be in this folder. You can trash this folder if you want, but it'll reappear every time you turn on the Mac.

Scrapbook file, Note Pad file — When you paste something into the Scrapbook or Note Pad desk accessories, behind the scenes, the Mac actually stores it in these files.

Startup Items, Shutdown Items — Fascinating, Captain. Anything you put into the Startup Items folder (a program, a document, a sound, a folder) gets opened with a mysterious automatic double-click whenever you turn on the Mac. If you don't do anything but word process, for example, drag the icon of your word processor into this folder. Thereafter, every time you power up for the day, your word processing program will be on the screen awaiting your brilliance.

Starting in System 7.5, you also have a Shutdown Items folder. Same deal, except anything in *here* gets run automatically when you *Shut Down* the computer. Automatic-backup programs come to mind.

A sound that says "Th-th-th-th-th-that's all, folks!" also comes to mind.

~ATM 68020/030 — Another component of Adobe Type Manager (see Chapter 4). Leave it here.

Top Ten Other Typical Pieces of System Folder Crud

Unless your Macintosh is brand new, you've probably got a bunch of other System Folder clutter I haven't mentioned. Usually, it's stuff that you (or your guru-friend) purchased and installed.

Remember, the vast majority of this stuff doesn't eat up any of your *memory;* it's only occupying *disk space.* Still, if some piece of unidentified System Folder crud really bugs you, you can always try moving it out of the System Folder for a week or so, long enough to see if your Mac still works without it.

1. **Aldus** — A folder full of stuff for programs made by Aldus (probably PageMaker or FreeHand).

2. **Claris** — A folder full of stuff used by Claris Corporation programs (ClarisWorks, FileMaker, and so on).

3. **CEToolbox** — A component of any program from a company called CE Software (DiskTop, QuicKeys, QuickMail, etc.).

4. **Suitcase** — A font-management program that lets you "turn on" or "turn off" sets of fonts very easily.

5. **GlobalFax** or **Teleport** or **PowerPort** or **Express Modem** or **FaxStf** — The software that controls your modem.

6. **After Dark Files** — After Dark is the famous automatic screen dimmer — see Chapter 8 — that features the famous Flying Toasters and Fish. This folder holds all of its different modules.

7. **32-bit Enabler** (or **Mode32**) — These are memory-related add-ons. You need one or the other if your Mac has more than 8MB of memory and it's a Mac II, IIx, IIcx, or SE-30. At this point, you probably don't know or care about memory; if you want to find out more, see Chapter 12.

8. **System Update** — Another one of those little tune-up gadgets Apple sends out from time to time in the hopes of making your Mac run better and faster. It only works if you have System 7.1 or later. The problems it fixes are unbelievably obscure, so don't work yourself into a frenzy if your Mac doesn't have it.

9. **At Ease Items** — The storage folder for aliases of everything you choose to list on your At Ease screen. See Chapter 10 for more about At Ease.

10. **HelvNar, PalatRom, etc.** — These wierd abbreviated-name icons are printer-font files. If you have System 7.1 or later, they belong in your Fonts folder instead; maybe they didn't get moved when you upgraded your System version. No harm done; it's only clutter.

Chapter 7

More Stuff to Buy and Plug In

*I*t's probably taken you at least a day to reach this part of the book, and I'll bet you're already chomping at the bit. "FileMaker — fiddlesticks! Printers — piffle!" you're no doubt exclaiming. "Give me something I, the Reader, can sink my teeth into!"

OK, O Reader. In this section you'll find out about several impressive and high-tech gadgets you can spend money on — yes, it's Credit Card Workout #4. These devices give the Mac eyes and ears, turn it into a national network, and turn it into an orchestra. You're not obligated to purchase any of them, of course. But knowing about some of the amazing things your computer can do will help you understand why a Mac is such a big deal.

Microphones

A few Mac models used to come equipped with a little microphone. It's the circular thing that looks like a Munchkin smoke detector, about two inches in diameter, with a thin cord trailing out.

For newer models, like the Power Macs and the 630 series, you have to buy the microphone separately for $20; it's a newer design, looking like a light-gray megaphone mashed in on one side. If you have a PowerBook or certain one-piece models like the Color Classic, maybe it's built right into the front of your computer.

Finally, if you have a much older Mac that doesn't even *have* a microphone miniplug jack in the back, a little money (as always) can remedy the situation. You can buy a MacRecorder. It plugs into the jack marked by a telephone (in back of your Mac), and it does everything the Apple mike can do, and more — it just costs more.

Anyway, you wouldn't be alone if you wondered what the point of a microphone was. Fact is, there isn't a whole heckuva lot you can do with it. Mainly what you do with it is record sounds — sentences, sound effects, belches, whatever you want. You'll find full instructions for enshrining your favorite audible emissions in Chapter 8.

If you ever see a sound icon like one of these, then you can play back the sound just by double-clicking its icon.

Otherwise, you can play back your recorded sounds by clicking their names in the Sound control panel. (Choose Control Panels from the menu, and double-click Sound.)

In this control panel, you can designate any sound to replace the beep the Mac makes when you make a mistake. (The offices of Mac freaks are filled with exclamations of *"Not!"* and "Bogus!" — the chosen error beeps of the Mac faithful. Again, for instructions, hie thee to Chapter 8.)

Casper, the friendly technology

If your Mac has *AV* or *Power Macintosh* in its name, you know pretty darned well why there's a microphone. Can you say *voice control?*

Yup, it's PlainTalk, formerly known as Casper, the speech-recognition ghost. You can actually *speak* to your Mac, and it will obey your commands. No, no, you can't just go randomly dictating your great American novel and expect the Mac to take it all down; the Mac can only recognize *menu commands,* mainly. And even then it doesn't respond to you for a moment or two. And this feature uses up a *huge* amount of memory (see Chapter 12). And it often doesn't even hear you correctly; if you say "Computer, close window," the Mac may just respond by opening, say, the Puzzle.

Despite all of this, voice control is extremely amazing and cool. If you get the right distance from the mike and speak the right way and don't set your expectations too high, you can get a serious fun-shiver out of this.

Scanners

You've actually seen scanners before. They're usually known by their technical name: *copying machines.* Yup. When you put a piece of paper on the ol' Xerox machine, the scanner part (glass, bright light, funny hum) takes a picture of your document. Then the printer part prints the copy. Well, if you strip out the printer part, what's left is a scanner.

If the point of a printer is to take something on the *screen* and reproduce it on *paper,* then a scanner is the opposite — its function is to scan an image on *paper* and throw it up on the Mac *screen.* After it's been scanned and converted into bits and bytes that the Mac understands (meaning that it's been *digitized)*, you can manipulate it any way you want. Erase un-wanted parts, make the back-ground darker, give Uncle Ed a mustache, shorten your brother's neck, whatever. The more dignified use for a scanner is grabbing real-world images that you then paste into your own documents, particularly in the realm of page lay-out and graphic design. Got a potato-industry newsletter to crank out? Scan in a photo of some fine-lookin' spuds, and you've got yourself a graphic for page one.

O Say Can U OCR?

Unfortunately, when you scan a page of *text,* the Mac doesn't see English words. It sees lots of itty-bitty dots in funny patterns. When the image pops up on your screen after being scanned, you can't correct a typo — because it's not really text anymore, just a *picture* of text. (Analogy time: If you take a Polaroid of a handwritten grocery list, you can't then erase *Charmin 8-Roll Pack* from the *photo* because it's no longer handwriting — just a picture of some writing.)

To convert that picture of text into a true text document, you need a piece of highly brainy software designed for *optical character recognition,* which is so unhelpful a term that people abbreviate it OCR out of sheer disgust. Using OCR, you can save yourself massive amounts of retyping; you can just roll the magazine article, book page, or other text document through your scanner, and wait while your OCR program examines each letter to decide its identity. The result is a text document that's about 98 percent correctly typed.

One in the hand

If you doubt you'll be needing to grab images or text every day, consider a *hand* scanner. Instead of being a huge piece of machinery, a hand scanner is a little hand-held doodad about five inches wide. Hand scanners have their limita- tions — the four-inch maximum scan width, for one thing, and the fact that you have to drag the scanner across the page absolutely straight. But they cost less than half what the big guns do.

So how much is all this gonna cost you? A serious black-and-white scanner, one with a big plate of glass like a copier, is around $700. Add another $400 for color. An OCR program costs between $200 and $800, depending on its sophistication.

Scannery row

Just one unhappy bit of advice about scanners: they're what are known as (shudder) *SCSI devices*. This means they attach to the fat, wide, menacing-looking jack in the back of your Mac. And *that* means that you have to be somewhat careful. For the full harrowing explanation, please see Chapter 12.

Modems

A modem is a phone hookup — a box that sits between the Mac and a phone jack.

After your Mac is connected by phone to another computer, all kinds of neat things can happen. You can have a conversation with somebody at the other end — everything each person types appears on both people's screens. You can transfer a file from your hard disk to somebody else's even if the person lives in Tulsa or Zurich. You can drop written messages into people's electronic mailboxes, which they'll read the next time they check in. (Such messages are called *e-mail,* from the exclamation "*Eeee*-hah! I don't have to send it through the *mail!*") You can make plane reservations, order disks, check your stocks, send cartoon renderings of your face worldwide, and get all kinds of other info by using an *online service.* (Examples of online services: America Online and CompuServe.)

Depending on how much of a computerphile you intend to become, a modem can be as exciting an addition to your life as, say, taking up aerobics or getting cable TV. If your printer blows up, you could scream for help on an electronic bulletin board, and you'd get it. If you have Macs both at work and at home, you can send documents back and forth over the phone wires. Some people phone *all* their work in to the office; these people are called *telecommuters* (or *lucky slobs,* depending on whom you ask).

In fact, if you have a PowerBook (a laptop Mac) with a modem, you can do something *really* neat. Suppose you're out in the Alaskan tundra and you realize you left those critical third-quarter sales reports on your regular office Mac in Chagrin Falls, Ohio. If the Ohio Mac also has a modem, you can actually dial in to your office, turn on the Ohio Mac automatically, get the documents you need, turn off the Ohio Mac — all by long-distance remote control. To do this, you need a program called AppleTalk Remote Access.

Coping with bauds

Just like computers, modems come equipped with different amounts of speed and power; just like cars, the more speed you have, the more the thing costs. Instead of miles per hour, which would probably be a more user-friendly measurement, modem speed is measured by its *baud rate.* (Note the spelling. *Bawd* rate is something completely different, having to do with barroom womanizing in 17th-century England.) I wouldn't try to explain what a baud is even if I knew. I *can* tell you, though, that the available modem speeds are 300, 1200, 2400, 9600, and 14,400 baud. (All right, you weenies. It's more correct to say 300 *bps,* 1200 *bps,* and so on, but who bothers?)

Almost nobody uses the lowest two speeds anymore. The 2400, 9600, and 14,400 (usually called 14.4) baud rates are the most common today. The 28,800 (28.8) type will certainly be the speed-o'-the-future (but at this point is way-2-expensive).

In addition to the modem, you'll also need some software. If you want to communicate directly to another Mac, you'll need a program like ClarisWorks, MicroPhone, ZTerm, SmartCom, or White Knight (and so does the person on the other end of the phone). If, instead, you want to hook up to an online service (see the section on online services later in this chapter), then you probably won't need to buy any software; the service you're subscribing to usually provides free software that works with their system.

And, of course, you'll need to rig some kind of phone-line connection for your modem, either by adding a Y-splitter jack to your existing phone line or by using a separate line.

Another stupid etymology worth skipping

Sorry to do this, but the weenies will claim I didn't do my job if I don't reveal the usual boring explanation for the word *modem*.

The word comes from the first syllables of the words *modulator* and *demodulator*. When a modem modulates, it's sending very rapid on/off pulses, kind of like a Morse code operator on a nicotine fit. That's how it talks to other computers. The computer on the other end translates (demodulates) those on/off signals back into intelligible text (or graphics or music or whatever you're sending).

Fax/modems

While we're talking about buying modems, you might also want to consider a *fax/modem*. Today, almost *every* modem is a fax/modem, meaning that instead of just being a modem, it can also turn your Mac into a big gray fax machine. A fax/modem can receive any kind of fax; the incoming document appears on your Mac screen, where you can read it, print it on your printer, or throw it away.

To *send* a fax, you prepare the document (that you want to send) on your Mac. For most people, that means typing it up in a word processor. This, of course, is the one major disadvantage to owning a fax/modem instead of a real fax machine: you can only send documents that are on the Mac. You can't fax someone, for example, an article from *MAD* magazine because it doesn't exist on your Mac screen. (Unless you go to the trouble of buying a scanner and scanning it in.)

Online services

One of the neatest things you can do with a modem is dial into an *online service*. The most popular ones are called America Online and CompuServe. You get a local phone number for each, so calling the service isn't a long-distance call. But you pay by the hour while you're connected to the service: about $3 per hour for America Online and about $10 per hour for CompuServe.

In reality, these services are gigantic rooms full of humming mainframe computers in Virginia (America Online) or Ohio (CompuServe) with gazillions of phone lines coming in so that thousands of computer users can dial in at the same time.

What you see on your screen, however, depends on the service you're using. America Online (and AppleLink, another popular one) looks just like the Mac screen you're used to: there are friendly icons and folders and buttons to click. Here's what the welcome screen might look like:

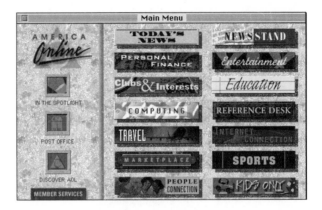

If you want to send an e-mail message to somebody, for example, you just click a button that says Send Mail.

CompuServe, on the other hand, has no graphics at all; it's basically some small text that scrolls endlessly up your screen. Most people would agree that CompuServe (like GEnie, Delphi, and other text-based services) is much harder to navigate and learn, *even* if they buy a program called CompuServe Information Manager that adds an icon-based front end to that Mother of All Networks.

On both kinds of services, though, there are some wicked-cool things to do. You can find up-to-the-minute news, sports, and weather reports, for starters. There's an electronic encyclopedia, for those middle-of-the-night bursts of curiosity about dead German philosophers. You can hook into the same airline reservation systems that travel agents use, so you can literally book your own flights. You can send faxes to anybody in the world for about a dollar a page (even though you don't have a fax machine or even a fax/modem). You can get help, overnight, for just about any computer problem.

What's especially fun about America Online is that you can have face-to-face meetings, live encounters, with up to 22 other people at once in an electronic "room." It's a real social encounter — wisecracks, social gaffes, falling in love, the whole bit — except you don't even have to comb your hair. Nobody knows your age, gender, weight, skin color, or whether or not there's spinach caught between your front teeth. There are also *private* rooms, where, legend has it, people from different parts of the world participate in the ultimate safe sex.

The 5th Wave — By Rich Tennant

"He must be a Macintosh user – there's a wristwatch icon etched on his retina."

Bulletin boards

Much less exotic, but especially practical, are local electronic bulletin board systems, known commonly as *BBSs*. A BBS is in your city and run by some computer guru. Since they're usually free, they're less polished than the expensive commercial services, but they make up for the glitz by being hotbeds of local information. You wouldn't have much luck selling your used printer on a national service, for example, but you could put an ad on your local BBS.

Like the commercial services, BBSs usually stock a huge amount of trial software free of charge, which you can transfer to your own Mac (in a process called downloading). This kind of software is called *shareware* (a computer term I actually *like*) because the programmer who wrote it wants to share it with fellow Mac owners everywhere. Instead of paying $400 for a beautifully packaged, heavily advertised program, you can download a piece of shareware from a local BBS and pay only $15 for it. And your payment is on the honor

A good solid paragraph of pathetic grubbing

If all this talk of modems and cyberspace interests you, by the way, I timidly recommend *MORE Macs for Dummies*. It was written by your humble present author, and it contains wonderfully funny, candid chapters on buying and hooking up modems, using America Online and CompuServe, tapping into the Internet, sending files to your pals, using e-mail, and other such delights.

system, at that: you only mail the guy his money if you really like the software. (Try *that* with a Microsoft program.) It's the ultimate try-before-you-buy, win-win, everybody's-happy system.

So how do you find out the number of a local BBS since that's probably the best way to try out your new modem? Well, you can ask around, of course. But a surefire (albeit roundabout) method is to call Apple at 800-538-9696 and ask them which Macintosh User Group is nearest to you. Once you know, call up the user group and ask *them* what some phone numbers of local BBSs are. Then dial away and have fun! I can almost guarantee it — you won't remember having tied up the phone for so long since you were a teenager.

CD-ROM

Nothing spices up a good discussion like a baffling computer equipment acronym, y'know?

Fortunately, you already know half of this one: CD stands for Compact Disc, just like the ones that let you play Ella Fitzgerald on your stereo. Instead of holding music, though, a CD-ROM disc holds computer information — *tons* of it. (Don't even worry about what ROM stands for. It'd leave you more confused than you may be already.)

If you have a CD-ROM player — a $300 gizmo that plugs into the back of your Mac — you can play CD-ROM discs. They contain pictures, sound, movies, graphics, and text . . . enough to keep you busy for days. Typical examples: One CD-ROM contains an encyclopedia, complete with color pictures, some of which are movies that show the motion of, say, the Venezuelan Sun Gekko. Another is a dictionary where you actually hear a guy read the pronunciation of each word. Another CD-ROM is a video game — an *interactive* one, like a TV show where *you* control where the main character goes next.

You can get a built-in CD-ROM player as an option on most Mac models. And there are more and more good CD-ROM discs worth sticking into them. A CD-ROM isn't a necessity — yet — but it'll become more and more valuable as we approach the millennium.

Speakers

Oh, yes indeedy: the Mac is more than high-tech — it's hi-*fi*. Most recent models churn out gorgeous *stereo* signals from their back-panel speaker jacks. When you listen to the Mac's tinny two-inch built-in speaker, though, you don't hear it.

If you get a pair of miniature speakers designed for the purpose, you're in for a tintinnabulating treat. If you play Mac games, particularly CD-ROM discs, you won't believe what you've been missing; the sounds are suddenly much richer and deeper. And, of course, in stereo.

If you don't do much more with sound than listen to your Mac's startup chord, don't bother buying speakers. And if you *do* want speakers, not just any old speakers will work. They must be *self-powered* and they must be *shielded;* the magnets inside normal stereo speakers are enough to distort the image on your monitor like the Sunday comics on Silly Putty. In other words, buy speakers designed for the purpose; Apple, Monster Cable, and Bose make a whole line of Mac-ready speakers.

Bonus *Macs For Dummies* 32-cent savings

I usually get a litter of letters about this chapter. They always contain the same two questions: "What CD-ROM discs should I buy?" and "Should I get a triple-speed (or quadruple-speed) CD-ROM drive?" Well, I'll save you the stamp.

First answer: Get *Myst,* a gorgeous, multiple award-winning, mysterious game/story set on an abandoned misty island. Get the Living Books discs (*Just Grandma and Me, Arthur's Teacher Trouble, The Tortoise and the Hare,* etc.) if you have kids of any variety. The encyclopedias are generally a disappointment, but the *World Book* and *Encarta* ones are pretty good. Get the *Microsoft Art Gallery.* You might consider *Street*

Atlas USA, which is a US map you can zoom in on, right down to the individual side streets — you can look up an individual street address and be shown where in the country it is.

Second answer: Don't buy the triple- and quadruple-speed CD-ROM players. These special drives are meant to play specially formatted discs. Unfortunately, there *aren't* any. You *can* play normal CD-ROM discs on 3x and 4x players. Here's the kicker, though: normal discs actually play *slower* on the 3x and 4x players than they do on *normal* CD-ROM players!

How's that for high-tech advice?

Of course, you can also plug your Mac into your existing stereo system. You just have to (a) get the right cables, and (b) learn to live with the cord trailing across the floor and into the back of your amplifier.

Music and MIDI

Oh, groan . . . it's another abbreviated computer term! All right, let's get it over with.

MIDI, pronounced like the short skirt, stands for Musical Instrument Digital Interface. What it *means* is "hookup to a synthesizer." What it *does* is let your Mac record and play back your musical performances using a synthesizer attached to it. When you record, the Mac makes a metronome sound — a steady click track — and you play to the beat. Then, when you play back the music, your keyboard plays *exactly* what you recorded, complete with feeling, expression, and fudged notes; you'd think that Elvis's ghost was playing the instrument, except that the keys don't move up and down.

The advantage of recording music in this way (yup, there's a term for this, too — it's *sequencing*) is that once you've captured your brilliant performance by recording it into the Mac, you can edit it. You can take *out* those fudged notes. You can transpose the piece into a different key. You can speed it up or slow it down *without* affecting the pitch. Why? Because this isn't a tape recording; it's a *digital* recording. Your musical MIDI information is a stream of computer numbers that describe each note you play; the Mac might instruct the keyboard, for example, to "Play middle C with this much volume. And hold the note for one-tenth of a second."

A one-person orchestra

In the real world, the most useful application of MIDI information, though, is that a single musician (or even semimusician) can make a recording that sounds like an entire band. How? you ask, eyebrows raised.

Simple: You record one musical line at a time. You play the bass line, for example; the Mac records it, nuance for nuance. Now, while the bass line plays back, you record the piano part. Then while those *two* tracks play back, you record the violins, and so on. Hate to break it to you, but virtually *all* popular music (and advertising jingles) are now recorded this way — by one Mac musician alone in a studio with a big pile of realistic-sounding synthesizers. (And I still haven't recovered from finding out, at age eight, that the whole band isn't actually at the radio station every time a song comes on.)

What you need

What you *don't* need to make MIDI music on the Mac is much musical ability. Remember, you can record something as slowly as you want, at a tempo that would slow a turtle's pulse. Then you can just change the tempo when the music plays back, and instantly you sound like you've got 18 fingers and six hands.

You do, however, need a little box that connects your Mac to the synthesizer. It's called a MIDI *interface,* and it shouldn't cost more than about $50. You also need a program that can record and play back the music, called a *sequencing program.* Some easy-to-use and inexpensive ones are EZ Vision, MusicShop, and Cubase Lite. And, of course, you need to get your hands on a synthesizer. Check out a music store and get jammin'.

Other things MIDI can do

Another popular use of the Mac is to make it write out your music for you in standard sheet music notation. Several *notation* programs (Finale, Finale Allegro, Encore) actually write down every note you play, let you edit it, add lyrics or chord symbols, and then print it out as gorgeous sheet music. These programs can even play back your music; you can listen to your masterpiece, correcting any wayward notes before committing them to paper. Presto, you're Mozart.

A Camcorder

"Say *what?*" you're saying. "This crazy author is suggesting I plug my camcorder into my computer? What's next, plugging my microwave into the vacuum?"

It's true. The hottest new use of a Macintosh is as a movie-making machine. You can actually plug your VCR or camcorder into the computer and watch in awe as your home movies pop up on the Mac screen. After you've captured your videos onto the Mac (or, more correctly, *digitized* them), with full color and sound, you can edit them, play them backward, edit out the embarrassing parts, or whatever. The technology and the movies are called QuickTime, and no other computer can do it.

The caveats of the proletariat

That's the end of the good news. QuickTime video editing takes some serious Mac horsepower: you need a fast color Mac. And unless you have a Mac model with *AV* in its name (or something with 630 in its name), you also need to buy a video *digitizing card* (the thing you actually plug your VCR into) and some movie-editing software. And you need a *lot* of hard-disk space: every minute of digitized movie on your Mac consumes about *15 megs* of disk space. (For those whose calculators don't work in megabytes, that's a hefty chunk of a typical hard disk.) Even with all that, the movies don't play back as smoothly as TV, and they play in a smallish window about the size of a Triscuit.

The very cheapest way to start making movies is to get a $100 QuickCam. It's a little mechanical eyeball that sits on top of your Mac. It only records in black-and-white, and the movies it makes are pretty jerky. But hey: *Jurassic Park* wasn't Spielberg's first movie, you know what I'm sayin'?

The next step up is the Video Spigot. It's a digitizing card (a circuit board you install into your Mac IIci, LC III, or whatever) that costs around $400. It records from your VCR or camcorder, in full color, and it makes fairly smooth movies. (It doesn't record sound, though, unless you have a microphone or a MacRecorder, as described earlier in this chapter.)

If you've got the bucks (more like $5,000), you can get one of the new generation of pro digitizing cards; instead of watching jumpy, Max Headroom-ish movies in a window on your screen so small you need a magnifying glass, you can watch very smooth, full-screen movies with stereo sound!

They still take up tons of hard-disk space, though. Of course, people just have to go buy additional hard disks to hold their movies. And when *those* disks fill up, then — hold on a second. Maybe it's time to talk about less expensive storage gadgets.

SyQuests, Bernoullis, and Tapes, Oh My!

There's only one thing wrong with hard disks: like closets, garages, and land-fills, they fill up. No matter how much of a neatness nerd you are, even if you promptly throw away anything you're finished working on, you'll gradually watch your "MB available" count go down, down, down over the months, until your hard disk is completely full. (Thousands of experienced Mac users all over the world are sagely nodding their heads in sorrowful acknowledgment.)

So what are you supposed to do? Go back to writing on Post-It notes? Well, you could buy another hard disk, of course. The one *inside* your computer is called an *internal* hard drive. If you buy another, you could plug it into the back of your Mac and have access to its contents as well. (This, as you may have guessed, would be called an *external* hard drive.) But that's an expensive proposition, and the darnedest thing of all is that *that* hard drive will fill up, too.

Remove it

For thousands of storage-starved people, the solution is to get a *removable-cartridge* system. This device looks just like an external hard drive, except when the spinning platters get full, you can just pull them out of the machine (they're sealed into a plastic cartridge) and put in a new, blank, virgin cartridge. Since an 88-megabyte cartridge only costs about $75, and a new hard disk costs $400, you can see why a removable cartridge is an attractive idea.

A removable-cartridge system solves another chronic problem, too: how to *back up* your data. To back up is to make a spare copy of your important files, so if something should happen to your main hard disk (or *you* do something to it) and all your files get erased, you haven't lost your life's work.

But placing a second copy of everything on the *same* hard disk doesn't make much sense; if the hard disk croaks, then you lose both copies. Many people copy their data onto floppy disks. That's certainly cheap, but it's inconvenient, especially if you work with large files that take forever to copy. With a removable-cartridge system, you can back up your entire hard drive in five minutes.

There are two primary makers of removable-cartridge systems: SyQuest and Bernoulli. Each makes cartridges — and the machines that play them — in various capacities; SyQuest drives cost from $300 to $500, and they take cartridges ranging from 44 to 270MB apiece. The huge advantage of SyQuest cartridges: they're extremely common. Thousands and thousands of people own them, and cartridges can be swapped back and forth, as long as swapper and swappee have the same-capacity drives.

Some say that a Bernoulli removable-cartridge drive is, technologically speaking, a slightly superior solution. (They're also more expensive than SyQuest drives.) The cartridges hold between 35 and 150MB of data, and the cartridges are incredibly tough and long-lasting. The possible drawback: there aren't as many Bernoullis in the world, so finding a fellow cartridge-swapper isn't easy (if, indeed, you care).

Another possibility for making backup copies is a *tape drive*. Instead of storing your information on metal platters, a tape drive stores it on a plain old cassette-like tape. The advantage: the special tapes are dirt cheap. The disadvantage: they're slow as frozen ketchup. Also, you can't easily retrieve just one file from a tape-backup cartridge because the computer can't easily jump from one place on the tape to another. I'm only telling you about tape backup so that you'll know to whom you're entitled to feel superior.

Networks

You already know what a *network* is. It's the television company that broadcasts stuff like *Melrose Place* so you'll have something to watch when you're burned out from computer work.

In the computer world, though, a network is defined as *more than one Mac hooked together*. In some offices, hundreds of Macs are all interconnected. Some advantages of being networked: You can send e-mail to other people, which pops up on their screens; you can have access to each others' files and programs; and you can save money by buying just one printer (or scanner or modem) for use with a whole bunch of Macs.

The goal of this book is to get you going with your *own* Mac. If you really, truly, honestly want to read about connecting Macs together (normally the domain of gurus, computer whizzes, and paid consultants), read *MORE Macs For Dummies*.

Plugging the Stuff In

Suppose you win the lottery. You buy every Mac add-on there is. Only two things left to do: give half your winnings to the IRS and figure out where to plug the stuff in. In Appendix A, you'll find a pretty good diagram of the jacks in the back of your Mac. Here's where everything goes:

- *Scanners, CD-ROM players, external hard drives, SyQuest drives, Bernoulli drives, tape-backup devices:* the SCSI port. It's the wide one with screws on each side. So how are you supposed to plug in so many different things if there's only one port? Simple — by *daisy-chaining* them, one to another. Daisy-chaining is an act of utter bravery, however, and should not be undertaken until after you've read the "Scuzzy SCSI" section in Chapter 12 and had a nice cool drink. Until then, plug *one* machine only into the SCSI jack of your Mac.

- *Apple microphone:* There's a special jack, a miniplug, just for this.

- *Modems, MIDI interfaces (music), label printers, MacRecorder, or other non-Apple microphones:* These all go into the modem port. It's the little round jobber marked by a telephone icon. So how are you supposed to plug more than one of these into your Mac? (No, there's no such thing as daisy-chaining modem-port devices.)

  You have two choices, both of which involve using only one device at a time. First, you can just unplug one device before using the next. Second, you can get an A/B switch box that acts like a Y-splitter; you plug both modem port pluggables into this box and then turn a knob to select which one you want the Mac to pay attention to. (You can even buy an A/B/C/D box that accommodates *four* devices if you've really gone crazy with this kind of peripheral.)

SCSI trivia not worth the paper it's printed on

Daisy-chaining is the act of connecting more than one peripheral gizmo to a single jack on your computer by plugging each into the back of another one. So called because, when you discover how frustrating it can be to connect multiple devices like hard drives, you'll be reduced to sitting in a field by yourself tying flowers together.

SCSI is the annoying acronym for Small Computer System Interface, pronounced even more annoyingly: "scuzzy." Actually, it refers to the wide jack with two rows of little holes located on the back of the Mac.

✔ *Camcorder, VCR:* There's no built-in jack for this, except on AV Macs. But after you buy a digitizing card and install it into one of your Mac's *expansion slots* (internal connectors), there will be a new little jack protruding from the back of the Mac (extending from the card inside).

✔ *Printer, network:* You've probably figured out, all by yourself, that the printer gets connected to the printer port (another small, round jack, next to the modem port, and marked by a printer icon). But it's good to know that this is where you plug in the cabling for a *network,* too, if you have one. (So then where does the printer go if your printer port is used up by a network connection? Easy — it gets hooked into the network so that anyone can use it. See your resident guru for details.)

Top Ten Non-Costly Mac Add-Ons

As with people, Macs that go unaccessorized are likely to be shut out of the most important social functions. But not every add-on has to cost a million bucks, as the following list demonstrates.

1. *A mouse pad.* It's a foam rubber mat that protects the desk and the mouse from each other, gives your mouse better traction, and keeps cookie crumbs out of the mouse mechanism. It often carries the same kinds of promotional graphics as T-shirts and bumper stickers.

2. *A dust cover.* Basically, it's a specially shaped bag you drape over your Mac at night to keep the dust storms out. You might get one for your keyboard, too.

3. *A glare filter.* I think they make the screen too dim, but lots of people use them and think they make the screen easier to look at.

4. *Disk boxes.* They hold your floppy disks. A nylon disk *wallet* holds about ten disks in a fold-up thing you can put in your breast pocket. Disk boxes hold between 10 and 100 disks, and come in every possible material from plastic to polished teak. (Actually, I've found that one of those colorful plastic Thermos-brand *lunch boxes* from Woolworth's makes the very best disk box. It holds 100 floppies perfectly, has a handle, and snaps securely shut. Just remember not to get it mixed up with your *kid's* colorful plastic Thermos-brand lunch box — peanut butter and jelly can impair the performance of your disk drives.)

5. *A carrying case.* For PowerBooks — and the older, one-piece Macs like the Classic or SE — these rugged, padded protective bags are extremely helpful in transporting your machine. Even if it's in one of these cases, don't ever check your computer as baggage on a plane (unless it's in the original cardboard box with its Styrofoam protectors).

6. *A trackball.* People who don't like computer mice often take great delight in replacing their Mac mouse with a trackball. A trackball looks like an eight ball set into a six-inch square base; you move the pointer on the screen by rolling the ball in place with your fingers. (Many PowerBook models have a built-in trackball in the center below the keyboard.)

7. *A surge suppressor.* This thing looks like an ordinary multiple-outlet extension cord from the hardware store, but it's supposed to have an additional benefit — circuitry that can absorb an electrical voltage surge, and thus protect your Mac from a wayward bolt of lightning. Not many people realize that the Mac already has a *built-in* surge suppressor, however. Furthermore, a surge suppressor's value has long been debated. (They're not designed to protect you from acts of God, though. I've known people with surge suppressors whose Macs got fried by lightning, as well as people *without* surge suppressors whose houses were struck by lightning without affecting the Mac.) Let your paranoia be your guide.

8. *A one-switch multiple-outlet box.* In other words, an extension-cord thing that lets you plug in your Mac, hard drive, printer, and so on, so that they all turn on when you flip a single switch. Such devices usually have a surge suppressor built-in, by the way. My favorite is the PowerKey, which is designed especially for the Mac, has four surge-protected outlets, and lets you turn the Mac on by pressing the big triangle key on your keyboard (even if you have a back-panel power-switch model, like an LC or a Quadra 605 or 630, whose big triangle keys usually do nothing).

9. *A paper clip.* Man, talk about low cost. Nonetheless, the true Mac cognoscenti keep a straightened paper clip next to their machines — it's the only way to remove a floppy disk that's stuck in the disk drive. (See the sidebar in Chapter 2, "Dweebs' Corner: Alternative disk tips.")

10. *Spare printer cartridges.* Have an extra ribbon, cartridge, or drum for your printer (depending on what it is) at all times. Murphy's Law, or whatever law governs computers, states that the printer cartridge you're using now will not wear out until you're halfway through a large printing project that's due shortly and all the stores are closed.

Chapter 8

Putting the Mouse to the Metal

• •

In This Chapter

▶ Uncovering the forbidden secrets of the Option key

▶ Duplicating, finding, and splitting the personality of icons

▶ Vandalizing your own Mac, without spray paint or a sledge hammer

▶ Utilities with no monthly bill

• •

*T*his chapter is about honing the basic skills you already have. It's about becoming more efficient in the way you work — shortcuts, hidden secrets, and slick tricks to astonish your friends. And it's about turning the basic Mac that *millions* of people have into one that's unmistakably yours.

Maybe it'd be better if I avoided the term that's about to apply to you . . . *power user.* Maybe those words will strike fear once again into your soul. But even if you started *out* as a Mac virgin, either leery or outright petrified about the alien technology before you, by now you've almost completely mastered the Mac. The only tidbits left to explore are the ones normally classified as — yes — *power-user secrets!*

The Efficiency Nut's Guide to the Option Key

Yeah, yeah, everybody knows that you can close a window by clicking its close box. But you didn't fork over good money for this book to learn something that's on page 1 of the Mac manual.

No, these tips are much choicer. They show you how to unlock the power of that most overlooked of keys, the Option key. It's been placed closer to you than any letter key on the keyboard — and that's no accident.

Closing all windows at once

Suppose that you've opened a gaggle of folders and their windows are lying open all over the screen. And suppose that the niggling neatness ethic instilled in you by your mother compels you to clean up a bit.

You could, of course, click the close box of each window, one at a time. But it's far faster to click only *one* window's close box while pressing the Option key. Bam, bam, bam — they all close automatically, one after another.

Windows and folders: Developing tunnel vision

When you're trying to find a document icon that's inside a folder inside a folder inside a folder, it's hard to avoid having COWS (Cluttered, Overlapping Windows Syndrome). By the time you finally arrive at the darned icon, your screen is filled with windows.

If you press Option while double-clicking each nested folder, though, the Mac will neatly close the *previous* window before opening the next one. Criminy — this computer even *cleans up* after you!

In the figure below, you could press Option while double-clicking the Oregon folder (left); the USA folder that contains it would automatically close as the new window opened (right):

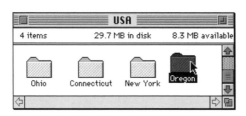 

OK. So here we are in the Oregon folder. What if we want to backtrack and go back to the USA folder (or the World folder)? There's a little-known trick that lets you jump to the folder that *contains* it: press the ⌘ key and click the window's title!

In the preceding figure, you ⌘-click the word Oregon at the top of the window. Now you slide down the pop-up menu that lists the nested folders from innermost to outermost. Let go when you reach the folder you want (following left); the Mac opens the folder you selected (following right).

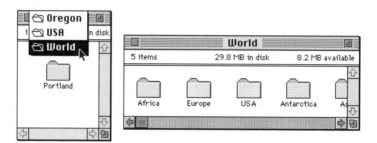

And, logically enough, if you press ⌘ *and* Option as you choose the new folder name, you'll simultaneously close the original nested window.

The silence of the Trash

Let's review: You drag an icon on top of the Trash can and the icon disappears. The Trash can bulges. You smile gently at the zaniness of it all. Then you choose Empty Trash from the Special menu, and a little message appears on the screen, saying something like:

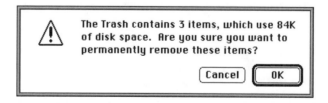

That's all very well and good, but busy Americans concerned with increasing their productivity may not always have time for such trivial information. Therefore, if you want to dump the trash, but you *don't* want that message to appear, press Mr. Option Key while you choose Empty Trash. (Option is also the key for emptying the trash when the Mac tells you there's something "locked" in the Trash can.)

'Smatterafact, you can shut up the Trash's warning permanently, if you're so inclined. Click the Trash can. Choose Get Info from the File menu. Turn off "Warn before emptying." What an improvement!

Multitasking methods

As you discovered early on, the Mac lets you run more than one program simultaneously. (Remember when you tried some tricks with both the Note Pad and the Calculator open on the screen at once?) You can switch from one program to another by choosing the program's name from the Application menu at the top right of your screen, marked by the ▣ icon (or the icon of whichever program is currently in front).

We haven't yet examined the other commands in this menu, such as Hide Others and Show All. These are anti-COWS commands that help keep your screen neat and clean. For example, suppose that you're trying to use the Calculator, but so many other programs are running that your eyes cross:

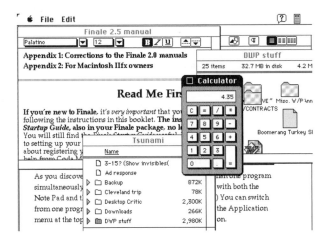

By choosing Hide Others from the Application menu, all windows that belong to other programs disappear, leaving the frontmost window all by itself:

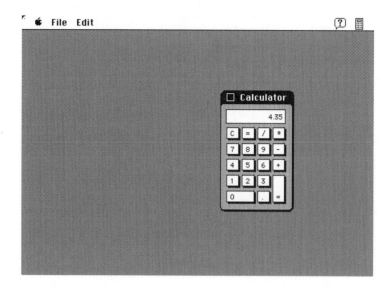

The other programs *are still running,* and they *do* still exist. But their windows are now hidden. You can verify this by checking the Application menu, where you'll see that their icons appear dimmed.

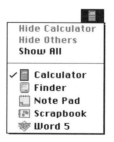

So how does the Option key play into all this? When you switch from one program to another, you can make the program you're *leaving* hide itself automatically. Just press Option while choosing the new program's name (or clicking in its window). That way you always keep nonessential programs hidden.

Making an instant document copy

In most Mac graphics programs, the Option key has a profound effect on a selected graphic item: it peels off a copy of the selected graphic as you drag the mouse. For example, the left eye (right) is selected and then Option-dragged to the right:

You can accomplish essentially the same thing in the Finder, making duplicates of your files instead of eyeballs. Normally, when you drag an icon from one folder to another *on the same disk,* of course, you simply move that icon. But if you press Option while dragging an icon to a new folder (or to the Desktop — the gray background), the Mac places a *copy* of the file in the new folder and leaves the original where it was, as shown here:

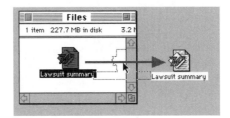

Alphabetize them icons!

For the neat freak, there's nothing worse than a mass of messy icons cluttering a window (next page, top). If you choose Clean Up Window from the Special menu, the Mac will align each icon to an invisible grid so that at least they're neatly arranged (next page, lower left). But (1) that won't alphabetize them, and (2) that won't maximize space in the window by eliminating gaps.

If you press Option while choosing Clean Up Window, though, it changes to say Clean Up by Name. And the effect is totally different — the Mac (1) alphabetizes your icons, and (2) moves them so that they take up as little window space as possible (above, right!).

Folder before cleaning up

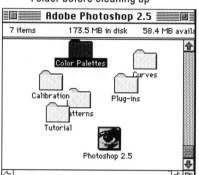

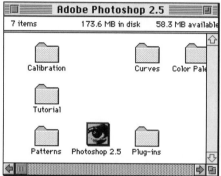

Normal Clean Up

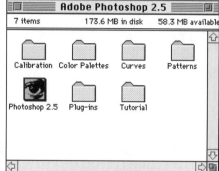

Clean Up using the Option key

Funny little hidden Option key stunts

Those wily Apple guys! The sneaky programmers! The funsters in Apple Land have buried all kinds of amusing little surprises in the control panels and other places (of System 7). Try these:

- The weird little Map control panel lets you find any major city by latitude and longitude, and tells you what the time zone difference is. If you Option-double-click the Map control panel, the map will appear at double size.

- Open the Monitors control panel (choose Control Panels from the menu and double-click Monitors). You use this panel to switch from color to black and white (if you have a color monitor). If you hold the mouse down on the little "7.0" (or "7.5") in the upper-right corner, you'll see a list of the programmers. Press Option while you do so, and watch the smiley face — you'll find out what they really think of you.

✔ When you're in the Finder, the first item under the ⌘ menu normally says About This Macintosh. Choose it to view some critical specifications about your machine — how much memory it has, for example. But if you press Option while choosing it, the command changes to say About the Finder and shows you a pleasant Silicon Valley scene. Wait long enough, and you'll eventually see some scrolling credits.

✔ Open the Memory control panel. See the part called Virtual Memory? (Some older Macs don't have this section.) Click the On button. Then, while pressing (what else?) the Option key, click the pop-up menu on the right side and keep the button pressed. And move the pointer to the right so that the submenus pop out. Wow — it's more fun than reading the phone book!

Buried Treasures

Did you enjoy those obscure, mostly useless Option key tricks? Then you'll really love these equally scintillating techniques, not one of which requires the Option key.

How to find a lost file

You haven't really poked around much with the Find command, but it's a doozie. Just choose Find from the File menu (or use the keyboard equivalent ⌘-F), and this box appears:

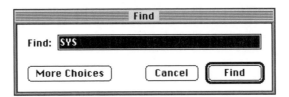

If you have System 7.5 or later, your Find box looks slightly different — flip back to Chapter 6 for a complete description.

Anyway, in the highlighted text box, type a few identifying letters of the name of the file you're looking for. For example, if (by some improbable cosmic acci-dent) you can't find your System Folder, you could just type *SYS* and then click

Find. It doesn't matter whether you type capitals or lowercase letters. The Finder will look for the nearest file that *contains* (not necessarily *begins with*) the letters you've specified.

You can buy any of a zillion programs and desk accessories that are designed to find lost files. But the Finder's Find command is the only one that actually produces the lost file's *icon*, opening its folder for you and highlighting the icon:

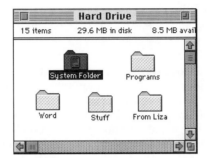

But what if there are several files on your disk that contain the same letters? Easy. Each time the Find command displays the wrong icon, choose Find Again from the File menu. Or just press ⌘-G, as in, "Guess again, diskbrain." The Mac will hunt through your files and highlight the next one it finds that contains those same letters. (Again, the ending is happier in System 7.5; you're shown the complete list of matching files to *begin* with. No ⌘-G necessary.)

If you click the More Choices button, the dialog box expands to show you some other search criteria, such as date, file size, and so on. You could, if you really wanted to, find a certain document whose name you couldn't remember, but that you're certain you created at 3 p.m. during a NoDoz-crazed fit on August 4th.

Make an alias of a file

In the File menu, there's a command called Make Alias. Although you might expect this command to generate names like One-Eyed Jake or Bubba Wilcox, the term *alias* in the Macintosh world represents something slightly different — a duplicate of a file's icon (but not a duplicate of the file itself). You can identify the alias icon because its name is in italics, as shown here. (The original file is on the left.)

What's neat about aliases is that, when you double-click an alias icon, the Mac opens the *original* file. If you're a true '90s kinda person, you might think of the alias as a beeper — when you call the *alias,* the *actual* file responds.

So who on earth would need a feature like this? Well, there's more to the story. An alias, for one thing, only requires a tiny amount of disk space (a couple of K) — so it's not the same as making an *actual copy* of the original file. (And you can make as many aliases of a file as you want.) Therefore, making an alias of something you use frequently is an excellent time-saver — it keeps the alias icon readily accessible, even if the real file is buried four folders deep somewhere.

Another very common trick: Place an alias of a program, or a document, into your menu, where you don't have to open *any* folders to get at it.

Here's the drill:

1. Click the real icon once.

2. Choose Make Alias from the File menu.

3. Open your System Folder.

4. Drag the alias into the folder called Apple Menu Items (within the System Folder).

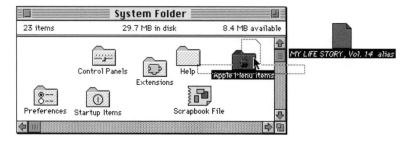

5. Now look in your menu.

Trash, aliases, and a word of caution

When you trash an alias, you're only deleting the alias. The original file is still on your disk. If you delete the *original* file, however, the alias icons will remain uselessly on your disk, rebels without a cause, babies without a mother, days without sunshine. When you double-click an alias whose original file is gone, you'll just get an error message.

Likewise, if you copy your inauguration speech file's *alias* to a floppy disk, thinking that you'll just print it out when you get to Washington, think again: you've just copied the alias, but you *don't* actually have any text. That's all in the original file, still at home on your hard disk.

Sure enough — there's your file! Choose it from the menu to open the original file.

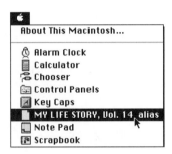

And yet, because you used an alias, the *real* file can be anywhere on your hard disk or on a different disk. You can move the real file from folder to folder or even rename it, and the alias still opens it properly.

Creating the L.L. Mac catalog

Every now and then, you might find it useful to create a list of files or folders on your disk. But it's hardly worth your time to go to the Finder, look at the first file's name, switch to your word processor and type it, and then repeat with the second file. Here's a much faster way:

1. Select the files whose names you want to copy. (You might want to use the Select All command in the Edit menu, at which point you can press the Shift key and click "off" the items you don't want.)

2. Choose Copy from the Edit menu (next page, left).

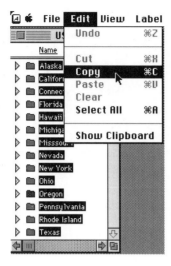

3. Launch your word processor (or even the Note Pad under the menu) and choose Paste from the Edit menu. Presto: a neatly typed list of file names (above, right)!

(P.S. — The list can't be a terrifically long one; the Mac copies only 256 characters of text at a time, but you can always repeat the process.)

Have it your way — at Icon King

You don't have to accept those boring old icons for files, programs, and folders. If you want anything done around the Mac, heaven knows, you've got to do it yourself.

1. Go into ClarisWorks or Kid Pix or some other program that lets you paint stuff. Make a funny little picture. And I mean *little* — remember, you're drawing a replacement icon for some hapless file. Like this guy here, for example:

2. Copy it to the Clipboard.

3. Go to the Finder, and click the file whose icon you want to replace.

4. Choose Get Info from the File menu so that this box appears:

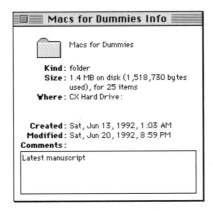

5. See the folder icon in the upper left? Click that sucker — and then paste away!

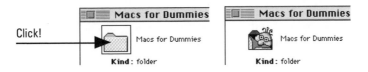

From now on, that little picture is the new icon for the file (or folder, or disk). To restore the original icon, repeat the Get Info business, but this time, after you click the icon, press the Clear key.

Taking a picture of the screen

In this book, you've probably noticed a number of pictures that illustrate objects on the Mac screen. Now I'll show you how to take your own snapshots of the screen.

It involves pressing three keys simultaneously: Command (⌘), Shift, and 3. You hear a satisfying *kachunk!* camera-shutter sound. After a moment, a new file appears in your hard disk window, called Picture 1. (If you take another shot, it'll be called Picture 2, and so on.)

If you double-click this Picture file, it will open in TeachText or SimpleText (which came with your Mac). Once TeachText/SimpleText opens, you'll see that you've successfully captured your screen image.

(If you have a more stalwart graphics program, such as Photoshop or Canvas, you can instead use *it* to view your Picture 1 file. Launch the program first and then choose Open from its File menu.)

Unfortunately, you don't have much control over this photo-session business: the ⌘-Shift-3 keystroke captures the *entire screen*. Once you're viewing the snapshot in TeachText or SimpleText, though, you can select a smaller portion of it. Just drag diagonally across the part you want.

Once you've got a shimmering rectangle, choose Copy from the Edit menu. That selected area is now on your invisible Clipboard. Open up the Scrapbook or your word processor or ClarisWorks or some other program. And then Paste (Edit menu). Your newly pasted screen shot appears.

Just say no

There's a wonderful keyboard shortcut that means *no* in Mac language. It could mean *No, I changed my mind about printing* (or copying or launching a program); *stop right now.* It could mean *No, I didn't mean to bring up this dialog box; make it go away.* Or: *No, I don't want to broadcast my personal diary over worldwide e-mail!* Best of all, it can mean *Stop asking for that disk! I've already taken it out of your slot! Be gone!*

And that magic keystroke is ⌘-period (.).

When you begin to print your Transcripts of Congress, 1952–1992, and you discover — after only two pages have printed — that you accidentally spelled it "Transcripts of Congrotesque" on every page, ⌘-period will prevent the remaining 14 million pages from printing. Because the Mac has probably already sent the next couple of pages to the printer, the response won't be immediate but will be light-years quicker than waiting for Congress.

Or let's say you double-click an icon by mistake. If you press ⌘-period *right away,* you can halt the launching and return to the Finder. And if the Mac keeps saying, "Please insert the disk: Purple Puppychow" (or whatever your floppy disk was called), you can tell it to shut up by doing that ⌘-period thing over and over again until the Mac settles down with a whimper. Show it who's boss.

Colorizing and Other Acts of Vandalism

The great thing about the Mac is that it's not some stamped-out clone made in Korea. It's one of a kind — or it will be after we get through with it. These tips illustrate some of the ways you can make the Mac match your personality, sensibility, or décor.

Changing the background pattern

When you first turn on a new Mac (Performas and System 7.5 Macs not included), the desktop area (the background) presents a lovely shade of uninteresting gray. You can easily change this to any other pattern of black-and-white dots — or, if you have a color Mac, to any elaborate arrangement of colored dots. Here's how.

From the menu, choose Control Panels. Double-click the General Controls icon, and you'll see this:

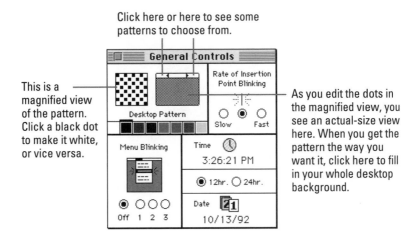

Click here or here to see some patterns to choose from.

This is a magnified view of the pattern. Click a black dot to make it white, or vice versa.

As you edit the dots in the magnified view, you see an actual-size view here. When you get the pattern the way you want it, click here to fill in your whole desktop background.

As shown in the diagram, the upper-left quadrant of the General Controls panel contains the tools you need to change the backdrop pattern. At left, there's a magnified view, which lets you easily edit each dot that constitutes the overall pattern. At right, you see the overall pattern — in other words, you see what's in the "magnified view" repeated over and over again.

Desktop vandalism for System 7.5 and Performa fans

As hinted above, you can't edit your desktop pattern in the General Controls panel if your Mac is a Performa or has System 7.5 (see Chapter 6 to find out what the heck that is). Or...can you?

If you have a pre-1995 Performa, open your General Controls control panel, exactly as described in "Changing the background pattern." There you'll see a pop-up menu of available desktop patterns, all prettier and more colorful than anything the non-Performa folk could ever hope for.

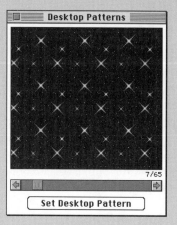

Use the scroll bar at the bottom to view the other possible patterns and textures. When you see one you like, click the Set Desktop Pattern button.

And if you want to make up your *own* patterns, you can do so easily. Use any program that can create graphics: ClarisWorks, Word, Photoshop, FileMaker, anything. Design a square's worth of artwork, and copy it. Open the Desktop Patterns control panel, as pictured above, and paste in your graphic! Now you can apply your own artwork to your desktop, and stare at it all day long.

Of course, you can't make your *own* patterns. Unless you get System 7.5 for your Performa.

In its Control Panels folder (which you open from the menu), System 7.5 has something called Desktop Patterns. When you open it, you get something like this:

If you have a color (or grayscale) monitor, you can use the row of eight colored squares beneath the magnified view. Double-click one of these squares to change the color it displays. Once that's done, treat these color swatches as a palette — click a swatch and then start clicking dots in the magnified view to change their colors.

Anyway, the point is that when you're finished editing the magnified view at left (to show, for example, your initial), you have to click in the normal-size view (to its right) to make the pattern "take" and fill in your desktop backdrop. Furthermore, you have to *double-click* the normal-size view if you want your new pattern saved for future use.

Here are a few pattern ideas to get you started.

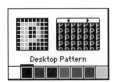 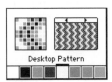 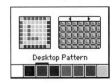

Color-coding your icons

There's another pretty neat colorization feature that hardly anyone uses, but it's still worth knowing about: color-coding. All you do is select an icon or a whole passel of them (below, left), and choose a color from the Label menu.

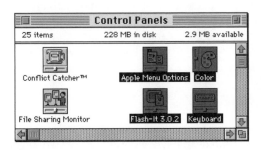 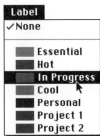

If you don't have a color monitor, you can still attach descriptive labels to your icons (Essential, Hot, In Progress, and so on), even though you won't see the colors.

Two questions, then: (1) How do you change the colors and labels into something more useful, and (2) what's the point?

Well, most people never bother with labeling their icons. You could argue, though, that it makes life more convenient since you can *sort* by label (you could see all your In Progress files grouped together in a window). You can also use the Find command to search for a file that has a certain label. You might give one label to everything related to, say, a certain book project — "Saddam Hussein: The Sensitive Side" — and then when it's time to back up your work, use the Find command to round up all files with the Hussein label, so you can copy them all at once. (Or, when the project is over, you could happily *delete* them all at once.)

Anyway, if you *do* want to use this feature, you'll probably want to change the labels Apple suggests (Essential, Hot, In Progress, and so on) to something more useful. To do that, choose Control Panels from the menu. When the Control Panels window appears, double-click Labels.

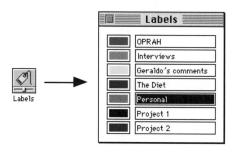

To change the wording of a label (remember, you're actually changing the wording of the Label *menu*), just double-click a label and type in something new. To change the color — if your monitor is thus equipped — click the color swatch; a dialog box appears where you can select a new color by clicking.

Blue language

Here's one more treat for color monitor owners: you can make highlighted text turn some color other than drab black. In other words, when you select some text in your word processor, it usually looks like this:

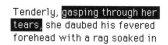

To change the highlighting so that it looks more like, well, a *highlighter,* choose Control Panels from the menu. When the Control Panels window appears, double-click Color. This control panel appears:

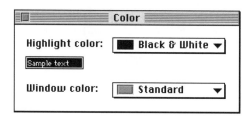

By choosing a new color from the upper pop-up menu, you can make your highlighted text any color you want, like this:

a vile mixture of Jack Daniels, sparkling water, and Pond's skin cream.

Let your innate fashion sense be your guide.

Views

Open the Views control panel. This baby is the control freak's best friend — it can change almost every aspect of the way the Finder displays icons.

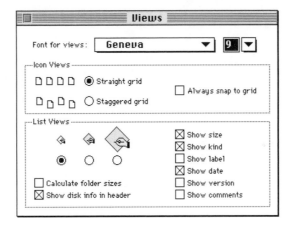

Using the font and size controls at the top of the window, you get to choose what text style you want the Mac to use for all icons in the Finder. If your vision is going — or you're trying to demonstrate the Mac to a crowd — make the font huge. If you want to make your icons as high as possible per square inch, pick a tiny, compact type style. Here's one possibility:

The Icon Views controls let you specify how icons should arrange themselves when you drag them around. If you select "Always snap to grid," icons will smartly jump into position whenever you drag them and let go, according to your Icon Views setting: "Straight grid" places them into neat rows, and "Staggered grid" offsets every other icon so that their names won't overlap when they're placed side by side.

The List Views control governs how icons appear when you're viewing them in a list format.

All those checkboxes on the right side ("Show size," "Show kind," and so on) control which pieces of information show up when you're in a list view. "Calculate folder sizes" is neat because it lets you see how much disk space each folder takes up. (If this checkbox isn't selected, then all you get is an unhelpful "—" in the Size column of a list view. On the other hand, some people think that turning on this option tends to make window contents appear more slowly.)

Finally, "Show disk info in header" puts a separate information strip at the top of each window, which shows you how full your disk is.

U R A recording studio

With many Macs, you get an Apple microphone (or you can buy one). It's not exactly the same one Madonna licks in her videos, but it's good enough for what we're about to do. And that is to change the little beep/ding sound the Mac makes (when you make a mistake) into some other sound, like "Oops!" or a game-show buzzer or a burp or something.

Here's how it works:

1. From the menu, choose Control Panels.

2. Double-click the Sound icon.

(Weird, convoluted note: If your control panel's *slider* is labeled Alert Sound Volume — instead of Speaker Volume — then read the sidebar called "Additional steps for the modern Mac owner.")

3. When you see the Sound control panel, click the Add button. (If your Mac has no microphone or CD-ROM player attached, the Add button is dimmed). Now you see this:

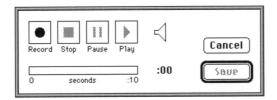

4. To record, just click Record and speak into the microphone.

Be ready to click Stop when you're done, or else you'll accidentally include a bunch of silence and fumbling at the end of your sound.

There's a plethora of ways to play back your new sound. You could, mnemonically enough, click the Play button. Then again, you could click Save and give the sound a title, so that you'll be able to preserve it for your grandchildren. When you return to the list of sounds in the Sound control panel, click your new sound's name to play it. If you leave it selected in the list, though, you've just selected it to be your new error beep.

A sound-playing fact for the detail-obsessed

Here's a way to play a sound that doesn't even involve opening a control panel. If you're a double-clicking kinda person, open your System Folder and then double-click the System *file*. It opens into a window showing all your fonts and all your sounds. Just double-click any sound's icon to hear it played.

Additional steps for the modern Mac owner

In their finite wisdom, the mad scientists at Apple Computer recently changed what the Sound control panel looks like.

Old style   New style with menu

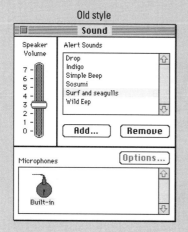 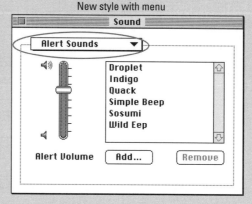

If you have the old-style panel, please rejoin the sound-recording instructions now in progress. If you have the *new* panel, first locate the little pop-up menu at the top. Click there, and choose Sound In.

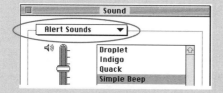 

Now the display changes to the one shown above (right). If you indeed have a microphone attached to your Mac, click the appropriate icon at the bottom of this screen. (Other sound sources that may show up here: your CD-ROM player; a MacRecorder; the microphone built into an AudioVision monitor; and so on.)

When you've selected the appropriate sound source, use the pop-up menu again. Go back to Alert Sounds. And then go back to step 3 in the sound-recording instructions.

Utilities with No Monthly Bill

Even as you've been taking your first tremulous steps on this most wondrous of computers, thousands of hackers, in a grand effort to make this insanely great computer even greater, have been slaving away late at night, for weeks at a time, subsisting primarily on three-cheese pizza and Jolt cola ("Twice the caffeine! And all the sugar!").

You'd be amazed at the things they come up with. Today you can buy programs that make your hard disk hold more, automatically type out your return address on cue, or — most important of all — send a squadron of aerodynamic toasters flapping across your screen. These are called *utility* programs; here's an overview.

Compression programs

Run a large file through a *compression* program, and it emerges from the other end at about half its original size. (Too bad you can't run the government through one.) Multiply that size-reduction process by all your files, and all of a sudden your hard disk can hold twice as much. It's almost like getting a second hard drive free.

Two of the best-known file-compression programs are StuffIt and the shareware program Compact Pro. The simplest and most useful, however (if you ask me), is DiskDoubler. This ultra-clever program adds a new menu to your menu bar in the Finder, containing Compress and Expand commands. To shrink a file, just click it and then choose Compress.

Best of all, DiskDoubled files decompress themselves automatically — a double-click does the trick. Why is that a big deal? Because in most other compression programs, you have to launch a special program each time you want to compress or decompress a file.

Oh, P.S.: Do *not* fall for the programs called things like Times Two and Stacker. They're advertised to make your disk hold twice as much information, but they use a scary method of doing so — you'll definitely slow your Mac down, and you'll also run the risk of losing all your files. "Other than that, Mrs. Lincoln, how did you like the play?"

Screen savers

If you've ever seen the ghost of a cash machine's welcoming screen permanently etched in the display, you'll understand the reason for *screen savers*. By automatically blanking the screen after a few minutes of disuse, these programs ensure that your Mac monitor won't suffer the same burn-in syndrome if you accidentally leave the computer on for the whole week you're in Acapulco. To signal you that the computer is still on, however, a screen saver must bounce some moving image around the screen. That's where the fun comes in.

The programmers of these utilities figure: if you've got to display some "I'm still on!" signal on the monitor, it might as well be entertaining. That's why today's screen savers let you choose from dozens of different patterns or animations to fill your screen while you're ignoring the Mac: wild, psychedelic lava-lampish images, sharks swimming back and forth, fireworks, swirling lines, slithering worms, and so on. The most popular commercial screen saver is After Dark, which displays the now-famous Flying Toasters in Space, or a Lawnmower Man whose riding mower gradually eats up whatever document you were working on. You get your regular screen back by touching the mouse or keyboard.

Do you really need one of these? Nah. You'd have to leave your Mac turned on for *months,* untouched, to get screen burn-in. On the one-piece Macs, you can just turn down the screen brightness; on many other models, you can use the Energy Saver control panel to black out your screen if you haven't used the Mac in half an hour. But frankly, screen savers are really, really neat, and sort of *de rigeur* among the computing elite. And they help you justify having bought a color monitor.

Anti-virus software

A computer virus, as you may have read, is a program written by some jerk from a dysfunctional family who seeks to bolster his own self-worth by gumming up other people's Macs. There have been a dozen or so Macintosh viruses — little self-duplicating programs that attach themselves to innocent software, whereupon they duplicate some more, until every disk that passes through your floppy-disk drive is infected. You can't get a computer virus unless you (1) swap disks with friends or (2) use a modem to connect to other Macs over the phone.

As you'll read in Chapter 9, no widespread Mac virus has ever destroyed files; they usually just make funny beeps or display some dumb message. But playing on virus paranoia, many companies offer anti-virus programs for sale, charging you money for an update every time a new virus is discovered. Virex, S.A.M., and Gatekeeper are a few.

I find those programs very disruptive, always interrupting your workday every time they (usually wrongly) suspect something unusual going on. If you're really worried about viruses, get Disinfectant, which is free. It watches over your Mac, tells you if you've contracted a virus, and wipes it out for you.

(Disinfectant comes from the usual sources of noncommercial software: your local user group has it, and you can get it from a dial-up online service or bulletin board. Or just send a disk to the author; I've provided his address in Appendix B.)

Top Ten Free or Almost-Free Utility Programs

Airborne appliances may be charming, but they cost money. Your other Mac utilities don't have to be. Here are ten good ones, all of them shareware. (In case you missed it, you get shareware from a user group, electronic bulletin board, or online service like America Online.)

1. *Before Dark.* Before Dark lets you plaster your desktop with a choice of 30 stunning, 3-D, brilliantly colored background textures and patterns that blow the standard set of Mac patterns out of the proverbial water.

2. *Disinfectant.* As described earlier.

3. *Compact Pro* or *StuffIt Classic.* File-compression programs. Not as convenient — and not as fast — as DiskDoubler, but then again much cheaper.

4. *SuperClock.* Puts a little digital clock at the upper right of your screen, in the typeface of your choice, so you'll always know exactly how late you are. (Built into System 7.5.)

5. *System 7 Pack.* When Apple upgraded its system software (i.e., all that junk in the System Folder) to System 7, many Mac owners rejoiced. But a few sighed because System 7 makes things in the Finder slower — things like opening windows and copying files. But System 7 Pack, written by a teenager in New Jersey, takes care of both problems. It makes windows open faster and makes your Mac copy files three times faster. (It's not so critical in System 7.5.)

6. *SCSI Probe.* You power up the Mac, but your hard-drive icon doesn't appear. If you have SCSI Probe (or the nearly identical SCSI Info), you can find out the make, model, capacity, and SCSI address of every SCSI device attached to your Mac, and more. It has a Mount button that can often bring a SCSI device on line if it's acting flaky. (SCSI is like that.)

7. *Save-O-Matic.* The software for the chronic Mac procrastinator: a safety net for people who forget to save their documents regularly. This thing'll do it *for* you, every five minutes or ten minutes or whatever you specify.

8. *Remember?.* It's a desk-accessory calendar thingie. You type your appointments into its clean, colorful calendar, and it actually reminds you of each

8. *Remember?.* It's a desk-accessory calendar thingie. You type your appointments into its clean, colorful calendar, and it actually reminds you of each upcoming event. If you want, it presents you with a list of the day's schedule when you turn the computer on in the morning. If anybody cares, I think it's as good as most of the high-priced calendar/reminder programs.

9. *Moire.* It's a screen saver, as described above. No, it doesn't have flying toasters or lawnmower guys. But what the heck — it's free, and the patterns it bounces around on the screen are plenty pretty.

10. *Color Switch.* Do you know how to switch your color monitor to black and white (and back again)? It's a long, boring process: choose Control Panels from the menu, double-click Monitors, and click Color or Black and White. The whole thing is much easier if you get Color Switch, which puts a new menu at the top of your screen, from which you choose any setting: black and white, color, whatever.

Chapter 9
Screamingly Important Things Nobody Tells You

• •

• •

*I*t's amazing anybody can use computers at all, really. You're sold a computer, you're handed a manual written by people who read *Popular Semiconductor*, and you get kicked out of the nest.

Think about every important lesson you've learned in life. You learned how to be careful in relationships only after having your heart broken. You learned about con artists only after being swindled. You learned to drive more carefully only after your first accident.

It's the same way with computers. Sure, you'll learn sooner or later; but most people have to learn everything the hard way. *You* get to sit back in your La-Z-Boy and *read* about it.

It Doesn't Need to Be Repaired.

Even if something funny's going on with your Mac, the machine itself is probably fine.

Most beginners, though, immediately suspect the circuitry. I understand the instinct. I mean, when VCRs, lawnmowers, or electric razors go on the fritz, you're right — you need a repair shop. But a computer's different; it has *software*. When your Mac starts behaving oddly, it's probably a *software* problem, not a mechanical one. That means you can fix it yourself, for free. Almost always.

In Chapter 12, you'll discover the steps you can take to restore your Mac's software to health. Until then, just remember: these machines are built like rocks and almost *never* "break." (PowerBooks are another story. You would be, too, if you were hauled around in a briefcase.)

Don't Buy Version 1.0 of Anything.

This principle isn't just true of software or Macs; it's true of cars and houses and medicines, too. The rationale is simple: if it's brand new, there's no way all the bugs and kinks have been ironed out.

Even if the software company's 20 paid testers can't find any problems, it's amazing what happens when 100,000 ordinary folks start banging away. Problems crop up from nowhere, hidden bugs emerge, and the "early adopters" (people who bought the 1.0 version) pay the price.

The 5th Wave   **By Rich Tennant**

"OH YEAH, AND TRY NOT TO ENTER THE WRONG PASSWORD."

The software company rushes to correct the problems, and they release a new version called something like 1.01. *That's* the version you should buy.

You Can Leave Windows Open.

There's no reason to close all your windows before you turn off the computer. Leave 'em open when you're done for the day! They'll be waiting and ready when you start up tomorrow. You save effort on both ends.

Press Option to Fax.

If your Mac has a fax/modem, you're in for a delicious treat. Faxes sent by a Mac come out looking twice as crisp and clean when they're received by a real fax machine. And sending faxes couldn't be more convenient for you — no printout to throw away, no paper involved at all. Your Mac sends the thing directly to another fax machine's brain.

Connecting a phone line to your fax/modem (or the phone jack on your PowerBook) is the easy part. Now you have to figure out how to *send* what you want to send. Sure, you could read the manual — but who's got the time?

Here's what you do. Begin by typing (or opening) whatever it is you want to fax. Usually, this means a letter you've written in your word processor. Make sure it's in front of you on the screen.

Now take a look at your File menu, and note where it says Print. Got it?

OK, let go of the mouse now. With one hand, press and hold down the *Option key* on your keyboard. With the other, go back up to the File menu and look at the word Print. If your fax/modem is like most, that word Print has now changed to say *Fax!*

File	Edit	View	Inser
New			⌘N
Open...			⌘O
Close			⌘W
Save			⌘S
Save As...			⇧F7
Print Preview...			⌘⌥I
Page Setup...			⇧F8
Print...			⌘P
Quit			⌘Q

Normal

File	Edit	View	Inser
New			⌘N
Open...			⌘O
Close			⌘W
Save			⌘S
Save As...			⇧F7
Fax Preview...			⌘⌥I
Page Setup...			⇧F8
Fax...			⌘P
Quit			⌘Q

With Option key

If you choose the Fax command, you'll be shown some kind of address book, where you can type in your friend's fax number; you'll also see a button called something like Send or OK, which will get the fax merrily transmitting away.

Now then. If your menu *doesn't* change to say Fax when you press the Option key, then maybe you don't have one of the standard modem brands. Try looking at the menu again while pressing the *Shift and Control* keys together. (That's the key combo if you have an Apple ExpressModem or a GeoPort adapter.) Or try it again pressing the ⌘ key.

If *none* of those combinations works, then something else is afoot. Maybe you don't have the fax/modem software installed; rustle up the original disks and install it. Maybe you have that one-in-ten fax/modem brand that doesn't have the Fax-menu feature at all.

The point, though, is that you should *not* have to open up the Chooser every time you want to send a fax! I'm afraid that thousands of people aren't aware of the Option-key (or Shift/Control-key) shortcut. They still open the Chooser in the ⌘ menu, switch to the Fax icon, send the fax, open the Chooser again, switch back to their printer — a colossal waste of time and effort.

Remember, the computer is supposed to *save* you time.

Submenus Are About Horizontalness.

A *submenu* is a mini-menu that springs out of a regular menu, like this:

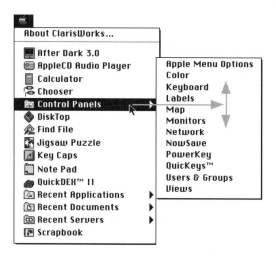

Getting one of these things to work is only slightly easier than tying your shoes with one hand.

The trick is patience. And horizontalness. Slide down to the main menu command (it's Control Panels in the figure above), and then *pause*. Now slide *directly to the right* onto the submenu; if you try to take a shortcut diagonally, the whole submenu will disappear and you'll have to start over.

Once you're squarely (and horizontally) onto the submenu, *now* you can move up or down to the command you really want.

A lot of work, I know, but it's the price we pay for progress.

A ".sit" File Has to Be Expanded.

Suppose, just for a moment, that you become a real Macintosh ace. You start using a modem to dial up the outside world. You visit America Online or a local electronic bulletin board system. You see something worth getting … maybe a program called FreeMoneyMaker 2.0. So you *download* it (transfer it to your own Mac).

FreeMoneyMaker.sit

But now you double-click the icon you got. And it says "Application not found." You've just been bit by the *.sit* bug.

A *.sit* file is one that's been compressed into a compact form, for use on modem services, using a program called StuffIt. The point is, of course, to make it smaller so it'll cost less to download or transfer to your Mac. America Online is *supposed* to unstuff *.sit* files automatically when you sign off. (It leaves the ".sit" file behind, though, so look for both the ".sit" and the expanded version when you're done using America Online.)

If, however, you somehow wind up with an un-expanded *.sit* file, you need to get your paws on a program that can expand it. There are millions of 'em. They're called things like UnStuffIt, StuffIt Expander, DropUnStuff, and, of course, StuffIt; many of them cost nothing.

And where do you get such a program? From wherever fine public utilities are vended: from those very same modem services, of course, or from a local Mac user group.

Fine print: You may occasionally see files that end with *.cpt* (created with Compact Pro), *.dd* (created with DiskDoubler), and *.sea*.

That last one — a *.sea* file — is especially likable. It's a *self-expanding archive,* which means that it expands when you double-click it. You don't need StuffIt or *any* other program to decompress it and start making FreeMoney.

Any New Program Must Be Installed.

Another real-life situation:

You buy a new program. Let's say it's *After Dark: The Oprah Winfrey Collection.* You admire the handsome disks, turning the cool plastic squares over and over in your hand until you get really bored.

At last you decide you want to install the software and start seeing talk-show characters parading across your screen. You manage to insert the disk correctly (metal side first, label side up). And then you stare dumbly at the screen, not knowing what to do next, and definitely not seeing any signs of Oprah.

Today's store-bought programs are much too complicated for the typical college-educated American to install correctly, having a multitude of files that must all be carefully deposited in specific places on your hard drive to work.

Therefore, the vast majority of them come equipped with some kind of automatic *Installer.* In other words, when you shove the disk into your Mac, you'll usually see something like one of these:

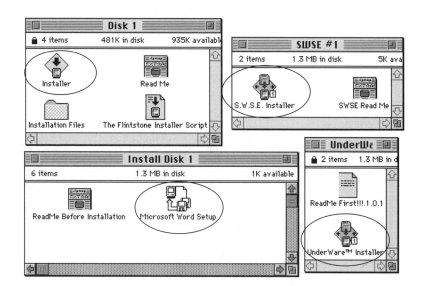

I'm sure you get the point: you're looking for the word *Installer* somewhere on your screen. Double-click whatever says Installer. (The exception, of course, is the Microsoft Word program shown above; Microsoft *never* does things the Macintosh way.)

From here on, you're on autopilot. The program will show you a few welcoming messages, explain what's about to happen, and maybe list what's about to be dumped onto your hard drive. Just keep smiling and clicking OK buttons until it's over. Along the way, you'll be asked to shove in any additional disks; just do what you're told. Keep Disk 1 handy, though. For some idiotic reason, you always have to re-insert Disk 1 when all the other disks are finished.

Do the Shift-Key Trick Before Installing.

One more thing about installing. Unless you find that computer headaches make life more interesting, do this. Before you install any new program, restart your Mac. As it's starting up again, hold down the Shift key until you read "Extensions off" on your screen.

You've just disabled any anti-virus programs or other startup programs that give most software Installers fits.

"Read Me First" = "Ignore Me First."

In the picture you saw a page or so ago, you may have noted that, along with an Installer, almost every program comes with a little icon that says Read Me First, ReadMe, *Lisez s'il vous plaît,* or something.

Most of the time, if you double-click this item, you'll be shown a screenful of fine print pertaining to the program you're about to install. Example: "Part 45. If you have a Performa 3100/23 with 45 MHz acceleration and no Shift key, and you've previously installed a 32-bit Addressing software, note that your screen saver may take two seconds longer to appear."

The point is that it's usually pretty trivial stuff. And it's usually pretty *technical* stuff. The software company is basically warning you about bugs you may be about to encounter.

So skim the material, but do *not* sweat it if you have no clue what they're talking about. Nobody else can understand programmers, either.

Most Stuff You Buy You'll Never Use Again.

This happens to be a proven fact. The vast majority of programs bought by computer fans wind up on the shelf, unused.

I guess that's perfectly understandable; after all, we retire old sweaters, appliances, and unlabeled jars in the refrigerator. Why not software?

Because it's darned expensive, that's why. Therefore, read the magazine reviews before you buy something; at $300 a pop, programs aren't sweaters. Also, buy software from a place (such as a mail-order joint) that will let you return it. They're insane to give you that opportunity. You may as well take advantage of it.

Don't Worry About Viruses.

There has never been a Mac virus that destroys files.

Read it again.

Oh, there have been viruses, all right. They've made Macs beep or burp or display quirky little messages. But there's never been one that wrecked anybody's files, let alone hurt the machine itself.

A virus *can't* physically hurt the machine, actually. A virus is a piece of software. Erase the disk it's on, and it's history.

In the preceding chapter, you read about anti-virus programs you can get. Fine. But if you're going to worry about owning a computer, there are much worthier worries: carpal tunnel syndrome, planned obsolescence, and Kid Pix-playing four-year-olds, for example.

Every Piece Of Equipment Needs Software in Your System Folder.

Your Mac is a regular little Ellis Island. It greets every piece of incoming add-on equipment with open little silicon arms. You can attach all kinds of things to it: printers, CD-ROM players, scanners, modems, musical instruments, or anything else described in Chapter 7.

When it comes to understanding and troubleshooting your Mac, though, here's a key piece of news: every single *hardware* item you add requires a corresponding *software* program. Think of it as the paperwork for newcomers.

These little programs, called *drivers,* translate between the Mac and whatever equipment you're attaching. They usually hang out in the folder called Extensions (inside your System Folder). If you look right now, you'll see one for your printer and probably a bunch for other printers. If you have a CD-ROM, scanner, modem, or whatever, you'll find corresponding files somewhere on your Mac for them, too.

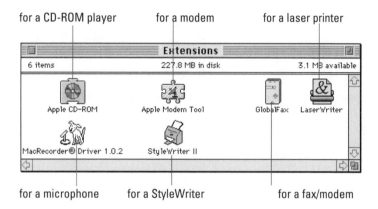

for a CD-ROM player   for a modem   for a laser printer

for a microphone   for a StyleWriter   for a fax/modem

Now you know the technical reason you can't just unhook *your* printer, attach it to *my* Mac, and expect it to work, without copying over that little driver file. (Another technical reason: I live in New York City.)

Error Messages Are Useless.

Every so often a representative of the United States Postal Service drops by bearing huge sacks of mail from readers around the world. Sure as spring follows winter, most of them ask the same question:

"What does 'Bad F-Line Instruction (Error Type -93)' mean?"

It means: "Does not compute."

Of *course* you know that. After all, you only *got* that message when something terribly wrong went down, and your cursor froze on the screen, and a loud electrostatic buzzing filled the room. What you really want to know is whether or not that "Bad F-Line, Error of Type -93" can help you figure out what happened.

And the answer is no. Oh, sure, they publish lists of these codes. But no kidding: they are *totally* unhelpful. Here are some examples:

Error code	Message	Meaning
–1	qErr	queue element not found during deletion
–2	vTypErr	invalid queue element
–3	corErr	core routine number out of range
–4	unimpErr	unimplemented core routine

OK? Now do you believe me?

As an Apple programmer once explained it, it's like finding a car smashed into a tree with its tires still spinning. All you can say for sure is that something went wrong. But you have no idea what *led up* to the crash. Maybe the guy was drunk, or distracted, or asleep. You'll never know.

Same thing with your Mac. The machine knows that *something* happened, but it's way too late to tell you what. Restart it and get back to business.

The More Popular It Is, The Cheaper and Better It Is.

Bummed out because your expensive music program is buggy? Frustrated when your medical-office software acts up?

Unfortunately, Economics 101 rears its ugliest head when it comes to Macintosh programs. If your interests are specialized — music, medicine, hair replacement — the pickings will be slimmer, more expensive, and less polished than general-interest stuff. For example, there aren't many bugs in ClarisWorks or WordPerfect; because so many people buy them (and because general software is a very competitive area), the companies have had the time to work out the wrinkles.

IBMs Are Not Cheaper.

There are two kinds of personal computers on earth: Macintosh and IBM-compatible. (Dell, Compaq, Gateway, Zeos ... they're all IBM-compatible, also known as PCs, DOS, or Windows.) Each kind has its following, which vehemently defends its own beliefs and purchases.

Incredibly, you still hear this one argument today: "I bought an IBM," some poor slob will tell you, "because Macs are more expensive."

First of all, it's simply not true. Look at the newspaper these days. A Power Macintosh model actually costs *substantially* less than an IBM compatible of the same speed (if there *are* any IBMs of the same speed).

Other Mac models cost about the same as IBM clones but run faster. Here's a quote from a 1994 study conducted by Ingram Laboratories: "The Macintosh Quadra 605 was priced like a 25MHz 80486SX [a DOS machine], but ran 16% faster."

But the *real* kicker is that when you compare sticker prices, you're comparing (you'll forgive me) Apples and oranges. Because an IBM-type computer doesn't *come with* as much stuff!

For example, a Mac has built-in sound circuitry, so you can play games and CD-ROM discs right out of the box; on a PC, you have to buy a $150 "sound card" and figure out how to install it. On a Mac, you can buy a piece of phone wire and connect several computers together (networking). You'd have to buy "networking cards" if you had an IBM. On a Mac, if you get a new hard drive, you just attach it to the back and it works. On a PC, you'd have to buy an "interface card" and spend a weekend installing and configuring it!

More fodder for Mac-vs.-Windows arguments

You'll often hear Mac-bashers say they use something called Windows, which is a program that's supposed to make the screen of an IBM clone look like a Macintosh, complete with menus and icons. Next time you hear that old saw, whip out *this* little tidbit. OK, it's a press release from *Apple,* but still:

"February 14, 1994—A new study released today demonstrates that Macintosh users are more productive than those who use personal computers running Windows. According to the study, from consulting firm Arthur D. Little, Macintosh is 'fundamentally a more productive platform' than comparable Windows computers for the broad range of computing tasks tested. Macintosh users completed the suite of tasks in 44% less time, and were almost 50% more likely to complete the suite of tasks correctly.

"The study took a group of 100 computer users and measured their productivity across 24 different computing tasks including editing documents, managing files and printing. Their performance was evaluated in two areas: time taken to complete a task, and success in completing the task correctly. Compared to their Windows counterparts, Macintosh users needed 68% less time to manage files, 33% less time to edit a document and 57% less time to print a document to different printers. Overall, Macintosh users completed 85% of their tasks correctly, while Windows users completed theirs only 58% correctly."

Finally, nobody ever considers the value of your *time*. Almost everybody concedes that the Mac is easier to learn and easier to use. You get stuff done in less time. Doesn't that count for something?

America Online Hangs Up on Everybody.

It's not just you. If you use your modem to dial into America Online in the peak hours of the evening, you're competing with 1.5 million *other* people trying to dial in. There just isn't enough space at the trough. You may get bumped off your connection, or you may not be able to dial in at all.

One thing's for sure: if you wait a little while — or a long while — and try again, you'll have much better luck.

Magazines Are Over *Everyone's* Head.

It's true: the major Mac magazines, *Macworld* and *MacUser,* simply drip these days with articles about 32-bit addressing and TCP/IP protocols. You don't get 'em; *I* don't get 'em. This despite the fact that the *huge* majority of Mac users are beginners! Are the editors crazy?

Nope; they do it on purpose. Magazines survive on advertising income. The more ads they sell, the fatter the magazine. (Interesting stat: the Mac magazines, exactly like other magazines from *Time* to *Log Cabin Living,* are rigidly controlled at 60 percent ads, 40 percent articles.)

To be a happy, healthy, thriving publication, therefore, the computer mags want to appeal to advertisers. So they're written to appeal to *people who buy a lot of stuff,* which will attract advertisers.

Well, who do you think buys the most stuff? Guess what: it's not Stella the student or Harry the home-office guy or Nancy the novice. It's Carl the corporate super-nerd. This guy doesn't buy one or two programs; he buys *500 copies at a time*, to outfit his entire company.

That's who the advertisers drool for; *that's* who the magazines write for; and *that's* why there are so many ridiculously high-tech articles about things most people couldn't care less about.

On the other hand, there's always at least a couple of articles that *are* useful to us. Furthermore, while most beginner-oriented Mac magazines have quietly croaked (because of — guess what? — not enough advertising), at least one of them is usually still struggling along. At this moment, the *Mac Home Journal* is alive and publishing, and not one of its articles is too technical.

1-800-SOS-APPL Is Worth Its Wait.

You *do* have that number magic-markered on your wall, don't you? It's the toll-free Apple help line. Twelve hours a day, a crack staff is at the other end who's willing to help you out of any crisis.

Unfortunately, they're also willing to help out twelve million *other* Mac users. As a result, before a live operator answers your call, you sometimes have to wait until the cows come home, make dinner, and get ready for bed.

But what do you care? It's toll-free, right? When you finally get live people on the phone, odds are high that they'll solve your problem. If your Mac is genuinely on the fritz, they'll schedule a repair; and if it's within a year since you bought your Mac, the repair is *free*. (If it's a PowerBook, they'll send you a shipping box; ship it to themselves overnight; repair the thing; and overnight it back to you, all for free. If it's any other Mac, they'll send somebody to *your house* to fix the Mac.)

Click the Label Instead of the Button.

Here's a wonderful shortcut. Whenever you're presented with a set of options, they usually look something like this:

Checkboxes	Radio buttons
☐ Rhinoplasty	┌─ Anesthetic ─┐
☐ Liposuction	○ Local
☐ Augmentation	⦿ General
	○ None

You're allowed to choose as many *checkboxes* as you want; a little X appears in each one when you click it. Like the pop-out buttons on a car radio, however, only *one* of the round ones — called radio buttons — can be selected at a time.

Anyway, your instinct is probably to click the little square or the little circle button to make your selection. But it's far quicker to sloppily slash away with your mouse at the *label* of a button instead of the tiny square or circle itself. Click the *words*, and the button gets clicked.

Click anywhere on the words

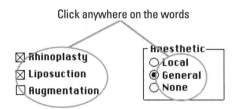

You Can't Rename or Trash a Window.

Computer experts, if you stop to think about it, are about the *worst* people to write computer books. Most of 'em have forgotten all about what it feels like at the beginning.

I recently went over to rescue a friend. He claimed that his new Mac was "a piece of worthless junk." When I visited his apartment, I saw why he thought so.

He had been trying to throw away files by moving them to the Trash. Nothing wrong with that, right?

But he hadn't been dragging their *icons* to the Trash — he had been dragging their *open windows!* There, in the lower right corner of his monitor, were several open windows, all piled up as close as they could get to the Trash can.

And you know what? That was a perfectly reasonable action on his part. Why *shouldn't* you be able to throw away a window?

Well, anyway, you get the point: you can't throw away a window. You can't rename it, either. You have to *close* the window and then rename (or trash) the *icon* that represents it.

Part III
Special Macs for Special People

The 5th Wave   By Rich Tennant

In this part...

1n 1984, you could have any Mac you wanted, as long as it was the beige, hard disk-free, 128K original Mac.

Fifty Mac models later, the line has begun to differentiate itself into peculiar breeds of Mac. A Performa is exactly like a regular Mac, only different. A PowerBook is exactly like a regular Mac, only smaller.

Chapter 10

Yo: It's Da Performa

Apple Computer has never seemed totally content simply to manufacture the greatest computer the world has ever known. No, they feel lonely over there in those rarefied computer stores. They wanna make it big. They want Apple products cropping up in department stores, mail-order catalogs, discount marts . . . it wouldn't surprise me one iota if, a year from now or so, we started seeing a chain of Apple casual-wear shops in America's finer malls.

Anyway, Performas (this chapter) represent one direction the company's plan for world domination is taking. PowerBooks are another (next chapter). In any case, I'll be concise in these chapters for two reasons. First, I don't want to bore everybody who *doesn't* own one of these specialty Macs. And second, as my cousin Anne always says, no computer book should weigh more than the machine it describes.

Principles of Performa

Your Mac is a Performa if (a) it says Performa on the front; (b) you bought it as an everything-included package for one price (monitor, keyboard, modem, software already installed); and (c) when you say your Mac's name, you sound like Sylvester Stallone trying to say "performer."

Most of this book applies equally well to Performas and non-Performas. This section, however, covers a few items exclusive to this, the Family Mac.

Crucially crucial note to System 7.5 users

I lied. This chapter *doesn't* cover items exclusive to the Performa.

It really covers items exclusive to the Performa — *and to System 7.5.* The Performa features were such a hit that Apple has made them available to all. (Well, to all who spring the $100 for System 7.5 ... or got it with their Macs.)

If, in Chapter 1 when you were supposed to figure out what kind of Mac you have, you learned that you have System 7.5, here's how you turn these features on and off.

From your menu, choose Control Panels. In the ensuing window, double-click General Controls. Here you can see the on/off switches for the three main Performa features: self-hiding programs when you switch; the Launcher window; and a Documents magnet folder.

Automatic window hiding

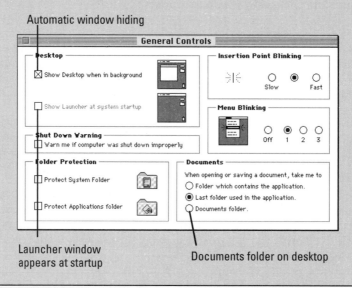

Launcher window appears at startup

Documents folder on desktop

The Deal

Buying a Performa is actually a great deal. It saves you hassle because you get the complete setup for one fixed price. It saves you money because you get a bunch of ready-to-use software programs already installed. And it saves you headaches because you get a year of *on-site* service. Know what that means? Some guy will actually come to your house to fix the computer for free if something goes wrong! (When, oh when, will electricians and plumbers adopt that policy?)

Despite all of these yummy freebies, there's also one thing you *don't* get: a set of those all-important white System disks to which I've referred about 1,000 times in this book. More on this topic later.

Just wanted to make sure you knew what you were getting into.

The Launcher

A Mac is, to be sure, a user-friendly computer. It's no longer the *most* user-friendly, though: a Performa is. Its System software (see Chapter 6) has been specially tinkered with to make it even simpler to operate. Case in point: the Launcher (called the Performa control panel on recent models).

What the Launcher *is:* a control panel, just like the ones described in Chapter 6. What it *does* is display a window containing jumbo icons for your programs.

As you know, you normally *double-click* an icon to launch a program. But anything in *this* window opens when you click it *once*. (This is progress.)

You can move, resize, or close the Launcher window just as you would any window (Chapter 1). Once closed, it will reappear if you double-click the little Launcher icon on the desktop (see the next figure).

So who decides which icons appear in the Launcher? You do. Inside your System Folder is a folder called Launcher Items. Any file or folder icon you put in Launcher Items shows up in the Launcher window. (Actually, more typically, you wouldn't put the icon itself into this folder; you'd put an *alias* of that item. See Chapter 8 for info on aliases.)

Super-hot power-nerd hot-rod Launcher tricks

The Launcher window has its charms. Not among them is the ritual of adding and deleting icons from its window. Every time you want to do so, you have to open your System Folder, find the Launcher Items folder, and open it.

There is a better way.

Hold down the Option key on your keyboard. With steely nerve, move the cursor over one of the topic buttons at the top of the Launcher window, as shown here. Note that your cursor changes shape ... to become a little tiny folder:

If you *click* now, the Launcher Items window will snap smartly into view. You just saved yourself several layers of folder-burrowing to find this window. Now you can add or remove icons as suits your fancy.

Once inside the Launcher Items window, you'll notice something else remarkable. Let's assume you bought your Performa after the middle of 1993, and therefore you *have* topic buttons across the top of the Launcher window, as shown in the figure to the left.

Here's the secret to those topic buttons: any *folder* inside the Launcher Items window whose name is preceded by a bullet symbol (•) will magically become a topic button in the Launcher window!

I realize that's an ocean of words to navigate, but try it and you'll see what I mean. Create a new folder inside the Launcher Items folder. When you name the folder, make the first symbol by pressing the Option key and typing the 8 key. Option-8 makes the • symbol.

Now have a look at your Launcher window. See the buttons across the top? My God, you're a programmer!

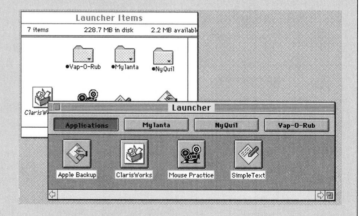

The Documents folder

For many people, the purchase of a Mac is a primal attempt to get their lives, so full of traffic and turbulent relationships and scraps of paper, into some kind of order.

Little do they know what awaits them on the typical Mac: their important documents get every bit as lost as their paper-based counterparts once did. Even the great Mac gurus of our time have, at one time or another, saved some document created on the Mac — and then found themselves unable to find it again because it got arbitrarily stashed in some hidden folder somewhere.

Enter the Documents folder. See its icon in the picture below? As you work with your Mac and create different documents, the Performa housekeeps for you by storing them *all* in this folder automatically. Every time you use a program's Open or Save command, you're automatically shown the Documents folder's contents.

In theory, you'll never lose anything again; everything you do will always be in one place. (That feature makes backing up your work simple, too; you just copy that one folder, and you know you're covered.)

If this document magnet bothers you, however, just rename the Documents folder. Then you'll have to file your documents in your own folders, just like everybody else.

Turning it all off

If any of the Performa features kind of bug you, it's a simple matter to turn one or all of them off.

Recent Performas

If you acquired your Performa after the end of 1994, it probably has System 7.5, just like all other new Macs. You can turn off the three Performa features — the Launcher, automatic window-hiding, and the Documents folder-magnet — the same way you do on any System 7.5 Mac. That is, choose Control Panels from your menu; double-click the icon called General Controls. There, as illustrated in a previous sidebar, you'll find the three on/off switches.

Mature Performas

If your Performa was born in 1993 or 1994, it probably doesn't have System 7.5. Instead, it has a special control panel called Performa. Choose Control Panels from your menu and take a look.

If you do have a Performa control panel, open it. Sure enough, you'll see the on/off switches (checkboxes) for the three Performa features.

Antique Performas

And if your Performa began life in the first part of 1993 or earlier, then you have, nestled in your Control Panels folder, a control panel called Launcher. *It's* responsible for creating all that Performa behavior: the Launcher window, the Documents folder, and the window hiding when you switch programs.

To kill off these antics, thus de-Performatizing your Mac, choose Control Panels from your menu. Drag the Launcher control panel clear out of the System Folder — onto the desktop, for example.

Now restart the Mac. From now on: no Documents folder, no program hiding. You *can* still use the Launcher window; double-click that Launcher control panel, wherever it is now (not in the System Folder), and the Launcher window will appear like always.

P.S.: You can also neuter only *some* of the features on your vintage Performa. For example, you can kill off only the Documents-folder feature by simply renaming the Documents folder on your desktop. You can also prevent the Launcher window from appearing every morning; open your System Folder, open the Startup Items folder, and drag the Launcher alias outta there. From now on, the Launcher window won't appear until you double-click the Launcher icon on your desktop.

Apple Backup

Apple saved itself a precious $7 by failing to give you System disks with your Performa. Instead, the System comes preinstalled on your hard drive, and you're supposed to back it up onto your *own* floppy disks using the Apple Backup program.

Two extremely important points:

(1) Do it! Call up Mac Connection (see Appendix B) and order a box of high-density disks. Use them to back up your System Folder as soon as possible.

(2) If your System Folder gets trashed *before* you've made a backup, call 1-800-SOS-APPL. Give them the bad news. Apple will Fed Ex you a free set of System disks. (Methinks they should just include these disks to begin with.)

All About At Ease

In addition to some cool work software like ClarisWorks, America Online, and so on, your Performa also comes with a fascinating piece of System software: At Ease. (You can also buy it for use on *any* Mac for $60.)

Remember all that talk of folders, windows, and disks that you slogged through in the beginning chapters of this book? It must've made your head spin at first. Now imagine that you're a six-year-old, and you'll understand why Apple invented At Ease. It's a sweet little program that *covers up* all that stuff you've spent so much time and effort learning: folders, the Trash can, dragging icons around, and list views. In fact, the entire Finder (the desktop) gets hidden when At Ease is running.

At Ease users: Read this or weep

To remove At Ease for good, *do not* just drag the At Ease files to the Trash. You'll mess up your Mac so badly it won't start up. (You haven't lost any of your files, and you haven't broken the computer. But you *will* need a set of system disks to get your Mac running again.)

Instead, open the At Ease Setup control panel (get to it by choosing Control Panels from the menu). Turn it *off* first!

Now you can safely drag the At Ease stuff to the Trash.

Want something safer than all that? Just find your original At Ease disk. Run its Installer. Click Customize, hold down the Option key, and click Remove. (See the At Ease manual for details.)

In its place, you see something like this:

Click here to see the screenful of document icons.

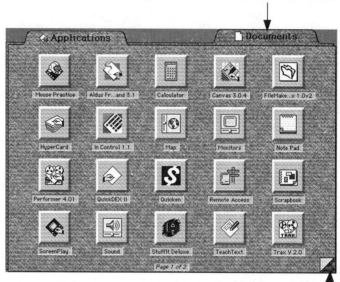

If there are more than 20 icons, click here
to see the next screenful of them.

What's neat is that, exactly as with the Launcher, you can open any program or document with a *single* mouse click, not a double-click. You hear a cool clicky sound when you click one of these icons.

When you launch a program, the At Ease window itself disappears, only to reappear when you quit that program. (What's also neat, for those who care, is that At Ease takes up 200K less memory than the regular Finder desktop, and that means 200K more memory for your programs to use.)

At Ease is designed for teachers, parents, or trainers who want to hide the confusing world of folders and icons from beginning Mac fans. It's also good for *protecting* your regular Mac universe from unwitting (or witting) disrupters. Because At Ease denies a user access to control panels, the Trash, or moving or renaming files, your hard drive is safe.

You can switch back and forth from At Ease to the regular Finder by choosing the appropriate command from the File menu (Go to Finder, for example).

If you want even *that* escape hatch closed, you can create a password so that only you, The Parent, can escape to the Finder.

Make Yourself At Ease

At Ease is a nice idea if you have kids, students, or visitors of any kind; it provides a lot of simplicity and reassurance if you don't want your normal Mac environment messed with.

Unfortunately, At Ease won't help *you* avoid learning the Mac; you still have to know the Mac just to install and set up At Ease. Here, then, for the sake of Ye Who Must Administer, is a step-by-step guide. (I'm assuming you've already installed At Ease by double-clicking the Installer icon on the At Ease disk and then restarting the Mac.)

1. From the ★ menu, choose Control Panels. When the Control Panels window opens, double-click At Ease Setup. This box appears:

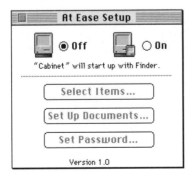

2. Click On. Then click Select Items. Now you see this:

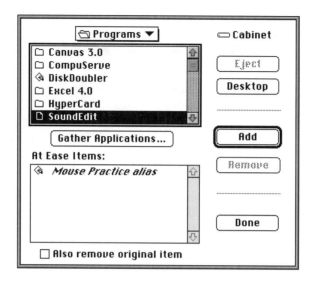

3. Using the upper half of the box, navigate to a program or a document you want to add. At Ease will eventually place its icon on the appropriate screen — Applications or Documents. It'll be listed alphabetically.

4. Double-click the name of a program or document. You'll see that its *alias* (an italicized reference to the original file) appears in the lower half of the box. These are the icons that appear when you use At Ease. If you ever feel like going mucking around in your System Folder, you'll find these alias's icons in the At Ease Items folder.

5. When you're finished adding items, click Done. Now restart the Mac ... you're in business! Remember that to get back to your old world, choose Go to Finder from the File menu.

To turn off At Ease, repeat step 1; but when you get to step 2, obviously, you should click Off and not On.

Chapter 11

The PowerBook Survival Guide

*I*t's a little bit mind-blowing that a tiny PowerBook Duo 280 has more computer horsepower than a hulking Quadra 900. Apple made almost no compromises: the speed, storage capacity, memory, and back-panel jacks on a PowerBook are almost exactly the same as those on regular Macs — but they're crammed into a book-size case that weighs four or six pounds and conceals dirt. You can get them with grayscale or color screens, and usually for less money than you'd pay for a regular Mac (hereafter called a *desktop Mac*).

In fact, working on a PowerBook is so much like working on a desktop Mac that you may forget to make certain allowances. Use the tips in this chapter to get extra mileage out of your machine and its battery.

Get A Case

The PowerBook comes with neither handles nor a carrying case. There are a million cases for sale, designed to carry and protect the PowerBook and accessories; call one of the mail-order companies, such as Mac Connection. Almost all of them are tough, attractive, and beautifully designed (the cases, I mean — not the mail-order companies).

Power Options

There are all kinds of ways to milk more juice out of your PowerBook battery. These methods are outlined in the Top Ten list at the end of this chapter.

In the meantime, consider buying a power accessory or two. Special car (or boat) cigarette-lighter adapters for the PowerBook are available. (Hot tip: Pick up a *regular* auto power adapter at Radio Shack; you can plug *any* appliance into this adapter, including the PowerBook.)

If you look in the pages of *Macworld* magazine, you'll also find ads for an absurd number of carry-along, external superbatteries that keep your PowerBook kicking for eight hours or more (compared with the regular battery's two hours). Keep that in mind the next time you have to fly to Europe.

My favorite alternative power product, though, is a second regular PowerBook battery. Not very innovative, I know, but you really get your $60 worth from the thing.

When Trouble Strikes

One of the best things that you bought with your PowerBook was Apple's emergency-repair program. For the first year, wherever you are, you can call Apple at 800-SOS-APPL. Apple will send a messenger to pick up your sick PowerBook, repair it in one day, and overnight it back to you, all at *no charge.* Ladies and gentlemen — an American bureaucratic program that really works.

Before you dial, though, you may as well know that burned-out *pixels* (the tiny square dots on your screen) may not qualify as being broken. Apple says that up to five burned-out pixels on any of the higher-priced PowerBooks (a PowerBook 540 or Duo 280, for example) are within its definition of "not really broken."

Yeah, well, I bet *their* PowerBooks don't have broken pixels.

Keeping An Eye on Juice

Mac insiders have known for years about SuperClock!, an ingenious control panel that puts a digital time readout in the upper-right corner of your screen, as shown below, left.

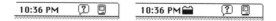

When you install SuperClock! on a PowerBook, though, a funny thing happens: you also get a battery "fuel gauge," like above, right, so that you can keep an eye on your battery life.

A solid black battery indicates a full charge. As the battery juice runs out, the blackness empties out of the little battery icon. (You get SuperClock! wherever fine shareware is sold: on electronic bulletin boards or from a local user group.)

Alternatively, of course, you can just leave the Battery desk accessory open on-screen in a convenient place. And if you have System 7.5, you have the wonderful Control Strip showing you the battery status at all times.

Those Darned X-Ray Machines

Airport X-ray machines can't hurt your PowerBook.

Airport X-ray machines can't hurt your PowerBook.

Airport X-ray machines can't hurt your PowerBook.

OK?

Sleep Is Good. We Like Sleep.

Do you have a PowerBook? Don't tell me you shut it down at the end of each day!

Yes, alas, thousands of people shut their PowerBooks off unnecessarily each day or — horrors! — even more than once a day. Don't do it!

Instead, put your PowerBook to *sleep* — that is, choose Sleep from the Special menu when you finish using the machine. The thing instantly blinks off. (Other ways to make a PowerBook sleep: If you have the Control Strip, click the Sleep Now icon; if you have SuperClock! in your menu bar, Control-click the battery icon; if you have a Duo, just close the lid!)

Sleep mode is almost like Off mode. You're not using the battery; nothing moves; all is calm; all is dark. But the advantages of letting a sleeping PowerBook lie are considerable. For example, when you want to use it again, you can just *touch any key* to wake it up. And when the thing wakes up, it doesn't go through the usual 45-minute "Welcome to Macintosh" startup process — instead, it takes you *right back to whatever you were doing*. If you were typing up a letter, you wake up to your half-finished letter, still on-screen. Great time savings.

You don't have to shut your PowerBook down for travel, either. The only time you need the Shut Down command is when you'll be storing the PowerBook for more than a couple of weeks. (You also have to shut it down whenever you plan to attach any major equipment to it, such as a scanner or a monitor. Most smaller attachments — printers, modems, microphone, speakers, a keyboard, a mouse, and so on — can be attached when the machine is sleeping.)

Losing network services — and your mind

Ever notice how sometimes, when you put your PowerBook to sleep, it doesn't go right off to dreamland? Instead, it gives you a goofy message about how you may lose some network services, and then you have to click OK before the machine nods off.

Annoying as hell, but easy to defeat.

You get that message *only if AppleTalk is turned on.* AppleTalk, of course, is the mystical technology that lets a Mac connect to a laser printer (or to another Mac). So if you have a laser printer, your PowerBook probably gives you that "network services" message when it goes to sleep.

Turning off AppleTalk is simple. Choose Chooser from the menu. In the lower-right corner, you'll see this control:

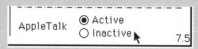

Just click Inactive. From now on, you won't get that network-services message anymore.

Turning off AppleTalk has another wonderful advantage: your battery charge lasts *30 minutes longer.*

Of course, turning off AppleTalk has one *bad* effect: you can't use your laser printer anymore (at least, not until you turn AppleTalk back on again).

Insta-Printer

You can get a fax/modem as an optional accessory for any PowerBook. (Apple, Global Village, and PSI make fax/modems for the PowerBook.)

That's not the tip, though. The tip is that if you have a built-in fax/modem, you really don't need to lug along a printer (even if you do have the money to spend on a portable Diconix printer). Instead, just fax the document that you want to print *to yourself,* using a fax machine at the airport or hotel to receive the fax that you're sending from the laptop. Ingenious, eh?

Desperate For A Fix

Now look, I don't want to get angry letters from spouses and significant others, blaming me for converting their beloveds into hermitic power nerds. What I'm about to tell you should be socked away in the back of your mind and used only in emergencies.

The tip is about airplanes and airports. You know that PowerBooks and airplanes were made for each other. What you may not know is what to do when the dreaded "Your screen has been dimmed" message pops up, warning you that you have only a few minutes of battery power remaining, while you're in the middle of a brainstorm.

First of all, I happen to know that there are publicly available power outlets at every gate of every airport (and at every bus and train station, too). The outlets are there, actually, for the benefit of the cleaning staff's vacuum cleaners; as such, the outlets are sometimes concealed on the side of a pillar. I also happen to know that the outlets are *never* convenient to a seat, so if your Mac habit is stronger than your pride, you're going to have to sit on the floor.

What's more, I know what to do when you run out of juice *on the plane.* That's right — I'm going to call to your attention the electric-razor outlet in the bathroom of almost every plane in America. You feel like an absolute idiot, of course, wedged in there on that toilet with your adapter cord snaking up to the plug above the doll-size sink while your laptop recharges.

Well, that's what I've been *told,* anyway. Naturally, *I* would never do anything that pathetic.

Cursing the lost cursor

The screens on some of the less expensive PowerBook models have a frustrating behavior that is well known to their owners: the cursor tends to get lost. Because of the ever-so-slightly-blurry nature of those particular screens, moving the mouse too quickly makes the pointer *submarine* (fade out momentarily).

Here are two solutions. One is free, and the other is, too.

First, get into the habit of designating a lost-and-found center for your pointer — the upper-left corner of the screen. Whenever you can't find the pointer, roll your trackball or touchpad furiously to move the cursor up and left. Sooner or later, your cursor, wherever it may have been, will bump up into the top-left corner of the screen. (Reunited, and it feels so good.)

The second solution is software. From a user group or an online information service (America Online, for example), you can get a pointer-fattening program such as FindCursor. When you're word processing, life's a lot easier with a fat cursor, as you can see from this before-and-after shot:

Before

> Roland puffed out his chest heroically as the beast's head tumbled to the marble floor, snakes still hissing and writhing. "That's for YOU, Beast!" he cried as the thunder clapped.
>
> He would regret those words.

After

> Roland puffed out his chest heroically as the beast's head tumbled to the marble floor, snakes still hissing and writhing. "That's for YOU, Beast!" he cried as the thunder clapped.
>
> He would regret those words.

Mano a Mano With the Duo

If you bought a PowerBook Duo, you must've turned this four-pound beauty over and over in your hands, mystified about where you're supposed to plug stuff in. There's no place to hook up a monitor; there's no SCSI connector for plugging in another hard drive; there isn't even a floppy-disk drive!

Then again, you don't *need* any of those items when you're sitting on an airplane typing, and that's exactly the point of the Duo. When you want to travel light, you can leave all the extra computer paraphernalia at home and carry only a lean, mean typing machine.

The great Duo myth

Q: So how do you get information into and out of a Duo?

A: You do *not* need to buy a hulking Duo Dock!

The Duo trio

The Duo has one great big wide jack on the back. Any of *three* things can be attached to it:

- *A floppy-disk-drive adapter.* Not a dock, mind you — just a three-inch, dark-gray, semicircular adapter, into which you can plug the external floppy-disk drive and a keyboard and/or mouse. The adapter and the disk drive probably cost $200 total.

- *A MiniDock.* This thing (about $400) looks like a three-ring hole punch. It clips onto the whole back of the Duo to provide a *complete* array of back-panel jacks. You can use the MiniDock to hook up a big-screen color monitor, keyboard, mouse, scanner, CD-ROM — anything (including the floppy drive, of course). Clip the Duo to a MiniDock, and presto: you can work merrily away as though the Duo weren't a laptop at all. Pretty cool. Flip one lever, and the Duo itself is free of all that wiring and gear, ready to nestle into your briefcase or carry-on bag.

- *The Duo Dock.* This is the one that everybody's heard of — a big, computer-size housing that contains expansion slots, a floppy drive, and every connector you can think of. When you come home from your trip with the Duo, you slide the laptop into an opening in the front of the Dock. The closed Duo gets slurped into the Dock like a videocassette. You've just handed all your data — and the Duo's brain — to the machine on your desk.

There are only two reasons to get a Duo Dock. First, get one if you plan to use its NuBus slots inside. (You'd have to know what those slots *are*, but you'd already know if you need to know.) Second, the Dock can display a richer palette of colors on whatever full-size screen is plugged into it. If you're into photo retouching and digital art, well, OK, get a Dock.

The one real jack

Oh, by the way, there *is* one normal jack on the Duo itself. (You have to flip down one of the Duo's little legs to see it.) You can use this jack to plug in *either* a printer *or* a modem — precisely the two items that you'd need most on the road.

In other words, you can get information into, and out of, a PowerBook Duo in three ways:

- ✔ Use a floppy-disk drive.
- ✔ Attach the Duo to a regular Mac, using the big, fat SCSI jack (and a special cable purchased for that purpose).
- ✔ Connect the Duo to another Mac, using that hidden printer jack — in other words, network the machines.

Top Ten Tips for Maximizing PowerBook Battery Power

Many new PowerBook owners are devastated to find that instead of getting "two to three" hours of life out of each freshly charged battery, they get only 90 minutes or so. These excellent tricks solve that problem in a hurry.

1. The backlighting for the screen uses up *half* the power. The more you turn backlighting down, the longer your battery will last.

2. I've actually heard PowerBook owners asking the airline gate agent for a seat not merely next to a window but on a particular *side* of the plane. Now I know why: they want to be where the sun will be shining. Bright sunlight is enough to illuminate a PowerBook screen, so you can turn the backlighting off.

3. As you go through life with your PowerBook (models 140 through 180), repeated partial chargings of your nickel–cadmium battery gradually decrease its potential life. The problem is called the *memory effect* (camcorder batteries do this, too); it occurs when you don't allow the battery to discharge fully before recharging begins.

To restore the battery to its good-as-new, virginal, strong-as-ever condition, deliberately let it run down to the ground. That's right — just keep your PowerBook on, not letting it sleep; click OK every time a message appears, telling you that the battery is running down. At the very end, the Mac literally tells you "Good night" and puts itself to sleep. You've now drained the battery — and undone the memory effect. Now it's OK to plug in the adapter to charge the battery.

When the battery is finally restored, it should last much longer. Do this routine once a month.

4. If you want to get serious about tip #3, you can buy a device that performs the whole sequence automatically. This device, called a Battery Reconditioner/Charger, is made by Lind. The device plugs into the wall; you put your battery in it, and it deep-empties the battery and then safely refills it to full. The whole cycle takes more than seven hours, but the company claims that it rejuvenates the battery even more than the process described in tip #3 does. (Lind also makes a charger for the PowerBook 100 battery, which is a lead–acid battery and therefore doesn't suffer from the memory effect.)

5. When you want to make sure that your battery is as full as it can be, allow all day for it to recharge — and don't trust the Battery desk-accessory fuel gauge. You see, the PowerBook battery gets charged 80 percent full in only two hours or so. At that point, the Battery gauge tells you that the battery is full. But to charge the battery fully — to charge that extra 20 percent — takes another *five or six hours* of what's called "trickle charging." (This isn't true of Duo, whose battery charges fully in two hours.)

6. Turn off AppleTalk — an incredible power drain that saps a half-hour of life from your battery. To do so, choose Chooser from the menu. In the lower-right corner, make sure that AppleTalk Inactive is selected.

7. If you're not going to use the machine, even for five minutes, put it to sleep by choosing Sleep from the Special menu.

8. If you have any PowerBook model numbered 160 or higher, open the PowerBook control panel and click the Options button. You'll be presented with two battery-saving options: Processor Cycling and Processor Speed. These options slow the Mac's brain, but they do eke out a few more precious minutes of battery juice per charge.

9. If your PowerBook has a built-in modem, quit your modem program promptly when you finish telecommunicating. Otherwise, as long as that program is open, the Mac is sending precious juice to the modem.

10. If your battery is so old that it no longer holds enough charge, recycle it at your Apple dealer and buy a fresh one.

Part IV
Becoming Your
Own Guru

The 5th Wave   **By Rich Tennant**

TOM'S COMPANY OCCASIONALLY CONDUCTED SPOT CHECKS TO MAKE SURE THE EMPLOYEES WEREN'T SNEAKING THEIR MACINTOSHES INTO THE OFFICE.

Pencil box,...Rolodex,...
large glowing chef's hat,
nope, no Macintosh here.

In this part...

Now it's time to take the bull by the horns, the sword by the hilt, the fish by the gills, and really take off. First, I bestow unto you Chapter 12, the Mother of All Troubleshooting Sections. And then you'll find out where to go from there, with your trusty Mac ever by your side.

Chapter 12

When Bad Things Happen to Good Machines

Introduction to Computer Hell

As a new computer owner, you probably aren't cheered up very much by the fact that this troubleshooting guide is the fattest part of the book.

But let's face it: computers are appliances. As such, they have minds of their own. And like other expensive appliances (cars, homes, pacemakers), they tend to get cranky at the worst possible times.

Fortunately, several million Mac users have been this way before, and they've already uncovered the most common glitches. You'll find those glitches and their solutions explained here. Again fortunately, most computer problems cost you nothing but time.

Some computer glitches, however, also cost you some data (that is, your work). Well, you've been told to floss if you want to keep your teeth; I'm telling you to *back up your work* if you want to keep your data, job, and sanity. Saving your work frequently and making backup copies minimize the number of midnight sobbing sessions you'll have when your important projects vanish into what's left of the ozone.

The three most common causes of computer problems

A guy once called a software company in a panic. "Help!" he told the help-line woman. "Your program made my monitor go out!"

The woman tried to soothe him. "Don't worry," she said. "A cable probably came loose. Why don't you look in back of the computer to see if everything's connected?"

The guy replied, "How can I look back there? It's too dark — the power in my building is out!"

That story is a tactful, nonthreatening way of introducing one very common cause of computer glitches: operator error. Nothing's actually *broken,* but there's something simple that you, the operator, may have overlooked. Be sure to read "The Top Ten Beginner Troubles" later in this chapter.

Another common cause of computer troubles arises when you attach other equipment (or *peripherals*, as the Mac intelligentsia call them) to the back of the Mac. Be sure to read "Scuzzy SCSI" for some chilling truths on this topic.

By far the most common and frustrating computer problem, though, is caused by software bugs. Writing a software program that works with *every* Mac model under *every* circumstance, and that is compatible with all *other* programs, is spectacularly difficult. It's like trying to work out the seating chart for a 100-guest dinner party at which no two people of different political, dietary, or hygiene habits can be seated together — and everyone, incidentally, happens to be schizophrenic. There are just too many variables, and in the computer world, everything changes all the time.

Therefore, even when Silicon Proboscis Software thinks that it's ironed out every single bug in its nose-imaging plastic-surgery program, *you* may have trouble with it because something on *your* hard disk is incompatible with that program. The result may be a system crash, a freeze, or something equally horrifying.

Shooting your own troubles

Therefore, what I'd *really* like to teach you is how to be your *own* Mac guru — how to ferret out the cause of a problem yourself.

There are only a certain number of ways that a person can set up a Mac. The variables are what model it is, how much memory it has, what printer it's connected to, what's in its System Folder, what order you take steps in, what program you're using, and how everything's wired together. When something doesn't work, the object is to try changing *one* of those variables and repeating whatever-it-is-that-didn't-work.

Example: Walter, a New Jersey tollbooth operator, tries to print out a picture he made of a Maserati flying off the highway at high speed — but nothing comes out of the printer. Flicking his earlobe, he wonders whether it's the *printer* that's not working or the *program*.

To find out, he goes to his word processor, types *TESTING TESTING*, and prints *that*. It works. Now he knows that the *printer* works fine; the problem is related to the drawing program. Next, he successfully prints a *different* document from the same drawing program. Therefore, he learns that the problem is with his Maserati *document,* not the drawing program in general.

Do you see the point? He never learned *what,* technologically speaking, the problem was. But he figured out *where* the problem was, and that's the first step to working around it and getting on with your life.

Here, then, is a chapter full of typical snafus that typical Mac users encounter. If you never need to refer to this section, the gods smile on you — but read it anyway, to find out how lucky you really are.

The most important factoid for troubleshooting

Get used to that computeristic-sounding word *extension*. Get used to its synonyms, too: *init* (pronounced "in NIT") and *system extension*.

An *extension* is a little file that lives in your Extensions folder (which is inside your System Folder). Each extension adds a specific new feature to the Macintosh: a screen saver, fax capability, and so on. You know those little icons that march across your screen when you turn on the Macintosh? Those are your *extensions*.

An extension runs *all the time*; it's like a program that you can't quit. It gets launched when the Mac turns on, and it's running in the background during your entire work day.

But the people who wrote the After Dark screen-saver program, for example, never met the programmers who wrote the FaxPlus faxing extension. Suppose that you have both After Dark and FaxPlus in your Extensions folder. Also suppose that each little extension program, in the background, simultaneously reaches for the same morsel of electronic memory.

"Sorry, a system error occurred."

In other words, *extension conflicts* (the technical term) are among the most common causes of problems on the Mac.

Ten Troubles That Don't Need Shooting

If you've read this book to this point, a couple of these troubles will seem obvious. But believe me, I've seen these typical troubles zap the confidence of many a first-timer.

1. *The screen is all gray, there's no window open, you can't find any files or folders, but the Trash can is in the corner.*

   If you want a window to appear, you have to open a disk icon. In the upper-right corner of your screen is an icon that represents a disk. Point to it and then double-click the mouse button to make the icon open into a window.

2. *You try to work, but nothing happens except beeping. Every time you click the mouse button, there's another beep.*

   When the Mac requests some information from you, it displays a *dialog box:* a box that contains some questions for you to answer. This one, for example, appears when you try to print:

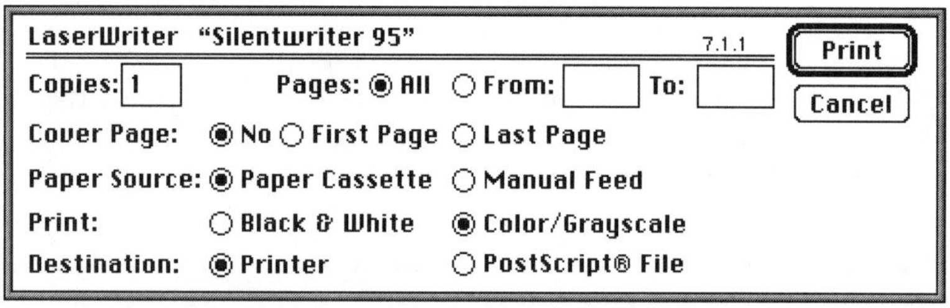

   ```
   ┌─────────────────────────────────────────────────────────────┐
   │ LaserWriter  "Silentwriter 95"            7.1.1  ┌─────────┐ │
   │                                                  │  Print  │ │
   │ Copies:│1│      Pages: ◉ All ○ From:│   │ To:│   │ └─────────┘ │
   │                                                  ┌─────────┐ │
   │ Cover Page:  ◉ No ○ First Page ○ Last Page       │ Cancel  │ │
   │                                                  └─────────┘ │
   │ Paper Source: ◉ Paper Cassette ○ Manual Feed                │
   │ Print:        ○ Black & White   ◉ Color/Grayscale           │
   │ Destination:  ◉ Printer         ○ PostScript® File          │
   └─────────────────────────────────────────────────────────────┘
   ```

   What's not very nice about dialog boxes, though, is the fact that they commandeer your Mac. You're not allowed to do *anything* until you answer the questions and get rid of the box. If you try to keep working, the Mac will keep beeping at you, and the box will sit on your screen until doomsday.

   Every dialog box, therefore, has a button that you can click to make the box go away. Usually, you can choose a button that says OK or one that says Cancel. (In the figure, the buttons say Print and Cancel.) Anyway, you have to click one of those buttons before the Mac will return control to you.

3. *You double-click an icon, but you get an irritating message that says "Application not found" (or something equally unhelpful).*

   This problem is a confounding one for beginning users. As it happens, it's also a confounding one for *experienced* users. So I'll refer you, at this point, to the same item in the section called "Error Messages."

4. *A whole document window just disappears.*

Every now and then — and this happens even to the greats — you'll be trying to do something with the mouse when your entire spreadsheet (or manuscript or artwork) suddenly vanishes, and you find yourself in the Finder. No message appears — no "Save changes?," no "System error," nada.

What probably happened is that in the process of clicking the mouse, you accidentally clicked *outside* the document window. Of course, clicking a window (or outside a window) is the universal Mac signal that you want to bring some *other* open program to the front.

If your arrow's aim misses the document window (usually when you're trying to use a scroll bar, as shown in the figure below), you're most likely to click the gray background: the Finder.

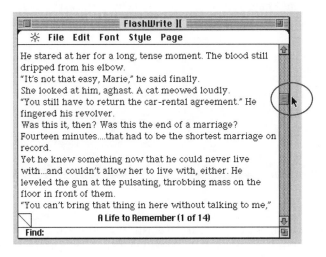

The Finder promptly jumps to the front, showing your folders and files, and the document that you were working on gets shoved into the background. (All together now: "It's a feature, not a bug.")

Now you know why, in the Performa Macs and in System 7.5, Apple offers an optional feature that makes the Finder get hidden *automatically* whenever you launch a program.

To bring your original program back, choose its name from the Application menu.

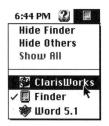

5. *There's a pile of stuff next to the Trash can.*

All the Mac books and manuals tell you how to chuck a file that you no longer want: drag its icon "to the Trash," meaning the Trash-can icon in the lower-right corner of your screen.

What's usually *not* made absolutely clear is that, as you drag the icon to the Trash can, you have to place the *tip* of the arrow cursor directly *on* the Trash-can icon. You have to see the Trash can itself turn black.

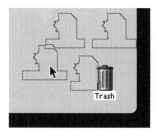 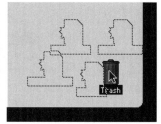

That may seem awkward, especially if you're dragging a whole group of icons at the same time. In the illustration above at left, for example, one of the icons being dragged is already bumping up against the edge of the screen.

You have to ignore that, though, and keep on moving the mouse until the arrow is directly on the Trash can (above, right).

6. *You're word processing, and all your text suddenly disappears.*

There are two possibilities, neither of which means that you've really lost your text.

First of all, not everyone is aware that when you fill a screen with text, a word processor automatically shoves that screenful up and off the top of your screen, in effect advancing you to the next clean sheet of paper. This diagram shows how the first page of text has scrolled off the top of the window:

As she slipped out of the silky almost-nothing she'd been
wearing, her shiny chestnut hair cascaded down across her
creamy shoulders.

"What you *don't* know about me, Arthur," she cooed, "is
that I'm not a woman at all."

An odor of electrical smoke touched his nostrils, and he
looked in horror as her graceful, womanly fingers—the very
fingers he'd kissed only moments before—grappled with a
seam near her collarbone. His breath quickened. A clock
ticked. Somewhere, in the distance, a wolf howled.

Attack of the Yuppie Aliens

ticked. Somewhere, in the distance, a wolf howled.

With a cold lick of fear, he realized that there would be
no attending the company picnic on Thursday.|

Page 1   Normal+...

Scroll upward to
bring the previous
page into view

But suppose that you *do* know all about scroll bars and scrolling, and you
scroll, and you decide that your text really *has* disappeared.

You may well be the victim of another not-immediately-obvious Mac
"feature": any highlighted text, from a single letter to a 4,000-page encyclopedia, is *instantly replaced* by the next keystroke that you type. Usually,
this arrangement is handy. If you want to replace the word *kickback* with
the words *incentive payment*, for example, you don't have to delete the
word *kickback* first. You just select it (see below, top) and then type
(below, bottom):

to accept the occasional kickback of
to accept the occasional incentive payment| of

The danger is that if you inadvertently (or advertently) select a bunch of
text and then touch any key — the spacebar, Return, or any letter key —
you'll replace everything that you selected with a space, a return, or a
letter. If this happens, the solution is easy: choose Undo from the Edit menu.

If it's too late for Undo — in other words, if you've done something else *since* deleting the text (Undo undoes only the *most* recent thing that you do) — you may be able to recover some of your text. Close your document *without* saving changes, and then reopen it. At least you'll see as much text as was there the last time you saved your work.

7. *There's a thin horizontal line all the way across your color monitor.*

   Believe it or not, *all* Apple 13-inch and 16-inch color monitors show this faint line (it's about a third of the way up the screen). It's a shadow cast by a wire inside. Just grit your teeth and remind yourself, "It's a Sony." (Sony makes these monitors.)

8. *You drag a file into a window, and the file disappears.*

   Once again, you have to watch your tip, if you'll excuse the expression. When you drag an icon, it's the cursor arrow's *tip* that actually marks where the icon is going, not the icon itself. What probably happened is that you accidentally released the icon when the arrow tip was on top of a *folder* within the window, as shown here:

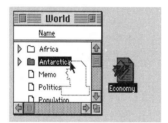

A word to writers

If you're a writer (or anybody else who plans to do a lot of typing), there's a way to protect yourself against *any* of the text-loss problems described earlier. Even if you (1) experience a system crash before you've had a chance to save your work, (2) accidentally replace all your text, or (3) *deliberately* delete some text but later wish that you hadn't, a little piece of software can save you. It's called Last Resort, and it lurks in the background of your Mac, silently logging everything that you type into a text file. You never see it and never notice it — *but* if the unmentionable happens, you can open the Last Resort text file and recover everything that you typed (ever since you installed Last Resort, in fact). See Appendix B, "The Resource Resource," for info. (Thunder 7 and Now Utilities have similar features.)

As a result, the Mac dropped the file *into* the folder, making it disappear from the screen.

9. *You can't print.*

There's a delightfully thorough discussion of printing problems later in this chapter.

10. *You become addicted to working with your Macintosh. The image of the Trash can gets burned into your corneas. Friends, family, and job recede and eventually fade away.*

Congratulations! You've graduated from this book.

Error Messages

Let's start the troubleshooting session in earnest with a few good old American error messages. Yes, kids, these are the '90s equivalent of "DOES NOT COMPUTE." These are messages, appearing in an *alert box* like the fictional one shown below, that indicate that something's wrong.

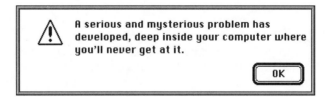

> ⚠ A serious and mysterious problem has developed, deep inside your computer where you'll never get at it.
>
> [OK]

"Application is busy or missing" or "Application not found"

I promised to return to this one. Here we go.

First resort: Not everything in the Mac world is meant to be a plaything for you; the Mac reserves a few files for its own use. If a thing came with your Mac — the Scrapbook file, the Clipboard file, and so on — you at least get *something* when you double-click its icon. The Clipboard file opens into a window where you can see the most recent stuff that you copied; the Note Pad file automatically launches the Note Pad desk accessory; and extensions or control panels at least identify themselves (by means of a message on the screen, such as "System Extension: This file adds functionality to your Macintosh").

But if you double-click an icon that belongs to *non*-Apple software — any icon in the Preferences folder, for example, or various other support-file icons for non-Apple stuff — you'll just get a beep and an unhelpful error message.

That's what's going on *most* of the time. (Review Chapter 6 for more information on double-clicking things in the System Folder.)

Second resort: Every now and then, you'll double-click a file that *you* created and *still* get the "Application not found" message. Refer to Chapter 3, where you learned about programs and the documents that they produce (like parents and children). In this case, you're trying to open a document (child), but the Mac can't find its parent (the program used to create it).

So if you double-click a ClarisWorks document, but the ClarisWorks program itself isn't on your hard disk, the Mac shrugs and asks, in effect, "Yo — how am I s'posed to open this?" To remedy the situation, reinstall the missing program on the hard disk.

Third resort: Sometimes, you get the "Application not found" message even if you're sure that the document's parent program is on the disk. (You double-click a ClarisWorks document, for example, and you're told that the application — ClarisWorks — can't be found, even though it's *sitting right there* on the disk in plain sight!)

In a situation like this, the Mac's genealogical gnomes have become confused: the computer has lost track of which program is associated with which kinds of documents. Don't ask me how such confusions happen; just rejoice that the problem is easy to fix. In the words of Mac gurus everywhere, "You gotta rebuild the Desktop."

Now, then, before you grope for your woodworking tools, let's analyze this concept of rebuilding the Desktop. The Desktop is a very important file on your disk. How come you've never seen it? Because the Desktop file is *invisible.* (Yes, Mac icons can be invisible. Remember that fact if you ever get involved in antiterrorist espionage activity.) The file is something that the Mac maintains for its own use.

The Mac stores two kinds of information in the Desktop file: the actual pictures used as icons for all your files and information about the parent-child (program-document) relationships that you're having trouble with.

If the Desktop file becomes confused (which results in the "not found" message), you have to reset it. Actually, you have to brainwash the file, forcing it to unlearn the misconceptions that are giving you trouble, and then to relearn the correct relationships between documents and the programs that gave birth to them. For instructions, see the "Rebuilding the Desktop file" sidebar.

Rebuilding the Desktop file

Turn the computer on. As it starts gearing up, press and *hold* the Option and ⌘ keys. Don't let go. Keep them down until the Mac explicitly asks you whether you want to "rebuild the Desktop." (Obviously, you should click OK.)

After that's done, your document double-clicking will work if, in fact, the parent program is on the disk. Also, your Mac, having been cleansed of all obsolete icons, will run faster and more smoothly.

Last resort: There's one more circumstance under which you'll get this message: if you try to open a generic text or graphics file that's not associated with *any* particular program.

(Sigh.) Yes, I know, this contradicts everything you've learned about programs and documents being like parents and children. But suppose that someone who isn't sure which brand of word processor you own wants to give you a memo that she wrote. The smart thing would be for her to give you the memo in *text-only* format: a generic, no-frills, raw-typing format. Text-only format is a text file or, as the weenies say, an *ASCII* (pronounced ASKie) text file. No matter which program was used to create this file, *any* word processor (even on non-Mac computers, for that matter) can open it.

A text file, however, isn't double-clickable. (Actually, in System 7, the Mac offers to open a text file with TeachText or SimpleText, but just pretend that I have a point here.) To read the file, launch your word processor *first*, and then choose the Open command from the File menu (below, left).

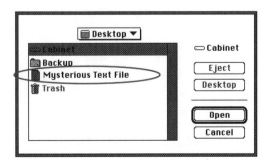

The usual list box appears, and you'll see the text file listed there (above, right). Double-click to open it.

The same applies to generic *picture* documents. The weenie word here is *PICT*; a PICT file is a generic, any-program-can-open-this artwork file. If you try to double-click a generic PICT file, you'll be told, "Application not found." Once again, the solution is to launch your graphics program (MacDraw, for example) *first* and then open the PICT file via the Open command.

"An error of Type 1 occurred" or "Bad F-Line Instruction"

This message, which is the equivalent of a 1950s-movie computer saying "Does not compute," conveys nothing. It simply means that something has gone terribly wrong inside and that you have to start over. See Chapter 9 for more information on this frustrating occurrence.

Turn the Mac off and then on again, or use the Restart switch (see "The Restart switch" sidebar later in this chapter).

As you've probably guessed, this message means that anything you typed — *and did not save* — is gone forever. Reality bites.

If you get a *lot* of these messages, however, it's time to wonder why. The Mac is not supposed to crash a lot!

Without question, the problem is your extensions. As you read earlier, having the wrong mix of extension files inside your System Folder is an invitation to conflicts and problems. Toward the end of this chapter, you'll find a section called "Extension conflicts," which shows you how to determine which ones are responsible for ruining your life.

"Sorry, a System error has occurred"

Once again, the most likely culprit is an extension, as described in the preceding paragraphs. Skip to "Extension conflicts" later in this chapter.

"You do not have enough access privileges"

First resort: Wow, does this message make people mad. "Not enough *access privileges!?*" they scream. "It's *my darned computer!*"

Right you are. If you have a Performa or System 7.5, however, your darned computer has a useful feature that can actually save your Mac from the marauding actions of children or ignoramuses. This feature is called Protect System Folder.

Choose Control Panels from your menu. Open the control panel called General Controls (on a Performa, it may be called Performa). There, you'll see the on/off switch for this System Folder protection business. You'll see a similar checkbox for protecting your Applications folder, if you have one.

```
┌─ Folder Protection ────────────────────┐
│                                         │
│  ☒ Protect System Folder       📁       │
│                                         │
│  ☐ Protect Applications folder  📁       │
│                                         │
└─────────────────────────────────────────┘
```

How, you may well ask, does this feature protect anything? All it does is prevent you from *moving* any of the icons in your System Folder. You can't throw them in the Trash; you can't put them in folders; you can't, in fact, do anything that would mess up your Mac.

If you try, you'll be told — yessirree — "You do not have enough access privileges." If you really *do* want to move something out of your System Folder or Applications folder, open the control panel again and turn the Protect feature off.

Last resort: If you *don't* have a Performa or System 7.5, there's only one possibility: you are, or have been, connected to another Macintosh (in the lingo, *networked*). Which means that in theory, you have remote-control invasion rights to somebody else's computer. Which means that in theory, the somebody else probably protected his stuff from over-the-network pillaging. Which ultimately means that sure enough, you don't have enough "access privileges" (i.e., permission) to root through that other Mac via network.

If you really, really want to know more about the headachy world of networking, fatter, finer books than this one are available for that purpose.

"Not enough memory to open Word"

This message is a biggie, so it gets a section all by itself; see "Out of Memory" later in this chapter.

"Application has unexpectedly quit"

You're probably out of memory. Again, see "Out of Memory."

Even if your Mac has plenty of memory, however, the individual *program* that just "unexpectedly quit" may not have enough memory allotted to it. To find out how to give your program a more generous helping of memory, see the upcoming sidebar called "Memory tactics."

"The disk is full"

This means that the disk is full.

It happens to the best of us: over time, your hard disk gets fuller and fuller. Then, with only a megabyte of storage space to go, you try to do something (like saving an important file), and you're told that there's no more elbow room.

You'll have to make some more room. From the Application menu (at the top-right corner of your screen), choose Finder. Root through your files, find some things to throw away, and drag them to the Trash can. Don't forget to *empty* the trash (by choosing the Empty Trash command from the Special menu).

"Can't empty trash"

First resort: There's probably a locked file in the Trash can. Press Option while choosing Empty Trash from the Special menu.

Second resort: It's possible that you're trying to throw away a document that you're still working on. Or maybe the Mac just *thinks* that you're still working on it. Be sure that the file isn't open on the screen. Sometimes, you even have to *quit the program* you were using before that document is considered to be trashable.

Third resort: Maybe the Mac has become confused about the trashability of some file in the Trash. Restart the Mac and try again.

Last resort: About once in every Mac user's life, the Mac gets *so* confused that it simply will not empty the Trash, even if you've tried all the logical things.

In this case, it's your System Folder that's having the psychotic break. The trick is to start up from *some other* System Folder — the handiest of which comes on your all-important Disk Tools (or Utilities) disk. This special startup disk comes with every Mac ever made, so you can't claim helplessness on this point.

Turn off the computer. Put Disk Tools (or Utilities) into the disk drive. Then turn the Mac on. When the computer is running, you should at last be able to empty the Trash.

"An error occurred while writing to the disk"

Something went wrong while you were trying to save a document — probably your disk was full, or it's a flaky floppy disk. (See "Floppy-Disk Flukes" later in this chapter for more information on flaky floppies.)

"Microsoft Word prefers 2048K of memory. 2000K is available"

Once again, you're out of memory. The Mac will give you the chance to launch the program anyway — but it'll run slowly and may crash if you get too ambitious with your work. See the "Memory tactics" sidebar for a more lucid explanation.

Out of Memory

As a service to you, the Tremulous Novice, I haven't even whispered a word about memory management, which is a whole new ball of wax. I hoped that you'd never need to think about it. Memory really becomes an issue only when you get the message "There is not enough memory to open Word" (or whatever program you're trying to open), and that's why you're reading about memory in a troubleshooting chapter.

Your Mac has a fixed amount of memory. Think of the Mac as a station wagon. You can pack it with camping gear, or you can pack it with your kid's birthday-party friends, but probably not with both. Even if you manage to cram in the kids and the gear, if you *then* try to cram in the dog, somebody in the family is going to say, "There is not enough room to take Bowser."

That's what the Mac is trying to tell you.

Each program that you open consumes a chunk of the Mac's limited memory. You're entitled to run as many programs as you want simultaneously — the Note Pad, the Calculator, your word processor, and so on — *provided* that they all fit into the amount of memory your Mac has. If you try to open one too many programs, you'll get that message about the dog. (*You* know what I mean.)

First resort: Quit programs

If you're told that you're out of memory, the easiest way out of the situation is to *quit* one of the programs you're already running. (You quit a program by choosing Quit from the File menu.) So if you're running Word and you try to open the Calculator, and you're told that there's not enough unused (free) memory, you'll just have to quit Word first.

Memory tactics

Here's how you can get a clue:

✔ Go to the Finder. From the menu, choose About This Macintosh. This helpful dialog box appears, showing several important numbers about your use of memory:

This is how much memory your Mac has. (If you want to convert this number to megs, mentally replace the comma with a decimal point.)

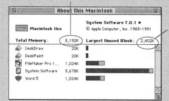

This is the largest chunk of memory you have left, intowhich you can open more programs. (There may be smaller chunks available, too.)

In the bottom part of the box, you can see what's already taking up memory and how *much* memory each program is taking up (see those bars?).

You may find it useful, however, to *change* the amount of memory that each of your programs uses. If you're experiencing a lot of system crashes, for example, the program may need a bigger memory allotment. If memory is at a premium, you may be able to give a program *less* memory, freeing some for other purposes.

Here's how:

✔ Quit the program whose memory appetite you want to change, and then click its icon.

✔ From the File menu, choose Get Info. This box appears:

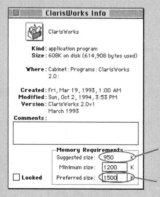

This is the amount of memory suggested by the programmers...

...but you can change the program's actual memory appetite by editing this number.

✔ Change the number in the Preferred size box (in older systems, it's called the Current size). This number is the amount of memory that the program will actually consume when you run it. Unless System crashes make your life more interesting, don't set the Preferred (Current) size much below the Suggested size, though.

Second resort: Make the Mac give back

Quitting programs, of course, isn't a very convenient solution — especially if having multiple programs open is part of what you're *trying* to do, such as copying numbers *from* the Calculator *to* Word. Therefore, your next attempt to solve the problem should be to make the Mac itself use less memory.

Yes, indeed, the Mac's own behind-the-scenes operations use memory like a silicon hog — at minimum, System 7 grabs 1.5MB of your memory. If your Mac has only 4MB to begin with, you can see why it's easy to run out of memory.

Here are some tricks to make the Mac use less memory:

- ✔ Use fewer *extensions* — the little auto-loading programs whose icons appear across the bottom of the screen when you start the Mac. Each extension that didn't come with your Mac (screen savers, menu clocks, virus checkers, and so on) eats up another nibble of your memory.

- ✔ Turn off File Sharing. Those of you who are advanced enough to be using this complicated feature know who you are. March right up to that Control Panels command in the menu, young man or woman, choose Sharing Setup, and click the Stop button. You'll immediately get back one-fifth of a megabyte of memory.

  And while you're shutting things off, open the Chooser (by choosing its name from the menu), and select AppleTalk Inactive, if it's not already selected. If you have a laser printer, you've just killed your ability to print, but you've reclaimed another one-fifth of a meg of memory. Turn AppleTalk back on when you have to print.

- ✔ Turn off Adobe Type Manager (ATM), if you have it. How do you know? Choose Find from the Finder's File menu, and look for it. This piece of type-enhancement software is amazing (see "Font format #2½: Adobe Type Manager" in Chapter 4), but it gulps up memory like there's no tomorrow. Either turn ATM off or turn it down (use its control panel to decrease its memory allotment).

- ✔ Got System 7.5 or later? Be aware that the much-heralded QuickDraw GX feature wolfs down an insane amount of memory: more than 1.5MB. (Check Chapter 4 for a description of this wonderful, but gluttonous, feature.)

  To turn off GX, open your System Folder. Open your Extensions folder. Drag QuickDraw GX out of there — onto the Desktop, for example. And then restart the computer. (Not everybody who has System 7.5 installed GX, though. If you don't see it in your Extensions folder, you didn't install it.)

Now you have that 1.5MB of memory back again. Of course, you no longer have QuickDraw GX doing its magic for you.

✓ Another potential memory stealer is the Disk Cache. This little gimmick is something that you can blissfully ignore for most of your computing days … until you start running out of memory.

Suppose that you're innocently word processing, and you make some text boldface. Because the word processing program resides on your hard disk, the Mac consults the disk to find out how it's supposed to create bold type. This disk-reading business takes, say, one second. If you use boldface a lot, those one-second disk searches are going to cumulatively slow both you and your Mac.

Therefore, the Mac reserves a piece of memory, called the Disk Cache, just for such frequent pieces of information. *Now* when you make text boldface, the Mac consults the disk (taking one second), but it stores the "how-to-make-bold" information in the Disk Cache. The *second* time that you need to create bold text, the Mac already knows how to do it; your text becomes bold in $1/100$ of a second (because memory delivers information to the Mac's brain 100 times faster than the disk does). Cumulatively, all the little tidbits of information that the Mac stores in the Disk Cache give you quite a speed boost.

The larger this piece of memory is, the faster your Mac will go. But there's the rub: if you make this Disk Cache memory *too* big, you'll use memory that you could be using to run programs.

Even if I've totally lost you, here's what to do when you're strapped for memory:

From the menu, choose Control Panels, and double-click Memory. Clicking the arrow, as shown below, makes the Disk Cache smaller (you can go all the way down to 32K).

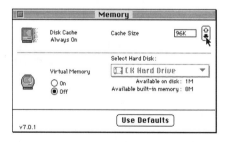

This has been a long explanation for a small reclamation of memory, I know, but it feels good to know what's going on behind the scenes, doesn't it?

Third resort: Defragment your RAM

Sometimes, the Mac will appall you. Here it is, the equivalent of a whole *roomful* of 1950s-style computers, yet it can't even add.

Here's the scenario. Your Mac has 5MB of memory, let's say. You know your System uses 1.5MB. And you're running Excel, which, let's suppose, takes 2MB.

Then you try to launch ClarisWorks, which we'll suppose needs 1.5MB of memory. You get the out-of-memory message. How can this be? After all, the System (1.5) and Excel (2) together use only 3.5 of your 5MB. There ought to be 1.5MB left over, right? What's going on?

Memory fragmentation is going on, if you must know. It works like this:

At noon, you start the Mac. Your memory usage looks like this:

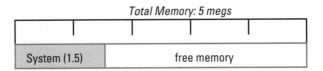

Then, at 12:05, you open the Calculator. For this example, let's say that its memory requirement is half a megabyte.

When you then launch Excel, your Mac's memory map looks like this:

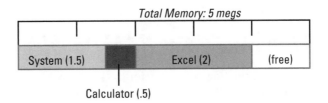

At 12:15, you close the Calculator. Your memory map looks like this:

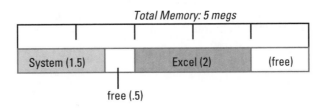

If you look at this last drawing, you'll see that you can't launch ClarisWorks (which needs 1.5MB) now because there isn't 1.5MB of *contiguous* memory left! Because of the sequence, you've inadvertently chopped your remaining memory into two smaller chunks, neither of which alone can accommodate ClarisWorks.

The solution to the I-*know*-I-have-enough-memory-to-launch-this problem is to *quit* all your programs so that only the Finder is running and *then* launch all the programs that are supposed to fit in your Mac's memory. This time, it will work.

Fourth resort: Starve your software

So far, we've assumed that each program has a certain memory requirement: 1MB, 2MB, three potato, four. What you may not realize is that *you* can determine how much memory a program eats up. For instructions, see the "Memory tactics" sidebar a few pages back.

Why is this useful? Sometimes when you install a program, the Current size (the amount of memory that it consumes) is set to a much higher number than it needs to be, which can only make your memory-shortage problems worse. Word 5.1, for example, comes set to 2048K (which equals 2MB), but it *really* only needs 1MB or less to run. Its programmers assumed that you'd be using all its fancy features: the grammar checker, the thesaurus, the automatic hyphenator, and so on. Besides, those programmers tend to do *their* work on Macs the size of a Buick.

If you *don't* plan to use these features, drag them out of the Word Commands folder, and by all means reset Word's memory allotment to something more reasonable.

Fifth resort: Get RAM Doubler

Here's a fascinating possibility for the RAM-shy Mac fan: buy a $50 program called RAM Doubler.

RAM Doubler uses several potent, deeply technical tricks to make your Mac *behave* as though it has twice as much memory as it really does. Most people who try it love it. The rest get their money back!

The only fundamental understanding of RAM Doubler that you need is this: it lets you run *more small programs at the same time*. It *doesn't* let you run one *big* program that requires more real memory than you have.

So Billy Bob, who has a 4-meg PowerBook and who wants to run ClarisWorks and Kid Pix at the same time, is made in the shade. He no longer has to quit Kid Pix just to free enough memory to launch ClarisWorks. RAM Doubler lets him keep both programs going.

Jenny Sue, however, wants very much to run Photoshop or Myst on her 4-meg LC. She's out of luck. Those programs require about 5 megs of memory apiece. RAM Doubler's double-memory tactics don't let you run any *big* programs that you couldn't run before.

Sixth resort: Use virtual memory

Here's another rather technical but interesting possibility for avoiding out-of-memory problems. Fortunately, this solution lets you run programs whose combined memory requirements add up to much more than your Mac should be able to handle. Unfortunately, it requires you to learn a new term. Ponder this tradeoff for a moment; then read on, if you dare.

The new term is *virtual memory.* (*Virtual* means *fake,* as in "virtual reality.") Under this scheme (unique to System 7 and later), the Mac attempts to use the hard disk as emergency memory.

Suppose that your Mac has 4MB of memory, but you want to run both LimerickWriter (which requires 2MB) and BrailleMeister (which also requires 2MB). Because your System requires 1.5MB by itself, you can see that 2 + 2 + 1.5 is going to equal more than your 4MB.

If you were using virtual memory, though, the Mac would allow you to run both programs simultaneously. Where would it get the extra 1.5MB of memory that it needs to fit everything in? It would use an empty hunk of hard-disk space.

Read this slowly: When you're in LimerickWriter, the Mac stashes the excess 1.5MB worth of BrailleMeister information on the hard disk. Then, when you bring the BrailleMeister window to the front, the Mac quickly feeds that 1.5MB worth of information back into actual memory, displacing the same amount of LimerickWriter instructions (which, needless to say, it writes back onto the hard disk). Each time you switch programs, the Mac juggles the overflow.

This switch doesn't take place instantaneously; that's a lot of information for the Mac to shuttle back and forth between memory and the hard disk. (Maybe it's time to reread Chapter 1^1/$_2$, which describes memory and hard disks in pulse-quickening detail.) In fact, there may be quite a lag when you switch from one program to another. But a little waiting sure beats not being *able* to run those two important programs at the same time.

For some mysterious technical reason, the amount of hard-disk space that the Mac needs to perform this stunt isn't just the amount of pretend memory you want to *add* to your real memory. That is, if your Mac has 5MB of memory, and you'd like your Mac to think that it has 8MB, you can't just set aside the difference (3MB) in hard-disk space. Golly, no. You have to allow a chunk of disk space that's the size of *all* the memory, real and imagined — in this case, 8MB.

OK. All that having been said (and read), let's get to the actual process of using virtual memory. Follow these steps:

1. From the menu, choose Control Panels; then double-click Memory.

   The control panel appears, like this:

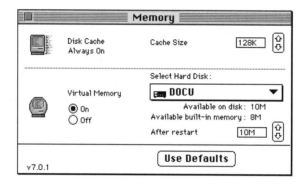

   See the Virtual Memory area? If not, your Mac isn't equipped for this feature. (Some of the older ones aren't, including the original Classic and the original LC.)

2. From the pop-up menu, specify the hard disk that you want the Mac to use as its temporary fake-memory dumping ground.

   If you have only one drive — the one inside your Mac — skip this step.

3. Using the little up-and-down arrows, specify how big you want that virtual-memory file (on your hard disk) to be.

   Remember: there has to be a chunk of empty hard-disk space that's big enough to hold the *total* of your real memory and the extra, phony memory that you'd like to have.

   Don't create total memory more than double your *real* memory. If you have 4MB of RAM, your total memory (including virtual) shouldn't exceed 8MB; things will get so slow as to be unworkable.

Oh, yeah: if you're going to set virtual memory *higher* than 8MB, you also need to turn on the 32-bit addressing switch (if your Mac displays one in the Memory control panel).

The Mac may tell you that there's not enough room on your disk. Maybe it's time to go on a cleaning binge.

4. When you're done with your virtual-memory setup, restart the Mac.

Last resort: Buy more

After a certain point, knocking yourself out to solve out-of-memory problems (like those listed in this chapter) reaches a point of diminishing returns. You get so worn out from workarounds that they're not worth doing.

At that point (or much sooner), just spring for the $40 per megabyte and *buy more memory*. You can get it from any mail-order company (such as Mac-Connection). You can install memory yourself, fairly easily, in many Mac II-something models. Installing memory in a one-piece Mac (such as a Classic) or a Quadra, however, is trickier and requires some funky tools. Anyway, when you call a mail-order company to buy memory, tell them what Mac you have and find out what you'll need. Sometimes, the company will send you a how-to video, which is very handy — and when you're done with it, you can use it to record *Seinfeld*.

Installing memory yourself is not difficult. But to please the lawyers, here's the warning: technically, if you cause any other part of the computer to malfunction as a result of your installation, you risk voiding the one-year Apple warranty.

Having lots of memory to kick around in is a joy. Your Mac runs faster, has fewer crashes and glitches, and acts like a new machine. It's a situation that I heartily recommend.

Starting Up

Problems that you encounter when you turn on the Mac are especially disheartening when you're a new Mac user. It does wonders for your self-esteem to think that you can't even turn the thing *on* without problems.

No ding, no picture

First resort: Chances are very, very, very good that your Mac simply isn't getting electricity. It's probably not plugged in. Or it's plugged into a power strip that has an On/Off switch that's currently set to Off. Or (if it's a Power-Book) the battery is completely dead; plug in the adapter for ten minutes before trying again.

Second resort: If you have a two-piece Mac, you normally turn the machine on by pressing the triangle key on the keyboard. Maybe the keyboard isn't plugged in. Check that.

Third resort: Here's another PowerBook possibility. It may be that the internal circuitry known as the *power manager* has gotten drunk again. Unplug the PowerBook *and* take its battery out. Let it sit like that for ten minutes. Then put it together and try again.

Last resort: If none of those steps solved the problem, your Mac is as dead as Elvis. Get it in for repair. But that's virtually never the actual problem.

Ding, no picture

If you hear the startup chime (or ding) but the monitor doesn't light up, something's wrong with the monitor.

First resort: Is the screen brightness turned up? On most Macs, there's a brightness dial on the edge of the monitor. On a Classic, you have to use the Brightness control panel.

Second resort: I don't mean to insult your intelligence — but is it possible that you have a screen-saver program installed? (You know, like After Dark ... flying toasters, all that?) To find out whether that's the cause of the current black-ness, click the mouse button. If the screen picture doesn't appear, read on.

Third resort: If you have a two-piece Mac, the monitor has to be (1) plugged into the Mac, (2) plugged into a power source, *and* (3) turned on. (Not every-body realizes that the monitor has an On/Off switch.) Often, the monitor is plugged into the AC outlet on the Mac itself; that's OK.

Last resort: Does your monitor require a graphics card? Some old models do. (Of course, if your Mac needs a graphics card, you would have discovered this problem the day you got your system.)

Picture, no ding

Every Mac makes a sound when it's turned on. In fact, even if you've set the volume level of your Mac's speaker to zero (by using the Sound control panel), you still get a sound when you start the Mac.

First resort: Look at the little speaker jack in the back of the Mac. If there's some kind of plug in it — some kid's Walkman headphones, a cord connected to a stereo, or a pretzel stick — no sound can come out of the Mac speaker.

Last resort: There's a remote possibility that somebody, mucking around inside your two-piece Mac, unplugged the speaker-wire cable. Find that person, yell firmly into his or her nearer ear, and insist that the cable (inside the Mac) be reconnected.

Four musical notes (or crash sound)

If you hear an arpeggio, a lick of the *Twilight Zone* theme, or a car-crash sound, something's seriously wrong inside the Mac (Apple's sense of humor at work).

Fortunately, 50 percent of the time, you hear this sound just after installing new memory. It means that one of the memory chips is loose or defective — something that you (or whoever installed the memory for you) can fix relatively easily. And 40 percent of the time, it's a SCSI problem. Read on.

First resort: If you've just installed or otherwise messed around with the memory chips in your computer, that's certainly the problem. Reopen the Mac. Carefully remove each memory chip and reinstall it, checking the little centipede legs to make sure that they're not bent. (Come to think of it, get someone who knows what he or she's doing to do this.)

Second resort: The other common source of funny startup notes is a SCSI problem of some kind. (Yes, I know that we haven't defined this in a while; for instructions, see "Scuzzy SCSI" later in this chapter.) For a quick fix, just unplug any external hard drive or scanner from the SCSI jack (the very wide one) in the back of the Mac, and try starting up again.

Last resort: If it's truly not a memory-chip or SCSI problem, call your Apple dealer. This baby's sick.

The Restart switch

Every Mac has this switch. Sometimes, there are two buttons side by side somewhere on the Mac's casing — and the one with a left-pointing triangle is the Restart switch. Sometimes, as on older PowerBooks, there are two little back-panel *holes* that you're supposed to stick a pin into. And on all the other models, it's a *secret* Restart switch; you press Control, the ⌘ key, and the On button (or key) at the same time.

In every case, pressing Restart is the same as turning your Mac off and then on again, except that it doesn't suddenly send a wall of electricity thudding into the machine's delicate electronics. Therefore, Restart is gentler to your Mac. It's good to keep the Restart switch in mind when you have a System freeze or crash, too.

A question mark blinks on the screen

The blinking question mark is the Mac's international symbol for "I've looked everywhere, and I can't find a System Folder anywhere."

If your hard disk, like most people's, is inside the Mac, the blinking question mark means that it's not working right — or that it's working fine, but your System Folder got screwed up somehow. In either case, here's what to do.

First resort: Panic. (Who are we kidding? You're going to do this anyway.)

Second resort: After ten seconds of that, turn the Mac off and try starting again, or just press the Restart switch (see the preceding sidebar).

Third resort: Find a floppy disk with a System Folder on it. The best bet is the white System disks (or the startup CD) that came with your Mac. The floppy called Disk Tools or Utilities usually does the trick. Put it into the disk drive, and turn the Mac on.

If you arrive at some kind of Installer screen, you must have used a System Software Installer disk, and (alas) it's not going to help you get going. If the screen says something about needing a newer version of the System software than 7.1, the disk doesn't have the little *Enabler file* that your Mac needs to run. (See Chapter 6 for a discussion of these important little rascals.)

But if the Mac happily accepts the disk, displays the smiling-Mac picture, and goes on to the familiar desktop, look for your hard disk's icon to appear. If it's there, in its customary upper-right-corner-of-the-screen position, reinstall the

System software (using those same white floppies, starting with the Install disk), and start over — first making sure that you have a copy of everything useful on the disk, of course.

Fourth resort: If the hard-drive icon still doesn't appear, read "Scuzzy SCSI" later in this chapter.

Fifth resort: This solution is really, *really* technical. I've never even seen it work. But repair people say that it could, theoretically, work. It's called — do *not* learn this term — *zapping the PRAM* (pronounced PEA-ram).

First, turn off (or restart) your Mac. Then turn it on again, but hold down four keys at the same time — ⌘, Option, P, and R — and don't let go until you hear the startup chime. Supposedly, this procedure can help.

Last resort: If nothing has worked, and you still can't make your hard-drive icon appear on the screen, your hard drive is sick. Call your local dealer or Mac guru, and do *not* freak out — chances are very good that all of your files are still intact. (Just because the platters aren't spinning doesn't mean that they've been wiped out, just as your Walkman tapes don't get erased when the Walkman runs out of batteries.)

In fact, you can probably rescue the data from your disk yourself. Buy a disk-recovery program, such as Norton Utilities or MacTools Deluxe. That'll let you grab anything useful off the disk and may even help heal what's wrong with it.

Some crazy program launches itself every time you start up

In the words of Mac programmers everywhere, "It's a feature, not a bug."

Inside the System Folder, there's a folder called Startup Items. Look inside it. Somebody put a program or document in there.

Anything in the Startup Items folder automatically opens when you turn on the Mac. This feature is supposed to be a time-saver for people who work on the same documents every day.

System Crashes and Freezes

There are two scary conditions that are enough to make even semipro Mac jockeys swallow hard and feel a little helpless. The first of these conditions, a system *crash*, occurs when this message appears on the screen:

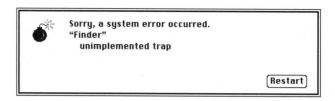

> Sorry, a system error occurred.
> "Finder"
>   unimplemented trap
>
>   [Restart]

Your current work session is over, amigo; you have to restart the computer. Anything that you've typed or drawn since the last time you saved your work is gone. (Safest way to restart is to press the Restart switch, as described in "The Restart switch" a couple pages ago.)

A System *freeze* is different — and, as horrific computer nightmares go, it's preferable. You get no message on the screen; instead, the mouse cursor freezes in place. You can't move the cursor, and nothing that you type changes anything. The Mac, as far as you can tell, has silicon lockjaw.

Escaping a System crash

You can't. Restart the computer. Don't even bother trying to click the Restart button on the *screen,* which doesn't do anything.

Escaping repeated System crashes

Ninety percent of the time, crashes are related either to memory or to *extension conflicts* — the dreaded topic that's looming only a few pages away.

First resort: Increase the amount of memory allotted to the program that you were using, as described in the "Memory tactics" sidebar several pages ago. Give the program 150K more, for example.

Second resort: Something, or several somethings, clashed in your System Folder. See "Extension conflicts," which is coming up. If you're in a hurry to get your work done and can't take the time, just restart your Mac while pressing the Shift key. That turns *all* extensions off.

Third resort: If the crashes still haven't stopped, it's possible that something in your System Folder got gummed up. You're in for a 20-minute, but *very* effective, ritual known as a clean re-install of your System Folder. For instruction, see the sidebar called "The beauty of a 'clean re-install.'"

The beauty of a "clean re-install"

This procedure is just a wee bit technical. But, look — if it'll save your Mac's life and won't cost anything, isn't it worth slogging through?

As the gears of your System Folder grind away day after day, little corruptions and rough edges can develop. The following procedure replaces your old, possibly corroded System Folder with a brand-spanking-new one. It's nearly *guaranteed* to wipe out any erratic, bizarre crashes or freezes that you've been having.

This process will, however, require your System installation disks: your pile of white Apple floppy disks, a startup CD-ROM disc, or your Apple Backup disks (for Performas). If you don't have those disks ready, get them. (If you're really stuck, you can always buy a replacement set of System disks, in the form of System 7.1 or 7.5.)

If you have System 7.5: Insert the first Installer disk (or the System 7.5 CD). Double-click the Installer icon. At the main installation screen — where you'd normally click the Install button — press ⌘-Shift-K, of all things. You'll be asked which you want: a *brand-new System Folder,* or just an updated *existing* System Folder. You want the whole new one. Click your choice, click OK, click Install, and then follow the directions.

If you have earlier System versions: Open your System Folder. See the Finder icon? The purpose here is to *hide* it, so that it's no longer in the same folder as the System *suitcase* icon. Drag the Finder into, for example, the Preferences folder, as shown here:

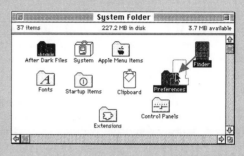

You're doing beautifully. Now close the System Folder window, press Return, and *rename* the System Folder. (Call it "Old System" or something like that.)

Finally, take the Install Me First disk (or Apple Backup disk, or startup CD), and insert it. Double-click the icon called Installer; then follow the directions on the screen, feeding floppy disks into the drive as requested.

Regardless of your System version: The result of all this is a virgin, clean System Folder, free of any corruptions. But all your customized fonts, control panels, preferences, and so on are stranded back in your Old System Folder!

Ideally, you should install each of these items from their original, store-bought floppy disks. If that's too much hassle, copy them, item by item, from your Old System Folder to your new System Folder. Do so with care, however, so that you don't simply reinstate whatever problems you were having.

Fourth resort: You may have a SCSI conflict on your hands, especially if more than one external gizmo is plugged into your Mac. See "Scuzzy SCSI" later in this chapter.

Fifth resort: If nothing so far has stopped the crashes, some weird memory-related thing may be going on under the hood. Some programs are allergic to virtual memory, for example; so your second step should be to turn off Virtual Memory (open your Memory control panel, and click the Off button). And if you're advanced enough to know what 32-bit addressing is, go to the Memory control panel and turn *it* off, if your Mac lets you. A lot of older programs break out in puffy hives when *that* is on.

Sixth resort: You don't, by any chance, have *two* System Folders on your hard disk, do you? That's like throwing two baseballs at the same time to a Little League shortstop; chances are that he'll panic and won't catch either one. Usually, people add another System Folder accidentally, in the process of copying new software to the hard disk from a floppy. If you don't want your Mac to (forgive me) drop the ball, use the Finder's Find command to search for *system,* to make sure that you have only one.

Last resort: If you're *still* having system crashes, particularly if they don't seem to be related to any specific program, the fault may lie in the way that your hard disk was prepared. Once again, I'm wading in waters that are technologically too deep for my comfort. But particularly if you purchased your Mac new in 1991 or before (in other words, before System 7), frequent system crashes are a telltale sign that you need to *reformat* the hard disk.

That tiresome task involves copying *everything* from the hard disk (onto a million floppies, for example, or just onto another hard disk) and then using a hard-disk formatting program to erase the disk completely. One such reformatting program is on the white Disk Tools disk that came with your Mac; it's called Apple HD SC Setup. Other popular programs are Drive 7 and FWB Hard Disk Toolkit. Also, if you bought an external hard drive, you may have a drive-formatting program on a floppy disk that came with the drive.

In any case, the main thing is to ensure that your formatting program is *System 7-compatible.* (All the programs that I named above are compatible.)

When you've erased and reformatted your hard drive, copy all your intellectual belongings back onto it. You'll probably be amazed by how many fewer crashes you experience.

Extension conflicts

OK, here it is — the long-awaited extension-conflict discussion.

See, each *extension* (a self-loading background program, such as a screen saver, that you install in your System Folder) was written by a programmer who had no clue what *other* extensions you'd be using. As a result, two extensions may fight, resulting in that polite disclaimer "Sorry, a System error has occurred."

These things are easy to fix, once you know the secret. Shut off your Mac, and then turn it on again (or just press the Restart switch). But as the Mac is starting up, hold down the Shift key, and keep it down until (1) you see the message "Extensions off" or (2) you arrive at the Desktop, whichever you notice first.

Your Mac probably won't give you trouble anymore — but now, of course, you're running without *any* of your cute little extension programs. No screen saver, no macro program, and so on.

If the point of this exercise is to pinpoint *which* extensions aren't getting along, you have two choices. One is free but takes a lot of time. The other costs $50 or so but works automatically.

The hard way: Burrow into your System Folder to find the Extensions folder, where these little guys live. Drag a few of their icons out of that folder onto the Desktop; that's how you prevent *selected* extensions from loading. You don't have to throw the extensions away; just take them out of the System Folder and then restart the computer. (Use the Restart command in the Special menu.)

If the Mac doesn't crash this time, you can pretty much bet that one of the extensions you removed was the guilty party. If the Mac *does* crash again, repeat the whole process, but this time take some more extension icons out of the System Folder.

Through trial and error, you eventually should be able to figure out which pair of extensions don't get along. Sometimes, just renaming one so that it alphabetically precedes its enemy is enough to solve the problem.

The easy way: A company called Casady & Greene offers a program called Conflict Catcher. This program does many useful things for managing your extensions, but its main virtue is catching conflicts. It can figure out, all by itself, which extension (or extensions) caused your Mac's problems. All you have to do is sit there, restarting the Mac over and over, each time telling Conflict Catcher whether or not the problem has been solved yet. By the time the process is over, the program will emblazon the name of the errant extensions on your screen; you then can dismember, disembowel, or trash them as you see fit.

System freezes

If your System freezes and your cursor locks in place, you can't save the work in the program that you were using. You don't, however, have to sell your Mac or even restart it. Instead, try this amazing keystroke: ⌘-Option–Esc. (This is about the only time that you'll ever use the Esc key.)

If it works, you'll get a dialog box that says, "Force [this program] to quit?" Click Force Quit, and you exit the program that you were working in.

So what's the big whoop? Well, if you had several programs running, this technique dumps only the *one* that you were working in — the one that crashed. You now have a chance to enter each of the *other* programs that are still running and save your work (if you haven't done so). Then, to be on the safe side, restart the Mac.

What causes a system freeze? Pretty much the same kinds of things that cause system crashes (see above).

Scuzzy SCSI

I've tried to shield you as much as possible from the term *SCSI* and all that it entails. But because it's one of the most common sources of trouble, it's time to put on the overalls and get dirty.

If there's nothing attached to your SCSI jack in the back of the Mac (for example, a scanner or a removable cartridge drive), you *have* no SCSI problems, and you should skip this entire section. You don't know how lucky you are.

What's SCSI?

They pronounce it "scuzzy," for some reason. Here on the East Coast, we used to pronounce it "sexy," which I prefer, but the Valley girls and boys held sway.

Anyway, SCSI stands for Small Computer System Interface (or *Serial* Interface, or *Standard* Interface, depending on where you look it up; it's such a messed-up technology that nobody can even get the *name* right). It describes the widest connector on the back of your Mac: the *SCSI port.* It also describes the fattest cable of any Mac appliance: the *SCSI cable.* It describes the kind of hard drives, scanners, SyQuest drives, computer CD players, and other gadgets that you attach to this jack: *SCSI devices.* It also describes the type of information that flows from those devices through those cables to that jack along the SCSI chain.

But frankly, the term that you hear most often is *SCSI problems*.

What's especially frustrating to people who write computer books is that you can't pin SCSI down. Even if you obey the "rules" (which I'll give you anyway), things still go wrong.

The only good thing to say about SCSI problems is that once you figure out the problem with your setup, that problem is gone for good.

System crashes, slow performance, CD-ROM won't work

These are only a few of the delicious symptoms that you have to look forward to in the world of SCSI problems. Here are some of the equally delicious solutions.

First resort: Unhook the SCSI devices from your Mac. That's right — put the Mac back the way it was when you bought it, bald and buck naked, with nothing attached. This way, at least, you can figure out whether SCSI *is* the problem. If the problem went away, you do indeed have a SCSI problem.

Second resort: Somewhere in this book, I've mentioned that you can string multiple SCSI devices together — or *daisy-chain* them, which is how you can use both an external drive and a scanner (for example), even though the Mac only has one SCSI jack. When the Mac attempts to talk to various devices along this SCSI train, it must be careful not to say "start scanning!" to the hard drive or "start spinning!" to the scanner. In other words, it has to address its messages carefully.

For that reason, every SCSI device in the world has a *SCSI address* between 0 and 7. Usually, there's a little number wheel that looks like a one-digit odometer on the back or the bottom of your SCSI device. Each SCSI device connected to your Mac must have a *different* SCSI number (address) so that the Mac can speak to each appliance individually.

The Mac, which is part of the chain, has a SCSI number, which is always 7. If you have an internal hard drive, it has a SCSI number, too — and that number is always 0. (If your Mac has a built-in CD-ROM player, its address is always 3.) So for your external drives, scanners, and so on, you can choose numbers from 1 to 6; just make sure that no two devices have the *same* number, or you're cruisin' for a bruisin'.

Third resort: I wish I didn't have to mention SCSI Rule #2: The last device on the chain has to be terminated.

When I say *terminated*, I mean taken out and shot.

But if you've paid good money for these things, I suppose that you'd prefer to keep them.

The second meaning for *terminated* is a little bit more complicated.

As the Mac sends its little instructions to the various SCSI devices attached to it, it shoves those instructions out the door with such force that they some-times go all the way to the end of the cable and *bounce back* toward the Mac. Sometimes, the instructions make it all the way back, in which case you get nutty problems like a hard-drive icon showing up *twice* on the screen.

To soak up any messages that were pushed with too much oomph, you're supposed to put an electronic shock absorber at the beginning and the end of the line of devices. This absorber is called a *terminator*, Arnold Schwarzenegger notwithstanding.

If your Mac has an internal hard drive, as most Macs do, you don't have to worry about the beginning terminator: your SCSI chain is already terminated inside. And if you also have only one SCSI device outside your Mac, you don't need a terminator on the outside end. (I'm perfectly aware that this contradicts Rule #2, but it doesn't contradict Rule #3, which is that these rules don't always apply. Including Rule #3.)

After you have two or more SCSI things attached to the back of your Mac, though, it's time to start thinking about termination. You add termination by attaching a three-inch stopper plug (called, obviously, a terminator) to the empty SCSI jack of the last device on the chain. Some devices, however, have a terminator *switch* on the back or bottom. You can just flip this switch between the terminated and unterminated positions.

Worst of all, some devices may or may not be *internally* terminated, meaning that you can't *tell* whether or not they're already terminated. Rule #4 is that you don't want a device in the *middle* of the chain to be terminated! The only way to find out whether a device is internally terminated (if that information is not in the owner's manual) is to call the cheap, lazy company that made it. If it *is* internally terminated, that device *must* go at the end of the SCSI chain. (Is this the most pathetic technology ever, or what?)

So if you have *two* devices, both of which are internally terminated — well, you're basically up the creek. You can't use both devices at the same time. You may be able to call the company that made the devices and have someone explain to you, over the phone, how you open the case and, with a pair of pliers, rip out the little circuits that terminate the device … but it's an ugly, unenviable operation.

I guess the point is that when you shop for hard drives, scanners, or other SCSI devices, you shouldn't buy one that's terminated internally. That only means trouble.

Fourth resort: Try rearranging the physical order of the devices in your SCSI chain. It makes no sense, and there's no Rule of SCSI about it, but sometimes, rearranging makes things work when nothing else does. Anyway, at this point, you're entitled to be a little irrational.

Fifth resort: If everything else seems hunky-dory, it's conceivable that the trouble is the *combined lengths* of your SCSI cables. They're not supposed to add up to more than 20 feet or so, and (like speeches and Willie Nelson songs) the shorter the better. Oh, and while we're talking about SCSI cables, you should know this: they go bad. It's true. One rich guy I know threw out an 800MB hard drive because he thought that it had died permanently. Upon rescuing it from the dumpster, an enterprising Mac buddy discovered that the drive was fine; the *cable* had been crimped by a piece of furniture. After he spent $30 on a new SCSI cable, the drive was as good as new. It's probably worth replacing, or at least switching, the cables if you're still having SCSI problems.

Another guy I know solved his SCSI woes by switching his cable from one SCSI jack on his CD-ROM player to the other (of the two identical SCSI jacks). It makes *absolutely* no sense, but that's what happened.

Last resort: OK, you've made sure that every device has its own address. If you have more than one external SCSI device, you've terminated the last one. But things *still* aren't working right.

In this case, try taking *off* the terminator. I'm perfectly serious. SCSI Rule #5 is: if a rule isn't working, try breaking it. Here at home, for example, I have both a hard drive and a SyQuest removable-cartridge drive plugged into the back of my Mac — and *no* external terminators. What sense does that make? I don't know — but I do know that if I follow Rule #2 and add a terminator, nothing works, and my hard-drive icon doesn't appear on the screen.

Someday, we'll laugh and tell our grandchildren, "Why, when I was your age, we used to have to *add terminator plugs to our external devices!*" Until that golden day, though, we have to put up with this cranky and unpredictable technology. Good luck to you.

For Mac IIfx owners only

You people have an additional SCSI rule to worry about. When it comes time for you to add a SCSI terminator plug at the outer end of your SCSI chain, you're supposed to use a special, black, IIfx terminator plug.

Truth to tell, though, my ex-girlfriend has a IIfx, and she uses a regular, gray, non-IIfx plug, which works fine. (Yet another SCSI rule that doesn't seem to work.)

Printing Problems

After the brutal experience of solving SCSI snafus, these'll seem like child's play.

"Printer could not be opened" or "Printer could not be found"

First resort: These messages appear when you try to print something without turning on the printer first (or letting it warm up fully). Turn it on, wait a whole minute, and then try again.

Second resort: Of course, it may be that you haven't performed the critical step of selecting the printer's icon in the Chooser desk accessory. (Even if you did, the Mac sometimes gets a little feebleminded and forgets what you selected in the Chooser. Just repeat the procedure.) See Chapter 4 for step-by-step instructions.

Last resort: Maybe a cable came loose. Track the cable from your Mac's printer port all the way to the printer. (Important: make sure that it's really the printer port, because the modem port looks exactly like it.) If it all seems to be firmly connected, try replacing (1) the cable or (2) the little connectors.

StyleWriter II: Blank pages come out

It's your cartridge.

First resort: Choose Print from the File menu. Click the Options button. See where it says "Clean ink cartridge before printing?" Click that.

StyleWriter II Print Options	1.2	OK
☐ Clean ink cartridge before printing		Cancel

Now try to print something normally. The StyleWriter will, in effect, blow its nose before trying to print, just in case your cartridge nozzle has dried up and clogged.

Last resort: If that didn't work, your cartridge is probably empty. Buy a new one.

To replace the old cartridge, pull open the front panel of the StyleWriter. Locate the existing cartridge — a little black square thing. Lift the blue lever to release the old cartridge, slip in the new one (after taking off the protective nozzle strip!), and lower the blue lever to lock it in.

StyleWriter II: Paper jams

Some people gape in shock to hear that *other* people have endless paper problems with a StyleWriter. Either yours works like a charm, or it doesn't.

First resort: The problem is your paper. Don't try to feed single sheets; put at least 20 pages or so into the feeder. If it's a humid day, fan the paper stack to separate the pages. Then resquare the pages and put them into the feeder.

Don't expect terrific results with stiff, textured, wedding-y envelopes, by the way.

Last resort: The problem is your feeder tray. On the left side is a sliding plastic thingy. You definitely want to slide this paper-edge-aligner right up to the edge of the paper stack. If it's too far away, the pages will tilt as they're pulled into the StyleWriter. If it's too close, the StyleWriter will have a struggle pulling pages through.

A million copies keep pouring out

This big-time hazard for novices has to do with background printing (see Chapter 4). When you print something, *nothing happens* for a minute or two. (The Mac is storing the printout behind the scenes so that it can return control of the Mac to you.)

Trouble is, your first time at bat, you probably don't *know* what the delay is; all you know is that the printer isn't printing. So you figure that you'll just try again. You choose Print from the File menu again. Still, nothing happens. So you print *again*.

The thing is, the Mac is duly *storing* all your printing requests; at some moment, when you least expect it, all those copies will start to print! To stop them, choose Print Monitor from the Application menu (the tiny icon at the far right end of your menu bar); select each document; and click Cancel Printing.

"Font not found, using Courier"

This problem is unique to laser printers. Your document contains a PostScript laser font (see Chapter 4 for excruciatingly detailed definitions), but the Mac can't find the printer font file for the font that you're using. Find the printer font (the file with the abbreviated name, such as FrankGothBol), and install it in your System Folder.

Nothing comes out of the printer

Sometimes, the Mac fakes you out: it goes through the motions of printing, but nothing ever comes out of the printer.

First resort: Go to the menu. Select Chooser. Click the icon for the printer that you're using, and make sure that your actual printer's name shows up in the list on the right side of the Chooser window. (This process is explained more patiently in Chapter 4.)

Second resort: Is there paper in the paper tray, and is the tray pushed all the way in?

If you're using an ImageWriter, is the little Select light on? If not, push the Select button.

Third resort: If you're using a laser printer: Alas, your document is probably overwhelming the printer's feeble memory, and the printer is giving up. You can try using fewer different fonts in the document. Try printing only a page at a time. Or try using fewer *downloadable* fonts — that is, fonts that aren't built into the printer (see #3 in "Top Ten Free Fun Font Factoids" in Chapter 4).

Fourth resort: If you're printing something complicated on your laser printer, there may be a messed-up graphic. Programs such as SuperPaint, FreeHand, and Illustrator are known for generating very complex, sometimes unprintable graphics. For example, here's a graphic from SuperPaint that won't print out:

If you're printing a document that includes both text and graphics, try removing your graphics and printing the same document. If it prints without the graphics, you know where the problem is. Call the graphics-program company and complain abrasively.

Last resort: If your laser printer truly has run out of memory, you can usually pay to have it upgraded with more memory. In the computer world, as always, a little cash can surmount almost any problem.

PrintMonitor won't go away

If you're using the generally wonderful Background Printing option, described in Chapter 4, you sometimes encounter the bizarro PrintMonitor program.

What's so baffling is that you never remember launching this program by double-clicking. But there it is, listed in your Application menu. And sometimes, it beeps at you, demanding some intervention on your part (such as when the printer runs out of paper).

Anyway, you can't make PrintMonitor quit on cue. To make it *really* go away, cancel any printing jobs that it's still working on (by clicking the Cancel button), and then go to another program. Eventually, PrintMonitor should disappear from your Application menu.

Streaks on laser printouts

If they're *dark* streaks, there's some crud on some element of the paper path inside the laser printer. Open the lid. Examine the rollers (but be careful if the printer has just been on; those rollers get incredibly hot). You're looking for a single blob of grit or toner dust. Clean it off with a Q-tip, preferably dampened with alcohol (the Q-tip, not you).

Also look for a series of thin, one-inch diagonal wires. Make sure that those wires are sparkling clean.

Then again, if this streaking business started after you returned from a three-month trip, the cartridge probably went bad from sheer loneliness. Replace it.

If there are *light* streaks on the printouts, open the printer lid. Remove the toner drum (usually, a big black plastic thing), and gently rock it from side to side. Basically, you're running out of toner dust; this procedure may give you a couple days' worth of extra time. But you'll be needing a new cartridge soon.

That stupid startup page

Every time you turn on your laser printer, it prints a dumb startup page with its own logo. This is an annoying problem, but easily fixed. See #8 in "Top Ten Free Fun Font Factoids" in Chapter 4.

Finder Foulups

The Finder, you'll recall, is your home base. It's the Desktop. It's the Trash can and icons and all that stuff. It's where you manage your files, rename them, copy them — and sometimes have problems with them.

The Find command doesn't find a file

The Find command is pretty literal. Suppose that you're looking for a letter called *Mr. Ted Smith*. You use the Find command, and where it says "Find what," you type **Mr. Smith**, **Mr.Ted Smith** (see the missing space?), **Mr Ted Smith** (no period), or **Mr. William Smith**. In any of these circumstances, the Find command will draw a blank. Try searching for *smi, Mr,* or any portion of the letters that you're certain of. (Capitalization *doesn't* matter.)

Of course, the problem may not be what you type in the "Find what" box. You may have misspelled the name of the file itself — say, **1993 Salries** — and no matter how many times you search for the word *salaries*, the Finder will always come up empty-handed.

You can't rename a file

The file is probably locked. Click it, choose Get Info from the File menu, and deselect the Locked checkbox.

You can't rename a disk

First resort: I'm gonna take a wild shot at this one. Despite your supposedly novice status, I'll bet you're using the Mac's networking feature. I'll bet you're plugged into another Mac. Right?

It's true: if you're using this feature (known as *file sharing),* you're not allowed to change your hard drive's name. You'd wreak havoc with the other people on the network, who are trying to keep straight who you are.

If you really want to bother, open your Sharing Setup control panel and turn *off* file sharing. Now you can rename your disk.

Last resort: In System 7, you can't rename those really old, single-sided, 400K disks. Period.

Floppy-Disk Flukes

Floppy disks are cheap and handy and make excellent coasters. But when they start giving you attitude, read on.

"File could not be copied

This one's a pain, isn't it?

First resort: If you were copying a whole group of files, try dragging the troublesome file by itself.

Second resort: Make a duplicate of the file (click it and then choose Duplicate from the File menu). Now try copying the duplicate.

Third resort: If the unruly file is a document, launch the program that created it. (If it's a Word file, for example, launch Word.) Now choose the Open command from the File menu, and try to open the file. If it opens, use the Save As command to save it to a different disk.

Fourth resort: Eject the disk. Open and close the sliding shutter a couple times. Manually rotate the round hub. Try again.

Fifth resort: Try inserting the obnoxious floppy into somebody else's Mac.

Last resort: With a little expenditure, you can almost certainly retrieve the file. The rescue programs are called things like 911 Utilities (the best for floppies) and Norton Utilities (the best for hard disks). These programs are listed in Appendix B, "The Resource Resource."

Mac keeps asking for a disk you've ejected

First resort: You probably ejected the disk by using the Eject Disk command in the Special menu. In general, that's a no-no, precisely because the Mac will continually ask for it.

You can get out of this scrape by pressing ⌘-period several times. Next time, eject a disk by choosing the Put Away command from the File menu (or by dragging the disk icon to the Trash can).

Last resort: Sometimes, even if you use Put Away, a ghost of the disk's icon remains on the screen; the Mac keeps asking for it, and pressing ⌘-period doesn't solve anything. In this case, you probably opened a file on that disk, and it's still open. As long as something on that disk is open, the Mac won't forget about the disk; it would be like canceling the space program while some astronauts were in the middle of a mission.

Choose the program in question from the Application menu, and make sure that you close all documents. Now you should be able to drag the disk icon to the Trash can.

You can't get a floppy disk out

First resort: Press ⌘-Shift-1. That should pop out the disk, even if you can't see its icon.

Last resort: Use the paper-clip trick described in the sidebar "Dweebs' Corner: Alternative disk tips" in Chapter 2.

"This disk is unreadable. Do you want to initialize it?"

If it's a brand-new disk fresh out of the box, there is *no* problem. *All* brand-new floppies are initially unreadable unless they have already been initialized. Go ahead and click Erase, and follow the disk-naming process that the Mac takes you through. But if it's a disk that you've used before, you certainly don't want to destroy it.

First resort: Click Eject. *No,* you do not want to initialize (that is, erase) the disk.

Second resort: Remember that there are three different kinds of floppy disks: single-sided (400K), double-sided (800K), and high-density (1,400K). If you have an older Mac (say, one made before 1990), it may not have a high-density disk drive, and you may be trying to insert a high-density disk that it can't read.

Actually, the situation is even more complicated than *that.* Another typical problem: you insert a new 800K disk into a high-density disk drive, go through the usual "Initialize?" routine, and then discover that the disk won't work in somebody else's old 800K disk drive! Strange but true.

In any of these cases, again, the main thing is that you do *not* give the Mac permission to erase the disk. Just take the disk to a more modern Mac, rescue the files, and bring them home on a kind of disk that *your* Mac can read.

Third resort: If it's a disk that you know contains data, and you have a disk drive of the right type, there may be something actually wrong with the disk. Eject it, shake it around a little, and try it a couple more times.

Fourth resort: Something may be wrong with your disk *drive* — not the disk itself. To find out, insert the disk into another Mac's drive.

If there turns out to be a problem with your drive, the culprit is often dust and crud. Some of my technoid friends say that it's dangerous (staticwise) to use a vacuum or blower in the disk-drive slot, but I've actually rescued a disk drive or two this way (and have never damaged one).

Fifth resort: Buy a recovery program, such as 911 Utilities. If anything can get your files off that disk, 911 can.

Sixth resort: You're not trying to insert an IBM PC disk into your Mac, are you? If you are (having read in the ads that any Mac can read a PC disk), give it up — it's not that simple. You're going to need some special software, described at the end of Chapter 5, if you want your Mac to read PC disks.

Last resort: If the problem is not your disk drive, and if even 911 can't get your data off the disk, the disk is really broken. Don't even erase it and reuse it: throw it away!

One occasional source of zapped floppies, by the way, is magnetic damage. Just like an audio tape, a disk stores information by magnetizing tiny particles of metal stuff. If the disk gets magnetized by accident, the metal particles get rearranged in some random pattern that the Mac correctly deems to be unreadable.

I know that this sounds crazy, but *somebody* has to put it into print: don't put refrigerator magnets on your Mac. That hard disk inside the machine is, after all, a disk, and magnets do to disks what gravity does to a watermelon dropped at 39,000 feet.

Your floppy disks don't hold the amount that they're supposed to

It's true — you can't fit 800K of information on an 800K disk or 1.4MB on a 1.4MB disk.

The missing storage capacity is filled by an invisible file, present on every disk, called the *Desktop file*. This file, which is the Mac's accounting department, is described in more detail in "Error Messages" earlier in this chapter.

The point is that the Desktop file takes up 7K or more on every disk. If it's taking up a lot more than that, you may have a *bloated* Desktop file; see the "Rebuilding the Desktop file" sidebar, also earlier in this chapter, for instructions on slimming it down.

Three Software Snafus

This section describes things that can go wrong while you're working — problems in programs, for example. Also see "System Crashes and Freezes" and "Error Messages" earlier in this chapter.

In FileMaker: Missing information

FileMaker, the world's most popular Mac database program, sometimes misleads novices into thinking that they've lost their information. That impression is a result of FileMaker's clever ability to *hide* data. For example, you can ask your Rolodex file to show you only the names of people who weigh more than 250 pounds or something similar; the name and address information for everybody skinnier will be *hidden*.

To restore all names to the screen, choose Find All from the Select menu. The names should reappear.

In Excel: ##### in a cell

In Excel and other spreadsheet programs, it's a simple matter to make a cell wider or narrower. But if you make a cell so narrow that it chops off the number inside it, the program displays #####. (Other spreadsheet programs display something similar.)

You can see why the program does this; otherwise, only *part* of the number would show up, possibly misleading you into thinking (for example) that your quarterly earnings are only $56 instead of $56,456,890.

In HyperCard: No menu bar

Actually, in certain HyperCard documents, the menu bar has been deliberately hidden by the programmer. You still can press ⌘-Q to quit the program, though.

If you'd like the menu bar to reappear, press ⌘-spacebar.

Hard-Disk Horrors

If you're like many Mac users, you wind up storing your whole life on that disk: appointments, finances, explosive secret diaries, the works. That's a lot of trust to place in an inanimate mechanical device that's all moving parts. Back up your work all the time — and rely on this section when things go wrong.

The hard-drive icon doesn't show up

If it's an external drive, either it isn't on, it isn't plugged in right, or its SCSI setup isn't right (refer to "Scuzzy SCSI" earlier in this chapter). If we're talking about the drive inside your Mac, it's probably a SCSI problem.

It's theoretically possible, too, that your drive is broken. Bummer.

Sluggish behavior

If copying, launching, and quitting programs (and opening and closing windows) seem to be taking longer than when you first bought your Mac, it's probably time to give your hard disk a physical. For instructions, see the sidebar "Defragmenting your disk" later in this chapter.

You threw something away by mistake

First resort: If you haven't chosen Empty Trash from the Special menu, you're in good shape. Just double-click the Trash icon. Its window opens, so you can rescue any files therein by dragging them back to your hard-disk icon.

Second resort: If you threw something away, emptied the Trash, and more or less *immediately* recognized your mistake, you're still OK. You won't find this in any manual, but it's a great trick:

Unplug your Mac.

Defragmenting your disk

Over time, you create and throw away a lot of files.

Your hard drive, if you'll indulge me, is like a closet maintained by a guy who's always in a hurry. When guests are coming over, he cleans up the living room and throws everything into the closet, although not particularly neatly. Every now and then, when he gets time, he unpacks the closet and repacks it neatly, putting everything in a tidy, organized place.

The hard drive, too, is in a hurry. When you ask it to save a file, it doesn't wait around: it shoves that file wherever it can find space. Sometimes, that even means sticking the file in *two* places, splitting it as necessary. Over time, more and more files are stored on your hard disk in pieces. It's no big deal: when you need that file again, the hard drive remembers where all the pieces are and is perfectly able to bring the file back to the screen.

But all this hunting for pieces slows the drive down. And like our busy closet keeper, you'll find it very satisfying, every six months or so, to reorganize the files on your disk so that they're each in one piece, neatly placed end to end on the hard-drive surface.

There are two ways to *defragment* your drive (which is the term for it). First, you can copy everything onto other disks, erase the hard drive, and copy the files back onto it. Second, you can buy a program just for defragmenting your drive. These programs are called things like Norton Utilities and DiskExpress.

That's right: just cut off the juice. When you restart the thing, holy moley, your Trash will be full again — and your file will have been brought back from the dead!

Last resort: If that unplugging bit didn't save your file, you're not out of luck. Chances are very good that you can still recover the last several dozen files that you threw away, using a *data-recovery program* like Norton Utilities or MacTools Deluxe. The more that you've used your Mac since you threw something away, the less chance you have of getting it back. See Appendix B, "The Resource Resource," for information on getting these programs, and see their manuals for instructions.

Hardware Headaches

These aren't the most common glitches that you're likely to encounter, but they're just as frustrating.

Mouse or trackball is jerky or sticky

This problem is very common. Like children, mops, and mimes, a mouse does its work by rolling around on the ground. It's bound to get dirty.

To clean it, turn it upside down in your hand. Very firmly rotate the round collar counterclockwise so that you can remove the trackball. (The idea is the same on a PowerBook. On a Duo, you may think that the collar ring is impossible to turn, but it can be done; push really hard against the soft curves of the ring around the trackball.) Dump the rubber or plastic ball into your hand, wash it off under the faucet, and let it air-dry completely.

In the meantime, go to work inside the socket where the ball usually is. With tweezers or something, pull out any obvious dust bunnies and hairballs. The main thing, though, is those three little rollers inside the cavity: you'll probably see stripes of accumulated gunk around them. With patience, a scissors blade (or a wad of sticky-side-out Scotch tape), and a good light, lift off that stuff, preferably making an effort not to let it fall inside the cavity. Keep turning the mouse right side up and tapping it on the table to dislodge stuff.

When you put everything back together, both you and your mouse will be much happier.

Double-clicking doesn't work

You're probably double-clicking too slowly, or you're moving the mouse a little bit during the double-click process.

Cursor freezes on the screen

This is a System freeze or System hang. Read all about it in the "System Crashes and Freezes" section earlier in this chapter.

Then again, your mouse (or keyboard) cable may have come loose. Plug everything in firmly.

Menus get stuck down

If it's not your Mac, or if it *is* your Mac and you just aren't very tuned in, the culprit may be a little add-on program that makes menus jump down when the cursor touches them, even when you're *not* pressing the mouse button. I've always thought that this kind of program is somewhat cruel, but some people claim that it saves them some effort.

If you're using a trackball, you may be the victim of a similarly stupid feature: a button on the trackball that, when clicked, makes the Mac think that you're pressing the mouse button *all the time*. For the rest of your computing day, the

Mac will think that the button is down, even if you frantically click the *regular* mouse button or try to quit the program or anything. Only when you again touch the click lock button does the Mac free the pointer from its bondage.

Nothing appears when you type

First resort: Well, obviously, you can't just type at any time and expect to see text appear. You have to be either in a word processing program or in a text-editing area (for example, in a dialog box or in the little text-editing rectangle that appears when you're renaming an icon).

Second resort: Check the cable between the keyboard and the Mac. Make sure that it's *very* firmly plugged in at both ends.

Incidentally, the keyboard and mouse cables are especially sensitive to being plugged and unplugged while the computer is on. Be religious about shutting off the Mac before plugging and unplugging the cables. (That's especially true of SCSI cables. The same is *not* true of modem and printer cables, though.)

The PowerBook or Duo modem (or printer) won't work

This note applies only if you have a PowerBook Duo or a PowerBook 500-something. These particular laptops don't have a printer jack and a modem-jack on the back, like all other Macs; instead, they have *one* combo printer/modem jack.

If your laptop is equipped with a built-in modem, you wouldn't think there'd be much problem. After all, your modem is built in, so you can use that single back-panel jack for your printer.

Soon you'll discover a bizarre and unfortunate gotcha, however: you can't use a StyleWriter printer and your modem at the same time! Each time you want to switch your Mac from one function to another, you have to

- Open your PowerBook Setup control panel.
- Choose Normal if you want to *print,* or Compatible if you want to use the *modem!*

While we're on the topic of StyleWriters: when you visit your Chooser (in the menu) and click StyleWriter or StyleWriter II, you'll note that you're asked to make a choice between two serial ports. One looks like a telephone, and the other looks like a little printer:

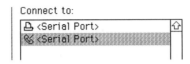

Which brings up a fascinating question. Your PowerBook only *has* one jack, so which port do you select on the screen: the modem (telephone) or printer port?

I'll save you five minutes of experimentation right here: select the modem port.

Your monitor shimmers

Of course, I don't mean that your monitor *itself* jiggles; I mean the picture.

First resort: Your screen's being subjected to some kind of electrical interference, such as a lamp, a fan, or an air conditioner running on the same circuit. Try a different plug, a different monitor location, or a different career.

Last resort: You live in an earthquake zone. Move to the Midwest.

The 5th Wave **By Rich Tennant**

"I'M GONNA HAVE A LITTLE TROUBLE WITH THIS 'FULL MOON' ICON ON OUR GRAPHICAL USERS INTERFACE."

Chapter 14

Beyond Point-and-Click: Where to Go from Here

A New Leash on Life: Upgrading

As I warned you in Chapter 1, your Mac's life span is limited — not in terms of usefulness but in terms of cutting-edgeness. As new models roll out of Silicon Valley, you'll find that your top-of-the-line Mac model becomes bottom-of-the-heap insultingly quickly.

The advice I'm about to give you may be difficult to follow, but it's something I firmly believe: If the Mac does what you need it to do, *you don't have to keep up with technology.* The impulse to keep your Mac current for its own sake will be strong, but I promise you that your personal worth does *not* ride on the processor speed of your Mac.

A woman in my building uses a 1984 Mac with one-eighth of a meg of memory. She owns one program — the very first version of MacWrite. She's in heaven.

Now then. If some *software* that requires a more powerful Mac comes out, and you require that program, that's a different story. At that point, you too will face: the Upgrade Paradox.

An aside to the superstitious

No, there's no Chapter 13. There's never a 13th floor, either. It's an American tradition.

The upgrade paradox

Here's the thing about upgrading your Mac: it's a psychological trap. Your *thinking* goes like this: "I've got so much invested in this thing, I'll just pay for a little bit of enhancement. That way, I retain my investment."

But the *reality* goes like this: While you were happily owning your Mac, prices of *new* Macs plummeted. Without your noticing, the price of a new, faster Mac has sunk so far, it costs *less* than accelerating your old one! Throw in the money you'd make by *selling* your current Mac, and the upgrade makes even less sense.

It's very true. Painful, at first, to accept, but delightful in practice. Here are a couple of examples.

Suppose you have a Centris 650. You've heard that, for $1500, you can buy Apple's upgrade that turns your Mac into a *Power Macintosh* 7100!

Only trouble is, at this writing, a *new* Power Macintosh 7100 costs about $2600, about $1500 of which you'd recoup by selling your Centris. (There are plenty of places to sell your Mac: the classifieds, user groups, bulletin boards at the library or the gym, and any of a number of national computer brokerages. These last advertise in *Macworld* and *MacUser* magazines.)

Do the math. If you upgraded your Centris, you'd have spent $1500. But if you *sold* your Centris and bought a *brand new* Power Macintosh 7100, you'd have spent $1100. Not only would you *save* $400, but you'd wind up with a new, updated machine with a new, one-year warranty.

No matter which example you choose, this surprising math keeps coming out the same way. Upgrade your Performa 400 to Quadra 605 speeds by buying a $580 Daystar accelerator card; you've spent $580. But sell your Performa for $400 and buy a brand new, *actual* Quadra 605 for $800, and you've only spent $400 — and gained new warranty, disks, and manuals.

Two great things about this reasoning: (1) It makes getting a cool new computer easier to justify to your spouse, and (2) it's actually true.

Nudgegrades

Now, despite the astounding genius of Pogue's New Upgrade Math, there *are* some Mac add-ons worth adding on. For example, if your hard drive has become full, and you're spending ten minutes a day weeding through old stuff to throw out, it's time to get another hard drive (or a removable SyQuest cartridge drive; see Chapter 8).

And if you're getting out-of-memory messages all the time, and you've tried all the tricks in Chapter 12 for making do with what you have, it's OK to consider installing more memory chips (known as SIMMs).

Those don't quite qualify for the term *upgrades,* really, but they do make using your Mac a happier experience for not much money.

Where to Turn in Times of Trouble

You *do* own the world's most forgiving, self-explanatory computer. But things will go wrong.

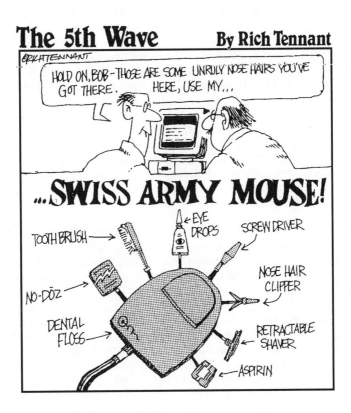

Up until a couple years ago, your official Answer Person was supposed to be —
ready for this? — the dealer from whom you bought your computer.

Yeah, right. Like this guy ever wants to see you again once the check clears.

Fortunately, Apple has gone from providing an absolutely wretched service
plan to an absolutely spectacular one. Any time during the first year you own
your Mac, they'll send somebody *to you* to fix the thing if it breaks. In your
house. For free.

And if it's a PowerBook, as I've mentioned, they'll send an overnight-package
person to your door to pick up the laptop, pay for the overnight freight to
Texas, fix it there, and overnight it right back to you. For free.

The magic phone number to get this kind of help, cleverly enough, is 800-
SOS-APPL. Get it?

Another tip: If you have a fax machine, you can use AppleFax, a great free
service; call 800-505-0171 by telephone, listen to the instructions, punch in your
own fax number when you're asked for it, put in a fresh roll of fax paper, and
stand back.

Otherwise, as I've no doubt etched permanently into your brain by now, your
next resort should be a local user group, if you're lucky enough to live in a
pseudo-metropolitan area. A user group, of course, doesn't exist to answer *your*
personal questions; you still have to do some phoning and hobnobbing and
research. But a user group *is* a source of sources. You can call up and find out
who will know the answer to your question.

The other great source of help, as I've said, is an electronic meeting place like
America Online, where you may get your question answered instantly — and if
not, you can post your question on a bulletin board for somebody to answer
overnight. As a matter of fact, *I'm* there, ready to receive your praise or, if it
must be, your wrath, for stuff I've gotten you into. My e-mail address there is Pogue.

As for your continuing education — after you spend a month's salary on a
computer, I'll bet you can afford $20 more for a subscription to *Macworld* or
MacUser magazine. As noted in Chapter 9, huge chunks of these rags will go
right over your head. But in every single issue, you'll find at least one really
useful item. You can learn all kinds of things just by reading the ads. And if
you're not in touch with the computer nerd world at least by that tenuous
thread — via magazine — then you might miss stuff like free offers, recall
notices, warnings, and other consumer-oriented jazz.

Buy a book — clothe an author

The publisher of this book has decided that, by gum, there's a market for this stuff, so he persuaded me to write two more. Such as *MORE Macs For Dummies*.

Everybody asks if *MORE Macs For Dummies* is just an updated version of this book. No, that's not it at all. Actually, it

✔ Describes and rates the top 200 most-advertised Mac programs

✔ Reveals a bunch more of those cool hidden Option-key stunts

✔ Shows how to connect two Macs together

✔ Teaches holistic hard-drive (and memory) health care

✔ Helps you fake your way through Photoshop, Quicken, Illustrator, Freehand, QuickTime, and Premiere

✔ Tells you how to work your modem, and what to use it for (connecting with America Online, CompuServe, your friends, and even the Internet)

✔ Talks all about AV Macs and Power Macs, and

✔ Walks you through exchanging stuff with IBM-type computers.

It has a money-back guarantee, a foreword by Carly Simon, and a really hilarious dedication.

And by the way: when you *really* become an expert, you'll be ready for *Macworld Mac & Power Mac SECRETS,* which has 1,100 pages, includes 40 great programs on three disks, and requires a forklift to move.

Then you'll be ready to write your *own* darned Mac books.

Save Changes Before Closing?

If you do decide to pursue this Macintosh thing, I've listed the phone numbers of major user groups, dial-up services, and magazines in Appendix B, the Resource Resource, along with contact information for the products I've mentioned.

But wait a minute — the point of this book wasn't to convert you into a full-time Mac rabbit. It was to get you off the ground. To give you just enough background so you'll know why the computer's beeping at you. To show you the basics and help you figure out what the beanie heads are talking about.

Don't let them intimidate you. So *what* if you don't know the lingo or have the circuitry memorized? If you can turn the thing on, get something written up and printed, and get out in time to enjoy the sunshine, you qualify as a real Mac user.

Any dummy knows that.

Top Ten Topics Not Covered in This Book

Here's a who's who of topics I don't think any new Mac user needs to bother with. If you have the slightest interest in any of them, the shelves are full of geekier books than this one.

1. Programming.

2. Networking.

3. Any add-on that costs over $2,000.

4. Color separations.

5. Multimedia.

6. Hard-disk partitioning. Too many syllables.

7. Publish and Subscribe.

8. How data is stored on a disk. (If you never need to know something, why bring it up?)

9. Security. There are all kinds of fancy ways to lock up your Mac. If you're really interested, call up Mac Connection and ask what they can sell you.

10. The terms *ROM, interleave, user-centric, initiate, V.32 bis, TCP/IP, user-definable, DRAM, implement, CDEV, nanosecond, kerning, VRAM, magneto-optical, token-ring, Ethernet, directory,* or *AUTOEXEC.BAT.*

Appendix A

How to Buy (and Set Up) a Macintosh

• •

*G*etting started with a Mac really involves three steps: deciding which model to get, figuring out where to buy it, and setting it up. This delightful appendix will guide you through all three steps with as few tension headaches as possible.

The Only Four Specs That Matter (Besides the Price)

You'll hear all kinds of numbers and specifications tossed around when you go Mac-shopping. But the only four that matter are (1) how big its hard drive is, (2) how much memory it has, (3) what processor chip is inside, and (4) how fast that processor runs.

✔ **Hard-disk space.** The first number that matters is the *size of the hard disk inside the Mac*. The size is measured in *megabytes*. (If you're at a cocktail party, you can say *megs* for short.) Larger disks are more expensive.

How much do you need? Well, the stuff that you'll be creating — letters, manuscripts, whatever — is pretty small. A 500-page book might take up 1MB (*MB* is short for *megabytes*) of your hard disk. But today's *software programs,* such as word processing programs, are huge. Count on each program's taking up a couple of megabytes by itself. (Count on anything from Microsoft Corporation taking up *10MB* all by itself.)

Whether you understand any of this or not, believe it: a hard disk fills up quickly. You can't even buy a hard drive smaller than about 80MB these days.

The first question you might ask in the computer store, then, is, "Yo — does this Mac have an 80-, 120-, or 250-meg hard disk?" No salesperson will take *you* for a ride.

✔ **Memory.** When you press Play on a VCR, the machine reads the videocassette's contents and throws the video information onto the TV screen. When the TV is off, you can't watch your movie, but you sleep well knowing that it's still safely stored on the tape.

Similarly, your Macintosh reads what's on the *hard disk* and throws an electronic copy of it up on your computer screen. There, you can look at it, make changes, whatever. While it's on the screen, it's *in memory.* (Details on this stuff are in Chapter 1^1/$_2$.)

What's confusing about memory is that it's measured in the *same units* as hard-drive space: megabytes. But memory is much more expensive than disk space, so you get a lot less of it. Whereas hard drives typically are 120MB or 250MB, a Mac usually comes with 4MB, 8MB, or 16MB of memory. The more memory you have, the more you can do with your computer simultaneously (type in one window, draw in another, and so on). In general, you need 4MB of memory to do even *one* thing at a time and 8MB to have a couple of programs going. If you have a Power Macintosh, double those numbers.

Intelligent Computer Question Number Two, then, is "How much RAM do I get in this Mac? Four megs? Forget it! I can't even *breathe* in four megs."

By the way, newspaper ads often give you both of these critical numbers (memory and disk space). You may read, for example, "PowerBook 4/120." In your newfound savvy, you know that this computer has 4MB of *memory* and a 120MB *hard drive* for permanent storage.

✔ **Processor model number**. The third important number is the name of the primary processor chip. (As endless *Newsweek* articles and specials on "Nova" have no doubt informed you, a *chip* is a rat's nest of tiny circuits etched into a piece of silicon the size of a postage stamp.) The heart of a Macintosh is a chip, about an inch square, that's actually manufactured in the millions by a completely different company. (It's Motorola; that's why *Apple* stock goes down when there are negative headlines about Motorola.)

Before the Power Macintosh line, several models of processor chips were used in Macs: 68000, 68020, 68030, and 68040. You don't have a choice for a specific model of Mac. The Quadra 630, for example, has a 68040 chip, and that's all there is to it. The higher the model number of this chip, the faster the Mac.

Power Macintosh models, on the other hand, use a newer kind of Motorola "brain" chip: the famous PowerPC chip. These chips have all kinds of names — 601, 604, 620 — but in this case, higher numbers *don't* mean faster Macs. To gauge the speed of a certain Power Macintosh, ignore its chip model number, and instead focus on the following item.

✔ **Clock speed.** This is the other variable that accounts for the performance differences among Mac models. A chip's clock speed is something like blood pressure; it's how fast the data moves through the machine's circuits. The range of speeds, measured (get this) in *megahertz,* is 16 (on a Mac Classic) to 100 or more (the latest Power Macs).

That explains why the Classic II, the IIsi, and the IIci (for example) run at different speeds, even though they use the same Motorola 68030 chip.

Until the Power Mac series, you didn't really know how fast a Mac was unless you looked at the fine print or bothered to ask. It's not so tough with the Power Macs, though: the clock speed is part of the Mac's name, appearing after the slash. So a Power Mac 8100/100, for example, is faster than an 8100/80. (See? 100 is higher than 80, so it's faster.)

Macintosh as a Second Language

To make newcomers feel as much like outsiders as possible, the computer stores and newspaper ads run all this information together in a cryptic little line. This is pretty important information for comparison shoppers, so I thought that a translation might be in order. Let's see how much of that tech talk you were able to absorb.

The newspaper-ad test

Stay calm. Don't let your eyes glaze over. You *do* know what this means. Take it morsel by morsel.

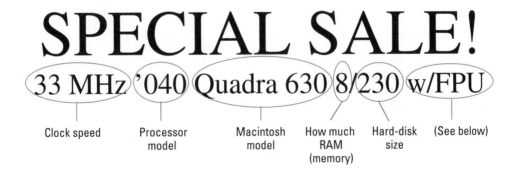

Translation: The **33 MHz** (megahertz) part is the speed measurement. The clock speeds of non-Power Mac models range from 16 MHz to 40 MHz, so this one, at 33, is pretty decent.

Next, there's the chip number. The non-Power Mac processor chips are 68000, 68020, 68030, and 68040 — so **'040** indicates a nice, fast brain. (The first three digits of the chip model number are left off.)

Then there's the Mac model number (**Quadra 630**). This number is pure marketing, concocted by some ad agency in California. It has nothing to do with the Mac's relative speed or anything. Just ignore it.

Finally, you see how much memory and hard-drive space you get in this computer (**8/230**). Both features are measured in megabytes. The memory comes before the slash, and the hard drive size after it.

What's an FPU 2U?

You sometimes run across the term *FPU*, too. This is a bonus chip, also called a *math coprocessor*. It pretty much does what it sounds like: it helps the Mac do math. Only the most expensive Mac models, destined for the desks of scientists and accountants, come with an FPU. For programs used by ordinary mortals — word processing programs, drawing programs, checkbook software, and most games — an FPU does *absolutely nothing* and isn't worth paying extra for.

Final exam

OK, let's see how fluent in Applespeak you've become.

In the grocery: "Nice to see you! Say, you ought to come over to my house. My husband just got a Macintosh PowerBook 520c 4/80. It's neato."

Translation: Well, you'll find out from the following discussion that a PowerBook with a *c* in its name has a color screen. So her husband got a middle-of-the-laptop-line color laptop computer with 4MB of RAM (just enough) and an 80MB hard drive — the 4/80 configuration. (He'll probably fill up that baby's hard drive with stuff in about six months.)

On a bulletin board: "FOR SALE: Macintosh Plus. Color monitor, 2 expansion slots. $3,000. Call Sid."

Translation: This guy has no idea what he's talking about. The Plus is black-and-white, it has no expansion slots, and that's about eight times too much to pay for that used machine!

If you understand that much, the worst is over. You're ready to begin your assault on the computer marketplace — informed, armed, and ready for anything.

The Product Line

Look, it's hopeless to try to keep up with Apple in a Mac book. Since the Macintosh first appeared on the scene, there have been *100* different models. Apple is still making something like 20 models — at *this* writing. Each one is available in several configurations.

For heaven's sake, Apple introduces a half-dozen new models *twice a year!* Who can keep them straight, let alone get them printed in a book that stays current?

Still, I think you should have some idea of what's happening on the Mac shelf when you walk into the computer store. One reason it's especially futile to keep track of the Macs in this world is that Apple often gives the *same machine* several different names! I mean, the Quadra 605, the Macintosh LC 475, and the Performa 476 are *identical Macs.*

Why on earth would Apple do something so silly? Because Apple thinks that people buy computers in three distinct ways. Kids, of course, buy them through their schools; the Macs for sale there are all called **LC**-something. Businesspeople buy computers at computer stores; their machines are all called **Quadra**-something, **Power Macintosh**-something, or **PowerBook**-something. And Mr. and Mrs. Family buy their computers at Sears and electronics stores; their Macs are all called **Performa**-something. So Apple figures it may as well sell the same models in as many different ways as possible!

Of course, this strategy is something new for Apple. Before the company came up with this scheme, there were a zillion other now-defunct model lines. Remember the olden days of 1993? Remember those crazy Mac II-series machines? And how about those nutty Classics? And oh, yeah — that wacky Centris line?

Anyway, here are some representative model names, past and present, along with information on what you might use them for. Remember that for a little *dinero*, you can upgrade almost any Mac at any time to make it faster. Also remember that within each family, higher numbers usually indicate faster, more recent models.

Black-and-white one-piece

Macintosh Plus
Macintosh SE and SE/30
Macintosh Classic and Classic II
Performa 200

These one-piece models, which Apple calls *compact Macs*, are about two feet tall. All you do is plug in the keyboard and the power cord, and you're off and running. All these models, which now cost $200 to about $600 (used), have been discontinued.

Techie note: All compact Macs run at a speed of 16 MHz, and all except the '030-based Classic II/Performa 200 and SE/30 are based on the 68000 processor.

The screen is built in. Apple calls it a nine-inch screen, but that's a diagonal measurement; the screen is actually about seven inches wide and five inches tall. You can see a five-inch-tall slice of a page all the way across.

One-piece Macs are inexpensive and relatively transportable (there's a handle built into the top). They weigh about 15 pounds; you can get a carrying case for them; and they fit into the overhead compartment of an airplane (just barely), especially if you take out the little foam pillows first. (In the compartment, I mean, not the computer.)

For word processing, the screen size is perfectly adequate. But art and graphic-design people go nuts if they can't see an entire page on the screen.

What they're good for

Word processing (but not with Microsoft Word 6); mail-merge operations (form letters); typing-instruction programs; black-and-white painting programs; dialing over phone lines with a modem; Rolodex and calendar programs; simple database files; flyer design; HyperCard stacks, such as kids' programs; and checkbook programs.

Color one-piece

Color Classic
Color Classic II (overseas only)
LC 500 series
Performa 500 series

These machines are bigger, heavier, and more expensive (in the $1,200-to-1,500 range) than the black-and-white compact Macs. On the other hand, they're easy to expand; and they have built-in, gorgeous *color* screens. Also, they're relatively fast because they're based on the 68030 chip at a speed of 16 or 25 MHz. The LC 500-line Macs also have built-in stereo speakers and a built-in CD-ROM player (see Chapter 7). Their screens measure 14 inches diagonally; the Color Classic's screen is 10 inches.

What they're good for

Everything listed for the preceding models, plus color games; kids' programs (especially CD-ROM discs); basic color painting and drawing; and playback of QuickTime digital movies, complete with sound and video, in a small window.

The LC series

Macintosh LC
Macintosh LC II (Performa 405, 410, 430)
Macintosh LC III (Performa 450, 460, 466, 467)
Macintosh LC 475 (Performa 475, 476)
Macintosh LC 630 (Performa 630,636,638)

Except for the 500 line, the LC (for *low-cost color*) Macs are two-piece Macs. In other words, you have to buy two pieces of equipment: the computer itself and a separate screen (the *monitor*). When computer nerds want to show off, they call the main box a *CPU.* Got that? You have two pieces to buy — a monitor and a CPU. (CPU stands for *Central Processing Unit.* Now *that* makes everything clear, doesn't it?)

You're not going to be able to transport *this* baby without the original shipping cartons (and a luggage cart). But buying a separate monitor grants you the power of choice: large or small, black-and-white or color, tall or wide. (If we're talking Performa, I take that back; every Performa comes with a monitor.)

The two-piece Macs, which Apple calls *modular*, are also easy to expand. The lid pops right off, just like the lid of a shoebox. Of course, the inside of the computer looks nothing like the inside of a shoebox. There are a lot of wires and chips and stuff, but they're very neatly arranged, and whatever you want to install (more memory, an accelerator card, whatever) slips into a very obvious place. Each LC has one *slot* — a rectangular socket into which you can plug a special-feature circuit board, such as an accelerator or a video card.

Today, Apple thinks of LCs as its educational line. An LC is no longer considered to be a cheapo wimp machine, either. The LC 475, for example, is the exact same computer as the Quadra 605, a respectably horsepowered machine. (Read about the LC 630 later in this chapter.)

Techie note: The LC models' speeds vary widely within the family, ranging from the LC (with an '020 chip) to the LC 575 (with an '040 chip); speeds run from 16 to 33 MHz. Prices for new and used LC computers range from $600 to $1,300 or so.

What they're good for

Everything listed for the previous models, plus page layout and graphic design (because you can attach a big screen, except on the 630 models, which max out at 15-inch monitors); music recording from a synthesizer; basic spreadsheets. (The LC 475 and higher-number models, of course, have the necessary horsepower for more challenging tasks. See "What they're good for" following the Mac II-series discussion.)

Mac II series

Macintosh II, IIx, IIfx, IIcx, IIsi, IIci
Macintosh IIvi (overseas only)
Macintosh IIvx (Performa 600)

All these models have been discontinued. These, too, are modular Macs; the screen is separate. Furthermore, most of these Macs have multiple expansion slots. The prices for used II-series Macs range between $500 and $1,000.

Techie details: All but the '020-based Mac II contain a 68030 chip running at speeds between 16 and 40 MHz. You can get a built-in CD-ROM player on the IIvx/Performa 600.

What they're good for

Everything listed for the previous models, plus complex spreadsheets, pro-level page layout, medium and complex databases, music notation (sheet music), QuickTime digital movie recording (with the addition of a $400 expansion card) and editing; and electronic mail (sent to other Macs in the office).

The Quadra series

Macintosh Quadra 605
Macintosh Quadra 610 (Centris 610)
Macintosh Quadra 650 (Centris 650)
Macintosh Quadra 700, 800, 900, 950
Macintosh Quadra 630 (LC 630,
      Performa 630-638)

If the PowerBooks are laptops, these are *floortops*. Most of them are so massive and powerful-looking that you're supposed to put them *under* your desk.

The name *Quadra* comes from the chip on which these Macs are based: the '040, which, when it debuted, made everybody's hair stand on end with its blistering speed. Only a couple of years later, this speed had become status quo, even for the PowerBooks. Then the Power Macintosh appeared, making even the '040 processor seem poky.

Anyway, the Quadras introduced one other notable feature: you can get other Mac devices, such as CD-ROM players and removable SyQuest cartridge drives, built right in. A Quadra 610 or 650 Mac can house one such device; Quadras 800 and higher are huge Macs, with enough room for two such built-in gadgets.

Most Quadra models also come with a feature called *Ethernet;* much as it may sound like the webbing of choice for anesthesiologists, Ethernet is actually a fast and fancy system of wiring the Macs in an office together (for sending electronic messages back and forth, sharing files, and so on).

Prices for new and used Quadras range from $700 to about $3,000 for the top-of-the-line, feature-packed 950, which is ready for use as the backbone of a whole office.

What they're good for

Everything listed for the previous models, plus color photo retouching and Photoshop (a professional painting program) art; 3-D graphics "rendering" (on-screen model making); morphing (making QuickTime movies that melt one image magically into another, as in Michael Jackson's "Black and White" video); high-level statistical analysis; programming; and use as an office *server* (a central Mac whose files can be accessed by every desktop Mac in the office).

The 630 has a couple of special properties; for example, you can watch TV on it and even record your own digital movies (if you buy optional accessory cards).

The AV series

Macintosh Quadra 660AV (Centris 660AV)
Macintosh Quadra 840AV

AV stands for *audiovisual*, and that describes these discontinued Macs perfectly. They can actually *speak* anything that you type for them, using a voice that actually has some expression and lilt (although it does sound like it has a permanent stuffy nose). These machines can also take orders from you; the microphone picks up any commands that you speak and executes them. Of course, it ain't exactly taking dictation; its comprehension of the things you say to it is, for the most part, limited to menu commands in your programs.

These are very fast Macs — particularly the Quadra 840AV, which has a 68040 chip that runs at a wild 40 MHz.

What they're good for

Everything listed for the previous models, plus a few specialized tasks that only AV Macs can perform: hooking up a VCR to record what you see on the screen; hooking up a cable and watching TV on your monitor; making QuickTime movies from a videotape or the TV without buying any extra equipment; and, with the purchase of a $100 adapter, serving as a full-fledged fax/modem (see Chapter 7).

PowerBooks

PowerBook 100, 140, 170
PowerBook 145, 145b,150, 160, 165, 180
PowerBook 520, 540
PowerBook 165c, 180c, 520c, 540c
PowerBook Duo 210, 230, 250, 270c, 280, 280c

PowerBooks are portable, laptop Macs. They're dark gray, two inches thick, weigh less than seven pounds, and are every bit as powerful as most of the models that you've read about so far. A PowerBook opens like a book when you're using it; one side has the keyboard, and the other has the screen. You can plug a PowerBook in or use the battery, which lasts about two hours per charge. (See Chapter 10 for additional PowerBook scoop.)

Typing on a PowerBook is slightly less comfortable than on a desktop Mac, and you can expand one only with considerable hassle and expense. But a Power-Book is indispensable for anyone who travels. And a PowerBook is definitely the Mac to have if you're trying to catch the eye of an attractive stranger across the airplane aisle.

What on earth could account for all the different models and prices? First, there's screen quality. Every PowerBook screen uses one of two technologies: *active-matrix* or *passive-matrix*. As is true of employees, agents, and brokers, active is better than passive. Active screens (models 180, 540, 270, and so on) are crisp and bright. Passive screens (160, 520, 230, and so on) are slightly murkier, slower to update the display (such as when you move the cursor), and a *lot* cheaper (to the tune of nearly $1,000).

Color also costs you. Those models whose names end in *c* (180c, 520c, 540c, and so on) show gorgeous full color. Most other PowerBooks can show, at best, different shades of gray, like a newspaper photo. Color screens also cost a lot more, drain your battery twice as fast, and weigh more than their paleface cousins do.

The biggest differences among PowerBook models, though, have to do with the *families* they belong to. The Duos, for example, are much smaller and lighter than regular PowerBooks. That's because you can leave a lot of the electronics — the floppy-disk drive and the back-panel jacks — at home on your desk and take just the computer itself on your travels.

Code name: Blackbird

Then there are the 520 and 540 (and the color versions of each). These sleek black PowerBooks don't just look futuristic; they *are* futuristic. They're way faster than the 100-series models. (Nerd note: It's because the 500s have an '040 chip inside.) Starting in 1995, you can replace the chip with a PowerPC processor chip for cheek-sucking speed.

These laptops have stereo speakers. They also offer a separate module socket into which you can insert your choice of accessory — a second battery or a fax/modem, for example. Finally, in place of the standard gray track/ping-pong ball, these special PowerBooks feature a *trackpad* that's a couple inches square. The trackpad lets you control the pointer just by dragging your finger — no doubt a response to the efforts of the powerful Long-Fingernailed Computer Users' lobby.

What they're good for

Everything listed for the Mac II-series Macs — and you can do any of those things while sitting comfortably in a plane, train, or La-Z-Boy recliner.

Power Macintosh

Power Macintosh 6100, 7100, 8100
Performa 6110, 6112, 6115, 6117, 6118

Apple's 1994/95 Mac models aren't based on those 68000-series processor chips, like all previous ones. Instead, the new Macs contain an *extremely* fast, very high-tech new chip called the PowerPC chip.

These Macs, called the Power Macintosh series, look, feel, and smell like the Macs that came before them. They work fine with all existing normal Mac programs. The speed doesn't exactly pin your ears back; when you run those pre-Power Mac programs, you'll think that you're using a Quadra 700 or something. But if you buy (or upgrade to) special PowerPC versions of your programs — the so-called "native" programs (doesn't that have a wild, jungly sound?) — these Macs *really* scream. Native programs run several times *faster* than on the fastest of yesteryear's Quadras.

In the coming years, every existing Mac model will be quietly snuffed out to make room for a new PowerPC-based model. Also in the coming years, practically every program will be available in a native version. Power Macs actually cost *less* than the Macs that came before them, and as the 1990s progress, Apple will crank out models built on faster and faster PowerPC chips.

If you already own a Quadra, a Centris, a recent LC or Performa model, or a PowerBook 500-something Mac, you can even upgrade your computer to have a PowerPC chip. Simply fork over between $700 and $2,000 to some smiling Apple-dealer technician.

What they're good for

Everything listed for the previous models — but *faster*. The Power Macs also have the hi-fi sound-recording features, the GeoPort, and speech-recognition options of the AV Macs (described earlier). If you buy your Power Mac with the AV option, you can also hook up your TV to the Mac for recording and play-back. Oh, joy.

Buying a Monitor

If you've decided to become the proud owner of a two-piece Mac (a Mac II-something, a Quadra, Centris, LC or equivalent), you have to decide what kind of screen (monitor) to get.

Black-and-white, grayscale, color

The least expensive screens show black writing against a white background, just like a typewriter does. For writing, finances, spreadsheets, music, data-bases, calendars, Rolodexes, and 90 percent of the other day-to-day Mac tasks, black-and-white is all you'll ever need. Black-and-white screens are also the fastest; you almost never have to wait for the computer to "paint" the screen from top to bottom, as you do when you're working in color.

On the other hand, you can't even *get* black and white anymore, either built into a Mac or as a separate piece, just as it's hard to find black-and-white TV sets these days. Like color TVs, color Macs have grown to dominate the market.

The next step up is a *grayscale* monitor. It doesn't just have black and white; it also displays many different shades of gray. Particularly in larger sizes, these Macs are less expensive than color monitors, but they can still give your icons a nice 3-D look.

Color monitors are the most expensive, and they make everything appear on the screen slightly slower. Some things absolutely demand a color monitor: games, color graphics, presentations and some business charts, most CD-ROMs, digital movies (called QuickTime movies), and so on. Certain pro-grams make clever use of color. For example, a drafting program may display light-blue graph-paper lines behind the black lines that you draw.

When you're choosing a monitor, remember that a color monitor is *also* a grayscale monitor *and* a black-and-white monitor. (An on-screen control panel lets you switch from one mode to another.)

How big is your view?

Your biggest buying headache, however, will be deciding what *size* monitor to get. Monitors are measured diagonally, and they're measured stupidly — that is, from edge to edge of the *glass,* not the *picture area.* (The outer inch of glass is always left black.) So much for the rise of marketing geniuses.

In any case, the common monitor sizes are 14, 15, 16, 17, 20, and 21 inches. (You may also hear "the old Apple 13-inch monitor" mentioned now and then. It's exactly the same size as the current Apple *14-inch* monitor; it got its name before the marketing people switched to rose-colored measuring tapes.)

By far the most common size is 14 inches (below, right). It's the most common because it's the least expensive. The screen is just shy of nine inches wide and seven inches tall.

Although most monitors are wider than they are tall (*landscape* orientation), some 15-inch screens come in *portrait* orientation. The point here is that you can see an entire 8¹/₂-inch × 11-inch page (below, left).

The remaining monitor sizes are called *two-page* displays because, obviously, they show two pages side by side (above, middle). Some monitors — such as, Apple's 15-, 17-, and 20-inchers — come with the fancy high-tech adjective *multisync* at no extra charge. This simply means that you can zoom in or out, magnifying or shrinking everything on the screen. Of course, when you're zoomed out, everything's smaller — but the advantage is that you can see a larger area. For example, you can zoom out the 17-inch screen and see two entire pages side by side.

For writing, virtually any size screen will do. Even if you can see only half a page at a time, you can always *scroll* the display up (or down) to see what you wrote on the preceding (or following) page. If you plan to do any graphic design — that is, page layout of brochures or newsletters — you'll probably want at least a full-page display. And if you're going to do professional page-design work, such as laying out a book, get a two-page display.

Getting it on paper

In the olden days (in other words, last year), seeing color on the screen would have been the end of the color story. You got to see great, rich, stunning color on the screen, but everything that you printed came out in black and white. Color printers cost way too much for any individual to buy.

Recently, though, the prices of color printers have plummeted. Now you can buy a high-quality color printer for $4,000 or one with a more limited palette of colors for $500. I wouldn't advise getting a color printer for everyday correspondence. But if you're ever hired to design rough sketches for a movie poster or something, keep those cheapie color printers in mind.

A bit about color bits

(Note: I'm providing the following discussion so that you'll understand the chatter in your favorite computer magazines. Unless you retouch photos for a living, there's no reason to know this stuff.)

The technobullies of the world have foisted several different *kinds* of color upon us: *8-bit, 16-bit,* and *24-bit* color.

All you need to know is that 16-bit and 24-bit color is relatively more expensive, slower to appear on the screen, and much more realistic. *Realistic* is a term that matters only if you plan to work with photos or movies on the screen. If not, 24-bit is for the pros; it's overkill for everyone else.

Which degree of colorness you have depends on your *Mac,* not the *monitor.* All of today's Macs provide 8-bit color: they can show 256 different colors on the screen. All you have to do is plug your monitor into the built-in jack. If you one day decide that you can't live without photorealistic colors on your screen, you can buy and install a *video card* (a circuit board) to get 16-bit or 24-bit color; you don't need a new monitor.

For pixel weenies only

You really, really want to know where terms like *8-bit* and *24-bit* come from? Don't say that you weren't warned.

Remember color theory from high-school physics? Mixing the three primary colors — red, yellow, and blue — is supposed to produce any color in the rainbow.

Well, to display a color picture, the Mac has to remember the precise amounts of those colors to mix for *each individual dot on the screen*. Think about it: dot number 15 is 21 percent red and 79 percent blue, and so on, for each dot. That's an awful lot of information to store for each of 307,200 dots.

To save expense, trouble, and memory, most Macs reserve only 8 bits of their brains to describe the color of each dot. (You can think of a *bit* as being one word of computer description — a unit of electronic information.) So even though a particular dot can be any color under the rainbow, the *total number of colors* that can appear on an 8-bit color monitor is 256. That may sound like a lot

of colors, but thousands more shades are needed to produce a convincing rainbow.

The pros, then, get much more expensive monitors that use far more information to describe the color of each dot — 16 or 24 bits, in fact. With that much description power, the Mac can display *millions* of different colors. In fact, every dot on the screen could be a different color, and you'd still have millions of colors to choose among that couldn't fit on the screen.

All this thinking and describing that the Mac has to do for 24-bit color (sometimes stupidly called *32*-bit color, by the way; it's the same thing) means that the screen gets painted pretty slowly. Of course, the Basic Rule of Computing states that whenever there's a computing inconvenience, some company will invent an expensive gizmo that solves it. The slow speed of 24-bit monitors is no exception: For a couple grand more, you can get an *accelerated* graphics card, which makes it possible to see 24-bit images almost as quickly as 8-bit ones on an *un*accelerated screen.

Where to Buy Your Mac

I'm going to assume that you're not in Donald Trump's tax bracket. I'm going to assume that you're looking for ways to get the most Mac for the least lira.

The Apple school discount

Apple grants hefty Mac discounts to students and teachers. In Apple's younger, healthier days, the discount was 40 percent; it's not nearly as much of a giveaway today, but there are still great deals to be had on Mac equipment. If you're affiliated with a college, find out whether the school's bookstore is a member of this delightful program.

Mail order

If you're not fortunate enough to be a student or faculty member, the next-least-expensive way to get a new Mac is probably through a mail-order company. These outfits take out big ads in the Macintosh magazines, such as *Macworld* and *MacUser*. Of course, you can't exactly browse the merchandise, so it's assumed that you already know what you want when you call one of these places.

If everything goes smoothly, mail order can be a nifty deal: You save hundreds by avoiding sales tax, you get a pretty good price, and you don't have to haul anything home in the car. The trouble with mail order, though, is that life can get pretty ugly if things *don't* go right. What if the thing is broken when it arrives? Suddenly, you've got the burden of packing it up, shipping it back, and persuading the company to replace the equipment (*if* they'll even consider it).

Mail order is for gamblers. You can score big, but you can also get shafted, and you won't have anywhere to turn for help.

Computer stores

A computer store is likely to have higher prices. You'll have to pay sales tax. But you also get a human being to blame when things get fouled up.

Unfortunately, buying a computer at a store is still a crapshoot: good dealers are relatively rare, and lousy dealers are everywhere. A notorious New York City dealership, for example, makes a regular practice of advertising rock-bottom prices. Then, when you show up, the salesperson mentions that you'll "probably also want to buy" several items that are normally included in the package — the mouse, for example, or a cartridge (if you're buying a printer).

So how are you supposed to know good dealers (and their repair guys) from bad? There's only one way: ask around. Depending on where you live, though, getting the word-of-mouth report may be easier said than done. If you're at a loss as to whom you should ask, start by finding the nearest Macintosh user group; call Apple's user-group-listing hotline at 800-538-9696.

Consumer stores

The Performa series of Macs aren't just sold at computer stores; they're also on the shelves of *non*-computer stores, such as Sears, Silo, Price Club, and office-supply stores. There they are, right next to the blenders and microwaves. Because the usual clerks can't be expected to know anything about computers, Apple covers you with toll-free phone numbers: one to call with questions and one to call if something breaks.

The Performas are essentially the same machines as Macs that are sold under other names. You're spared the hassle of choosing a keyboard and monitor; both devices are included in the total price. It's about the same price that you'd pay for a non-Performa system, except that you get free software. If you aren't too grossed out by the word *Performa*, the Performas are a good deal (see Chapter 10 for details).

Used Macs

Finally, you can buy a used Mac. Once again, the luck of the draw determines how satisfied you'll be. To a certain extent, you can tell how much abuse a Mac has taken by looking at it. But a visual exam won't tell you about the funny noise that the hard drive makes only after it's been on for 20 minutes, or about the monitor that's been in for repairs three times already, or about the ball of cat hair wedged inside the disk drive.

In other words, there are three rules for buying used equipment:

- First, determine whether you're willing to forgo the comfy Apple warranty for the sake of saving money.

- Second, be sure that the asking price really is low enough to make the savings meaningful, particularly on discontinued Mac models (such as the SE/30 or the LC). Some naïve sellers who don't understand the Inviolable Rule of Instant Obsolescence think they can recoup the full purchase price when they sell their used Macs. Don't fall for it — be sure to compare the asking price with a computer store's new-Mac price.

- Finally, test the Mac as much as possible before you buy it. Above all, test the disk drive (by inserting a floppy disk and copying a file onto it), the printer port (by printing something), and the mouse (by rolling it around on the desk).

Credit cards

It doesn't thrill me to break the news to you, but you're going to be spending a lot of money even *after* you buy your Mac. We haven't even discussed buying a keyboard yet. You're also going to need software. As hobby costs go, computing isn't exactly crocheting.

As long as you're committed to this plunge, a word of solemn advice: put everything on a credit card, especially when you're buying by mail order. Thousands of Mac users have avoided getting ripped off by the occasional fly-by-night operation because they charged it. (As you probably know, the credit-card company doesn't pay your bill if you're disputing the charge. This is an incredible layer of protection between you and companies that send you the wrong item, a broken item, and so on.)

I Took Off the Shrink Wrap! Now What?

Setting up the Mac should take less than 20 minutes; all you have to do is plug in a few cables. (See Chapter 4 for instructions on plugging in your printer.)

Ergo . . . ergonomics

First, figure out where you're going to put the most expensive appliance that you've ever bought. In my opinion, the principal principle is this: when you're seated at your desk and you're in typing position, *your elbows can't be lower than your wrists.* Otherwise, if you plan to do a lot of work at the computer, you may wind up with a nasty and painful ailment called Carpal Tunnel Syndrome, which never goes away until you stop using the computer.

The next ergonomic lesson is one learned from the painful experience of thousands of home-office users: don't put the monitor in front of a sunny window. It turns out that your pupils shrink to accommodate the bright window light. But because you're trying to focus on the relatively dim Mac screen, your optic system gets confused and strained, and it's hello, headache.

Finally, I suppose that I should mention ELF. No, this elf isn't the little man inside the Mac who runs around obeying your every command; it stands for Extremely Low-Frequency radiation. A few scientists have been saying (without much hard proof one way or another) that electrical appliances emit a very subtle, low dose of radiation. If you sit very close to an appliance for a very long period of time, the theory says, your cancer risk increases. (Computers are supposedly the biggest risk; not many people sit hunched in front of their *blenders* all day.)

Macworld magazine tests discovered that you have to sit *really* close to your Mac to get any of this radiation. In fact, by the time you move 28 inches away — that's arm's length — the level of ELF radiation is zero. If ELF radiation concerns you, just stay arm's length from the nearest monitor, and you'll be OK. (Further-more, all this radiation stuff applies primarily to two-piece Macs; the compact Macs and PowerBooks don't emit anything but good vibes.)

Getting plugged

Your manuals, of course, are the best source of instructions for setting up the Mac. But here are the basics.

Everything plugs into the back of the Mac. Take a look: there's a whole assortment of plugs back there. The plugs labeled with little symbolic pictures called *icons.* (Get used to icons; they're the cornerstone of the Mac's graphical nature.) The sidebar in this section shows the back of a typical Mac and what you can plug into it.

If your new Mac is a laptop (PowerBook), there's nothing to set up. Plug it in, open the back panel, press the round On/Off button, and flip back to Chapter 1.

If your Mac *isn't* a PowerBook, study the diagram in the sidebar. Using it as your guide, plug the power cord into the power jack and the keyboard into the ADB jack. Most people then plug the mouse into the other side of the keyboard, but some Macs have a second ADB port for the mouse. Do whatever feels good.

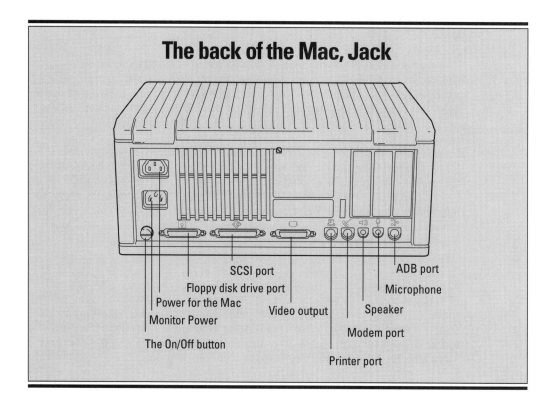

The back of the Mac, Jack

If you have any form of Classic, Mac Plus, SE, LC, or Performa 500-something, your installation is complete. Flip back to Chapter 1.

If you have a two-piece Mac, plug the monitor's two cables into the monitor-power and video-out jacks, as shown in the diagram. You're all set.

If you bought an old, used Mac that requires a video card, you have to open the cover and install it. Call whoever sold it to you for help.

You're ready for business. For instructions on hooking up your printer, see Chapter 4.

Switching the Mac on

Quick! Flip to Chapter 1!

Top Ten Things That You Get Free with Your Mac

Enjoy this list — this is the last time in your entire computing career that you'll get anything free.

1. A mouse.

2. A floppy-disk drive built into the machine.

3. HyperCard Player. (See Chapter 5.)

4. A one-year warranty that covers parts and labor at *any* Apple dealership — or at your house or office.

5. A set of white System software disks, or a startup CD-ROM disc (except Performa models).

6. A power cord.

7. A coupon for a free mouse pad or a subscription to *Macworld* magazine.

8. Instruction manuals.

9. A guided-tour program (Macintosh Basics or Mouse Practice).

10. A registration card. Fill it out and send it in.

Appendix B

The Resource Resource

Magazines

Mac Home Journal
415-957-1911

Macworld
800-234-1038

MacUser
800-627-2247

MacWeek
609-461-2100

User Groups

Apple User-Group Info Line
800-538-9696 ext. 500

Arizona Macintosh User's
Group
602-553-8966

Boston Computer Society
BCS/Mac
617-625-7080

BMUG
415-849-9114

Apple Corps of Dallas
214-357-9185

Houston Area Apple Users'
Group
713-522-2179

Los Angeles Macintosh
Users' Group
213-278-5264

New Jersey Macintosh
Users' Group
201-893-5274

New York Macintosh Users'
Group
212-645-2265

Products Mentioned in This Book

1-2-3 for Macintosh
Lotus Corp.
617-577-8500

911 Utilities
Datawatch Corporation
Triangle Software Division
919-490-1277
919-490-6672 (FAX)

**Adobe Type Manager
(ATM)**
Adobe Systems
415-961-4400
800-833-6687

After Dark
Berkeley Systems, Inc.
510-540-5535

America Online
America Online Inc.
800-827-6364

Bernoulli
Iomega Corporation
801-778-1000
800-456-5522

Bose Speakers
Bose Corp.
508-879-7330
800-444-2673

Central Point MacTools
see MacTools Deluxe

**ClarisWorks
ClarisDraw**
Claris Corp.
408-727-8227
408-987-3932 (FAX)

ColorIt
MicroFrontier
515-270-8109

CompuServe
617-661-9440
800-873-1032

Conflict Catcher
Casady & Greene
408-484-9228
800-359-4920

Cubase Lite
Steinberg
818-993-4091

DeskWriter
Hewlett-Packard
415-857-1501
800-752-0900

Disinfectant
Freeware: John Norstad,
author. Available from any
online modem service, or
send a self-addressed
stamped sturdy envelope
and an 800K disk to the
following address. People
outside the U.S. may send an
international postal reply
coupon instead of U.S.
stamps (available from any
post office).
John Norstad
Academic Computing and
Network Services
Northwestern University
2129 Sheridan Road
Evanston, IL 60208

DiskDoubler
Symantec Corp.
408-253-3570
800-441-7234

Encarta
Microsoft
206-882-8080

Encore
Passport Designs
415-726-0280

Excel
Microsoft Corp.
206-882-8080
800-426-9400

EZ Vision
Opcode Systems, Inc.
415-856-3333

Finale, Finale Allegro
Coda Music Technology
612-854-1288
800-843-2066

Flight Simulator
Microsoft Corp.
206-882-8080
800-426-9400

FreeHand
Aldus Corp.
206-622-5500

Gatekeeper
Available from online
services

Hard Disk ToolKit
FWB Incorporated
415-474-8055

HyperCard
Apple Computer
408-996-1010
800-776-2333

Illustrator
Adobe Systems
415-961-4400
800-833-6687

KidPix
Broderbund Software
800-521-6263

Last Resort
Working Software
408-423-5696
800-229-9675

Living Books
Broderbund Software
800-521-6263

MacConnection
800-800-4444

MacDraw
see ClarisDraw

MacLink Plus
DataViz
203-268-0030
800-733-0030

MacRecorder
Macromedia
415-442-0200
800-288-4797

MacTools Deluxe
Central Point Software
503-690-8090
800-964-6896

MacWarehouse
800-255-6227

Mac Zone
800-248-0800

MenuFonts
Dubl-Click Software, Inc.
818-888-2068

MicroPhone
Software Ventures
415-644-3232
800-336-3478

Microsoft Art Gallery
Microsoft
206-882-8080

ModuNet
Data Spec
818-772-9977
800-431-8124

MusicShop
Opcode Systems, Inc.
415-856-3333

MyAdvancedLabelMaker
MySoftware Company
415-325-9372

Myst
Broderbund Software
415-382-4400
800-521-6263

Nisus
Nisus Software
619-481-1477
800-922-2993

Norton Utilities
Symantec Corp.
408-253-3570
800-441-7234

Now Up-to-Date
Now Utilities,
Now Compress
Now Software
503-274-2800

PageMaker
Aldus Corp.
206-622-5500

Painter
Fractal Design
408-688-8800

Persuasion
Aldus Corp.
206-622-5500

PhoneNet
Farallon
510-596-9100
800-344-7489

Photoshop
Adobe Systems
415-961-4400
800-833-6687

**PowerBook Battery
Recharger**
Lind Electronics Design
612-927-6303
800-659-5956

**PowerBook Car/Boat
Adapter**
Empire Engineering
805-543-2816

PowerKey
Sophisticated Circuits
800-827-4669

QuarkXPress
Quark Inc.
303-934-2211
800-356-9363

QuickCam
Connectix Corp.
800-950-5880
415-571-5100

Quicken
Intuit/Microsoft
415-322-0573
800-624-8742

QuicKeys
CE Software
515-224-1995

RAM Doubler
Connectix
415-571-5100
800-950-5880

SilverLining
La Cie
503-520-9000
800-999-0143

Street Atlas USA
DeLorme Mapping
207-865-4171
800-452-5931

StuffIt, StuffIt Expander
Aladdin Systems, Inc.
408-761-6200

Suitcase II
Symantec Corp.
408-253-3570
800-441-7234

Super QuickDex
Casady & Greene, Inc.
408-484-9228
800-359-4920

SuperPaint
Aldus Corp.
206-622-5500

**Symantec Utilities for the
Macintosh (SAM)**
Symantec Corp.
408-253-3570
800-441-7234

SyQuest
SyQuest Technologies
510-226-4000
800-245-2278

Thunder 7
Baseline Publishing
901-682-9676
800-926-9677

UltraPaint/ArtWorks
Deneba Software
305-596-5644
800-622-6827

VideoSpigot
SuperMac Technology
800-345-9777
408-245-2202

Virex
Datawatch Corporation
Triangle Software Division
919-490-1277

White Knight
The FreeSoft Company
412-846-2700

Word
Microsoft Corp.
206-882-8080
800-426-9400

**WordPerfect for the
Macintosh**
WordPerfect Corp.
801-225-5000
800-321-4566

WriteNow
WordStar International, Inc.
800-523-3520

Appendix C
The Techno-Babble Translation Guide

• •

accelerator — The pedal that you press while driving to pick up your very first Mac. Also, an expensive circuit board that you can install to make your Mac faster and slightly less obsolete.

access privileges — Permission to do something on the Mac. Appears only in the context of "You can't do that because you don't have access privileges." Pertains either to File Sharing (you haven't been allowed access to a certain networked folder) or Performas (somebody turned on "System Folder protection" in your Performa or General control panel).

active window — The window in front. Usually, only one window can be active; you can recognize it by the stripes across the title bar, like this:

ADB — An acronym (for *Apple Desktop Bus*) that describes the cables and jacks used by the keyboard and mouse, as in "Can you believe that dimwit!? He plugged his printer into the ADB port!"

alert box — A message that appears on the screen; the Mac's attempt to maintain an open and communicative relationship with you. Unfortunately, as in most relationships, the Mac tends to communicate only when something is wrong. An alert box is marked either with the International Exclamation Point or a warning hand, like this:

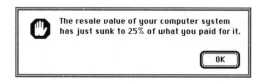

alias — A duplicate of a file's icon (not of the file itself). Serves as a double-clickable *pointer*, or reference, to the original file, folder, or disk. A feature of System 7 or later. Indicated by an italicized icon name.

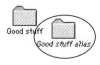

Apple menu — The menu at the far left end of your menu bar, marked by the symbol — a piece of black or multicolor fruit. In the menu, you'll find a list of your desk accessories (miniprograms, such as the

Calculator), as well as any files, folders, documents, control panels, and even disks (or their aliases) that you care to see there. To add something to the menu, drop its icon into the Apple Menu Items folder within your System Folder.

AppleShare — Some kind of trademarked name for the way that interconnected Macs communicate with one another. (You'll never need to know this.)

AppleTalk — Another trademarked name, also having to do with Macs talking to one another. You *may* need to know this term if you have a laser printer because AppleTalk is the language that it speaks to your Mac. To print, you must make sure that AppleTalk is active. Choose the Chooser from the menu, and you'll see where you turn AppleTalk on or off.

application — Nerd word for *program*.

Application menu — The rightmost menu in the menu bar (if you have System 7), marked by an icon. This menu lists whichever programs you have open and displays a check mark next to the frontmost program. You can switch from one program to another by choosing names from the Application menu.

ASCII — The most interesting thing about this term (which means *text file*) is its weird pronunciation: ASKie. Good name for a Labrador, don't you think?

ATM — Short for *Adobe Type Manager*, a piece of software that makes certain fonts look really great on the screen (and in nonlaser printouts). It's free, for only $7.50.

background printing — A feature that returns control of the Mac to you immediately after you use the Print command; the

Mac will print your document, taking its own sweet time, always giving priority to what you're doing on the screen. The alternative, known as *background printing is off*, takes less time to print but takes over the Mac, preventing you from working and displaying a "now printing" message until the printing is over.

back up — To make a copy of a file for use in case some horrible freak accident befalls your original copy (such as your throwing it out).

Balloon Help — A feature of System 7 and later. See the little question mark in the upper-right corner of your screen? It's a menu. Choose Show Balloons from it; then point to various elements of your little Mac-screen world. Cartoon balloons pop out to identify what you're pointing at.

baud rate — The speed of a modem (see *modem*). Directly related to the price.

BBS — An electronic bulletin-board system. That's where a Mac in somebody's house is connected to a phone line or two so that you can dial in with a modem (see *modem*) and post messages for other people to see. You can also read other people's messages. A BBS is a good place to advertise that you're selling your used Mac stuff and to get dates.

beta test — Means *test*, but adding a Greek word makes it sound more important. Used exclusively when applied to software: When a program is still so buggy and new that a company doesn't dare sell it, the company gives it away (to people who are called *beta testers*) in hopes of being told what the bugs are.

binary — Capable of counting only up to 2: how a computer thinks. Or anything that can only be in one of two conditions, such as a Morse-code signal, a light switch, or a public restroom.

bit — You'd think that it's the past tense of *byte* (see that entry). Actually, it's a tiny piece of computer information that's not even big enough to bother with.

bitmap — A particular arrangement of black dots on your white screen. To your eye, a particular bitmap may look like the letter *A* (bitmapped text) or a coffee mug (a bitmapped graphic); to the computer, it's just a bunch of dots whose exact positions it has to memorize.

boot — (1) (v.) To start the computer. (2) (n.) Western footwear. (3) (v.) To fire somebody for having accidentally erased the hard drive, as in "He was booted out of here so fast, you could have heard a résumé drop."

bps — Bits per second. The technically proper way to measure the speed of a *modem* (instead of *baud,* which everybody still says out of force of habit).

bug — A programming error in a piece of software, caused by a programmer too wired on Jolt and pizza, that makes the program do odd or tragic things when you're working to beat a deadline.

bus — A form of public transportation. Any other questions? No, really, it's a connection between any two components *inside* your computer.

button — There are two kinds of buttons that you'll have to deal with: the big square one on the mouse, and the many oval or round ones on the screen that offer you options.

byte — A piece of computer information made up of bits. Now *that* made everything clear, didn't it?

CAD — An acronym for *computer-aided design* (i.e., architectural programs).

Caps Lock — A key on your keyboard that's responsible for messing up pages and pages of manuscript if you're one of those people who doesn't look up from the keyboard much. Caps Lock makes every letter that you type come out as a capital; it doesn't affect numbers. Press it to get the capitals; press it again to return to normal.

cdev — Short for *control panel.*

CD-ROM — A computer compact disc that requires a special $300 player. CD-ROMs can show pictures, play music or voices, display short animations and movies, and display reams and reams of text. (A typical CD holds 600 megs of information; compared with the measly 230-meg hard disks that come in the more expensive Macs.)

character — (1) A single typed letter, number, space, or symbol. (2) The scoundrel who got you into this Macintosh habit.

Chooser — A desk accessory, therefore listed in the   menu, that lets you specify what kind of printer you have. Failure to use this thing when you set up your Mac is the #1 reason why beginners can't print.

click — The cornerstone of the Macintosh religion: to point the cursor at an on-screen object and then press and release the mouse button.

clip art — Instead of possessing actual artistic ability, graphic designers can buy (or otherwise acquire) collections of ready-made graphics called *clip art* — cutesy little snowmen, city skylines, Santa Clauses, whatever — that they can use to dress up their newsletters, party invitations, and threatening legal notices.

Clipboard — The invisible holding area where the Mac stashes any text or graphics that you copy by using the Copy command. The contents of the Clipboard get vaporized when you turn off the Mac (or copy something new).

clock rate — The speed of your computer, measured in megahertz, and determined by the studliness of the main processor chip inside.

close box — The little square in the upper-left corner of a window (as opposed to the little square who sold you the Macintosh), which, when clicked, closes the window.

close box

Control Panels		
32 items	201.1 MB in disk	29.8 MB availabl
Name	Size	Kind
Conflict Catcher™	444K	control p.
Apple Menu Options	56K	control p.
Color	12K	control p.
ColorSync™ System Pro...	24K	control p.

color separation — The technique used in offset printing, where four separate metal plates (each one sopped in ink of a different color) are used to print a full-color image.

command — Something that you'd like the Mac to do, such as Print or Save or Make Me Rich. See also *menu.*

Command key — The one on your keyboard, right next to the spacebar, that has a ⌘ (Command) symbol on it. When you press this key, the letter keys on your keyboard perform commands instead of

typing letters — for example, ⌘-P = Print, ⌘-S = Save, ⌘-Q = Quit, and ⌘-Z = Undo. (Well, they can't *all* be mnemonic.)

Control key — A keyboard key that does absolutely nothing.

control panel — A little window full of settings that pertain to some aspect of the Mac's operation. There's a control panel for the mouse, another for the keyboard, another for the monitor, and so on. To view the selection of control panels, choose (what else?) Control Panels from the menu.

Copy — The command that places a copy of something (whatever text or graphics were first *selected*) in the invisible Macintosh Clipboard. Accomplishes nothing unless you then click somewhere and *paste.*

CPU — What it *stands for* is *central processing unit.* What it *means* is the actual computer — in the case of two-piece Macs, the box that contains the real brains. As distinguished from things like the monitor, the printer, and the keyboard.

crash — A very ugly moment in every Mac user's life when the Mac abruptly malfunctions, usually with scary-looking sounds and visuals. Requires restarting.

CRT — Man, those geeks really get into cryptic acronyms for simple things, don't they? The CRT is the screen. If you must know, it stands for *cathode ray tube.*

cursor — The pointer on the screen whose position you control by moving the mouse across the desk.

DA — Short for *desk accessory.*

daisy chaining — The act of stringing together a bunch of different add-on appliances, such as a CD player, a hard disk, and a scanner. Involves plugging one into the back of the next, very much like an elephant conga line.

data — Isn't he that white-makeup guy on *Star Trek: The Next Generation*?

database — An electronic list of information — for example, a mailing list — that can be sorted very quickly or searched for a specific name.

default — (1) The factory settings. For example, the *default* setting for your typing in a word processor is single-spaced, one-inch margins. (2) De blame for hooking you on de Mac hobby.

defragment — To restore, in one continuous chunk, something that's all broken up and scrambled. Usually refers to the information in memory or on a hard disk, but can also be applied to hamburger meat.

Delete key — In the typewriter days, this key was named Backspace. In my opinion, it still *should* be called that. I make it a habit to magic-marker the word *Backspace* on every keyboard that I encounter.

deselect — To *un*highlight some selected text or graphic. (You usually do it by clicking someplace else.)

desktop — (1) The top of your desk, where the Mac sits, as in "I don't want a laptop; I want a desktop computer." (2) *(Capitalized)* The home-base environment, where you see the Trash can, icons, and all that stuff. Also known as the Finder. (3) The actual (usually gray) background of that home-base view. You can drag an icon out of its window and onto this gray tablecloth, and announce to your coworker that you've just placed an icon on the Desktop.

desktop file — A file the Mac maintains for its own use, in which it stores information such as what your icons should look like and which kinds of documents can be opened by which programs. This file is invisible, but when it becomes damaged or bloated and starts causing problems, it's not quite invisible enough for most people.

desktop publishing — The act of cranking out nice-looking printouts from your Mac instead of paying to have the work typeset. Despite the fact that the PowerBook is equally adept at creating beautiful printouts, the term *laptop publishing* still hasn't quite caught on.

dialog box — The message box that the Mac puts on the screen when it needs more information from you (for example, the one that appears when you print, asking how many copies you want). Because the Mac doesn't, thank God, actually talk back to you, and instead just listens to what *you* say, a better name might be *therapist box*.

digitize — Computerese for *digest*. It's what happens to sound, pictures, video, and any other kind of real-world sensory experience after the Mac converts it in its own numerical digestive tract.

digitizing board — A circuit board that converts video or TV pictures into files on your Mac.

disk — Oh, come on; you know *this* word.

disk cache — A secret feature for making your Mac faster at the expense of memory. The Mac memorizes a few things that you do a lot and keeps them in a wad of memory called the *disk cache*, where they'll be immediately accessible. You set the size of the disk cache (the amount of memory reserved) in the Memory control panel.

disk drive — The machinery that actually reads what's on a disk. If we're talking hard disk, the disk and the drive are built into a single unit. If we're talking floppy, the disk drive is the slot in the face of the Mac into which you insert a floppy disk.

document — A file that you create with a *program.* Examples: a memo (using a word processing program), a logo (using a graphics program), or a spreadsheet (using a spreadsheet program).

documentation — A five-syllable way of saying *user's guide.*

DOS — Synonym for *IBM-style computers,* meaning the computers of the world that aren't lucky enough to be Macs. Stands for Disk Operating System.

dot-matrix — A kind of low-quality printer, such as the ImageWriter, and the printouts that it makes.

dots per inch — A gauge of visual clarity, both on printouts and on the screen. The Mac's crystal-clear screen became famous for having a very high resolution — 72 dots per inch, or 72 *dpi.* A laser printer is much sharper, though, capable of printing at 300 dpi.

double-click — One of the most basic Mac skills, without which you can't do anything but stare at the blank screen. Double-clicking involves placing the on-screen pointer on an icon and, without moving the mouse, pressing the mouse button twice quickly. If you double-click an icon, it always opens into a window. In word processing, you double-click a word to select it.

download — To transfer a file from one computer to another over phone lines. If you're on the receiving end, you *download* the file. If you're on the sending end, you *upload* the file. If you're the phone company, you *love* the file.

downloadable font — Every laser printer comes with a basic set of typefaces built into it. You're welcome to use fonts that aren't in that built-in set, but the Mac has to send them to the printer (the printer *downloads* them) before the printer can start spitting out pages.

drag — (1) To position the cursor on something, hold down the mouse button, and move the mouse while the button is still down. (2) What it is when your disk drive breaks the day after the warranty expires.

drawing program — A graphics program (such as MacDraw or ClarisDraw) that creates circles, squares, and lines. The Mac stores each object that you draw as an object unto itself, rather than storing the status of each screen dot. See also *painting program* and *bitmap.*

driver — A smallish file on your disk that tells the Mac how it's supposed to relate to a specific piece of equipment (such as a printer or a scanner) that it's never heard of before. A translator.

E-mail — Electronic mail; messages that you read and write on the Mac screen without ever printing them. May also be short for *Earth-mail,* because no paper (and no rain-forest acreage) is involved.

Enter key — A key (obviously) with the word *Enter* on it. It almost always does the same thing as the Return key.

EPS file — A type of graphics file. Characterized by extremely sharp, smooth printing on a laser printer; a large file size on the disk; and, often, difficulty in printing.

expansion slot — The new notch that you have to add to your belt when you've been putting on weight. Also the connector socket for an add-on circuit board inside most Mac models.

extended keyboard — A slightly more expensive keyboard than the "standard" one. The extended keyboard has a row of function keys (F1, F2, and so on) across the top, which don't do anything, and a little bank of keys that say Page Up, Page Down, and other stuff.

extension — Miniprogram that you install by dropping it in your System Folder (whereupon the Mac puts it in the Extensions folder). From that moment on, the extension will run itself when you turn on the Mac and will be on all the time. Examples: virus protectors and screen savers.

fax/modem — Like a modem (see *modem*), but also lets you send or receive faxes from your Mac screen.

field — Computerese for *blank,* such as a blank in a form.

file — The generic word for one of the little icons in your Macintosh. There are two kinds of files: *programs,* which you purchase to get work done, and *documents,* which are created by programs. See also *program* and *document.*

file compression — Making a file take up less disk space by encoding it in a more compact format, using a *file-compression program* such as StuffIt or DiskDoubler. The trade-off: stuffing something down (and expanding it when you need it again) takes a few seconds.

File Sharing — A built-in feature of System 7, wherein you can make any file, folder, or disk available for other people to go rooting through (as long as they're connected to your Mac by network wiring).

Finder — The "home-base" view when you're working on your Mac. It's the environment where you see the Trash, your icons, and how little space you've got left on your disk. Also known as the Desktop or "that place with all the little pictures."

FKEY — One of those cool techno-sounding words that nobody's ever pinned down to one meaning. Can refer to (1) the row of keys across the top of some keyboards: the *function* keys, labeled F1, F2, and so on. Or (2) a special built-in keyboard shortcut involving the ⌘ and Shift keys plus a number. The ⌘-Shift-3 function key, for example, takes a snapshot of the screen, and ⌘-Shift-1 ejects a floppy disk.

flat-file database — A shopping list, Rolodex, or phone book; a simple collection of information. On a Mac, you can do things to your database like search or sort; *flat-file* means that the database doesn't have fancy interconnections to other lists, as a "relational" database does.

floppy disk — The hard 3½-inch-square thing that you put into your disk-drive slot. Comes in three capacities: 400K (single-sided), 800K (double-sided), and 1,400K (quadruple-sided, or high-density). After being accidentally zapped by a refrigerator magnet, often used as a windshield scraper.

folder — In the Mac world, a little filing-folder icon into which you can drop other icons (such as your work) for organizational purposes. When you double-click a folder, it opens into a window. Also the name of the high-speed machine that creases and envelope-stuffs the junk mail that you're going to start getting from computer companies.

A folder

font — (1) Apple's usage: a single typeface. (2) Everyone else's usage: a typeface *family* or package.

Font/DA Mover — An obsolete, obtuse, and obstinate utility program that came with every Mac for years. Used for adding/removing fonts to/from your Mac (and for adding or removing desk accessories). With System 7, thank God, the Font/DA Mover is history.

FPU — See *math coprocessor*.

fragmentation —When something gets broken up into little pieces. Usually refers to the files on your hard disk (which, over time, get stored in little pieces all over the disk, making it slower) or to the memory in your computer (see *defragment*). Also can apply to your window after you throw the computer through it in frustration.

freeze — When your cursor becomes immovable on your screen, you can't type anything, your Mac locks up, and you get furious because you lose everything you've typed in the past ten minutes.

function key — See *FKEY*.

gig — Short for *gigabyte,* which is 1,024 *megabytes,* or a *very* big hard drive.

grayscale — A form of color image or color monitor on which all the colors are different shades of gray, like all the images in this book.

grow box — Slang for *resize box* (see that entry).

hang — (1) Freeze (see *freeze*). (2) Knack, as in "Hey, I'm actually getting the hang of this. I'm no dummy!"

hard copy — A synonym for *printout.* A term used primarily by the kind of people who have car phones and say, "Let's interface on this."

hard disk — A hard drive.

hard drive — A hard disk. That is, the spinning platters, usually inside your Mac but also available in an external form, that serve as a giant floppy disk where your computer files get stored.

hardware — The parts of your computer experience that you can feel, and touch, and pay for. Contrast with *software.*

header — Something that appears at the top of every page of a document, such as "Chapter 4: The Milkman's Plight" or "Final Disconnection Notice."

highlight — To select, usually by clicking or dragging with the mouse. In the Mac world, text and icons usually indicate that they're selected, or highlighted, by turning black. In the barbecue world, things indicate that they're *ready* by turning black.

HyperCard — A program that once came with every Mac; sort of a Rolodex gone mad. Can be an appointment book, a diary, a kid's game … whatever you make of it.

icon — A teensy picture used as a symbol for a file, a folder, or a disk.

ImageWriter — A low-cost, low-speed, low-quality, high-noise Apple dot-matrix printer.

INIT — The dweeb's word for *extension* (see that entry).

initialize — To prepare a new disk for use on your computer. Entails *erasing it completely.*

insertion point — In word processing, the short, blinking vertical line that's always somewhere in your text. It indicates where your next typing (or backspacing) will begin.

↓

the insertion point is right before this word.

jaggies — Ragged or tiny stairstepped edges on lettering or graphics, appearing either on the screen or in your printouts. Usually solved by switching to a TrueType font or by getting Adobe Type Manager working. See also *ATM.*

K — Short for *kilobyte,* a unit of size measurement for computer information. A floppy disk usually holds 800K or 1,400K of data. All the typing in this book fills about 1,500K. A full-screen color picture is around 1,000K of information. When your hard disk gets erased accidentally, it's got 0K (that's not OK).

kerning — In type-intensive Mac work, such as creating a newspaper headline, the act of squishing two letters slightly closer together to make better use of space so that you can fit the phrase AN ALIEN FATHERED MY TWO-HEADED BABY on one line.

label — A System 7 text tag or color tag, used to identify icons by category.

landscape — Used to describe the sideways orientation of a piece of paper. Also the natural environment outdoors that you gradually forget about as you become addicted to the Mac.

laptop — Where a PowerBook computer is when you're working on the plane.

laser printer — An expensive printer that creates awesome-looking printouts.

launch — To open a program, as in "He just sits at that computer all day long, moving icons around, because he hasn't figured out how to launch a program yet."

LCD — The technology that creates the flat screen on the PowerBook laptop computer, marked by the tendency for the pointer to fade out if it's moved too quickly. Stands for either *Liquid Crystal Display* or *Lost the Cursor, Dammit.*

leading — (*LEDding*): The vertical distance between lines of text in a document. Single-spaced and double-spaced are measurements of leading. Example: "His term paper was 33 pages short, so he increased the leading and hoped that the professor wouldn't notice."

LocalTalk — The hardware portion of a Macintosh network: the connectors and cables that plug one Mac into another.

logic board — The main circuit board inside your Mac. Often at fault when your Mac refuses to turn on.

MacOS — The System software (the behind-the-scenes operating software) that makes a computer act like a Mac. As distinguished from DOS or Windows.

macro — A predefined series of actions that the Mac performs automatically when you press a single key — such as launching your word processor, typing **Help! I'm being inhabited by a Mac poltergeist!**, and printing it — all by itself. Requires a special macro program such as QuicKeys or Tempo.

MacroMaker — A macro program that used to come free with your Mac. Doesn't work with System 7.

mail merge — Creating personalized form letters with a word processing program. Considered to be perfectly polite unless somebody catches you.

math coprocessor — The kid whose algebra homework you used to copy. (Just kidding.) Actually, a specialized chip inside certain high-level Macs that kicks in to handle certain very intense number-crunching tasks — data analysis and stuff. Does nothing for word processing and other normal tasks. Also called an *FPU* (floating-point unit).

MB — Short for *megabyte*.

megabyte — A unit of disk-storage space or memory measurement (see *K*). Used to measure hard disks, memory, and other large storage devices. There are about 1,000K in a megabyte.

memory — The electronic holding area that exists only when the Mac is turned on; where your document lives while you're working on it. Expensive and limited in each Mac.

menu — A list of commands, neatly organized by topic, that drops down from the top of the Mac screen when you click the menu's title.

menu bar — The white strip, containing menu titles, that's always at the top of the Mac screen. Not to be confused with *bar menu*, which is a wine list.

modem — A phone attachment for your Mac that lets you send files and messages to other computer users all over the world, and to prevent anyone else in the house from using the phone.

modifier keys — Keys that mess up what the letter keys do. Famous example: the Shift key. Other examples: ⌘ (Command), Option, Control, and Caps Lock.

monitor — What you should do to your blood pressure when you find out how much computer screens (*monitors*) cost and weigh.

motherboard — See *logic board.*

mount — A term used mainly in error messages: to bring a disk's icon onto the Desktop so that its contents may be viewed or opened.

mouse — The little hand-held gray thing that rolls around on your desk, controls the movement of the cursor, and is such an obvious target for a rodent joke that I won't even attempt it.

mouse button — The square or rounded plastic button at the far end of the top of the mouse.

mouse pad — A thin foam-rubber mat that protects the mouse and desk from each other and that gives the mouse good traction. Often bears a logo or slogan, such as "Sony Disks: We're always floppy."

MultiFinder — Before Apple invented System 7, you could run only one program at a time. To paste a graphic into a letter, for example, you'd have to quit your graphics program, launch the word processing program, and paste the picture. Using MultiFinder, a special optional software add-on, you could have the graphics and word processing programs open at the same time. (In System 7, you can *always* have more than one program open, provided that you have enough memory.)

multimedia — Something involving more than one medium, I guess. Mainly an advertising gimmick. On the Mac, anything that gives you something to look at *and* listen to, such as a CD-ROM game.

native software — Specially written programs that run amazingly fast on a Power Macintosh.

network — What you create when you connect Macs to each other. A network lets you send messages or transfer files from one Mac to another without getting up and running down the hall with a floppy disk in your hand (a networking system fondly called *SneakerNet*).

Newton — A small hand-held computer made by Apple. Has no keyboard; you write on it with an inkless pen. Can exchange names, addresses, and notes with your Mac.

NuBus — The special kind of expansion slot (see *expansion slot*) found in any Mac II-style computer and most Quadra-style computers. Contrast with *PDS,* the slot in a Macintosh LC. (And no, there was never an OldBus.)

NumLock — A goofy key, named by numskulls, on the keyboard. Pretty much does nothing except in Microsoft Word, where it switches the functions of the keys in the number pad.

OCR — Short for *optical character recognition*. You run an article that you tore out of *Entertainment Weekly* through a scanner, and the Mac translates it into a word processing document on your screen, so you can edit it and remove all references to Cher.

online — Hooked up, as in "Let's get this relationship online." In Mac lore, it means hooked up to another computer, such as America Online.

painting program — (1) A program with the word *Paint* in the title (for example, MacPaint or UltraPaint) that creates artwork by turning individual white dots black on the screen. (2) An adult-education course for would-be watercolorers.

partition — To use special formatting software that tricks the Mac into thinking that your hard disk is actually *two* (or more) disks, each with its own icon on the screen. Like subdividing a movie theater into a duplex, but less expensive.

paste — To place some text or graphics (that you previously copied or cut) in a document.

PC — Stands for *personal computer,* but really means any non-Macintosh (i.e., inferior) computer; an IBM clone.

PCI — A 1995-era new style of NuBus slot in certain Mac models (see NuBus).

PDS — Stands for *processor direct slot* and is the kind of *expansion slot* (see that entry) in a Mac LC. Incompatible with *NuBus* (see that entry, too).

peripheral — (1) Any add-on: a printer, scanner, CD-ROM drive, dust cover, and so on. (2) The kind of vision by which you'll see your spouse leave you forever because you're too consumed by the Mac.

PICT — A confusing-sounding acronym for the most common kind of picture file, as in "Just paste that image of Sculley's head into your word processor, Frank; it's only a PICT file, for heaven's sake."

pixel — One single dot out of the thousands that make up the screen image. Supposedly derived from *pi*cture *el*ement, which still doesn't explain how the *x* got there.

pop-up menu — Any menu that doesn't appear at the *top* of the screen. Usually marked by a down-pointing black triangle. Doesn't actually pop *up;* usually drops down.

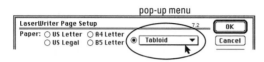

pop-up menu

port — (1) A jack or connection socket in the back of your Mac. (2) Where boaters dock so that they can recharge their PowerBook batteries.

portrait — A right-side-up piece of paper; the opposite of *landscape* (see that entry). Also a right-side-up monitor that can display a full page (as in "a portrait display monitor").

PostScript — A technology, a printer, a trademark, a kind of font, a computer code language for displaying or printing text or graphics, a way of life. All of it means high-quality type and graphics, and all of it means heaping revenue for Adobe, the company that invented it.

PowerBook — A Mac laptop and the first of many Apple trademarks to contain the word *Power.*

Power Macintosh — A Mac whose primary brain is the PowerPC chip.

PowerPC chip — The very fast main processor chip inside a Power Macintosh.

PowerTalk — A special feature of System 7.5, designed for very sophisticated network setups in offices. Provides a desktop mailbox icon for electronic messages sent to you by your officemates (and may

someday also be able to receive your messages from services such as America Online). Absolutely impossible to figure out.

PRAM — *Parameter RAM*: the little piece of memory maintained by your Mac's battery. Helps explain why the Mac always knows the date and time even when it's been turned off.

printer font — The printer half of a PostScript font (the other half is the *screen font*). Must be in your System Folder, and you must have one printer font for each style (bold, italic, and so on). An eternal nuisance.

PrintMonitor — A program that launches itself, unbidden, whenever you try to print something when background printing is turned on (see *background printing*). Print Monitor is also the program that tries to notify you when something goes wrong with the printer, such as when a piece of paper gets horribly mangled inside.

program — A piece of software, created by a programmer, that you buy to make your Mac do something specific: graphics, music, word processing, number crunching, or whatever.

Publish and Subscribe — A fancy new version of copy-and-paste that's part of System 7. Lets you paste information (such as a graphic) from one document into another (such as a memo) in such a way that when you make a change in the original (the graphic), the copy (the memo) is changed automatically.

QuickDraw — A behind-the-scenes technology used to draw all the familiar pictures on your screen, such as lettering, windows, and icons.

QuickDraw GX — A very sophisticated feature for System 7.5 and later. Permits certain "GX-savvy" programs to manipulate type on the screen in neat ways. Also puts an icon on your Desktop for each printer you own, so you can specify which printer to use by dragging your document icon onto it. Not really worth the trouble until more programs are upgraded to work with it.

QuickTime — The technology (and the little software extension) that permits you to make and view digital movies on your Mac screen. Does nothing by itself; requires QuickTime recording, playing, and editing programs.

quit — To exit or close a program, removing it from memory. Or to exit or close your job, having gotten sick of working in front of a computer all day.

radio button — What you see in groups of two or more when the Mac is forcing you to choose among mutually exclusive options, such as these:

A System error has occurred. What result would you like?

○ Loud, static buzzing
◉ Quietly blink to black
○ A two-minute fireworks display

RAM — Term for memory (see *memory*) designed to intimidate non-computer users.

RAM disk — A way to trick the Mac into thinking that it has an extra floppy disk inserted. The RAM disk is actually a chunk of memory set aside to *resemble* a disk (complete with an icon on the screen). A built-in option on most Macs and PowerBooks.

reboot — Restart.

rebuilding the Desktop — One of several desperate methods that you can use in the event that something screwy goes wrong with the Mac. Involves holding down the ⌘ and Option keys while the Mac is starting up.

record (n.) — Other than its obvious definitions, the computer word *record* refers to one "card" in a database, such as one person's address information. Contrast with *field,* which is one *blank* (such as a ZIP code) within a record.

relational database — A complex information list that you hire somebody to come in and set up for you, in which each list of information (such as a mailing list) is connected to another list (such as People Who Never Pay on Time).

removable cartridge — Like a hard drive with free refills: a storage device (usually made by SyQuest or Bernoulli) that accepts huge-capacity disks, so you never run out of disk space (until you run out of the ability to buy more cartridges).

ResEdit — A free program that lets anybody do some hacking in any program — changing what the menus say, altering the keyboard shortcuts, or really screwing up the works.

resize box — The small square in the lower-right corner of a window that, when dragged, changes the size and shape of your window.

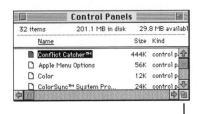

resize box

resolution — (1) A number, measured in dots per inch, that indicates how crisply a printer or a monitor can display an image. (2) A New Year's vow, such as "I will spend five minutes away from the computer each day for family, exercise, and social activity."

restart switch — A little plastic switch, marked by a left-pointing triangle, on the case molding of most Macs that, when pressed, safely turns the Mac off and on again.

RISC — Stands for *reduced instruction-set computing* and means a very fast processor chip, such as the PowerPC chip inside a Power Macintosh.

ROM — A mediation mantra that you can use when contemplating the ROM chips, where the Mac's instructions to itself are permanently etched.

sans serif — A font, such as Helvetica or Geneva, with no little "hats" and "feet" at the tip of each letter. See Chapter 4.

scanner — A machine that takes a picture of a piece of paper (like a Xerox machine) and then dis-plays the image on your Mac screen for editing.

Scrapbook — A desk accessory, found in your menu, used for permanent storage of graphics, text, and sounds. (Not the same as the Clipboard, which isn't permanent and holds only one thing at a time.) To get something into the Scrapbook, copy it from a document, open the Scrapbook, and paste it. To get something out of the Scrapbook, use the scroll bar until you see what you want, and then copy it (or cut it).

screen saver — A program (such as After Dark) that darkens your screen after you haven't worked for several minutes. Designed to protect an unchanging image from burning into the screen, but more often used as a status symbol.

scroll — To bring a different part of a document into view, necessitated by the fact that most computer monitors aren't large enough to display all 60 pages of your annual report at the same time.

scroll bar — The strips along the left and right sides of a Mac window. When a scroll bar's arrows, gray portion, or little white (or gray) square are clicked or dragged, a different part of the window's contents heaves into view (*scrolls*).

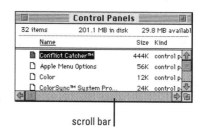

scroll bar

SCSI — Stands for Small Computer [something] Interface. The second *S* may stand for *standard*, *system*, or *serial*, depending on whom you ask. Used only in the following five terms.

SCSI address — Refers to a number that you must give each SCSI device (see *SCSI device*) that's plugged into your Mac, using a little switch or thumbwheel on the back. The address can be between 0 and 7, except that the Mac is always 7 and the internal hard disk is always 0. If two SCSI devices have the same SCSI address, you're in big trouble.

SCSI cable — A fat cable with a 25- or 50-pin connector at the end, used to join SCSI devices. The total length of all your SCSI cables can't be more than about 20 feet, or you're in big trouble.

SCSI device — A scanner, CD player, external hard drive, printer (sometimes), removable-cartridge drive, external floppy-disk drive (sometimes), or other piece of equipment that you attach to the wide SCSI port in the back of your Mac. When you attach more than one of these devices (by plugging each into the back of the preceding one), you have to obey certain rules (outlined in Chapter 12), or you're in big trouble.

SCSI port — The wide connector in the back of your Mac.

SCSI terminator — A plug that is supposed to go into the last SCSI device attached to your Mac. If you don't use one, you're in big trouble; although sometimes you're in big trouble if you *do* use one. See Chapter 12.

serif (n., adj.) — A term used to describe a font that has little ledges, like little "hats" and "feet," at the tip of each letter, such as Times or this font.

shareware — Programs that are distributed for free, via an electronic bulletin board or on a floppy disk, from user groups. The programmer requests that you send $10 or $20 to him or her, but only if you really like the program.

Shut Down — The command in the Special menu that turns off your Mac.

SIMM — Stands for *Single In-line Memory Module*, which I suggest that you immediately forget. It refers to the little epoxy mini-circuit board that you install into your Mac when you decide you need more memory.

sleep — A command, and a condition, that applies only to PowerBooks or the Mac Portable. Sort of like Off, except that the Mac remembers everything that you had running on the screen. When you want to use the computer again, you just touch a key; the whole computer wakes up, the screen lights up, and you're in business again. Used to conserve battery power.

slot — An *expansion slot* (see that entry).

software — The real reason you got a computer. Software is computer code, the stuff on disks: programs (that let you create documents) and documents themselves. Software tells the hardware what to do.

spooler — A program that allows *background printing* (see that entry).

spreadsheet — A program that's like an electronic ledger book; you can type columns of numbers in a spreadsheet program and have them added automatically.

stack — A document created by the HyperCard program.

startup disk — *A* startup disk is a floppy or hard disk that contains a System Folder (including a particular set of fonts, desk accessories, and settings for running your Mac). *The* startup disk is the one that you've designated to be in control (in the event that you have more than one to choose among). The Startup Disk *control panel* is what you use to specify *the* startup disk.

stationery pad — A System 7 feature. Click a document icon, choose Get Info from the File menu, and select Stationery Pad. Thereafter, when you double-click that icon, it won't open; instead, an exact *copy* of it opens. This saves you the hassle of pasting the same logo into every memo that you write because you can paste it into your Stationery Pad document just once.

StyleWriter — A quiet, low-cost, high-quality, slow-speed Apple inkjet printer.

submenu — In some menus, you're forced to choose among an additional set of options, which are marked in the menu by a right-pointing triangle. When your pointer is on the main menu command, the submenu pops out, like this:

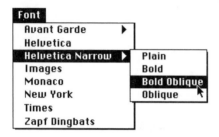

SuperDrive — The kind of floppy-disk drive in every Macintosh except the Plus and the early Mac IIs and SEs. Called Super because it can read high-density (1.4MB) floppy disks instead of the unsuper 800K disks and because it can (theoretically) read IBM-format disks.

System 6 — One version of the Mac's controlling software. Faster, but harder to use, than System 7. Requires 1MB of memory or less.

System 7 — The more recent version of the Mac's controlling software. More attractive, easier to use, more powerful, and slower than System 6. Requires at least 2MB of memory and, because it's a lot of software, a hard disk (it doesn't fit on a floppy). Generically, refers to any flavor of System 7: version 7.0, 7.1, 7.5, or whatever.

System 7.1 — The first version of the Mac System software that's not free; you have to buy it. Adds two features to System 7: a Fonts folder, which contains all manner of font files (TrueType, screen fonts, and printer fonts); and WorldScript, which enables you to convert all Mac screen elements to a different language, such as Japanese. (WorldScript requires special drop-in language modules.) System 7.1 is also modular; you can add new features to it just by dropping in plug-in software tidbits as they become available.

System 7.5 — Yet another version of the System Folder, which, again, you must purchase unless your Mac came with it. Under the hood, System 7.5 is much the same as System 7.1. But it comes with about 50 new control panels and extensions that perform stunts such as giving submenus to your menu to providing a floating "control strip" for your PowerBook. Has one huge new feature: AppleGuide, which walks you through basic Mac functions (such as printing). Also has PowerTalk and QuickDraw GX, which take major computer geniuses to figure out.

System crash — When something goes so wrong inside your Mac that a bomb appears on the screen with the message "Sorry, a System error has occurred" — or not. Sometimes, the whole screen just freaks, fills with static, and makes buzzing noises, like a TV station that's going off the air.

System disk — A *startup disk* (see that entry).

System file — The most important individual file inside a System Folder. Contains the Mac's instructions to itself, and stores your fonts, sounds, and other important customization information. A Mac without a System file is like a broke politician: it can't run.

System Folder — The all-important folder that the Mac requires to run. Contains all kinds of other stuff that's also defined in this glossary: the System file, the Finder, fonts, desk accessories, printer fonts, and so on. Always identified by this special folder icon:

System Folder

telecommunication — Communicating with other computers over the phone lines. Requires a *modem* (see that entry).

telecommute — To work in T-shirt and slippers in a messy apartment, spending not one penny on transportation, and sending work to the office over the phone lines. Requires a modem and an ability to be alone for days on end without going insane.

terminator — See *SCSI terminator*. Or see an Arnold Schwarzenegger movie.

third party — (1) A company other than Apple, as in "You didn't get a mouse pad with your Mac? Well, of course not; you buy that from a third party." (You, by the way, are the second party.) (2) The New Year's Eve get-together at which you get the drunkest.

TIFF — Stands for *tagged image file format* and is the kind of graphics-file format created by a scanner.

title bar — The strip at the top of a window where the window's name appears. Shows thin horizontal stripes if the window is *active* (in front of all the others).

toner — The powder that serves as the "ink" for a laser printer. Runs out at critical moments.

trackball — An alternative to the mouse. Looks like an 8-ball set in a pedestal; you roll it to move the pointer.

TrueType — A special font format from Apple that ensures high-quality type at any size, both on the screen and on any printer. Rival to PostScript but costs much less (nothing, in fact; it comes with System 7).

upload — To send a file to another computer via modem. See also *download.*

user group — A local computer club; usually meets once a month. Serves as a local source of information and as a place to unload your obsolete equipment to unsuspecting newcomers.

video card — A circuit board that most Mac II-series Macs need to display anything at all on the monitor.

virtual memory — A chunk of hard-disk space that the Mac sets aside, if you want, to serve as emergency memory.

virus — Irritating, self-duplicating computer program designed (by the maladjusted jerk who programmed it) to gum up the works of your Mac. Easily prevented by using Disinfectant or another virus barrier.

volume — A disk of any kind: floppy, hard, cartridge, or anything represented on your Desktop by its own icon.

VRAM — Stands for *video RAM*. Memory chips inside your Mac that are dedicated to storing the screen picture from moment to moment. The more VRAM you have, the more colorful your picture (and the more you paid for your Mac).

window — A square view of Mac information. In the Finder, a window is a table of contents for a folder or a disk. In a program, a window displays your document.

word wrap — A word processing program's ability to place a word on the next line as soon as the current line becomes full.

WYSIWYG — Short for *what you see is what you get* — one supposed reason for the Mac's superiority over other computers. Theoretically means that your printout will precisely match what you see on the screen (but isn't always true).

zoom box — The tiny square in the upper-right corner of a window (in the title bar) that, when clicked, makes the window jump to full size.

zoom box

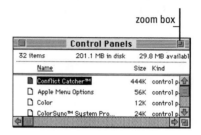

Index

IDG BOOKS WORLDWIDE REGISTRATION CARD

RETURN THIS REGISTRATION CARD FOR FREE CATALOG

Title of this book: Macs For Dummies, 3E

My overall rating of this book: ❑ Very good [1] ❑ Good [2] ❑ Satisfactory [3] ❑ Fair [4] ❑ Poor [5]

How I first heard about this book:

❑ Found in bookstore; name: [6]　　　　　　　　　　　❑ Book review: [7]

❑ Advertisement: [8]　　　　　　　　　　　　　　　❑ Catalog: [9]

❑ Word of mouth; heard about book from friend, co-worker, etc.: [10]　　❑ Other: [11]

What I liked most about this book:

What I would change, add, delete, etc., in future editions of this book:

Other comments:

Number of computer books I purchase in a year:　❑ 1 [12]　❑ 2-5 [13]　❑ 6-10 [14]　❑ More than 10 [15]

I would characterize my computer skills as: ❑ Beginner [16] ❑ Intermediate [17] ❑ Advanced [18] ❑ Professional [19]

I use ❑ DOS [20] ❑ Windows [21] ❑ OS/2 [22] ❑ Unix [23] ❑ Macintosh [24] ❑ Other: [25]_____
(please specify)

I would be interested in new books on the following subjects:
(please check all that apply, and use the spaces provided to identify specific software)

❑ Word processing: [26]　　　　　　　　　❑ Spreadsheets: [27]

❑ Data bases: [28]　　　　　　　　　　　❑ Desktop publishing: [29]

❑ File Utilities: [30]　　　　　　　　　　❑ Money management: [31]

❑ Networking: [32]　　　　　　　　　　　❑ Programming languages: [33]

❑ Other: [34]

I use a PC at (please check all that apply): ❑ home [35] ❑ work [36] ❑ school [37] ❑ other: [38] _____

The disks I prefer to use are ❑ 5.25 [39] ❑ 3.5 [40] ❑ other: [41]_____

I have a CD ROM: ❑ yes [42]　❑ no [43]

I plan to buy or upgrade computer hardware this year:　❑ yes [44]　❑ no [45]

I plan to buy or upgrade computer software this year:　❑ yes [46]　❑ no [47]

Name:　　　　　　　　　Business title: [48]　　　　　Type of Business: [49]

Address (❑ home [50] ❑ work [51]/Company name:　　　　　　　　　)

Street/Suite#

City [52]/State [53]/Zipcode [54]:　　　　　　Country [55]

❑ **I liked this book!** You may quote me by name in future
IDG Books Worldwide promotional materials.

My daytime phone number is _____

IDG BOOKS

THE WORLD OF
COMPUTER
KNOWLEDGE

❏ YES!

Please keep me informed about IDG's World of Computer Knowledge.
Send me the latest IDG Books catalog.

Macs For Dummies, 3rd Edition

Cheat Sheet

Working with Icons

Finding a file

Each file you create is represented by an icon and is usually stored inside an electronic folder, which looks like a file-folder on your screen. Beginners and pros alike occasionally lose files or forget where they filed a certain file.

1. Choose Find from the File menu.

2. Type a few letters of the missing file's name.

   You don't have to type the whole name . . . only enough to distinguish it; type *Wonk* to find the file called *Willy Wonka Quarterly Earnings*. Capitalization doesn't matter.

3. Press the Return key, or click the Find button.

   The Mac roots through your files. It either displays the first icon it finds that matches your request, or shows you a list of *all* icons that match.

4. If the Mac found the wrong file, choose Find Again from the File menu.

Keep choosing Find Again until you find what you're looking for, or until the Mac beeps, telling you that it's done searching.

Renaming a file

1. Point to an icon's name, and click the mouse button.

   The icon's name is now highlighted (selected).

2. Type a new name.

   A file's name can be up to 31 letters long. If you make a mistake, backspace over it by pressing the Delete key.

   Note to IBM types: A Mac file name can have any kind of letters you want (uppercase, lowercase, symbols — anything but a colon) and doesn't have to have a period in it.

3. Press Return when you're done typing.

To insert a floppy disk

1. The metal part goes in first.

2. The label side should be up.

3. Push it into the Mac's disk slot until it makes a *chunk* sound.

Copying a file onto a disk

1. Drag the icon (below left) onto the disk's icon (below right), and let go.

Alternatively, you can drag the file into the disk's *window*, instead of on top of the disk's icon.

Locking a disk

1. Eject the disk.

2. Slide the small square tab in the corner of the disk so that you can see through the hole.

A disk you've locked in this way can't be erased, and nothing on it can be thrown away.

What to Do When You See Something Like This:

They call this box a *dialog box* because the Mac is asking you some questions it needs answered. Here are the elements of a typical dialog box and what they do.

Radio buttons

Paper: ⦿ **US Letter** ○ **A4 Letter**
  ○ **US Legal** ○ **B5 Letter**

Named after the pushbuttons on a car radio, where only one can be pushed in at a time. If you push a different one, the first one pops up. Likewise, only one Mac radio button can be selected at a time.

Checkboxes

⊠ **Text Smoothing?**
⊠ **Graphics Smoothing?**

Used to indicate whether an option is on or off. Click once to place the X in the box; click again to remove the X (and turn off the option).

Text fields

Reduce or
Enlarge: `100` %

You're supposed to type text or numbers into these blanks. To move from one blank to another (if there's more than one), you can either click in a blank with the mouse or press the Tab key to jump from one to the next.

Pop-up menus

When you see some text in a rectangle, marked by a down-pointing triangle, you're seeing a *pop-up menu*. Point to the text, hold down the mouse button, and make a selection from the mini-menu that drops down.

Buttons

Some buttons, like Options (in the dialog box above), make *another* dialog box appear, where you can make even more choices.

Every dialog box, though, has a clearly marked button or two (usually OK and Cancel) that make the box go away — your escape route.

Click OK (or Print, or Proceed, or whatever the main button says) to proceed with the command you originally chose from the menu. Click Cancel if you want to back out of it, as though you'd never issued the command.

And a power-user tip: See the thick black outline around the OK button picture above? That's your cue that you don't have to use the mouse to click that button; you can press either the Return or Enter key on your keyboard instead.

Macs For Dummies, 3rd Edition

COMPUTER BOOK SERIES FROM IDG

Cheat Sheet

What've You Got There?

Your Mac's model name is painted on the front. For the System and memory info, choose About This Macintosh from the menu; details in the first two chapters.

Your Mac model: _____

Your System version: _____

How much memory it's got: _____

Surviving the First Half Hour

You may only need this information at the very beginning of your Mac career — but you'll *really* need it.

Turning on the Mac

1. Press the On button. For most Macs, it's either the big key on your keyboard with a left-pointing triangle, or a rocker switch on the back panel (Chapter 1.)

Turning off the Mac

1. If you've typed or drawn anything, make sure it's safely stored on your disk by choosing Save from the File menu.
2. Choose Quit from the File menu.
3. From the Special menu, choose Shut Down.

```
Special
Clean Up Window
Empty Trash

Eject Disk      ⌘E
Erase Disk...

Restart
Shut Down
```

4. Most models shut off immediately. On some models, you'll now be told to turn off the power, using the same switch you used to turn it on.

Working with Several Programs

One of the handiest features of the Mac is that it lets you run more than one program at once. If you keep launching programs, eventually you'll be told you're out of memory. Until then, here are some pointers. (See Chapter 3 for info on *getting* programs.)

Launching a program

1. Find its icon.

   The icon for a program is usually diamond-shaped. Here are some typical program icons:

   Microsoft Word   DiskDoubler   TeachText   Claris Works

2. Put the cursor on the icon, and double-click the mouse button quickly.

Determining what programs are running

1. Put the cursor on the icon in the far upper right of your screen, and hold down the mouse button.

   The *Application menu* drops down, listing all the programs you've launched. The frontmost one, the one you're working in, is indicated by a check mark.

Working with Windows

Opening or closing a window

A window is simply your view into something that's normally closed. When a window is closed, it's not a window at all — it's represented by an icon (of a disk, a folder, or a file).

1. Double-click any icon to open its window.
2. To get rid of a window, click the *close box* in the upper-left corner.

```
Hard Drive
5 items          29 MB in disk
```

Moving a window

Point to its striped *title bar* (where the name of the window appears). Hold the mouse button down, and drag the window into a new position.

Bringing concealed icons into view

Sometimes a window is too small to show you all the icons within it. If that's the case, you'll see gray *scroll bars* along the bottom and right side.

1. Point to one of the small arrows on the scroll bar, as shown, and press the mouse button continuously.

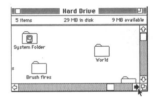

Your view of the window will slide in the direction of the arrow, showing you what's hidden beyond the edges.

2. To make the window as large as necessary to view all the icons (limited by screen size), click the *zoom box*, as shown.

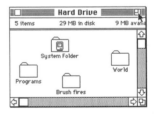

Making a dimmed window active

1. Click in it.

IDG BOOKS

...For Dummies: #1 Computer Book Series for Beginners